More Praise for *The First-Year Teacher's Survival Guide*

"This survival guide is one of the best that I've seen for new teachers. This experienced teacher knows firsthand what new teachers will encounter during that important first year in the classroom. She provides practical strategies and ready-to-use materials to make sure that the common pitfalls of discipline, organization, time management, lesson planning, grading and assessment, working with other teachers, and job burnout are avoided. Julia Thompson also knows that teaching is one of the most challenging as well as one of the most rewarding jobs in the world. From what I've read, her mission is to keep talented new teachers in the classroom and not pursuing other careers. Thank you for writing this book!"

—Darlene Mannix, special education teacher, Crichfield Elementary School, Indiana

"Julia Thompson earns an A+ for her practical and comprehensive *First-Year Teacher's Survival Guide*. This veteran educator skillfully provides effective classroom-tested strategies to guide the new teacher through the possible problems and potentially stressful situations often encountered during that memorable first year of teaching. . . . *First Year Teacher's Survival Guide* should be required reading for all new teachers!"

— Jack Umstatter, veteran teacher of thirty-five years and educational consultant, Islip, New York

"I can't think of anything this guide doesn't have! It's common knowledge that the first year of teaching presents endless challenges and a plethora of questions. Thompson's *First-Year Teacher's Survival Guide* will prove to be an invaluable tool for new teachers. Seasoned teachers will love it for its new and innovative ideas. I would have one available for each teacher on opening day!"

— Gloria Smith, early childhood staff developer, District 7 Bronx, New York

"I found Julia Thompson's *First-Year Teacher's Survival Guide* provides it all. She has written a remarkable guide that any teacher will enjoy having. The ideas and suggestions she has gathered provide a 'compass' of usable and practical information. This guide will help keep new professional educators focused on what is most important: the mutual positive development of their students and themselves."

— Dr. David E. Hutt, superintendent, Buellton Union School District, California

"First-year teachers—and veterans too—will find an abundance of resources in this well-stocked survival guide. Julia Thompson's down-to-earth ideas are based on years of classroom experience, seasoned judgment, and a strong sense of professionalism. This book is like having a personal mentor to guide new teachers through the demanding process of becoming educators. Experienced teachers will also find fresh insight that can transform effective instruction from instinctive to intentional."

— Elisabeth H. Fuller, coordinator of grants, budget, and resources, Isle of Wight County Schools, Virginia

"*The First-Year Teacher's Survival Guide* offers a true insight into handling the challenges of our profession. As a university supervisor with student teachers for over twelve years, I would make Julia Thompson's book mandatory reading for beginning teachers. Her approach to planning and classroom management is very relevant to today's students. This book will enable the new teacher to have a foundation for a stable, rewarding first year."

— **Pamela J. Edwards, supervisor, Teacher Education Services, Old Dominion University, Virginia**

"*The First-Year Teacher's Survival Guide* is a comprehensive guide filled with practical advice for new teachers. From detailing how to work effectively with students, colleagues, and parents to maintaining balance in personal life, this Guide covers virtually every concern and problem a new teacher may have. It even includes numerous helpful resources, such as online forums and education databases. *The First-Year Teacher's Survival Guide* can help new teachers not only survive, but flourish, setting the stage for a successful and rewarding career. It should be required reading for all new teachers."

— **Gary Muschla, author and former sixth-grade teacher, Appleby School, New Jersey**

"What an extraordinary book! With this one resource, Julia Thompson addresses the needs of all beginning teachers. Elementary, middle, and high school teachers—both new and experienced—can find beneficial information on every page. Not only are there tips on how to manage the 'science' of education—seating charts, lesson plans, daily routines—but also tips on how to master the 'art' of this profession with sections devoted to classroom management, motivation, professional expertise, and learning how to be part of a team of professionals. Beginning teachers need this valuable resource. Certainly, in my early years of teaching, I could have benefited immensely from having this book on my desk."

— **Pam Leigh, English teacher, Spotswood High School, Virginia**

Jossey-Bass Teacher provides educators with practical knowledge and tools to create a positive and lifelong impact on student learning. We offer classroom-tested and research-based teaching resources for a variety of grade levels and subject areas. Whether you are an aspiring, new, or veteran teacher, we want to help you make every teaching day your best.

From ready-to-use classroom activities to the latest teaching framework, our value-packed books provide insightful, practical, and comprehensive materials on the topics that matter most to K–12 teachers. We hope to become your trusted source for the best ideas from the most experienced and respected experts in the field.

JOSSEY-BASS

The First-Year Teacher's Survival Guide

Ready-to-Use Strategies, Tools & Activities for Meeting the Challenges of Each School Day

SECOND EDITION

JULIA G. THOMPSON

BICENTENNIAL 1807 WILEY 2007 BICENTENNIAL

John Wiley & Sons, Inc.

Published by Jossey-Bass
A Wiley Imprint
989 Market Street, San Francisco, CA 94103-1741 www.josseybass.com

Jossey-Bass books and products are available through most bookstores. To contact Jossey-Bass directly, call our Customer Care Department within the U.S. at 800-956-7739, outside the U.S. at 317-572-3986, or fax 317-572-4002.

Jossey-Bass also publishes its books in a variety of electronic formats. Some content that appears in print may not be available in electronic books.

The Library of Congress Cataloging-in-Publication Data has been applied for.

ISBN 978-0-7879-9455-6

Printed in the United States of America
SECOND EDITION
PB Printing 10 9 8 7 6 5

About the Author

Julia G. Thompson received her B.A. in English from Virginia Polytechnic Institute and State University in Blacksburg, Virginia. She has been a teacher in the public schools of Virginia, Arizona, and North Carolina for more than twenty-five years. Thompson has taught a variety of courses, including freshman composition at Virginia Tech, English in all of the secondary grades, mining, geography, reading, home economics, math, civics, Arizona history, physical education, special education, graduation equivalency preparation, and employment skills. Her students have been diverse in ethnicity as well as in age, ranging from seventh graders to adults.

Thompson currently teaches in Greenville, NC, and presents new teacher and classroom management workshops nationally and internationally. She also publishes a web site with tips for teachers (www.juliagthompson.com).

Acknowledgments

I am grateful to my editor, Marjorie McAneny, for her generous patience, kind encouragement, and perceptive insights during the preparation of this book.

Thank you to Patricia A. Bonner, Ph.D., for her useful suggestions concerning Internet resources available for first-year teachers.

Thank you to Erin Muschla for her astute observations regarding professional development for first-year teachers.

Thank you to Susan Kolwicz for her continuing interest and support.

Thank you to the faculty, staff, and students of Windsor High School in Isle of Wight County, Virginia, for their unconditional encouragement—something every teacher needs.

Special thanks to the following thoughtful teachers who offered their wise counsel because they can remember what it's like to be a first-year teacher:

Paige Adcock
Carolyn Marks Bickham
Dawn Carroll
Sandra Councill
Melinda Cummings
Edward Gardner
Charlene Herrala
William Leigh
Stephanie Mahoney
Deborah McManaway
Patty Muth
William N. Owen
Nancy Parker
Yann Pirrone
Carole Platt
Sabrina Richardson
Julie Savoy
Luann Scott
Marlene Stanton
Kay Stephenson
Sarah Walski

J.G.T.

About This Survival Guide

When *First-Year Teacher's Survival Kit* was published five years ago, the professional life of a first-year teacher was different in many ways from the life of a beginning teacher today. The national teacher shortage was just beginning; the Internet was not the easy-to-use educational resource it is now; and the No Child Left Behind Act had not yet affected most classroom teachers. For new teachers, professional development five years ago meant reading an occasional book about teaching.

Some things remain the same, however. If you are like other first-year teachers, you probably feel a mixture of exhilaration and uncertainty as you face each new school day. You know what you and your students are supposed to achieve, but you are not always sure how to proceed. Some days increase your confidence in your teaching skills, while others test your dedication.

Almost everyone begins a teaching career with the same emotions. Many veteran teachers also suffered through the tough days when they didn't know what to do and gloried in the days when they were able to engage every student in the magic of learning. The daily barrage of pressures on first-year teachers can be so exhausting and defeating that some eventually choose another career that is not as difficult nor as rewarding.

On the other hand, the first years of your teaching career can be immensely satisfying ones. Your students are intriguing and challenging. Every day is a new opportunity to make a difference in a child's life. Your first years as a teacher can be years of dynamic professional growth and personal fulfillment as you achieve your own dreams while helping your students achieve theirs.

Helping you enjoy success in the first years of your career is the goal of *The First-Year Teacher's Survival Guide.* The suggestions and strategies in these pages can help you develop into a skillful classroom teacher who remains enthusiastic about the possibilities in every student. For instance, in this resource you'll find

- Helpful ways to efficiently manage paperwork and other time robbers so that you can focus on teaching
- Guidance on translating your state's standards into interesting lessons that will engage all of your students
- Many motivational strategies designed to help you involve every student in purposeful learning activities
- Assistance in identifying your professional responsibilities and establishing personal priorities in order to accomplish them
- Tools for examining your current teaching skills and establishing achievable goals for your professional life
- Inspiration, insight, and practical advice from successful veteran teachers
- A wide variety of innovative and time-tested classroom management activities, strategies, and techniques to help you create a positive learning environment
- Confidence in your ability to find the satisfaction that a career in education can bring

This second edition reflects the changes of the last five years, providing information that today's beginning teachers need, including expanded and new material on

- How to collaborate with colleagues in discussion groups
- How to access information and resources about the No Child Left Behind Act
- How to share a classroom or teach in a mobile unit
- How to find teacher freebies and create classroom storage on a budget
- How to find information about creating a class Web page
- How to use technology to design and deliver innovative, appealing lessons
- How to use innovative strategies such as WebQuests, essential questions, and "I" messages in your class
- How to help students prepare for standardized tests
- How to help struggling readers
- How to reach students through educational games, toys, and learning centers
- How to use peer pressure to help students with self-discipline
- How to fulfill your legal responsibilities and protect yourself from lawsuits
- How to reach out to at-risk students
- How to help students whose first language is not English
- How to solve many behavior problems that all teachers face

The First-Year Teacher's Survival Guide was written to help K–12 teachers meet the challenges that each school day brings. In these pages, you will find the answers to the most common how-to questions that many first-year teachers have:

How can I develop into a successful professional?	Section 1
How can I fulfill the responsibilities inherent in my new profession?	Section 2
How can I develop successful professional relationships with my colleagues and with the families of my students?	Section 3
How can I organize my time, tasks, and classroom before school begins?	Section 4
How can I guarantee that my students and I will have a fantastic first day together?	Section 5
How can I develop a meaningful relationship with each of my students?	Section 6
How can I design lessons that will meet the needs of my students?	Section 7
How can I deliver instruction that will fully engage my students in learning?	Section 8
How can I evaluate my students' progress accurately and fairly?	Section 9
How can I motivate my students to succeed?	Section 10
How can I help my students develop the study skills they need to become independent learners?	Section 11
How can I use class time so that my students are on task from the start to the finish of class?	Section 12
How can I help students who struggle with reading?	Section 13
How can I prevent discipline problems from disrupting the positive learning environment that I want to establish?	Section 14
How can I successfully manage discipline problems once they occur?	Section 15
How can I meet the needs of each child in my diverse classroom?	Section 16
What are the common problems that can happen in any classroom, and how do I cope with them?	Section 17

The First-Year Teacher's Survival Guide is meant to be a working resource, full of classroom-tested knowledge for you. What is the most effective way to use this book? The answers to this question are as varied as the teachers who use it.

- ✔ Browse through this guide section by section, gathering ideas to enrich your classes and strengthen your teaching skills. This method allows you to pick and choose from the practical advice and activities you'll find included here.
- ✔ When you have become familiar with the format and contents, use this book as a desktop resource. You can use the table of contents or the index to quickly look up solutions to specific problems that are of immediate concern.
- ✔ Work through a section at a time, learning, applying, practicing, and adapting the information as you go. While you can't learn how to be an excellent teacher all at once, you can benefit from this systematic approach.
- ✔ When you have had a discouraging day, look over the practical advice from experienced educators, who offer strategies and insights to help you keep your troubles in perspective and solve the day's problems.

However you choose to use this book, it was designed to be an interactive experience. Use a pencil to fill in the assessments, set your goals, and scribble notes as you read each section.

Highlight. Underline. Dog-ear the pages. Place bookmarks in the sections that appeal to you. As you go through the process of learning the intricacies of your new profession, refer to this book when you need assistance with the daily problems that can rob even the most stalwart educator of confidence.

The ultimate goal of the information in these pages is to help you become the self-assured and knowledgeable educator that you dreamed of being when you chose your new career. From the first day of school to the last day, you can be one of the greatest assets that our nation can have—an effective teacher.

With patience and practice, you can realize your professional dreams. Millions of others have done it; you can, too. Your first years as a teacher can set you squarely on the path to achieving the satisfaction that only a career in education can bring.

Best wishes for a gratifying and enjoyable first year!

Greenville, North Carolina
May 2007

Julia G. Thompson

For more information on how you can have a successful first year,
visit www.juliagthompson.com.

Do you want to use *The First-Year Teacher's Survival Guide* to train your new teachers?
A free staff development study guide is available at
www.josseybass.com/go/First-YearTeacher.

Contents

SECTION ONE

Get a Good Start in Your New Vocation

In this section, you will learn

- ✔ How to avoid ruining your career
- ✔ How to be the best teacher you can
- ✔ How to promote your new profession
- ✔ How to boost your confidence
- ✔ How to establish a discussion group

"Welcome Back!" Those signs in schools across the nation apply to teachers, too—especially new teachers. As a first-year teacher, you will have an exciting and memorable year. You will face new challenges and have lots of fun with your students.

Fun? Yes, teaching is fun. Many teachers have fun every day at school, contrary to what many people think. Believing that teaching cannot be fun is just one of the many ways that people hold misconceptions about teaching. As a new teacher, you will join millions of others in a profession that is probably one of the most universally misunderstood.

The rest of the world believes that teachers enjoy short hours and long summer vacations, that we must have taken courses in how to answer seemingly endless questions with unflinching patience, that we enjoy eating in a cafeteria with children who left their table manners at home, that we must like wearing clothes stained with red ink, crayon, and chalk.

The rest of the world doesn't know that teachers spend their free time grading papers, writing lesson plans, and taking classes for recertification. The rest of the world does not realize how hard it is to find words that can inspire as well as scold. The rest of the world does not understand that teachers weep when a school erupts in violence, because it could have been their school, any school.

Your life as a new teacher will be a paradox. You will have to be strict and loving at the same time. You will be exhausted and exhilarated. Best of all, you will receive more than you can ever give, no matter how generous you are.

As a teacher, you will never be rich, even if your district has the wisdom to offer you a signing bonus. However, you will be rewarded repeatedly because you will help students achieve their dreams, and in doing so, you will achieve your own. Teachers don't just "touch the future," as bumper stickers promise; education is far more than that. Teachers see the promise of the future in the unruly classrooms of the present.

It's not easy being a teacher. You will need to develop heroic qualities: the stamina of an Olympic athlete, the diplomacy of a head of state, and the courage of a soldier. It is a tremendous challenge, but other teachers have done it, and so can you. After all, someone had to teach those other heroes. Olympic athletes, heads of state, and soldiers are not just born that way. Standing behind them—behind every hero—is another hero: a teacher.

Welcome to your new vocation.

Your Teaching Career: The Good News

"You're a teacher? Boy, I don't see how you do it. I could never be a teacher." Perhaps you have already heard this several times since you announced that you have signed a teaching contract. Media reports are full of grim news about the teacher shortage, embarrassingly low teacher salaries, controversies over standards and standardized testing, and, worst of all, school violence.

While these reports are not exaggerations, there is a great deal of unreported good news about education. Day after day, well-behaved children learn what they are expected to learn—and even exceed their teachers' expectations. There are many positive aspects to being a teacher:

You are part of a large supportive team of caring professionals. The good news about being a teacher today is that you are not alone. Teachers are members of a team of supportive adults who care about and work with all students in a school. Depending on the size of your school and your district's policies, you may work with social service workers, support committees, student mentors, parole officers, counselors, or other caring adults.

You have access to an increasing amount of educational research. Since the 1970s, there has been an enormous increase in educational research. Because of this extensive research, we can better understand students' differing needs. Educators can quickly find solutions to many of the problems that teachers face every day. We now know that teachers play a much more important role in shaping students' futures than we once thought. Another benefit of this increased research is that much of it is available online or through conferences, professional organizations, or books.

You have access to technology that can connect you and your students to the world. One of the best things about being a teacher in the new millennium is the technology available for educators. Not only do we have access to sophisticated technology, but so do our students. Even if there is a shortage of equipment in your school, there are remedies to this problem. Along with the advances in equipment, there are countless education resource sites on the Internet that give you access to hundreds of thousands of other teachers who are willing to share ideas and who are just a few keystrokes away. You can visit Web sites, read blogs, and find innovative lesson plans and materials online.

You can rise to the challenge of the No Child Left Behind Act. One of the most controversial education topics in recent years is implementation of the No Child Left Behind Act (NCLB) and the accountability measures that accompany it. Although coverage of this issue tends to be sensational and negative, much about NCLB is positive. While school districts are under enormous pressure to improve academic performance, students and teachers who rise to the challenge of closing the achievement gap can only be enriched by their efforts.

Today's teachers reach out to all students. In years past, educators reflected the social climate of their time by not fully including all children in the education process. Students were discriminated against because of many factors, including gender, race, ability, and national origin. Today's teachers include all students in their instructional efforts. We even teach the children who make it clear to everyone around them that they are not interested in an education.

The best reason to teach is the simplest: children. Although the preceding examples of the recent news in education are positive ones, they are not the best feature of your new career. The very best news about the teaching profession is that you get to be with children all day long. Whether the children in your class are bored seniors or energetic kindergartners, they are still the best reasons to go to school each day.

Core Values of Professional Educators

No matter where or when teachers gather, inevitably the conversations all seem to revolve around the same topics: students and classroom issues. Why does this remarkable similarity occur? It is not a coincidence that teachers everywhere have the same concerns and interests. While our students and schools may be very different, the same core values shape our teaching experiences. Here are the essential beliefs, the core values of professional educators:

- All children can learn; however, not all children learn at the same rate or in the same way.
- Lowered expectations kill the hope of success.

- Success breeds success in the classroom as well as in life.
- All teachers are role models all the time.
- The three P's of success are planning, preparation, and prevention.
- Teachers control what happens in a classroom, the good as well as the bad.
- Teachers can make a difference in the life of a child.

You Are Not Alone

Given the purpose of your work and the diverse personalities, needs, and backgrounds of your students, problems are inevitable. Some will be simple to resolve, others will take longer, and still others will not have workable solutions. To examine your assumptions about problems you may have as you begin your teaching career, use Self-Assessment 1.1.

> **When you have a bad day, know in your heart that you did something to affect a student in a positive way.**
>
> *—Nancy Parker, 31 years' experience*

On the days when your life as a teacher seems beset with serious problems, take comfort in knowing that you are not alone. All teachers have problems. First-year teachers, experienced teachers, teachers at every grade level and every ability level have to cope with problems, no matter how ideal their school situation.

Anytime you feel overwhelmed, remember that all teachers have had to deal with what you are going through. The following problems are ones that all teachers experience:

- Stacks of tedious paperwork
- Fatigue and burnout
- Frequent class interruptions
- Difficulty in contacting parents
- Not enough equipment or materials
- Students with overwhelming family problems
- The threat of school violence
- Uncertainty about the right course of action to take
- A culture or generation gap with students
- Not enough productive time with students
- Lack of practical solutions to discipline problems
- Overcrowded classrooms

SELF-ASSESSMENT 1.1

What Are Your Assumptions About Teaching?

Below you will find some common assumptions that many first-year teachers make about teaching.

✔ Put a checkmark in the box beside each statement that you think is valid.

✔ Check the information at the end to see how much you really know about your new profession.

☐ 1. It's important that my students like me.

☐ 2. The advice that more experienced teachers have been giving me—"Don't smile until Thanksgiving"—makes sense.

☐ 3. Lawsuits happen to other teachers.

☐ 4. Many of my students come from broken homes with busy parents who do not take an active interest in what is happening at school.

☐ 5. All year will be as tough as the first semester.

How Veteran Teachers View Popular Assumptions

1. **It's important that my students like me.** We all want our students to like us. However, as a teacher, you will often have to ask students to do things they do not want to do. You will also have to enforce rules they must follow. It is not your role to be a student's well-liked friend. It is important that students respect you and your role as a teacher, too. Work to maintain a balance between students' liking you and students' respecting you.
2. **The advice that more experienced teachers have been giving me—"Don't smile until Thanksgiving"—makes sense.** Why shouldn't you smile? No one likes a grouch. Besides, students will not respond any better or behave any better if you show no sense of enjoyment in teaching them and being with them. Balance the need to be strict with a cheerful presence.
3. **Lawsuits happen to other teachers.** Lawsuits are one of the hazards of modern life, and teachers are not exempt from the threat. Do not be lulled into thinking that a lawsuit can't happen to you. You can protect yourself by keeping your documentation in order and by being professional in your conduct at all times.
4. **Many of my students come from broken homes with busy parents who do not take an active interest in what is happening at school.** You should not assume that single parents or guardians are less concerned about their children than other parents. Parents or guardians who are too busy to be concerned about their child's welfare, fortunately, are very rare. Treat all students and their parents or guardians with consistent and respectful dignity.
5. **All year will be as tough as the first semester.** The first few months of any job are the most difficult. Every day of your first semester and first year will be an opportunity for you to learn and grow. Although neither activity is always comfortable, before long you will be handling your role as a teacher with confidence and ease.

You Are the Solution

While some people believe that schools are hotbeds of social, behavioral, and academic problems, you are the solution to those problems. While it is exciting to think of the powerful influence you can have on your students, it is just as unnerving to accept the challenges that accompany your importance.

Countless studies have proved that teachers are the most significant factor in any student's schooling. Although you may be tempted to think that sports, peer pressure, or a student's physical environment have more influence than you do, consider the many ways in which you play a role in your students' lives:

- Inspiring students to believe they can achieve their goals and dreams
- Keeping defenseless students safe from bullies
- Encouraging a lifelong interest in learning
- Guiding students in building a better life
- Offering comfort and guidance
- Teaching students to read, to write, to think
- Modeling how to be a good citizen and a successful adult
- Helping students believe in themselves
- Encouraging students who get little encouragement elsewhere

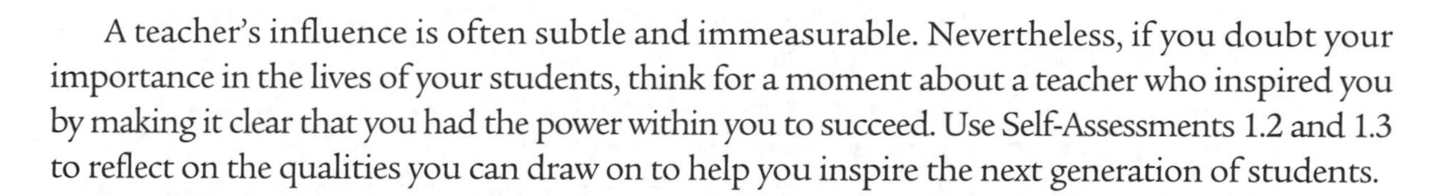

A teacher's influence is often subtle and immeasurable. Nevertheless, if you doubt your importance in the lives of your students, think for a moment about a teacher who inspired you by making it clear that you had the power within you to succeed. Use Self-Assessments 1.2 and 1.3 to reflect on the qualities you can draw on to help you inspire the next generation of students.

> One day in the cafeteria, I noticed a young man who was not his usual fun self. I walked by, stopped, and asked him quietly if everything was all right. He said yes, but I knew it wasn't. I told him he knew where I was if he needed me, then moved on. The next morning, I found a note on my desk, all folded, teen style. In the note, this young man thanked me for asking him if he was OK. He said he had been struggling with some very hard news and was really thinking of doing something stupid, but I had made him rethink his decision. I was awed at the power. As teachers, we never, ever know the full extent of our effect on those lives entrusted to us. We must truly exercise caution in how we interact with young people. I carry that note, now twenty years old, in my wallet every day of my life, to remind me of this moment. The good news: this young man is now a productive member of our community with a lovely wife (who was also my student) and three great children. What greater reward could any teacher desire?
>
> *—Luann Scott, 31 years' experience*

SELF-ASSESSMENT 1.2

Character Traits of Successful Teachers

Place a checkmark in the box beside each character trait you already possess. After you have made this quick self-assessment, look over the list again to determine how to develop other characteristics that will help you become a competent, successful teacher.

Successful teachers are

- ☐ Patient with their students, their colleagues, and themselves
- ☐ Able to let their students know they care about them
- ☐ Energetic and willing to work
- ☐ Able to engage children whose attention span is brief
- ☐ Optimistic that what they do today affects the future
- ☐ Successful at listening to students both in groups and individually
- ☐ Able to make quick decisions on a variety of issues all day long
- ☐ Enthusiastic about their subject matter and about their students
- ☐ Efficient at planning, organizing, and managing time
- ☐ Not afraid to ask for help

SELF-ASSESSMENT 1.3

How Will You Rate as a Teacher?

Before you begin, remember that good teachers are not just born that way; instead, they make deliberate choices to become the teachers that they are. You can do the same. As a first-year teacher, you should commit yourself to developing as many of the following qualities as possible as quickly as you can. See where your strengths lie and which qualities you need to develop further by following these steps:

1. Put a checkmark in the box before each characteristic in the following list that applies to you every day that you are at school.
2. When you are finished, total the number of checkmarks.
3. See the rankings at the end of the assessment to see how you rate.

Good teachers:

☐ Enjoy their students

☐ Inspire their students to want to know more

☐ Return papers promptly

☐ Use a variety of interesting activities in a lesson

☐ Keep students engaged in meaningful work throughout class

☐ Make sure students know how to do an assignment well

☐ Know their subject matter

☐ Are a reliable role model

☐ Maintain an orderly classroom

☐ Are prepared to teach every student every day

☐ See themselves as part of a team

☐ Commit themselves to professionalism

☐ Make their students feel capable

☐ Handle paperwork efficiently

☐ Stay open-minded

Total number of checkmarks: ______________

How to Use Your Results

13–15: You are on the right track! Keep up the good work!

11–12: Begin by choosing one or two qualities to improve. Make a plan, set your goals, and work to develop all the attributes of a successful teacher.

10 or less: Remember that improving your performance as a teacher takes time and deliberate choices. Begin by selecting the qualities that are most important to you right now. Set your goals for developing each one.

How to Avoid Ruining Your Career

As a first-year teacher, you will make many mistakes. Some of these mistakes will be small ones: a poorly worded question on a quiz, a misplaced teacher's edition, a misspelled word on a handout. While such mistakes are an unavoidable part of your learning process, other mistakes are serious ones that could jeopardize your career. Just like the small mistakes, these serious mistakes may seem expedient or not very important at the time, but you should never doubt that they are indeed grave errors that can cause irrevocable harm. Follow these suggestions to avoid the possibility of ruining your career:

- Don't allow small problems to become large ones.
- Don't refuse to honor school rules even if you don't agree with them.
- Don't touch a student in any way that could possibly be misconstrued.
- Don't model a lack of integrity. Follow the rules for photocopying material and showing movies at school.
- Don't ever leave your students unsupervised.
- Don't overlook serious student problems such as substance abuse or bullying.
- Don't give students free time in which they have nothing to do.
- Don't allow students to harass each other or to engage in horseplay.
- Don't agree "not to tell" when a student tells you confidential information. You may be required to report it to an administrator or counselor.
- Don't neglect to monitor students who are engaged in a strenuous activity.
- Don't allow a student to leave the school with an adult who is not legally authorized to take the child.
- Don't break laws on confidentiality and privacy of student information.
- Don't neglect to learn and abide by school policies and procedures.
- Don't act in anger.
- Don't be inconsistent in implementing your behavior policies.
- Don't call in sick when you are not.

Love every child. *Your love may be the only love some children get.* Remember that many, if not most of the children you teach, bring a lot of baggage to school that was never even close to being a part of your world growing up and that you don't understand. Teach them anyway.

—Charlene Herrala, 24 years' experience

How to Be the Best Teacher You Can Be

How can you develop into the kind of teacher you want to be? The answer is simple: be a student again.

Just as you worked hard to be an excellent student, you will now have to work to be an excellent teacher. Both endeavors require the same skills. Study, concentrate on your objectives, believe in yourself, seek help, do your homework, work well with others, take notes, and, above all, pay attention to the excellent teachers all around you!

Ten Skills All Teachers Should Have

In addition to the innate and learned characteristics that all teachers need, there are many skills that all teachers should develop as quickly as possible.

Teachers should be able to

1. Break down material in a variety of ways appropriate to the age and abilities of their students
2. See past a misbehavior to the whole child
3. Establish goals and set priorities for their students and themselves
4. Encourage, inspire, and chastise all at the same time
5. Make quick adjustments when a lesson is not working well
6. Treat all students with affection even when they misbehave
7. Diagnose and remediate a child's learning difficulties
8. Work with parents and other caring adults on behalf of students
9. Multitask in front of a crowd
10. Find joy in being with their students

How to Promote Your New Profession

Similar to those working in other occupations, educators are expected to be cheerleaders for their school, their students, their co-workers—in short, for their profession. Showing your enthusiastic and positive attitude can only enhance your ability to work well with others. Here are a few ways to promote your new profession (and enhance your own image as a caring teacher):

- Shop and transact other business in the community where you teach. Become part of community life.

- Leave your complaints about school at school. People who are not involved with your school district should not hear indiscriminate negative comments about area schools, teachers, and, especially, students. Be positive instead.
- Attend school events, and be sure to take friends and family members with you.
- When you send information home, proofread it to make sure it is well expressed and professional.
- If you can take your students on field trips in the community, do so. Let the members of your community see how well behaved local children can be.

Common-Sense Steps to Boost Your Confidence

As you go through the first year of your new career, there may be times when you lose confidence in yourself and in the choice you made to be a teacher. Such a lack of confidence is stressful and may cause you to consider other, less rewarding professions.

You can do many things to reassure yourself about how well you are adjusting to the changes of a new career. Follow these suggestions, and enjoy the rewards they will bring.

- **Dress the part.** If you look like a veteran educator, then your professional image will speak for you in the moments when you are too shy, overwhelmed, or uncertain to think of just the right things to say.
- **Be prepared for class.** There is a great sense of accomplishment in knowing that you are prepared for questions, have the correct number of handouts, and know just how to interest your students in the day's lesson.
- **Listen more than you speak.** This does not mean that you should never speak up; it just means that the veteran teachers around you have a great deal to offer to novice teachers who are willing to listen to what they have to say.
- **Keep it simple at first.** Do not plan elaborate class activities such as lengthy collaborative learning exercises or overnight field trips until you have gotten to know your students well enough and have enough experience to ensure that the activities will be successful.
- **Pay attention to your successes.** It is very easy to dwell on your failings at work. Make a conscious effort to focus on the improvements you make in your first year. Keep a list of the things you did correctly each week, or reward yourself when you have mastered a professional goal.
- **Seek support from your colleagues.** Novice and veteran teachers all can offer encouragement and advice. Often it is comforting to know that other teachers are experiencing the same problems. Use the "Talk It Over" information at the end of each section of this resource to create your own discussion group or join an online forum.
- **Set professional goals for yourself.** By setting goals, you will not only improve your teaching skills, but you will also give yourself a psychological boost because you will

> **Enjoy this time. Teaching can be a lot of fun when you connect with a student. Do not expect instant payback. You are laying the foundation for years to come both in and out of school.**
>
> —*Edward Gardner, 36 years' experience*

feel a greater sense of control over your professional life. Keep your goals manageable, and track your progress.

- **Stay organized!** When you are organized at work, you will avoid many stressful situations because you will be in control of your environment and you will appear competent and professional.
- **Smile and act as if you have things under control.** Your students do not need to know that you are having a bad day. They just want a teacher who is in control of the class.
- **See opportunities instead of disasters.** You will need to develop an optimistic and resilient attitude in order to feel confident as a teacher. Instead of dwelling on your mistakes or on what went wrong during the day, see such occasions for what they really are: opportunities to learn and grow.

Talk It Over

How to Get a Good Start in Your New Vocation

According to conventional wisdom, you will learn more from other teachers than from any other source. To become the kind of teacher you want to be, you should develop strong professional relationships with other teachers. Even the most experienced teacher cannot do his or her job without the support of others. Every successful professional needs a supportive working environment.

Unfortunately, one of the biggest hurdles that novice teachers face is a lack of this necessary support. The isolation that can accompany a teaching career is especially evident in the first few years when teachers are adjusting to their new profession. Being out of the loop can be a drawback for anyone, but it is especially detrimental to inexperienced teachers, who stand to benefit most from the support of friendly, knowledgeable colleagues.

Look past your department or grade level to see just how many colleagues you really have. Every adult involved in education is a potential source of support; mentors, outstanding teachers, other new teachers, teachers in other grade levels, or even people you meet at conventions or conferences can be part of your professional support network.

When you do create a supportive network, you will benefit in several ways:

- Other teachers will have many of the same problems you experience and can offer insights and solutions.

- ▶ Other teachers can reinforce your idealism with their own.
- ▶ Other teachers will understand your successes and failures, your joys and frustrations.
- ▶ Other teachers will offer a new perspective as they share strategies, techniques, and advice.

Fortunately, it is easier than ever to form professional relationships with other educators. An excellent way to connect with teachers in school districts across the nation is through an online blog, chat room, or discussion forum. One advantage of this method is that teachers everywhere share many of the same experiences, so you can receive insights from a wide range of perspectives and look at local problems from a fresh point of view. If you are interested in trying this type of networking, here are two excellent online sites to explore:

- **A to Z Teacher Stuff (http://forums.atozteacherstuff.com).** This discussion site is teacher-designed and teacher-friendly. Anyone can view a forum posting, but to reply or post your own new topic, you must register. Follow the helpful guidelines and tips to start connecting with other teachers across the nation.
- **Editorial Projects in Education Blogboard (http://blogs.edweek.org/teachers/blogboard/).** Part of a larger site maintained by Editorial Projects in Education, which publishes *Education Week* and *Teacher Magazine,* among others, this site offers links to dozens of interesting blogs about current educational issues.

A second way to form strong professional relationships with your colleagues is to establish a discussion group with some of your co-workers. You will learn a great deal if you can meet regularly to discuss common concerns. A local teacher discussion group could center on a shared discipline, shared students, or shared interests. Here are some suggestions for creating your own local discussion group:

- ▶ Begin with just a few people, so that everyone's opinion matters.
- ▶ Establish a regular meeting time and place. Set the times when your meeting will begin and end. Weekly meetings that last thirty minutes will be more effective than monthly meetings that are so long that everyone loses interest.
- ▶ Set ground rules about acceptable topics; for example, the meetings should not be gripe sessions but discussions whose purpose is to study school-related topics.
- ▶ Arrange a system in which group members share responsibility for facilitating the meetings.
- ▶ For best results, determine the topics you want to discuss in advance of the meeting, so that all of the participants have a chance to think about them and can come prepared to share.
- ▶ You do not have to limit your group to faculty members. Consider involving other interested staff members when appropriate.

Although the specific topics of discussion will reflect the makeup of the group, some of the topics you should consider talking about include innovative lesson plans and materials, classroom management strategies, how to develop collaborative lessons, current educational issues, and solutions for school problems.

At the end of each section of this resource, you will find a list of ten discussion questions specific to the material in that section to talk over with your colleagues. You can use these questions as a springboard for discussions that will help you and your discussion group members grow and develop professionally.

Discuss these questions about your new vocation:

1. What qualities have you observed that allow teachers to be successful? Share your beliefs about good teachers.
2. What are your professional goals this term? What plans do you need to make in order to achieve them? How can your colleagues help?
3. When have you experienced the most growth as a teacher? What did you learn that helped you grow?
4. Talk about a person in your building whom you admire. What have you learned from this person?
5. What can you do to boost your confidence in your ability to be a competent teacher? What actions can you take to develop the confidence you need?
6. Categorize the ways in which good teachers are also good students. What can you learn from this?
7. Which teachers in your past empowered you to believe in yourself? How can you model your own career on this inspiration?
8. What meaning does the expression "teaching is a deliberate act" hold for you? What can you conclude about successful teachers from this statement?
9. Compile a list of problems you can anticipate as you begin your career. How can you begin to cope with them? Work together to brainstorm possible solutions for each one.
10. What beliefs about teaching do you share with the colleagues in your discussion group? How do your beliefs differ? How can you learn from each other?

SECTION TWO

Develop Your Professional Expertise

In this section, you will learn

- ✔ How to fulfill state and district guidelines in your classroom
- ✔ How to develop professional work habits
- ✔ How to manage the information, policies, and procedures you need to know
- ✔ How to become an efficient teacher
- ✔ How to be proactive in avoiding burnout

Just as in any profession, a teacher's first year can be a difficult one. Everything is new, and it is not always easy to know the right course of action to take. However, if millions of other teachers have not only survived their first year but gone on to help their students realize their dreams, so can you. One of the best ways to not just survive but thrive in your first year is to develop professional expertise.

Professional expertise can be as simple as not losing your class keys and as complex as working well with a mentor. Developing professional expertise means having the skills and attitudes of a competent educator. It is evident in many tangible ways, such as how you dress, organize your materials, or grade papers. Students and colleagues can tell at a glance that you are in control of your situation and of yourself. However, the hallmarks of professional expertise are mostly intangible ones, such as good work habits or how skillfully you convey a seriousness of purpose about your new career.

As you face the hardships of your first years as a teacher, take them as opportunities to learn and overcome challenges. Retain your sense of humor, expand your sense of adventure, work hard, and develop into a professional educator. Even the most seasoned experts had to begin somewhere.

Advantages to Enjoy in Your First Years as a Teacher

While it is true that a teacher's first years can be difficult, there is much about this time in your career to appreciate. Here are five important benefits to being a novice teacher that you can take advantage of right away:

1. **You have up-to-date training.** You have probably taken courses designed to help you earn a teaching license recently. This gives you a tremendous advantage over faculty members who may not be aware of some of the newest trends and changes in education.
2. **You have enthusiasm.** Your inexperience allows you to be enthusiastic about things that some jaded teachers may no longer find interesting. Don't lose your enthusiasm! Let it be infectious! If you can always carry it in your heart, you will ensure your success as a teacher.
3. **You have not yet developed poor work habits.** You are starting with a clean slate. Now is the time to develop the good work habits that will lead to successful teaching. Use this stage in your professional life to learn how competent teachers accomplish their teaching objectives successfully.
4. **Your colleagues will be generous to a new teacher.** The experienced teachers you work with can recall their own difficulties during the first few years of their careers and will likely be generous in offering you the help you need. As a new teacher, you will find that others will offer you materials, advice, and support.
5. **Others will be more understanding of your mistakes.** Simply because you are a new faculty member, other staff members will not expect you to have the same level of knowledge or expertise that experienced teachers have. This does not mean that you should not work as hard as you can to become a competent teacher; rather, it means that other staff members will understand when you do not know some things that they take for granted. Enjoy this small benefit, and remember to return the favor when you are an experienced teacher.

In addition to the advantages that all beginning teachers enjoy, you bring your own valuable traits, skills, and attitudes to your first year of teaching. Use Self-Assessment 2.1 to assess your strengths.

SELF-ASSESSMENT 2.1

Assess Your Strengths

What is the current state of your professional expertise? Below you will find a brief list of some of the positive attributes that teachers need to be successful. Use the following three-point scale to assess how well you are doing:

1 = I need to develop this attribute.

2 = I have some experience with this attribute, but I need to work on developing it fully.

3 = I have mastered this attribute.

______ I have established several professional goals.

______ I value the differences among my students.

______ I want each of my students to have a positive attitude about school.

______ I am an organized person who is in control of my class.

______ I can handle almost all of the problems I have at work each day.

______ I can successfully prevent or cope with discipline problems.

______ I have a thorough knowledge of my content area.

______ I control my attitude about work.

______ I have a supportive group of people to whom I can turn for help.

______ I want my classes to be dynamic and enjoyable.

______ I encourage students to cooperate with each other and with me.

______ I see problems as challenges rather than obstacles.

______ I allow enough time to balance my career and my personal responsibilities.

______ I believe courtesy is important in successful professional relationships.

______ I believe my students are worthwhile people who can learn and succeed.

- First, identify all the areas in which you scored a "3," and be proud of yourself for your current strengths as a teacher.
- After you have examined your successes, turn your attention to the areas in which you only gave yourself a "1" or a "2." These scores indicate the attributes for you to work on as your career progresses.

Your Classroom Responsibilities

Education is a complex undertaking. It differs from many professions in the multitude and variety of daily tasks that teachers must accomplish. As a teacher, you not only have to master the art of interacting successfully with others at all times, but you also face a wide range of other responsibilities.

> **Let kids know that they are special to you and that time with them is special.**
>
> *—Carole Platt, 35 years' experience*

One of the most difficult tasks you face as a new teacher is learning how to manage all of your duties successfully. To accomplish this, you should first focus on your classroom responsibilities. Use Self-Assessment 2.2 to help you brainstorm about strategies for managing your tasks. In addition, here are some suggestions:

- **Become thoroughly familiar with the content you are teaching.** You must be the authority on this material in the classroom. If you do not know the material, then your students cannot learn.
- **Quickly develop and maintain a positive relationship with every child.** This is a sure way to a successful school year for students and teachers alike.
- **Develop interesting, innovative strategies for teaching the material your students need to know.** You should include a variety of activities to meet the needs of every student every day.
- **Establish clear objectives for your students.** Clear objectives will focus your instruction and allow your students to concentrate on what is essential for mastery in each lesson.
- **Learn to deliver instruction effectively.** You can and should learn to speak with poise and precision in front of a class.
- **Teach your students the study strategies they need to do their work well.** Teachers who teach study strategies such as outlining, summarizing, and successful time management empower their students to become responsible for their own learning.
- **Recognize and address the diverse needs of students in each of your classes.** Your teaching should take into account your students' skill levels, preferred learning styles, and previous knowledge.
- **Provide appropriate, helpful, and timely feedback.** Make it your goal to return graded papers to your students within three days and to provide helpful rather than critical comments.
- **Provide an orderly and safe environment in which courtesy is the order of the day.** Successful classroom management requires consistent effort on your part. It does not happen by chance.
- **Accept your role as classroom leader.** You are the primary positive force in your classroom and in the lives of many of your students. When you accept responsibility for what happens in your class, all of your students benefit.

SELF-ASSESSMENT 2.2

Manage Your Classroom Responsibilities

While it can be difficult to know how to begin meeting each of your many classroom responsibilities, you can avoid many problems in your workday if you create strategies for accomplishing each responsibility. Use the spaces below to plan how to begin each task.

Classroom Responsibility 1: Be familiar with the course content (see Section Seven)
Strategies for meeting this responsibility:

Classroom Responsibility 2: Develop a positive relationship with every child (see Section Six)
Strategies for meeting this responsibility:

Classroom Responsibility 3: Incorporate innovative teaching strategies (see Sections Seven and Eight)
Strategies for meeting this responsibility:

Classroom Responsibility 4: Establish clear goals for students (see Section Ten)
Strategies for meeting this responsibility:

Classroom Responsibility 5: Deliver instruction effectively (see Section Eight)
Strategies for meeting this responsibility:

Classroom Responsibility 6: Teach study strategies (see Section Eleven)
Strategies for meeting this responsibility:

Classroom Responsibility 7: Address the diverse needs of students (see Section Sixteen)
Strategies for meeting this responsibility:

Classroom Responsibility 8: Provide appropriate feedback (see Section Nine)
Strategies for meeting this responsibility:

Classroom Responsibility 9: Provide an orderly and safe environment (see Sections Fourteen and Fifteen)
Strategies for meeting this responsibility:

Classroom Responsibility 10: Accept responsibility as classroom leader (see Sections One and Two)
Strategies for meeting this responsibility:

Go observe the teachers in your building. A lot can be gained from watching an experienced teacher, especially a great one.

—*Debbie McManaway, 12 years' experience*

Look Ahead and Set Goals

It is important to establish your professional goals as you start a new school year. Use Self-Assessment 2.3 to help you reflect and plan.

How to Fulfill State and District Standards in Your Classroom

States and districts, in recent years, have outlined the standards you are expected to cover if your students are to meet the benchmarks indicated by the No Child Left Behind Act. When you read these standards for the first time, your heart may sink at the enormity of the task before you. However, other teachers have been able to reach the goals described in the standards, and you will also be able to do so.

First, you must accept the importance of the standards to your students, to your school, and to your school district. Your students will be tested on how well they have mastered the objectives outlined in state and district standards.

There are many ways for you to improve how well you teach and how well you can help your students master the material in the standards. Here are several strategies to help you incorporate them into your own teaching style:

ATTEND CONFERENCES

As a first-year teacher, you may not believe that attending a professional conference is a good use of your time when you have so much work to do that you struggle not to be overwhelmed. However, conferences provide an opportunity to learn new strategies and network with other professionals. If your school district offers you an opportunity to attend a conference, accept the offer.

Keep your fresh innocence alive. Don't fall victim to the negativity of those who no longer seem to be able to find a bit of good in the world.

—*Dawn Carroll, 10 years' experience*

LEARN THROUGH READING AND RESEARCH

The next way you can learn how to teach the standards is through your own reading and research. Public libraries and college libraries abound with useful materials for teachers. You can also use the extensive resources on the Internet to learn more about the material you are expected to cover.

SELF-ASSESSMENT 2.3

Create Your Vision of the Year Ahead

Even though you may change your ideas, you should formulate your own vision of the successful year that lies ahead of you. To turn this vision into actuality, ask yourself the following questions:

How will my teaching skills be different at the end of the year?

____

____

____

____

____

____

What can I do to develop these skills?

____

____

____

____

____

What knowledge do I most want to acquire this year?

____

____

____

____

____

What can I do to acquire this knowledge?

____

____

____

____

____

INVESTIGATE THE NATIONAL BOARD FOR PROFESSIONAL TEACHING STANDARDS

As a first-year teacher, you may yet not be eligible to work toward national certification, but it is a positive choice for all teachers to make as early in their career as they can. As you work to improve your overall teaching skills, you will also learn how to effectively teach the material in your state and district standards. You can learn more at the Web site of the National Board for Professional Teaching Standards (www.nbpts.org).

Don't be afraid to ask for help. Experienced teachers are more than willing to help; they just don't know you need it until you ask.

—Patty Muth, 14 years' experience

FIND ROLE MODELS

All teachers need role models. To learn not just how to integrate standards into your lessons but how to become a better educator, you should find your own role models. Fortunately, you probably will not have to look far to find other teachers who are already skillful at teaching your state's standards. If you look around your school, you'll find many role models. Ask for their advice.

The No Child Left Behind Act and You

On January 8, 2002, President George W. Bush signed into law educational reform legislation known as the No Child Left Behind Act (NCLB). This monumental reform in education has had a dramatic impact on teachers and students in all fifty states.

Designed to close the gap between the highest and lowest achievers, NCLB seeks to ensure that all students receive the education they deserve, regardless of factors such as gender, race, age, or socioeconomic status. The federal mandate is simple: by the 2013–2014 school year, all students will read and perform math at grade level.

NCLB has four important components. The first is accountability. Each year, states test students to see whether they have met the benchmarks for their grade level. If students do meet the benchmarks, then they have made adequate yearly progress (AYP).

The next component of NCLB is its emphasis on scientific research. Teachers now have access to information about the best instructional practices for all grades and subjects. NCLB encourages schools to use programs that have been proved to be successful.

The third component of NCLB is increased involvement of parents in their children's education. From notifying parents of their child's progress to reporting on a school's achievement, NCLB reaches out to all parents.

The final component is the local control that states and school districts have to meet the demands of the law. To meet the requirements of NCLB, states and local districts have increased flexibility in how they spend federal funds.

How does NCLB affect you?

Teachers can no longer teach courses that they are not qualified to teach. This means that all teachers should be "highly qualified" under the terms of NCLB. Highly qualified teachers have a bachelor's degree in the subject they teach; they have full state accreditation to teach that subject; and they have demonstrated competence to teach through a state-mandated test or through their collegiate courses.

NCLB also affects you through its emphasis on increased professional development for all teachers, based on the belief that teachers are one of the most important factors in a child's academic success.

NCLB Strategies for Success in Your Classroom

As a new teacher, you will continue to learn much about how NCLB affects you and your students. Try these strategies to make sure the effects of the reform are positive ones for you and your students:

- Make sure you know the curriculum standards that apply to your students.
- Be sure to follow your state and district guidelines in teaching the standards.
- Familiarize yourself with the standardized tests your students will take.
- Teach your students how to take standardized tests. Teach them test-taking strategies, and provide them with plenty of opportunities to practice.
- Raise your students' awareness of the importance of standardized testing.
- Check with your local school district about your school's status. Find out how this will influence your teaching methods.
- Make sure you are aware of the requirements of your teaching certificate so that you know whether you need to meet additional requirements to be considered "highly qualified." Check with your local school district or state department of education to learn more about what your state requires.

WEB RESOURCES TO HELP YOU WITH THE CHALLENGES OF NCLB

While a great deal of information (and misinformation) is available for teachers concerning the challenges of NCLB, responsible educators avoid the rumor mill. To learn more about NCLB, excellent primary source materials for teachers are available online:

- **U.S. Department of Education (www.ed.gov).** The U.S. Department of Education maintains a large Web site that offers information, news, policies, and practical resources for educators. Try learning more about NCLB at these two links within the larger site:

- **What Works Clearinghouse, U.S. Department of Education (http://whatworks.ed.gov).** Learn about successful research-based teaching practices here. The What Works Clearinghouse, which was established by the U.S. Department of Education, maintains this excellent site packed with practical information that all teachers can use.
- **No Child Left Behind, U.S. Department of Education (www.ed.gov/nclb).** To stay informed about NCLB, try the U.S. State Department of Education's Web site, which provides up-to-date information that may be relevant for your school, your students, and you.

School Information, Policies, and Procedures You Need to Know

All teachers must learn a great deal of nuts-and-bolts information quickly, often as early as the first day of school. Although most of this information is available in your faculty manual or through the initial district and schoolwide meetings at the start of the school year, you will have to learn some of it by talking with your mentor or colleagues. Here are some of the information, policies, and procedures you need to know:

- ☐ Acceptable student behavior
- ☐ Attendance procedures
- ☐ Audiovisual aids procedures
- ☐ Behavior rules for common areas
- ☐ Bell schedules
- ☐ Children with special needs
- ☐ Chronic attendance problems
- ☐ Class party policies and procedures
- ☐ Class schedule
- ☐ Detention policies and procedures
- ☐ Discipline policies and procedures
- ☐ Dismissal procedures
- ☐ Duty assignments
- ☐ Emergency safety codes and procedures
- ☐ Faculty attendance policy
- ☐ Faculty committees
- ☐ Faculty handbook information
- ☐ Family vacation policies for students
- ☐ Field trips

- ☐ Fire drills
- ☐ Food in the classroom policies
- ☐ Guest speaker policies and procedures
- ☐ Handling student injury
- ☐ Homework policy
- ☐ How late you may stay in the building
- ☐ How to collect money
- ☐ Janitorial concerns
- ☐ Lesson plan format
- ☐ Library use policy
- ☐ Lost textbook policy
- ☐ Lunch procedures
- ☐ Parent conference procedures
- ☐ Professional organizations
- ☐ School organizations
- ☐ School staff members
- ☐ Student absence procedures
- ☐ Student folder access procedures
- ☐ Substitute teacher procedures
- ☐ Supply policies
- ☐ Support staff procedures
- ☐ Tardiness policies
- ☐ Teacher duties and responsibilities
- ☐ Teachers' manuals and materials
- ☐ Technology use policies
- ☐ Textbook distribution procedures
- ☐ Tornado drills
- ☐ Withdrawal from school procedures

Professional Information, Policies, and Procedures You Need to Know

In addition to being part of a school community, you are also, of course, part of larger educational communities, including those of your local district, state, and nation. The information, policies, and procedures of these larger professional communities affect your school life every day in a variety of ways. All teachers should quickly learn about these topics:

- ☐ Achievement gap reduction
- ☐ Adequate yearly progress records
- ☐ Definition of "highly qualified" teacher
- ☐ District curriculum guidelines
- ☐ District mission statement
- ☐ Emergency school closing procedures
- ☐ Geographic areas covered by your school district
- ☐ Grading policies
- ☐ In-service meeting schedules
- ☐ Insurance policies
- ☐ Local school calendar
- ☐ Location of district offices
- ☐ Locations of other schools in your district
- ☐ Members of local and state school boards
- ☐ Names of key staff members
- ☐ No Child Left Behind Act
- ☐ Payroll department personnel and location
- ☐ Reporting periods and procedures for grades
- ☐ Retention and promotion policies
- ☐ Staff attendance policies
- ☐ Staff evaluation policy and procedures
- ☐ Standardized testing schedule
- ☐ Teaching certificate information
- ☐ Teaching contract information
- ☐ Tenure policies
- ☐ When and where the local school board meets

How to Share Space, Materials, and Equipment

To be a responsible colleague, you must share space, materials, and equipment in a fair and professional manner. After all, every teacher must work with others if students are to be successful. Here are some tips to help you successfully share space, materials, and equipment at school:

- Don't be messy. Other people should not have to clean up after you or work around your untidiness. Remind yourself to pick up your own trash. Wipe up anything you spill in the lunchroom. Encourage your students to leave the classroom tidy.

- If you are sharing an office area or classroom, be aware that others may be trying to work. Keep your voice down, and try not to disturb them.
- Don't borrow anything without permission.
- If you do borrow an item, be sure to return it promptly and in good condition. Be sure to thank the lender.
- There is rarely enough equipment in a school. Be reasonable about what you request.
- Follow procedures for checking out equipment. If you are expected to sign up to use a projector three days in advance, for example, do so. There are usually very good reasons for procedures concerning materials and equipment.
- If a piece of equipment is broken, report it immediately so that others will not have to wait for it to be repaired.

OPTIMIZE YOUR USE OF THE PHOTOCOPIER

Few things can annoy an entire school staff more than a broken photocopier. Because so many people depend on a copier, the professional etiquette surrounding this important piece of machinery is clear-cut:

- Never make others wait unnecessarily while you run off hundreds of copies or arrange items on a handout. If you do either of these, expect the line behind you to become an angry mob.
- Avoid cutting and pasting your handouts at the copier. If you do need to cut and paste, prepare as much as you can in advance and then step away from the copier to work, so that others can use it.
- Be generous in allowing people with only a few copies to precede you in line if you have many copies to make.
- Take care not to be the cause of a breakdown. Use the correct paper or transparency type. Remove all staples, tape, and paper clips. Be careful not to make the situation worse when clearing paper jams.
- Try to avoid peak photocopying times: before the term begins, in the morning before class begins, at the end of the day, and right before exams or standardized tests.
- Don't violate copyright laws. Not only do you put yourself at risk for legal action, but you set a bad example for your students.
- If paper or the number of copies you can make are limited, be careful to use the amount that you are allotted wisely. Plan ahead, to make sure you will have enough when you really need to copy.

HOW TO SAVE PAPER

One of the chief expenses in most schools is paper. From construction paper to photocopy paper, the cost of those sheets can mount up quickly. Instead of being part of the problem, you can choose to be part of the solution by making an effort to save paper. Here are some tips to help you:

- The most obvious way to cut paper use in half is to use both sides of a sheet. If you use both sides when you photocopy and also allow your students to write on both sides, not only will you save paper, but you will encourage good environmental stewardship in your students.
- If you can present material on an overhead projector, a video monitor, or in another way that enhances learning and does not require paper, do so.
- If the situation is appropriate, allow students to share handouts.
- Make it a class project to devise ways to save paper. When your students become involved, you are on the way to successfully conserving paper.
- If an assignment is a brief one, have students tear a sheet in half and share.
- Ask students to reuse paper whenever they can, and model the same responsible behavior.

HOW TO ENCOURAGE STUDENTS TO RECYCLE

Making recycling part of the culture of your classroom can be a significant way to forge a connection with your students as well as encourage them to be responsible citizens. Fortunately, recycling paper and other items in a classroom is very easy. Follow these strategies to encourage your students to recycle:

- Raise student consciousness about the problem. Even very young students can be involved in recycling. Hold a discussion with students about the importance of recycling. You might even consider inviting a guest speaker from a local waste management service.
- Ask students to share ideas about how their class can recycle. Encourage them to set a reasonable goal and work toward that goal.
- Place a bin for recycled paper near the trash can so that students can choose to recycle instead of throwing away papers.
- Let students see you recycle by reusing folders, binders, shoeboxes, cans, and other items.
- Allow students to have as much control and ownership of the issue as you can. In this way, you empower them for the future as well as in your classroom.

Become an Efficient Teacher

No messy classroom. No missing papers. No forgotten phone calls. As a novice teacher you may be tempted to think that the art of teaching is intrinsically more worthwhile than the numerous details that lead to being an efficient teacher. Not so. Both are essential to a successful educator. Being an efficient professional simply means that you can handle your numerous non-instructional responsibilities in the most efficient manner.

With so many new responsibilities, you need to develop a system to manage them. Although this may be common sense, in the daily press of starting a new career, many new teachers do not take the time to plan how to accomplish the many tasks they face each day. The result is wasted time, unfinished work, and stress.

If you find yourself overwhelmed by new responsibilities, remember that other teachers have figured out solutions to the problems that confound you. Before long you will be able to handle those problems like a pro, too. Follow these tips in order to use your faculty handbook wisely, eliminate procrastination, and manage your time:

TIPS ON USING YOUR FACULTY HANDBOOK WISELY

Too often a beginning teacher will skim through the faculty handbook at the start of the year and then shove it in a desk drawer until the end of the term. However, a faculty handbook is a practical place to keep much of the information you will receive or create in the course of a school year. Reorganize the handbook with your own divider pages and tabs. You can use them to create your own sections for many items, such as

- The curriculum guidelines, standards, or objectives provided by your state and local school board offices
- The procedural information in memos, directives, school calendars, special notices, and meeting minutes from the state, the district, or your own school administrators
- A statement of your own teaching philosophy, vision, and professional goals
- Inspirational ideas: quotations, humorous sayings, positive comments from your supervisors and students
- Those great teaching ideas you would like to try once you gain more experience

TIPS ON ELIMINATING PROCRASTINATION

- **Identify the problem.** Quickly jot down the tasks you tend to put off. Some of the ones common to many teachers include phoning parents about problems, filing handouts, and grading papers.
- **Ask yourself why you procrastinate.** You don't procrastinate because you are lazy. Do you lack the supplies to get the job done well? Do you know how to do the task? Do you need a specific deadline? Whatever the reason for your procrastination, address the problem. (Do it today.)
- **Realize that you can break the procrastination habit with just a bit of consistent effort.** It is a habit that you can control, not an innate life force.

- **Before you begin a job, break it into smaller parts.** You will then be able to see how easy it is to accomplish the job one step at a time.
- **Just begin.** Remember the old proverb, "A journey of a thousand miles begins with one step." Often just the act of beginning to work on a project will break the inertia that has caused your delay and stress.
- **If you have a due date for a project, give yourself an earlier due date.** Sometimes this simple trick will encourage you to work at a task until it is complete.
- **Prioritize your responsibilities.** A to-do list can help you accomplish tasks in a timely fashion.
- **Get in the habit of doing your work *now*.** If you spend too much time thinking about something you have to do and why you are not doing it, the task becomes increasingly onerous. Instead, if you have something to do, just do it now.
- **Reward yourself once you have accomplished a burdensome task.** While the accomplishment may not seem important to others, you know how hard you worked to get it done. Take time to recognize your achievement with a reward.

TIPS FOR MANAGING TIME

- If a task will take less than three minutes, do it right away.
- Keep your calendar in an accessible spot, so that you can refer to it often. Use it to record tasks, appointments, and other information you'll need to remember as you plan your workdays. Don't just plan for a day, but for the week, for the month, for the semester, and for the year.
- Refuse politely when someone asks you to give time you cannot spare (see Section Three).
- Remember to use your biological clock whenever you can. If you are not a morning person, don't set aside time in the morning to accomplish detailed work. Do it later instead.
- Follow the old business rule: touch each sheet of paper only once.
- Keep your keys in the same location each day.
- Deal efficiently with mail. Act immediately on items that require a written response. Throw away or recycle junk mail. File catalogues for later use.
- Set up equipment early, in case there are problems.
- Be sure to use electronic files to save time and paper whenever you can.
- Consider keeping a binder in which you store your hard copies of lesson plans, handouts, and other materials for each class. If you have this material all together, you won't have to waste time searching for missing papers.

Use Small Blocks of Time Wisely

One of the frustrating aspects of a teacher's life is that there is never enough time to accomplish everything. While the general shortage of extra time seems to be a problem, large blocks of time are in especially short supply. Interruptions and schedule changes fill a teacher's days.

You can cope with this reality by learning to be an expert at accomplishing much in small moments. This is possible with determination, preparation, and practice. You will be surprised at how much you can accomplish; those minutes add up.

Still not convinced? Here are just some of the things that a focused teacher can accomplish in just a few minutes.

In fifteen minutes, you can

- Grade the objective portion of a set of test papers
- Create a quiz
- Create a review sheet
- Answer e-mail
- Create warm-up exercises for the entire week

In ten minutes, you can

- Call a parent
- Write a lesson plan
- Grade some essay questions
- Average grades
- Check homework papers

In five minutes, you can

- Create a dynamic closing exercise
- Write a positive note and send it home with a student
- Use the hole punch on a set of papers
- Write a positive comment on at least five papers
- Review key points in a lesson

In three minutes, you can

- Record grades
- Drill your students with flash cards
- Put stickers on a set of papers
- Praise a class for good behavior
- Have students write an evaluation of the day's lesson

In one minute, you can

- Erase the board
- Display a cartoon about the day's lesson
- Have students tidy the room
- Select the student of the day or week
- Write an inspirational message on the board

- Don't arrive too early or too late to meetings or duty assignments.
- Delegate as much as you can. Even very young students can accomplish many routine tasks, such as putting up posters or keeping the supply area clean.
- Have an up-to-date set of emergency lesson plans ready—just in case.
- Maintain order in your classroom so that you do not have to spend time dealing with behavior problems.

Arrive a Little Early, Leave a Little Late

One of the biggest mistakes many new teachers make is to arrive at school just in time to sprint to class, drop their briefcase, and begin teaching. While students chat idly, their stressed-out teacher rushes to take attendance, find the grade book, and scribble an assignment on the board.

In the afternoon, the same inefficient work habits can hamper teachers who race from the building the minute the last bus pulls away from the curb. The stress from arriving late and leaving early builds until many teachers suffer significant distress. There are better ways to begin and end your school day.

Plan your arrival time so that you can be in your classroom at least fifteen minutes early. Use this time to organize yourself for the day. If you plan to stay after school for just a few extra minutes every day, you will also benefit. You can finish any extra work you do not want to complete at home, leave the room ready for the next day, and complete any of those pressing tasks that are always waiting. Here are just some of the activities you can do in just a few minutes either before or after school:

- Grade papers
- Schedule a parent conference
- Check your calendar
- Return phone calls
- Record grades
- Preview a video
- Check e-mail and voice mail
- Write lesson plans
- Straighten file cabinets
- Write the assignment on the board
- Arrange papers and materials
- Find resources for lesson plans
- Organize your desk
- Write a quiz

Arrive at school as early as you can manage. Never make it a habit to arrive on time; be early. Be available to help an administrator solve an issue with a student or a parent that may have occurred after hours the day before. It's much less stressful to solve a problem before the buses arrive than after your school day begins.

—Yann Pirrone, 15 years' experience

Manage Stacks of Paper with Ease

One of the most stressful aspects of a teaching career is the heavy load of paperwork. Like many other professionals, teachers have to document progress, write plans, and keep accurate records. And like other professionals, teachers complain about the proliferation of their stacks of paperwork.

In the last few decades, the amount of paper all professionals have to handle has multiplied. During the course of just one school year, the average teacher will have to handle more than ten thousand student papers. When you consider the notices, directives, printouts, purchase orders, letters, forms, catalogues, and publications that are received each day, the amount of paperwork that confronts a teacher is staggering.

You can learn to stay ahead of paperwork by creating your own system for managing those stacks. For any sheet of paper you receive, you have three choices: act on it, file it, or throw it away. Get in the habit of acting quickly, and you will never have to face towering piles of papers.

Though all professionals may have to cope with heavy loads of paperwork, the largest and most stressful part of a teacher's paperwork is unique: student papers. Planning will make this part of your school day much easier. Student papers should follow a consistent path:

Step 1: Have students place them in a designated area.

Step 2: Move them to a color-coded folder to be graded.

Step 3: Grade them.

Step 4: Record the grades.

Step 5: File or return to students.

HOW TO ORGANIZE AND MANAGE FORMS

Like many other professionals, teachers have to contend with forms for just about every aspect of their work life. To be a competent teacher, you must be able to organize and manage all of those forms efficiently. This is not a difficult task, but it does require effort and attention.

First, you must allocate a space for the forms you must manage throughout a school term. Many teachers use a file drawer or part of one to store forms. Others use three-ring binders or a combination of binders and file drawers.

When you file forms, the ones you use often should be easily accessible. These forms may include attendance reports, lunch counts, positive notes for parents, or hall passes. (Be sure that you do not put hall passes where students can have access to them without your permission.) Other forms that you should keep on hand include ones that involve disciplinary matters: detention notices or referral forms.

Forms that you do not need to use often can be stored in a less accessible spot, such as the back of a file drawer. These may include blank progress reports, blank report cards, student inventories, receipt books, purchase orders, field trip permission forms, or textbook inventories.

Next, make sure to file forms containing sensitive or confidential information in a drawer that can be locked. These include forms such as Individualized Education Plans for children with special needs, completed progress reports, completed report cards, and medical histories.

To maintain all forms with a minimum of stress, make it a habit to file them away promptly each day. Allowing forms and other papers to pile up on your desk will make finding the right form when you need it needlessly difficult.

TIPS FOR MANAGING STUDENT INFORMATION

In addition to the many forms you will have to keep track of, you will also have to manage the information about your students that comes to you from a variety of sources throughout the term. While there are a number of ways to manage this information, many teachers have found that the following simple approach works well because it is easy to maintain.

1. Set aside space in a lockable desk or file drawer.
2. Create a folder for each student, and arrange the folders alphabetically.
3. Promptly file every piece of information you receive about a student. Date each item. Place new papers behind other items in a file folder so that you don't have to shuffle through all of them to find a particular one.
4. To stay organized, make a point of filing papers daily.

Your Teacher Binder

Many teachers have found that staying organized is easier if they organize all of their daily tasks in a combination of calendar, planner, and address book similar to the daily planners that other professionals use. Although you could purchase and use a planning system designed for executives, you can also organize your responsibilities in a simple binder.

Materials You Will Need

- A sturdy three-ring binder with pockets
- Dividers
- Paper
- Self-adhesive notes
- Pens and pencils
- Calendar

The Outside of the Binder

- ▶ Make sure that the binder is sturdy enough and big enough to hold all of your important papers. (Rings should be at least two inches in diameter.)
- ▶ Label the binder with your name, school, and room number so that it can be returned to you if you misplace it. If you select a binder with a clear pocket on the cover into which you can slip a sheet of paper with identifying information, make sure that the paper you use is very bright so that you can find your binder easily.

The Inside of the Binder

Pockets

- ▶ Use the pockets to store notepads, pens, pencils, computer disks, or adhesive notes.

Dividers

- ▶ Insert dividers to keep your calendar, to-do lists, grade book, and address lists separate so that they are easy to use.

Calendar

- ▶ Find a calendar with spaces large enough to record information comfortably. School districts often offer these at the start of the new school year, or you can purchase or even make one yourself.
- ▶ Consider using pencil for appointments that may be changed or canceled. Use ink for appointments that you know will be permanent. Use colored ink for appointments that you want to highlight.
- ▶ Use adhesive notes to help you recall vital information. Use small ones that you can stick within a calendar block to help you stay on track.
- ▶ Make it a habit to check your calendar several times each day. At a minimum, you should check it when your day begins, at the start of your planning period, and right before you leave for the day.

Address Lists

- The first address list you need is one that includes the addresses, e-mail addresses, and phone numbers of the teachers and administrators you need to contact when you will be absent or when you have questions about school. Be sure to include your mentor in this list.
- The second address list should include the addresses, e-mail addresses, and phone numbers of your students' parents or guardians so that you can quickly contact them from school or from your own home. You can create a spreadsheet with this information, or you can just photocopy the student information sheets in Section Five.

Grade Book or Grade Printouts

- You may want to slip your grade book or a printout of your students' grades into your binder so that you will have easy access to it when you are speaking with parents or guardians.

To-Do List

- Photocopy or adapt the sample teacher's to-do list in Self-Assessment 2.4 to help you plan your work and keep a record of what you do each day. This will be invaluable if you forget to document a parent conference and need to know its date later in the year.

SELF-ASSESSMENT 2.4

A Teacher's To-Do List

Date ______________________________

Phone Calls Concerning Students

Student	Parent's Name and Number	Reason	Time

Other Phone Calls

____

____

____

____

Parent Conferences

Student	What	When	Where	Outcome

Other Meetings

____

____

After-School/Extra Duty Responsibilities

____

____

Items to Duplicate

____

____

Lesson Plans or Projects to Complete

____

____

Notes/Reminders/Errands

____

____

Find Your Mentors

To find a mentor, begin by looking for competent teachers who have high standards for themselves and who are comfortable being observed by other teachers. An effective mentor is good-humored, tactful, knowledgeable, and eager to share ideas with you. In short, look for a mentor who is enthusiastic about teaching, about students, and about helping you learn to be a better teacher.

What should you ask of a mentor? While novice teachers will obviously have a wide range of needs, there are some common concerns that all teachers share. These usually can be divided into two levels of questions that you will discuss with your mentor.

The first is the practical level: the daily concerns that are so difficult to manage at first. Here are just a few of the day-to-day concerns that you can discuss with your mentor:

- Planning procedures
- Curriculum issues
- Where to find materials
- How to work with parents
- Where equipment is stored
- How to group students successfully
- What is expected of teachers in your school

The second level of help that you should ask from a mentor focuses on more complex issues. After you have settled into the school term and mastered the general information you need to manage a class, you will be able to expand the focus of your concern to the art of teaching. Some of the complex issues your mentor can discuss with you include these:

- Solving common classroom problems
- Helping students with special needs
- Increasing student motivation
- Handling diverse classrooms
- Learning about NCLB issues
- Managing group discussions
- Evaluating students fairly
- Incorporating a variety of teaching strategies
- Enhancing student self-esteem

One of the most common problems that people in a mentoring program experience is the lack of time to work together. You and your mentor should plan to meet on a regular basis. While it is not always easy to find the time to work together, here are a few suggestions for coping successfully with this problem:

- Use e-mail
- Call each other in the evening
- Write notes to each other
- Eat lunch together
- Share rides
- Arrange to observe your mentor's class during your planning period

College will never, ever prepare you for real teaching. Find a mentor, someone you respect, and stick to that person like glue. No question is too silly for a first-year person to ask.

—Paige Adcock, 10 years' experience

Professional Organizations for Teachers

One of the best ways to acclimate yourself to your new profession is to join an organization just for teachers. Joining a professional association is a way to stay abreast of the latest developments and trends in education. Through collaboration and networking, you learn from other teachers with shared interests and concerns. Here is a list of some of the professional organizations open to teachers:

American Federation of Teachers (AFT)
555 New Jersey Avenue
Washington, DC 20001
www.aft.org
The AFT is a teachers' union allied with the AFL-CIO. With 1.3 million members, AFT has been a strong voice supporting the classroom teacher for decades.

Association for Supervision and Curriculum Development (ASCD)
1703 N. Beauregard Street
Alexandria, VA 22311
www.ascd.org
This group is a nonpartisan, nonprofit national and international organization for educators at all grade levels.

Coalition of Essential Schools
1814 Franklin Street, Suite 700
Oakland, CA 94612
www.essentialschools.org
This organization provides professional development and networking opportunities, conducts research, and serves as a policy advocate for public education.

National Association for the Education of Young Children
1313 L Street, N.W., Suite 500
Washington, DC 20005
www.naeyc.org
This organization is the nation's largest organization for early childhood educators. Its focus is to provide support and resources for the educators of young children.

National Board for Professional Teaching Standards (NBPTS)
1525 Wilson Blvd., Suite 500
Arlington, VA 22209
www.nbpts.org
NBPTS is an independent nonprofit organization. Its purpose is to advance the quality of teaching by developing professional standards and creating a voluntary system to certify teachers.

National Education Association (NEA)
1201 16th Street, N.W.
Washington, DC 20001
www.nea.org
With almost three million members, the NEA is the largest organization for public school teachers in the United States. It provides strong national support for educators at all grade levels.

National High School Association
6615 E. Pacific Coast Highway, Suite 120
Long Beach, CA 90803
www.nhsa.net
This nonprofit association is dedicated to improving the professional knowledge of high school educators.

National Middle School Association (NMSA)
4151 Executive Parkway, Suite 300
Westerville, OH 43081
www.nmsa.org
With over 30,000 members, NMSA is the largest national education association committed to the educational needs of young adolescents.

Teachers Network
285 West Broadway
New York, NY 10013
www.teachersnetwork.org
Teachers Network is a nationwide nonprofit organization that supports and assists teachers in public school systems.

Journals to Help You Grow Professionally

Just as joining a professional organization can help you develop professional expertise, so can reading professional journals. Through such reading, you can learn a great deal about the interests you share with others in your field. Subscribing to one of these journals will enrich your teaching experience in many ways.

Education Week
Educational Projects in Education
6935 Arlington Road, Suite 100
Bethesda, MD 20814
www.edweek.org
This journal is a weekly periodical devoted to up-to-the-minute news about education.

Educational Leadership
Association for Supervision and Curriculum Development
1703 N. Beauregard Street
Alexandria, VA 22311
www.ascd.org
This journal is the voice of ASCD and a useful resource for teachers at all grade levels.

Instructor
Scholastic, Inc.
557 Broadway
New York, NY 10012
www.scholastic.com
This widely read magazine devoted to K–8 educational concerns offers practical support through a variety of timely articles.

Learning
The Education Center
3515 W. Market Street, Suite 200
Greensboro, NC 27403
www.learningmagazine.com
This is another supportive resource for teachers of younger students, offering practical advice on a wide range of topics.

Phi Delta Kappan
Phi Delta Kappa
408 N. Union Street
P.O. Box 789
Bloomington, IN 47402
www.pdkintl.org
This professional journal addresses issues of policy and serves as a forum for debates on controversial subjects.

Teacher Magazine
Educational Projects in Education
6935 Arlington Road, Suite 100
Bethesda, MD 20814
www.teachermagazine.com
This K–12 magazine offers news, commentary, and practical support for teachers.

Using the Internet as a Teaching Resource

One of the most significant changes in education in recent years is the growth of the Internet as a resource for educators at all levels of expertise and experience. No longer do teachers have to spend long hours trying to find materials and bits of information about their subject matter. With a few clicks of a mouse, the world can come to your classroom.

The Internet can provide teachers with lesson plans, advice, forums, and a wealth of resources that were unheard of just a few decades ago. Much of the potential drudgery of teaching vanishes when teachers can ask other teachers across the country for advice, download materials for next week's lesson, keep in touch with parents through a class Web page, or perform numerous other tasks online. Students, too, benefit when their teacher brings technology into the classroom. Students working at computers tend to be more actively engaged in their lessons because of the fast-paced hands-on work they are required to do.

One problem with the Internet is that it is so information-rich that it is hard to know where to begin. Another problem with using the Internet as a teaching resource is that it changes continually as new information is developed, making it is hard to keep up with the latest developments. To combat this, you should work with your colleagues to share information about new technology and helpful Web resources.

To get your first year off to a good start, here is an alphabetical list of some of the best general sites for teachers (at the time of publication of this resource) for you to explore:

- **A to Z Teacher Stuff (http://www.atozteacherstuff.com).** Here you will find thousands of plans, thematic units, advice from other teachers, downloadable materials, and much more.
- **Education World (http://www.education-world.com).** Offering thousands of resources for teachers, this site calls itself "The Educator's Best Friend." At Education World, you can find lesson plans, materials, professional development activities, technology information, and many other resources for educators and students.
- **EduHound (http://www.eduhound.com).** "Everything for Education K–12!" At EduHound, you will again find thousands of resources: clip art, lesson ideas, links to virtual exploration sites, downloadable worksheets and forms, and information divided into easy-to-search topics.
- **Federal Resources for Educational Excellence (http://www.free.ed.gov/).** Over thirty federal agencies contribute to the extensive collections of this Web site each

month. You can search the array of materials, activities, and information for teachers and students.

- **GlobalSchoolNet (http://www.globalschoolnet.org).** This site connects students in 194 countries in a worldwide approach to problem solving, project-based learning, and online collaboration. The materials for teachers of students of all ages will connect your classroom to the world.
- **Kathy Schrock's Guide for Educators (http://school.discovery.com/schrockguide).** Kathy Schrock, Discovery School's technology expert, provides much helpful information for teachers and students. The information is divided into an enormous range of content areas that are easy to search. From specific information categories to helpful strategies for teachers, this site has it all.
- **Kindergarten Connection (http://www.kconnect.com).** Specifically for teachers of primary students, this site offers plans, supportive teaching tips, and many links to other resources and materials for young children.
- **Mid-Continent Research for Education and Learning (http://www.mcrel.org).** Here you will find a wide range of excellent lesson plans and links to curriculum resource sites aligned with state standards.
- **Teachnology (http://www.teach-nology.com).** Teachnology offers access to printable worksheets, educational games, hundreds of teaching strategies, advice from other teachers, education news, and more than 25,000 lesson plans.
- **Thinkfinity (http://www.marcopolo-education.org/home.aspx).** At this site, you will find several content-specific areas with lesson plans, interactive activities for students, downloadable worksheets, links to other excellent Web sites, and additional resources. The high quality of the comprehensive resources at this site makes it exceptional.
- **U.S. Department of Education (http://www.eduref.org).** The Educator's Reference Desk offers resources such as AskERIC, lesson plans, archived information, and links to hundreds of diverse education sites.

Burnout Can Happen to You

Part of the professional expertise you need to develop during your first year as a teacher is how to cope with the daily stresses that accompany a career in education. Teachers who learn to manage their stress levels enjoy school and find its challenges enjoyable. Teachers who do not are the ones who stress out, burn out, and leave the profession to find a less challenging but less rewarding career.

Burnout begins slowly. The combination of work stresses and inadequate coping skills leads first to exhaustion and then to an increasingly negative attitude. As a teacher struggles to cope, a common mistake is to work longer hours in an effort to fix the problem. This only increases mental, emotional, and physical fatigue.

All educators are at risk for burnout; you do not have to be inexperienced or have a difficult schedule or have the worst behaved students in the school. Although even the best

> **Remember that in a twenty-day working month, fifteen days will be average. Three will be tops, but you will have two bad days. The longer you teach, the more tops days you will have.**
>
> —*Edward Gardner, 36 years' experience*

teachers can experience burnout, it does not have to happen to you.

You can take proactive measures to prevent stress from having a negative effect on your life and your career. Because this stress is not going to vanish overnight, it is up to you to protect yourself from burnout. No one else can do it for you.

PROACTIVE ANTI-BURNOUT STRATEGIES

You have many effective tools in the battle against burnout, and you should be proactive in avoiding the damage it can cause. One place to begin to learn more about the stressors particular to teachers is this Web resource:

Teachnology (http://www.teach-nology.com/edleadership/burn_out/). Here you will find several supportive and practical articles to help you prevent burnout and be proactive in dealing with your daily stress.

You must prevent the buildup of the small stresses that eventually lead to distress and burnout. Consider some of the following strategies when you create a proactive plan to prevent toxic stress from taking over your life:

- **Place great value on your personal time.** Working long hours every day is a sure path to burnout. You need time to just be yourself.
- **Allow yourself time to make effective transitions from one class to another.** This is particularly difficult when you have many classes each day. One way to manage this is by having an opening routine that your students can do independently. This will free you to make the mental, emotional, and physical switch from one group of students to another.
- **Keep a flexible attitude.** Get into the habit of looking for solutions instead of dwelling on your problems. If you are open to alternatives, you will be able to assess your options much more quickly.
- **Plan ahead.** When you know that you are approaching a tough time at school, find opportunities to solve problems and not just suffer through them. Plan to thrive and not just survive.
- **Don't procrastinate.** Resolve to accomplish the items on your to-do list before they become a problem. Small problems are less stressful than large ones.
- **Change your thinking!** Adjust your mind-set to accept that you will never be free from professional responsibilities during the school term.

- **Plan how you will cope with stress.** A good way to do this is to make a list of stress reduction strategies and keep it on hand for times when you need to defuse anxiety and distress.
- **Plan activities that you and your students can anticipate with pleasure.** Few teachers experience burnout while they are having fun.
- **Learn to pace your instruction to allow for some less intense teaching periods.** For example, you should not lecture day after day. Instead, allow your students time for independent work, small-group work, or even activities such as viewing films related to the subject under study. Being "on" all of the time will quickly exhaust you.
- **Work consistently to have a well-disciplined class.** This not only will save you daily stress but will benefit your students as well.
- **Add structure to your life.** Routines will prevent many problems. For example, if you always place your classroom keys in the same spot in your desk each day, you will avoid the stress of looking for them.
- **Establish a network of supportive and positive people who can help you.** Being connected to others is an important way to avoid the isolation that often accompanies burnout.
- **Take command of your school life.** Establish realistic goals for yourself, and then strive to achieve them.
- **Keep up with grading papers.** Passing back papers quickly will allow you to remedy areas of weakness before they become serious.
- **Think before you act.** If you plan your responses to unpleasant situations, you will prevent many problems. Situations that you should think about before you act include incomplete homework assignments, angry parents, defiant students, cheating incidents, tardy students, and other classroom disruptions.

> Go home and relax: shop, exercise, read, watch television—whatever. Then think about what you could have done differently to change the situation that made the day so bad and plan for tomorrow to be better. Bad days happen, but we don't have to let them rule our lives.
>
> *—Charlene Herrala, 24 years' experience*

TURN PROBLEMS INTO OPPORTUNITIES

In every problem at school, even a very stressful one, there are opportunities to change, to learn, to grow, and to solve problems. Instead of viewing your problems as disasters, you can choose to see them as challenging opportunities. You can react in a negative way, or you can choose to solve a problem.

Here is a six-step plan to follow whenever you are presented with a potential disaster that you want to turn into an opportunity:

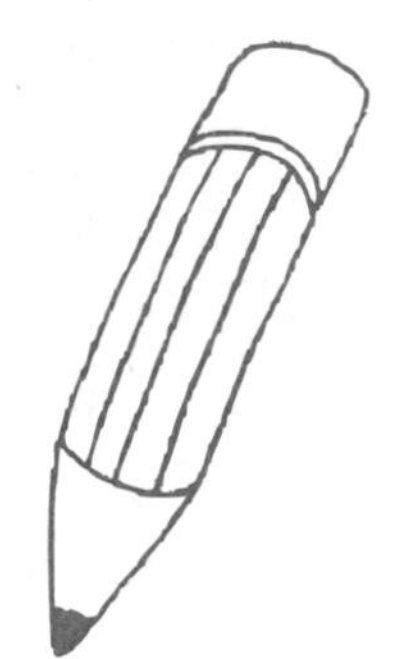

1. Choose to see a situation as an opportunity instead of as a problem.
2. Take an objective look at all sides of the situation.
3. Look for options by brainstorming as many solutions as you can.
4. Carefully examine your possible solutions. Select the best solution.
5. Set your goals, and make a plan to implement the solution.
6. Put your plan into action.

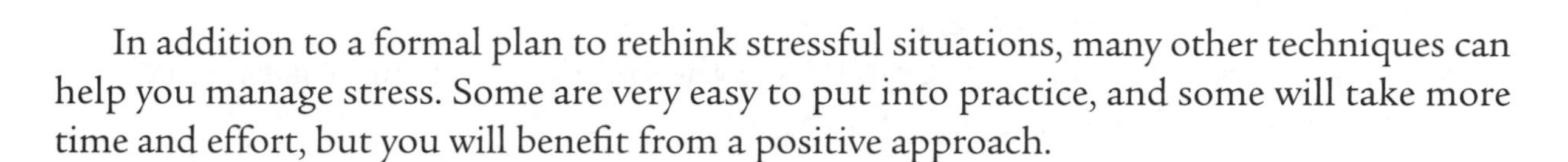

In addition to a formal plan to rethink stressful situations, many other techniques can help you manage stress. Some are very easy to put into practice, and some will take more time and effort, but you will benefit from a positive approach.

- Ask yourself how realistic you are when faced with a tough problem. Are you too optimistic about what you can accomplish in a single day?
- Make a list of what you can learn from a troublesome situation.
- If your students are disruptive or defiant, refuse to take it personally. The cause of the problem may have nothing to do with you. (Also see Section Six.)
- Stop and ask yourself what you might have done to cause a stressful situation and what you can do to prevent it from happening again. Take the opportunity to learn from your mistakes instead of dwelling on them.
- Ask yourself: Is a career in education what is causing your stress, or is it the way you are handling the day-to-day grind? Facing a career with many troubling demands is not easy, but other careers have their own difficulties. Before you allow yourself to burn out or leave teaching, carefully consider whether another career will satisfy your needs.

The Safety Net of Professionalism

Professionalism means being the very best teacher that you can be every day. When you choose to conduct yourself in a professional manner, you send the message that you are in control of your classroom and yourself. You earn the respect of your students and colleagues in the process. Although it is not always easy to be a professional educator, especially when you are just starting out, professionalism is one of the best tools that you have to prevent stress.

These are just some of the professional behaviors that can enhance stress prevention:

- Treat your students with respect. Don't be a pushover or play favorites.
- Accept criticism from your supervisors in a calm and professional manner. Do not be defensive. Instead, work to correct the problem.

How to Stay Healthy

It is common wisdom that first-year teachers are particularly vulnerable to the illnesses that plague their students. You do not have to join your students in sniffles or flu if you use common sense to take good care of yourself in the following ways:

- Exercise at least three times a week.
- Get enough rest.
- Practice stress reduction techniques.
- Eat well. If you pack your lunch, be sure to include foods that are good for you. Avoid too much sugar and fat.
- Keep disinfectant handy, and use it.
- Keep tissues and hand sanitizer on hand.
- Keep your hands away from your face.
- Wash your hands as often as you can. Be extra careful to do this when you are grading papers or using shared pens or pencils.

- Take your workday appearance seriously. Dress comfortably but neatly. Your appearance sends a message to your students that you take your position seriously.
- Greet everyone you meet with a friendly word and a smile. Project an air of confidence, and soon you will feel confident.
- Become an organized and efficient worker so that you can accomplish all of your paperwork chores.
- Take charge of your classroom with sound discipline policies.
- Be known as a punctual person who does not miss school without a good reason.
- Plan lessons that are meaningful, interesting, and based on your district's or state's curriculum guidelines.
- Never shout at your students. If you are tempted to do this, stop and reassess the situation.
- Admit it when you make a mistake. Ask for help.
- Be careful about what you say and how you say it. Use Standard English. Never allow students to curse in front of you.
- Make sure that the goals you set for your students are attainable and that you teach the skills needed to reach them.
- Have high expectations for your students.
- Take pride in your profession. Share this attitude with your students.

- Follow all school rules.
- Let students know that you care about their welfare. Don't give up on them when things are difficult.

Talk It Over

How to Develop Your Professional Expertise

Use these questions as a springboard for discussions that will help you and your discussion group members grow and develop professionally. Discuss these questions about how to develop your professional expertise:

1. Discuss your group's definitions of *professional expertise.* What are the most important characteristics of a professional educator?
2. What advantages does a new teacher have that more experienced staff members do not have? What are the disadvantages of a lack of experience?
3. What resources are available to you as you develop your professional expertise? How can you find out about other resources?
4. Discuss the skills you need to fulfill your classroom responsibilities. How can you develop these skills? Who can help you?
5. What is your vision for the year ahead?
6. How would you rate your current work habits? Which ones serve you well in your new career? Which ones do you need to improve? How can your colleagues help you with this?
7. Being well organized is not a characteristic that happens by chance. Categorize your organizational skills. What do you still need to work on? To whom can you turn for assistance?
8. What steps can a new teacher take to establish a positive working relationship with a mentor? What suggestions do your colleagues have for working well with mentors?
9. What are the most important professional qualities that teachers can develop? How can you develop them?
10. Discuss this statement: "You must teach in order to learn."

SECTION THREE

Become a Valuable Team Player

In this section, you will learn

- ✔ How to build your teamwork skills
- ✔ How to manage the evaluation process successfully
- ✔ How to work well with colleagues, parents, and guardians
- ✔ How to make a good impression through correspondence
- ✔ How to conduct successful parent conferences

For many people, it will come as no surprise to find out that the reason many employees are fired is not poor job performance but the inability to work well with others. School employees must learn to work well with others, too.

Schools are much more complex than many organizations, however. Each school is an ever-changing mixture of clerks, custodians, technical assistants, nurses, counselors, coaches, media personnel, paraprofessionals, and police liaison officers as well as teachers, students, and students' families. These complex communities extend far beyond the boundaries of the schoolyard. The challenge for teachers is to work well with all members of their school community.

Teamwork Skills That Build Success

According to an ancient Japanese proverb, "None of us are as smart as all of us." Teams make the workload easier and the task more pleasant only if all of the team members have the skills to work well together. Just what does it take to be a good team member? Teachers who are good team members

- ✔ Treat all people in their work community with courtesy
- ✔ Listen to others' opinions before making decisions
- ✔ Commit themselves to the good of the school
- ✔ Are quick to celebrate the hard work and success of others
- ✔ Are cheerleaders for their school

Use Self-Assessment 3.1 to set your goals in the area of teamwork.

What Your Co-Workers Expect from You

Your colleagues expect you

- ✔ To be courteous and cooperative
- ✔ To work toward shared goals
- ✔ To be understanding and supportive
- ✔ To conduct yourself with professionalism
- ✔ To be willing to collaborate
- ✔ To clean up after yourself
- ✔ To be on time for everything
- ✔ To keep your promises
- ✔ To value their experience
- ✔ To be willing to do your share of extra duties
- ✔ To be a good listener
- ✔ To be interested in others but not a gossip
- ✔ To admit when you're not sure of something
- ✔ To have a sense of fun
- ✔ To keep trying to improve

ON-THE-JOB COURTESY

Now that you have minded your manners long enough to make it through the job interviews that resulted in your new career, it is time to develop the business manners that will guarantee your success. Follow these suggestions in order to present yourself as a courteous professional.

SELF-ASSESSMENT 3.1

Set Goals to Improve How You Work with Others

The first year of your career is a terrific time to improve how you work with others. You have a new relationship with all the teachers in the building—even those you may already know well. Get off to a good start by establishing goals to improve your working relationships with others.

Goal 1: Treat all people in the building with courtesy
Steps I can take to achieve this goal:

____

____

____

Goal 2: Listen to all other opinions before making decisions
Steps I can take to achieve this goal:

____

____

____

Goal 3: Be committed to the good of the school
Steps I can take to achieve this goal:

____

____

____

Goal 4: Be quick to celebrate the hard work and success of others
Steps I can take to achieve this goal:

____

____

____

Goal 5: Be a cheerleader for my school
Steps I can take to achieve this goal:

____

____

____

- Refer to other adults in the building by their title and last name when you are with students.
- Greet absolutely everyone you meet with a pleasant smile.
- Pay attention during faculty meetings.
- Be known as a punctual person.
- Plan carefully, so that you don't have to ask to cut in line at the photocopier.
- Be careful to say "please" and "thank you." Take extra care to remember this during stressful times.
- Don't repeat gossip.
- Leave your work area clean. If you use the paper cutter, pick up scraps; if you spill food at lunch, wipe up the mess.
- Answer the phone or respond to an intercom message in a businesslike manner.
- Be polite to all cafeteria staff members, and expect your students to do the same.
- If you are having a disagreement with a colleague, be careful to remain calm and professional. Never raise your voice. Never air such a disagreement in front of students.
- If you see another teacher struggling with books, papers, or any of those other packages teachers lug around, offer to help carry a couple of items, or hold the door.

Don't be hung up with the sour grapes and bad apples at your school.

—Edward Gardner,
36 years' experience

- If you borrow something, return it promptly.
- Keep the noise in your class at a reasonable level so that you do not disturb other classes.
- Meet your students at the door with a friendly word.
- Share your materials, supplies, and other resources.
- Respect the class time of other teachers. Unless there is an emergency, try not to interrupt another teacher's instruction.
- Do not make students late to another teacher's class or ask that they be allowed to miss another class to come to yours.
- Share the phone lines. There will never be enough phones in a school, so be careful to limit your phone conversations to business matters.

TRUSTWORTHINESS

You will have to learn to work well with every adult in the school; they are all your colleagues. One of the best ways to work well with others is to be a trustworthy person.

One of the most important facets of your professional reputation—one that you should establish as quickly as possible—is the perception that you are a dependable teacher. Good teachers are the people on whom other staff members can rely for both big and small tasks. The rewards of this reputation are enormous.

Keep your promises. Because this is so important, be very careful not to make promises you cannot keep. It is very easy to become caught up in the enthusiasm of a moment and agree to something you may regret later. Take your time, and ease into your new responsibilities.

Diversity in the Workplace

Many people may think that the expression *global classroom* refers only to the access that teachers now have to classrooms and resources all over the world through the Internet. Not so.

One of the most intriguing trends in American education in recent years is the push to hire teachers of differing cultures and ethnic backgrounds in more and more schools. Many school districts even actively recruit and hire teachers from other countries. As a first-year teacher, the chances are excellent that if you look around at your opening faculty meetings, you will see a mixture of people whose culture and background are very different from your own.

Everyone in a school benefits from the diverse perspectives offered by a multiethnic faculty. New perspectives combat stereotypical thinking, which is dangerous to all members of a society, and contribute to greater understanding. Students and teachers benefit from exposure to a faculty that values other cultures.

However, the benefits of a diverse workplace cannot be realized unless all members of the school community agree not just to accept one another's cultures but to value and embrace them. All members of a school community should be aware of how easily intolerance can create an unfriendly work environment. Suspicion, misunderstandings, and fear of rejection are all problems that can affect any workplace, especially a diverse one.

What is your role as a first-year faculty member in a diverse workplace? While the parameters of your workplace will dictate the specific actions your school will take to include all faculty members in the common goal of educating students, the following guidelines will help you to become a team player in the global classroom.

- **Examine your own unintentional biases.** Even the most tolerant and well-intentioned person can be biased at times. Make an effort to be aware of subtle negative attitudes about cultures and ethnicities other than your own that you may have.
- **Keep an open mind.** You can learn a great deal from people whose background is very different from yours. Work with your students to help them learn to value people from other cultures. Everyone benefits when a diverse workplace is successful.
- **Make sure that your language is appropriate.** Be aware that the names you use and the things you criticize when referring to people of other cultures are very real reflections of your own thinking. Make sure that your language reflects an open-minded, well-educated person who values people of other cultures.
- **Reach out!** If you sometimes feel ill at ease in your school environment, think how much more difficult it might be for a teacher of another culture. Be friendly to everyone. Show a genuine interest in and respect for another person's culture.

The following books offer more information, guidelines, strategies, and advice on how to thrive in a diverse workplace.

- *Building on the Promise of Diversity: How We Can Move to the Next Level in Our Workplaces, Our Communities, and Our Society* by R. Roosevelt Thomas (AMACOM, 2005)
- *The Diversity Toolkit: How You Can Build and Benefit from a Diverse Workforce* by William Sonnenschein (NTC Publishing Group, 1999)
- *Becoming Multicultural Educators: Personal Journey Toward Professional Agency* by Geneva Gay (Jossey-Bass, 2003)

How to Fit In

Sometimes it is overwhelming to be a new teacher. Every staff member seems to know everyone else and to have a wealth of interesting experiences to share. Even the most outgoing person might be intimidated in circumstances such as these. However, with just a bit of thought, you will soon be able to be a part of the team of professionals at your school. Here are some easy-to-follow suggestions to help you fit in:

- Be the first to greet other teachers.
- Even though you may be tempted to stay in your room, eat lunch with other teachers.
- Be respectful of the customs of your school. For example, if Fridays are casual dress days, you should dress casually on Fridays.
- Don't give in to the urge to gossip in an effort to find out about your colleagues.
- Be available before and after school. If you are only at school during required classes, it will be difficult for you to meet others.
- Share a little bit about yourself so that your colleagues can get to know you.
- Attend after-school activities. Show that you care about your school.

BE ASSERTIVE IN A POSITIVE WAY

As a new teacher, you can expect to be asked to perform various nonteaching duties. Schools need staff members who are willing to take on responsibilities other than classroom instruction, such as sponsoring clubs, tutoring after school, or coaching sports.

It is common for a new teacher to agree to an extra duty but later to find that the time required by the additional responsibility makes it difficult to be an effective classroom teacher. To prevent this from happening to you, take measures to ensure that you are involved in school activities without having to give up too much of the time that you should be devoting to learning how to be an effective classroom teacher. These strategies may be helpful.

- When you are asked to assume an after-school responsibility that you are absolutely not comfortable doing, respond by saying something like "I'd love to help you, but I need to focus on classroom instruction right now."
- Volunteer to assume an additional duty that you know you can manage well. For example, if you were a member of the honor society in high school, volunteer to sponsor that group. Or if you are a fitness buff, volunteer to teach an after-school exercise class.
- Consider being a co-sponsor with another teacher. Sharing responsibilities with another person will reduce the amount of time you have to spend on an after-school task, allow you to ease into your new professional responsibilities, and show that you are willing to work hard for the good of the school. Being a co-sponsor also gives you an opportunity to get to know one of your colleagues.

BEHAVE PROFESSIONALLY AT MEETINGS

No matter how informal your school's atmosphere is, faculty meetings are serious business. If you have never had a job in which routine staff meetings were scheduled, adjusting to professional faculty meetings may be difficult for you at first. While you may quickly become bored with information you have already heard many times, do not give in to the temptation to act on this feeling. Here are a few rules for presenting a professional image at meetings:

- Be on time.
- Always attend; faculty meetings are not optional. Many administrators take attendance. Even if no one calls roll, you can be sure that your absence will be noted.
- If your school has a set time for meetings, mark them on your calendar so that you can plan appointments around them.
- If you have to be absent, contact the people in charge of the meeting to let them know that you will not be there.
- Sit near the front, and take notes. Make sure you bring along paper and a pen.
- Do not chat while the speaker is leading the meeting. Not only is it rude to the speaker and to the people around you who are trying to hear, but it marks you as unprofessional.
- Even though you may have a tall stack of tests to grade, it is rude to grade papers or do other paperwork in a meeting.
- Turn off your beeper or cell phone so that ringing from your book bag does not interrupt the meeting.

AVOID THE HARM THAT GOSSIP CAN DO

While it's natural to want to know about your colleagues, being a gossip is not the best way to accomplish this. Spreading rumors and discussing the intimate affairs of fellow staffers are not worthwhile activities for a professional educator. Here are a couple of other reasons why you should avoid gossip at school:

> **Find out where the teachers' lounge is located, and stay away from it!**
>
> —*Yann Pirrone, 15 years' experience*

- As a new staff member, you do not yet know the relationships among your colleagues or where their loyalties lie. If you gossip about one staff member, you may be inadvertently making an enemy of another.
- You do not want to develop a reputation as a person who likes to dish dirt; few actions can damage your reputation as quickly.

If you want to learn more about a staff member or a situation at school, you should take a professional approach by speaking with your mentor or a trusted colleague.

WORK WELL WITH DIFFICULT COLLEAGUES

People in all professions have to learn to deal with difficult colleagues, and teachers are no exception. Some colleagues may be so difficult to get along with that you find it very challenging to work with them.

Many people make up a school community. You may form close friendships with some and never quite hit it off with others. To be a successful professional and part of an effective team, you need to work well with every colleague.

The best guideline to follow in trying to work well with difficult colleagues is recognize that you share a common goal: the education of the children entrusted to your care. If you hold this common goal in mind, you have little choice but to work well together, because the alternative could result in failure, for students and for you.

How to Maintain a Private Social Life

Be very careful what you reveal about yourself to your colleagues and even more so about what you reveal to your students. If you are indiscreet about sharing details of your personal life, expect to have those details not only gossiped about in homes all over your school district but wildly embellished. Follow these guidelines to keep your social life private.

- It is not a sensible idea to purchase alcohol, tobacco products, or other very personal items in a place where you could run into your students, their family members, or unsympathetic colleagues.
- If you eat in a restaurant, limit your alcohol intake. In fact, to avoid hearing rumors of how you were publicly intoxicated, avoid purchasing alcohol in places where you could meet someone connected with your school.

How to Get Along with Difficult People

- Don't rush to judgment. For example, if you meet someone at the start of the term, you are probably meeting a harried, stressed colleague with too much to do. Be patient, and wait until you know the person better before making a judgment.
- Look for the good traits in your colleagues. Though everyone has irritating personality quirks, they also have appealing ones. Be on the lookout for these positive traits in every person you work with.
- Do not gossip about a person you find difficult. If you are unsure of the best course of action to take with a difficult person, ask a close colleague or a mentor for advice.
- The best way to handle a colleague who is a bully is to use the same technique you probably learned in grade school: stand up for yourself. Do not try to argue with a bully; just make your point firmly.
- Negative people are that way for many reasons. Their chief harm is that they encourage you to be negative, too. Because it is almost impossible to cheer up people who are determined to be negative, avoid them.
- Don't be one of the difficult people in your school! Listen more than you talk, and be as tolerant of others as you can.

- Avoid sharing too much information about your personal life at work. It is one thing for your colleagues to learn that you have a new puppy; it is quite another for you to relate how the puppy accompanied you and a date on a romantic weekend adventure.
- Do not make personal phone calls or send personal e-mail messages at school. The phone calls may be overheard, and school e-mail is not private.
- If you decide to date a staff member, keep your relationship as private as possible. Your students should have absolutely no idea that you are involved with a fellow staff member.
- The less you say about the details of your personal life to your students, the better. Instead, model acceptable and mature behavior. Before you reveal anything about your personal life, ask yourself, "Would I be comfortable revealing this if a school board member were in the room?"

Mistakes No Teacher Should Make in Social Situations

Although the culture of your school and the preferences of your administrators will determine many of the attitudes about suitable social behavior for teachers, certain actions are never acceptable:

- **Drug use.** This means avoiding illegal substances at any time. Also avoid alcohol or tobacco at school or when they could cause negative attention.
- **Engaging in illegal or criminal behavior.** Breaking the laws of your community or state is clearly not acceptable for a role model. If you are arrested, you are required to report it to your principal.
- **Talking about students.** You should not talk about students when you are not at school. When you do this, you violate their privacy and your professional ethics.
- **Talking about other staff members in an unpleasant way.** In a social setting, it is not acceptable for you to discuss the failings of other staff members. People who do not work at your school should not be privy to the disagreeable quirks of your co-workers.
- **Rehashing a disagreeable incident.** When something unpleasant happens at school, it is tempting to discuss it. Discussing your school's problems around people who are not involved is not acceptable. You will only spread ill will about your school if you do so.

The Support Staff

As a new teacher, you will have to learn many new faces and names as quickly as possible. While it is sensible to learn the names of other faculty members first, it is a mistake to think that they are your only colleagues.

A school community is composed of many different people in many different positions. Each of them deserves your cooperation and respect, because you all work toward the same goal: the good of the children in your school.

You can do much to encourage a spirit of teamwork with your colleagues. Here is a brief list of just some of the actions that you can take right away to treat all staff members as colleagues:

- Learn the names of the support personnel in your school as quickly as possible. Greet each by name when you meet. Treat each person in the building with the same courtesy that you would like to receive.
- Develop professional relationships with your colleagues. Learn the roles that various people play in your school and how they contribute to the overall picture. By doing this, you will be able to be supportive when they need your help.
- Encourage your students to respect the work of support personnel by modeling that respect yourself. Speak courteously to the cafeteria, clerical, and custodial staff. Make sure that your students leave their work area clean. Let them see you picking up trash in the hall.
- Never make a disparaging comment about the work of support staff members when you are with students. This courtesy means that you should go as far as avoiding making unkind remarks about the food served in the cafeteria, the media

ordered by the school librarian, or the computer glitches that technicians can't solve quickly.

- Be as cooperative as possible. If a colleague requests that you hand in reports, grade sheets, attendance information, or other paperwork, respond promptly.
- Respect your colleagues' time, equipment, and other resources. If the school secretary asks you to not tie up a phone line, respect that request, even though you may have a very important call to make.

The Chain of Command

In order to work well with your supervisors and other staff members, you must know and follow the chain of command at your school. Few things annoy other employees as much as a person who does not have enough respect for their position to follow the chain of command when things are not going well.

Not following the chain of command may win you a momentary victory, but it will be a hollow one. For example, if you have requested certain repairs to your classroom and these repairs have not been made, you may be tempted to speak to the principal about this problem. If you do this instead of speaking with the custodian in charge of your classroom, you may have been unfair to that person. There may be a good reason for the incomplete repairs. As a rule of thumb, you should always talk over a problem with your mentor or the person who directly supervises you before requesting additional assistance.

Working Well with Your Supervisors

The supervisory staffs of your school district and of your school building depend on faculty members to make things run smoothly. While it is only natural that there will be problems, it is up to you to work well with your supervisors.

There is a specific hierarchy of supervision at any school. It is likely that you report to a department head, lead teacher, or grade level leader who serves as a liaison between staff members and administrators. Assistant principals make up the next level. At the top of the hierarchy in your school is the principal, who is the instructional leader of your building. At the district level, your supervisors may differ in their titles but will include curriculum coordinators and assistant superintendents who report to their supervisor, the superintendent of schools. The hierarchy does not end there. The school board supervises all employees, including the superintendent.

If you want to establish positive relationships with your supervisors, you will need to take positive action. Do not just hope that no one will notice you because you are a first-year teacher. In fact, you are particularly noticeable just because you are a first-year teacher!

Follow these suggestions in order to establish a positive working relationship with all of your supervisors.

- **Behave in a professional manner at all times.** This will win the support of administrators because it makes their job easier. In addition, if you maintain a solid reputation, it is easier for them to support you when you make mistakes—and more likely that they will want to offer their support.

- **Take time to familiarize yourself with the information in your faculty manual.** This will help you avoid mistakes that may lead to negative interactions with your supervisors.
- **Remember that administrators are responsible for the entire school and you are responsible for only a very small part of it.** If you can maintain this point of view, you'll find it easier to understand some of the policies you might otherwise find confusing. Accept the fact that while you are not always going to agree with the decisions and actions of the administrators with whom you work, public criticism of their actions might seriously damage your professional reputation. Think before you voice public criticism.
- **Don't threaten to send your students to the office instead of resolving the problem through other, more successful methods of discipline.** Maintain control of your classroom so that when you have to send a child out of class, the action will have meaning for students as well as administrators.
- **Remember to be professional in your dealings with administrators.** Always present a calm and competent image, not an image of a furious teacher who lacks self-control. Regardless of your personal feelings toward a supervisor, always model respect.
- **When you make a mistake, be truthful in discussing it with your supervisors.** If you can do this before they find out the bad news from someone else, you should do so.
- **Share your successes with your supervisors.** Help them create positive public relations for your school by letting them know noteworthy news about your students.

The Evaluation Process

As a teacher, you can expect to be evaluated on a variety of criteria every year. The evaluation process has several components. First, you can expect one of your supervisors to discuss your goals and progress with you in a pre-observation conference. This is a good time to mention any particular problems you are having and to solicit advice.

Sometime after your pre-observation conference, your evaluator will make a planned classroom observation. At this point, the evaluator will be looking for your strengths and weaknesses as an educator.

After the observation, you will meet with your evaluator again. At this conference, the evaluator will talk with you about the lesson you taught as well as your strengths and weaknesses as a teacher.

There will be other observations during the course of the year. The number varies from school district to school district. Expect to have many informal visits from administrators over the course of your career, but especially during your first few years, when you are not a tenured teacher.

Near the end of the school year, you will have a final evaluation conference. This conference will involve more than just the formal classroom observations you have had throughout the year; it will address your overall effectiveness as an educator. There should be no surprises in regard to your final evaluation. If your supervisors believe that you are not an effective teacher, you will certainly receive some indication of that before the final meeting.

PREPARING FOR AN OBSERVATION

In many ways, informal visits by evaluators are much easier to get through than the planned, formal observations. You do not have time to worry about an unannounced visit, whereas knowing that an administrator is going to observe you in a few days gives you time to feel anxious. It is normal to feel nervous about being observed. Use Self-Assessment 3.2 to help you prepare. In addition, taking the following steps can help you feel confident both before and during the observation.

- **Be proactive.** Make sure that you have a copy of the supervisor's observation form if there is not a copy in your faculty manual. In fact, you should do this as early in the term as you can. Study the form so that you will know what the observer will be looking for as you teach.
- **Clean up your room.** This will give you a psychological boost as well as a positive mark on your evaluation form.
- **Keep your lesson simple so that you can do it well.** The observer will want to see you interacting with your students, so do not plan a test or a video. Experimenting with a class skit or collaborative groups may not highlight your skills early in your first year.
- **Tell your students what is going to happen.** Tell them that there will be a visitor in the classroom and that you would appreciate their cooperation.
- **Write out your lesson plan, and collect copies of all handouts, textbooks, or materials for the lesson.** Select an unobtrusive place for your visitor, and place this material there. Be ready to show your lesson plan book as well as your grade book.
- **Get control of your anxiety (see Section Two).** This is the most important step in your preparation. If you are ready and have a well-planned lesson, you do not have to worry. Expect to be nervous, but also expect to do well because you have prepared thoroughly.

SELF-ASSESSMENT 3.2

How Observers Will Evaluate You

During a classroom observation, your observers will make notes on a form that has been approved by your school district. While these forms vary from district to district, certain items are common to most of them. You can be proactive in how you prepare for an observation by looking at yourself as an evaluator does. Choose a particular class session in which to evaluate your own teaching. Rate your performance on each of these positive qualities by circling the number that best fits your assessment of your own skills. Use this scale:

1 = I had no problems in this area.
2 = I had a few problems in this area.
3 = I really need to work on this skill.

TEACHER

1	2	3	I followed the district's curriculum.
1	2	3	I had objectives for the lesson.
1	2	3	I made the purpose of the lesson clear to my students.
1	2	3	I delivered accurate and appropriate information.
1	2	3	I showed a depth of understanding of the material.
1	2	3	I made use of all available class time.
1	2	3	I kept all of my students on task.
1	2	3	I allowed time for transitions between activities.
1	2	3	I used a variety of teaching strategies.
1	2	3	I demonstrated effective questioning skills.
1	2	3	I had an assessment instrument for the lesson.
1	2	3	I motivated my students to succeed.
1	2	3	I established the relevance of the lesson.
1	2	3	I provided timely feedback.
1	2	3	I monitored my students effectively.
1	2	3	I encouraged and assisted students.
1	2	3	I interacted in a positive way with my students.
1	2	3	I maintained an orderly classroom.
1	2	3	I minimized disruptions.
1	2	3	I incorporated critical thinking activities in the assignment.
1	2	3	I had classroom rules posted.
1	2	3	I enforced classroom rules.
1	2	3	I made sure that procedures for routine tasks were in place.
1	2	3	I delivered clear instructions.
1	2	3	I projected a professional image.

MAKE EVALUATIONS WORK FOR YOU

Evaluations can be of enormous benefit to you, or they can turn you into a nervous wreck; the difference is in your attitude. If you want to grow as a teacher, then adopt the attitude that your evaluators only offer you advice in areas in which you need to improve.

Remember this: no teacher is perfect. Every teacher has areas of performance that can be improved. One way to identify those areas is through evaluations. You can suffer through the process, or you can benefit from it. The choice is yours.

TURN CRITICISM INTO A POSITIVE EXPERIENCE

Hearing negative things about yourself is never pleasant, and hearing them from your supervisor is even less so. Here are several ways in which you can turn criticism from a negative experience to a positive one:

During an Evaluation Conference

- Go into your evaluation conference with paper, pen, and an open mind. Be prepared to hear negative as well as positive comments about your performance.
- Listen objectively. Most of the criticism will probably cover issues you have already started to address yourself. Before you become defensive, stop and make an effort to remain objective.
- Listen more than you speak. During an evaluation conference, ask for advice and suggestions for improvement, then listen carefully, write them down, and follow them.

After an Evaluation Conference

- Ask a mentor for suggestions on how you can handle specific areas that need improvement.
- Release your negative emotions by talking with a friend, not by venting in the lounge.
- Some time after the conference, when you have had an opportunity to correct some of your weaknesses, keep the administrator updated on your progress in following his or her suggestions.
- Ask a colleague to observe you. Tell the observer one or two specific problems that you know you have, and ask him or her to offer suggestions.
- Whenever you have the opportunity to observe another teacher or to substitute in another teacher's classroom, take advantage of the chance to learn more about what others are doing in order to teach effectively.

> **Stay upbeat. Form your own opinions of young people. Don't be ashamed to admit mistakes. Seek help from the doers on the staff.**
>
> —*William N. Owen, 43 years' experience*

Develop a Plan to Correct Weaknesses

While you have begun the process of self-evaluation, it is not enough to make yourself aware of your weaknesses. You must plan how to correct them. Here's how:

1. Choose three of the areas you intend to work on; list them on a sheet of paper.
2. Brainstorm as many ways as you can to improve these weaknesses. Remember that brainstorming works best when you keep generating ideas beyond obvious solutions.
3. Go over your list again and decide on the steps you need to take to correct your weaknesses. Write them down.
4. Put the list in a conspicuous place so that your personal improvement plan is easily accessible.

Working Well with Parents and Guardians

All parents have the right to remain informed about their child's behavioral and academic progress. Not only is it their right, but you will find that your job is much easier when you make parents part of their child's success team. Because they want their children to be successful and look to you for help in achieving this success, parents and guardians can be enormously helpful.

Without a doubt, parental support is a major influence on students' attitudes about school. When students know that the important adults in their lives present a united front, they are less likely to misbehave and more likely to strive for success.

It is your responsibility to reach out first to your students' parents. Although reaching out makes extra demands on your time, it is time well spent. Always remember to treat parents with careful respect even if you disagree with the way they express their concern for their children.

Working well with the parents and guardians of your students is sensible if you want to create a positive learning climate in your classroom. If you make the effort to work successfully with parents and guardians, you will find them more willing to support you as you work with their children. Follow these suggestions in order to create a strong connection with the significant adults in your students' lives.

- Be careful to make your first contact with your students' parents a positive one. A good example of how to make initial contact is sending home a letter containing information about how parents can help their children adjust to school.
- If there is a crisis in a student's family, express your concern and offer assistance. For example, if there is a death in the family, send a condolence note and offer to stay after school to help the student catch up on missed work.
- Encourage parents to drop by your classroom often. They can volunteer or be guest speakers.

- Some experienced teachers send out class newsletters or have a Web page for their class. You might try this after you have adjusted to your teaching responsibilities.
- Take the time to make positive phone calls at the start of the term. Send home positive news as often as you can. Parents who hear good news will be more willing to work with you when a problem develops.
- Return phone calls to parents or guardians as soon as possible. Make it a rule to call back within twenty-four hours.
- Take the time to be a good listener when you talk with parents. Together, you can work out many problems while they are still small ones.
- When you talk with parents, realize that their own past negative experiences with school may affect their perception of you. Be as positive and professional as possible in order to help them overcome their negative feelings.
- Don't give out your home phone number. Keep your relationship with parents businesslike. You have a right to protect your privacy at home.
- Notify parents or guardians as soon as you begin to notice a problem developing. Many parents complain that teachers wait too late to call.
- When you call parents at work, ask if they have a moment to talk instead of plunging in with an account of the problem. This small courtesy will enable them to focus on their conversation with you.

What Parents and Guardians Expect from You

When you are a novice teacher who is just beginning to work with the families of your students, you may find it hard to decipher what they expect from their child's teacher. Some may want you to be a tough disciplinarian, while others expect you to take an "anything goes" attitude. As confusing as these extremes can be, however, most parents and guardians are reasonable in their expectations. Here's what parents and guardians expect you to do:

- ✔ Treat their child fairly
- ✔ Teach the material their child needs to succeed
- ✔ Work with them for the good of their child
- ✔ Communicate with them early about problems
- ✔ Show that you value their child
- ✔ Keep their child safe from harm
- ✔ Act in a professional manner at all times
- ✔ Respect their rights and efforts as parents
- ✔ Agree to reasonable requests that benefit their child
- ✔ Make school a pleasant experience

- Avoid becoming confrontational with parents, even when they are unpleasant and confrontational first. Continue to show your concern and caring.
- Never discuss another person's child with a parent. This violates the child's privacy and is unprofessional. It is acceptable to compliment the parents or guardians of a child to other people, and you should feel free to do this; however, it is not acceptable to criticize them.

BE POSITIVE WITH PARENTS AND GUARDIANS

There are many ways to make positive contact with the parents and guardians of your students. Although it may take time to follow through on these little actions, the benefits will repay the time you spend on them. Start with a few of the ones you find easy to manage, and reach out from there.

- Call at the start of the term to relate a positive message.
- Send home positive updates as often as you can.
- Have parents sign papers with good grades as well as bad ones.
- Create a newsletter to relate the good things that happen in your class.
- Compliment parents to other people. Do not hesitate to let students know that you think highly of their parents.
- Make it a habit to thank parents and guardians of your students for their support whenever you see them.
- Call or e-mail parents with good news.
- If you have school voice mail, record a positive message to parents and guardians.
- Hold a Thank-a-Parent Day at your school, and encourage students to join in.
- Send home a thank-you note after a conference.

One of the most effective ways to be positive with the parents of students at all grade levels is by sending home positive messages as often as you can. Even older secondary students will appreciate the effort you take to recognize their hard work and successes.

Create your own "positive postal," or try one of these Web sites:

- **A to Z Teacher Stuff (http://www.atozteacherstuff.com/printables).** This is a good site to search for printable positive message templates to download. A to Z Teacher Stuff is a teacher-created site where you can find thousands of online resources quickly and easily. It provides numerous templates for students of all ages.
- **Teachnology (http://www.teach-nology.com/worksheets).** This Web portal offers a wide variety of free and easy-to-use resources, including printable templates. It also provides links to other sites about best practices in education.

Sample Positive Message to a Parent

Although many formats can be used to notify parents of student achievements, it is best to keep your message simple. Adapt the format of this sample for your own students.

To the Parents [or Guardians] of ______________________________

I am writing to let you know how pleased I am with your child's recent success in my class. You will be proud to know that______________________________

____

____

I know you are as proud of this effort and achievement as I am. Thank you for your support.

Sincerely,

The Importance of Keeping Parent Contact Records

By now, you are probably convinced that you will spend all of your free hours at school documenting things you took for granted in your own student days. There are forms for just about every interaction you will have with your students, and you must complete each form accurately and promptly.

It is sensible to keep accurate records of the times when you have contacted parents and guardians. Even the very best teacher could be asked to provide proof that he or she did all that could be done to help a particular student. Every year, there are countless cases in which frustrated parents sue teachers in an attempt to find a simple cause for a complex problem. Although it may be upsetting to think that this could happen to a dedicated teacher, it does happen.

Fortunately, you can help to protect yourself with just a few minutes of planning and paperwork. You can enhance your professional reputation by being able to provide documentation that you have contacted parents appropriately. Keeping a record of parent contacts does not have to be time-consuming. Photocopy or modify the sample documentation form (Form 3.1), and keep plenty of copies on hand so that you can complete one each time you contact a student's parent or guardian. Fill out the form, and file it in a folder or binder with the other paperwork for that student.

FORM 3.1

Documentation Log for Parent Contact

Student ______________________________ Parent ___________________________________

Date and time of contact ____

Person who initiated the contact ____

Type of contact:

______ Phone call

______ Letter

______ E-mail

______ Open house/Meet the Teacher

______ Meeting with administrator

______ Note home

______ Home visit

______ Detention notice

______ Informal meeting

______ Meeting with counselor

Topics discussed:

____

____

____

Steps parent will take:

____

____

____

Steps teacher will take:

____

____

____

Additional notes:

____

____

____

____

____

____

____

Open House

Your school district will probably arrange several opportunities for parents and teachers to meet during the course of the school year. You may have Meet Your Teacher Day before school starts so that parents and students can introduce themselves to you. Some parents may just stop by your classroom to introduce themselves, especially at the start of the term or if their children have special needs.

While these opportunities are helpful to students, parents, and teachers who want to work well together, they don't have the impact of an open house. During an open house, parents can come to school to meet their child's teachers. In some places, this event is referred to as "Back to School Night." No matter which term your district uses, this meeting can generate good will for you all year long.

An open house can be stressful for you as a teacher. You will have much to do in preparation, and you will be on display for several hours. Both of these can be exhausting when you must do them at night, after you have already put in a long day.

However stressed you may feel about an open house, it is your chance to connect with parents and guardians in a positive and professional way. It is an effective way to build a strong team of support for your students and an excellent opportunity to generate the good will that will sustain you in the days ahead, particularly when some of your students need extra help and guidance.

A FEW GENERAL GUIDELINES FOR AN OPEN HOUSE

- At an open house, you should expect to meet many parents and guardians. The number will vary with your school population and how successfully your school district has promoted the event.
- You will have to give a brief presentation that will probably be five to fifteen minutes long, depending on your school's schedule.
- You must avoid talking about specific students and their concerns; instead, you will need to set up later appointments for parents who want to discuss their children or your class policies in more detail.

HOW TO PREPARE FOR AN OPEN HOUSE

- Clean up your classroom! Parents and guardians want to see a spotless room that shows that you are a well-organized professional who is in control of your environment. You may not be able to do anything about graffiti from previous years, but you should make the room as attractive and clean as possible.
- Plan and practice your presentation. Rehearse what you are going to say. This is not the time to try your skill at winging it.

- Start collecting student work on the first day of class, and display it on the walls of your classroom. Parents expect to see their child's work on display, no matter how old the child.
- Photograph your students as they work. If you use a digital camera, you can run a continuous computer slide show or PowerPoint presentation featuring your students.
- Use the overhead projector to display your rules and procedures. You can also display the main points of your presentation in an overhead transparency or on the board.
- If you have the technical skill and the equipment, show a videotape of your students at work.
- Prepare a handout with general information about the course, homework, important dates, classroom policies, and contact information.
- Have copies of the text available.
- Prepare a sign-in sheet and place it near the door. Include a column for the student's name as well as one for the adult's name so you will know which child's parents attended.
- Dress in your professional best, in order to present yourself as a competent professional educator.

WHAT TO INCLUDE IN YOUR PRESENTATION

- Tell parents what general topics you will cover in class before the end of the term. Give a quick overview, so they will not be surprised about what their child is learning.
- Explain your class rules, policies, and procedures.
- Inform parents of any major projects and approximately when these will be assigned. Parents and guardians should have advance warning about projects such as major term papers, class trips, or science fairs.
- Ask parents to contact you if a problem arises. Make sure you give out your school voice mail, e-mail, and phone numbers.

PRESENT A PROFESSIONAL IMAGE

- Meet parents and guardians at the door. Pleasantly greet any latecomers.
- Begin your presentation promptly.
- Be upbeat, enthusiastic, and positive.
- Be very careful not to mention any problems you have with specific students. Protect their privacy, and do not embarrass their parents or guardians.

- Plan to run out of time. Create a presentation that will last the entire time that you have to speak. If you open the floor for questions, you may run into a sticky situation in which parents can attack you for reasons you may not be prepared to defend in a large group.

Time Line for a Successful Open House

One Week in Advance

- Send home open house announcements.
- Display student work.
- Begin preparing presentation.
- Create and photocopy handouts.

Three Days Before

- Make up computer presentation.
- Create transparencies.
- Create sign-in sheet.

Two Days Before

- Begin practicing presentation.

One Day Before

- Practice again; you cannot be too polished.
- Begin straightening room.
- Get enough rest for the long day tomorrow.

On the Day of an Open House

- Dress professionally.
- Adopt a positive attitude.
- Tidy the classroom one final time.
- Make sure all equipment is working.
- Put the sign-in sheet near the door, with a pencil nearby.
- Have textbooks and handouts ready.

Take Care to Interact Professionally with Parents

By making an effort to work well with parents and guardians, you can create a team of allied adults whose purpose is to work together for the good of the students involved. It is important to always interact professionally with parents and to take care of specific areas of these delicate relationships that may require special attention. Interacting with your students and their families in a professional way in every situation is not always easy, but it will be worth the effort.

ASSIST PARENTS AND GUARDIANS WHO DO NOT SPEAK ENGLISH

At some point in your career, whether you teach in a small town or in a large city, you will have to communicate with parents or guardians whose primary language is not English. This situation can be awkward and confusing for everyone if you are not prepared to offer assistance.

Although it is likely that your school district made efforts to provide assistance when the student enrolled, it is up to you to find a way to communicate effectively if you cannot find an adult interpreter.

One solution is to have students translate for their parents. This is effective if the child is trustworthy and old enough to handle the task. Another solution is to involve an older sibling of the student, if that person is dependable.

You can also use technology to help with this problem. Many Internet sites are available to help you translate what you need to communicate to parents or guardians. Some are so helpful that you can type in what you want to say and it will be translated quickly into another language. Try visiting iLoveLanguages (www.ilovelanguages.com) the next time you need a translator. This site is a comprehensive catalogue of more than 2,400 language-related Internet resources. Click on the "Languages" tab at the top of the home page to find sites that can translate bits of text free of charge.

BE A GOOD LISTENER

To build positive relationships with your students' parents and guardians, it is important to develop good listening skills. Try these simple suggestions for improving your listening skills, and enjoy the benefits of improved communication.

- Stop talking. Allow the other person to speak without fear of interruption from you.
- Give nonverbal cues to indicate that you are paying attention. Nod your head, look the person in the eye, or lean forward in your seat. When appropriate, prompt the speaker by asking questions.
- Jot notes so that later you will be able to recall what was discussed. Before you begin, tell the other person that you are going to take notes in order to help you recall the conversation.
- Make sure that you fully understand the other person by asking for clarification if you need it. Say, "I am not sure I understand what you are saying. Do you mean . . . ?" or "I think I hear you saying . . . "

HANDLE ACCIDENTAL MEETINGS GRACEFULLY

Few situations are as awkward as making a quick trip to the grocery store, dressed in your oldest clothes, and hearing, "Do you remember me? We met at my son's open house." The collision between your personal life and your professional life can be unsettling. How can you handle such meetings gracefully? Try these suggestions:

- Be friendly and poised. Act glad to see the parent.
- Make the necessary introductions of friends who may be accompanying you. Try to avoid introducing your friends by naming the role they play in your life. For example, instead of "This is my girlfriend, Jill Smith," simply say, "This is Jill Smith."

- Keep the meeting friendly and brief. Move on as quickly as you can without appearing desperate to get away.
- Don't discuss school business in public places where others can overhear your conversation. Instead, arrange another time to discuss specific concerns.
- If you are in a potentially embarrassing situation—with a grocery cart full of beer when you suddenly realize that the PTA president is ahead of you in the checkout line, for example—be prepared for embarrassment. You should also brace yourself for the potentially damaging gossip that will result.
- The best way to keep accidental meetings as graceful as possible is to avoid situations in which you appear less than professional in public.

DEAL WITH THE GIFT DILEMMA

While it is gratifying to receive presents from students, you should never encourage students to give you gifts at any time of the year, for a variety of reasons: some students cannot afford them; some students will give gifts only to curry favor; and the practice creates undue pressure on students who simply don't want to give their teacher a gift.

One way to head off the problem is to involve the entire class in a project that helps those who are truly needy. Discuss this with your students, mentioning that the best present they can give you and each other (in addition to good behavior and academic effort) is to participate in the project.

However, if a student does give you a gift, be careful to be gracious about receiving it. Be discreet; don't call attention to it in front of other students. Thank the student in person and then later with a thank-you note.

Reach Out to Parents and Guardians

As a caring teacher, you should be the first to reach out to your students' parents and guardians. With just a bit of effort, sending professional correspondence, making effective phone calls, and creating informative class newsletters or Web pages can be rewarding ways to forge a strong bond between home and school.

MAKE A GOOD IMPRESSION THROUGH EFFECTIVE CORRESPONDENCE

If you thought that your English teachers in high school were quick to catch your grammatical errors, you have not yet experienced the embarrassment of sending home a note with a misspelled word. With a bit of careful effort, you can spare yourself this humiliation.

When you send home a note or letter or send an e-mail message, it represents your effectiveness as a teacher. The correspondence you send home should be businesslike because it reflects your professional competence. Follow these suggestions for making a good impression with effective correspondence:

- Before going into detail in writing about an incident at school, consider phoning the parent instead. Often you can clear up confusion quickly with a friendly phone call.
- Make sure that what you write in a letter is accurate; verify the dates, times, and other details.
- Be brief, but not brusque. Cover your points quickly. Use bulleted lists or other businesslike writing techniques to make your letters easy to follow.
- Appearance counts! Photocopy with clean edges and with enough ink or toner to make clean and clear copies. Avoid cute graphics or unusual fonts whenever you can. Use letterhead stationery when appropriate.
- Grammar and word usage matters a great deal in letters home. Have a colleague proofread your correspondence before you send it out.
- When you send home handwritten notes, write legibly. Use a dark ink for readability, and take the time to proofread your work.
- Never give in to the temptation to fire off an angry e-mail or send a hasty note home. Cool off before you contact a parent.

> **Every teacher needs to be able to communicate with parents with honesty, in a polite manner, and without condescension. Always document conferences, whether phone conferences or face-to-face conferences.**
>
> —*Charlene Herrala, 24 years' experience*

MAKE TELEPHONE CALLS WITH CONFIDENCE

Phoning parents or guardians when there is a problem is one of the unpleasant tasks teachers must do well. Even experienced teachers dread the occasional angry parent who makes phoning a student's home a negative and upsetting experience. However, as disagreeable as this task can be, phoning a parent or guardian is a necessary and often helpful action. There are several strategies you can adopt to make phoning parents easier:

- To save time, use the contact information you collected from your students early in the term instead of searching database records in the school office.
- Plan what you want to say and what information the parent needs to know so that you can work together to solve the problem.
- Find a phone at school where you can make the call with at least some privacy and where you are not likely to be interrupted.
- Be sure to have a pen and the notes you have made about the situation with you.
- Don't hesitate to call a parent at work. However, be careful not to reveal too many details to the parent's colleagues. Protecting their privacy shows respect for parents, making it more likely that they will be cooperative when you ask for their help.

- If you call while parents are at work, begin the conversation by asking, "Do you have a few minutes right now?" so that they can set their work aside long enough to listen.
- Remember that the purpose of the phone call is not to allow you to vent your frustration on the parent but rather to solve a problem by working with the parent.
- Begin with a positive statement about the student, and then say that you would like to enlist the parent's help in solving a problem: "I had a problem with Jim today, and I wonder if you could help me?"
- Be very specific about the problem. Don't just say, "Jim is acting odd today." Try, "Jim laughed out loud at inappropriate moments six times today and fell asleep right before lunch."
- Next, state what you have done to correct the problem. Again, be very specific, and give the result of your actions.
- Ask for parents' help. Listen while parents explain what they know about the situation. Make sure to listen carefully and clarify any points you do not understand.
- Never lose sight of the fact that you and the parent are working together to solve the problem. A team approach is the best one to take.
- Finish the call with a positive statement, expressing your appreciation that a solution has been devised.
- Before you go on to your next task, document the call. Complete a contact log sheet (see Form 3.1) so that you have a record of the conversation and what each party decided to do.

SEND HOME CLASS NEWSLETTERS

Class newsletters have played a strong role in classrooms for many years. While they are most often used by teachers of younger students, newsletters are a valuable tool for all teachers who wish to connect with parents and guardians in a meaningful way.

Newsletters can serve many purposes—for example, to keep parents informed about what is happening in their child's class, to inform parents of upcoming events, or to include parents in creating a caring environment for learning.

Newsletters can be written entirely by a teacher, or they can be managed by students in an authentic writing activity. Either way, parents and students gain new insights as they communicate with each other and with you. To make sure that the newsletters you send home represent your professional best, try including some of these items:

- A message from you
- Clip art
- Student art
- A review of the work covered in class since the previous newsletter

- A list of topics currently under study
- Student work samples
- Creative writing samples
- Student success stories
- Upcoming events such as conferences or field trips
- A word of the week
- Ways that parents can help students study
- A survey of parents and students on a relevant topic
- An inspirational message
- A request for donations
- A thank-you note from you

CREATE A CLASSROOM WEB PAGE

Another terrific way to connect with students and their families is through a class Web page. In recent years, it has become easier and easier for teachers to create an attractive, useful Web page that will connect classroom and home as never before.

If you are still not sure about creating a class Web page, consider these incentives:

- With just a bit of work, you will have an easy way to contact the parents and guardians of your students. With just a click, they will know to send in the permission slip for a field trip or that there really is a test scheduled for Monday.
- If you post homework assignments online, students can stay caught up with the rest of the class when they are absent.
- You can display your students' work. The positive relationships you develop with students and their families when they can see students' artwork or writing published online are successful motivators and can even prevent behavior problems.
- Older students can learn to manage the site as part of their classroom chores.

Fortunately, there are many helpful sites to get you started on creating a class Web page. Here are three that other teachers have found easy to use:

- **Teachers.Net Homepage Maker (http://www.teachers.net/sampler/).** This free site offers systematic instructions on how to make a page that is easy to establish and maintain.
- **Education World (www.schoolnotes.com).** This free site offers a user-friendly format and appealing features and options.
- **ClassNotesOnline (www.classnotesonline.com).** This free Web resource makes Web pages easy to set up and manage.

Conduct Successful Parent Conferences

Parent conferences can produce high-level anxiety for everyone involved: students, parents, and teachers. Despite the anxiety they produce, face-to-face meetings can be a very effective way to solve problems.

Teachers who want to communicate well realize that parents and guardians want to be reassured that their child is doing well and can succeed in school. Even if that is not what is happening at the moment, parents want teachers to work with them to help their children. A strong connection with your students' parents and guardians is achievable if you make sure that your goals for conferences are clear.

Five Essential Goals to Accomplish in a Parent Conference

Goal 1: Parents should see you as a friendly and knowledgeable teacher who has their children's best interests at heart.

Goal 2: Parents should feel an atmosphere of cooperation and support when they are meeting with you.

Goal 3: Parents should leave a conference with all their questions answered and all the points they wanted to discuss covered.

Goal 4: You and the parents should have a sense of mutual respect and an understanding of each other's problems and viewpoints.

Goal 5: Workable solutions to any problems should be agreed on, and everyone involved should agree to work together to help the student.

GUIDELINES FOR EFFECTIVE PARENT CONFERENCES

A parent conference is much more involved than a quick chat after school. Successful conferences require planning, attention to details, and effort. Use the guidelines that follow to guarantee that the parent conferences you have this year are positive and productive.

Actions to Take Before a Parent Conference

- Make sure you have a clear purpose for the conference and a clear understanding of the outcome you would like.
- Plan the points you want to cover. Write them down.
- Gather samples of student work or other evidence that you would like to show parents in the conference. Include progress reports and other information related to grades or behavior.
- Review cumulative records and report card information.

- Make notes on the student's strengths and weaknesses as well as any other special information you would like to present.
- Anticipate a parent's reactions and questions, and jot down notes about possible answers that you may be too nervous to recall in the conference.
- Create a seating arrangement that will be comfortable for adults. Arrange chairs around a table or desks large enough for adults in a circle. Do not sit behind your desk.
- Make sure you provide a pen and paper for everyone.
- Remain calm before, during, and after the conference. If you lose your cool, you will gain nothing.
- Make a neat "Do Not Disturb" sign; post it on your door so that you can meet without distractions.
- Meet parents and escort them to your room.

Actions to Take During a Parent Conference

- Be prepared to begin promptly. Do not make parents or guardians wait while you shuffle papers.
- Begin by expressing your appreciation that the parents have come to the conference. Try to establish a tone of good will and friendly cooperation as quickly as you can.
- Use language that will make parents comfortable. Do not use educational jargon.
- Begin with positive remarks about the child. Talk about the student's aptitude, special talents, improvements, and potential. Focus on strengths even if there is a serious problem. Never lose sight of the fact that the child is very important to his or her parents.
- Convey the attitude that the child's welfare is your primary concern.
- State any problems in simple, factual terms. Express your desire to work with parents for a successful resolution.
- Discuss specific examples of a problem. Show examples of work that illustrates or give details about the student's behavior.
- Always allow upset or angry parents to speak first. After parents have had the opportunity to say everything they need to say, then—and only then—can they listen to what you have to say or begin to work on a solution to a problem.
- If you have discussed a problem before, let the parents know of any improvement.
- Be sure to state what you have done to try to correct problem situations.
- If you want to solve a problem, you need to give your full attention throughout the entire conference. Your nonverbal language is crucial for success. Be friendly and attentive.

- Don't put parents on the defensive by becoming angry or by asking personal questions.
- Don't try to outtalk parents. You may make your point, but the parents will not listen to you. Do not give in to the temptation to interrupt.
- End the conference gracefully by recapping the points that you have covered.
- Determine what you will do to follow up on the conference and to keep in contact with the parent.
- Express appreciation again for the parents' concern and the time they have spent with you in the conference.

Actions to Take After a Parent Conference

- Immediately complete your notes and the documentary evidence of what was discussed and the agreed-on decisions. Spend enough time on this so that your records are complete. Should you need to refer to this material later, you may not remember details accurately if your notes are not complete.

Take a breath and think before speaking or deciding on something.

—*Yann Pirrone, 15 years' experience*

WHY SOME PARENTS AND GUARDIANS MAY NOT RELATE WELL TO YOU

As you gain experience, you will find that not all parents and guardians are supportive of you and the other teachers in your school. While your first tendency may be to take this personally, there are many possible reasons for such negative attitudes:

- Some parents and guardians may have had unpleasant experiences in school themselves.
- Their child may have told them something objectionable (though probably exaggerated or false) about you.
- One of your lessons may have contained information they find inappropriate.
- You may not have presented yourself as professionally as possible when you first met them.
- You may have allowed a problem to escalate by not contacting them as quickly as you should have.
- They may be reacting out of their own frustration with their child's behavior, particularly if the problem is a long-standing one.
- They may disagree with you about the consequences of their child's behavior.
- They may feel embarrassment at their child's behavior or lack of success.

- Their child may have had unsympathetic or unsupportive teachers in the past.
- Previous teachers may have reacted negatively to their efforts to parent the child.
- Your uncertainty and lack of confidence may be obvious.
- They may want to protect their child from potential embarrassment or punishment.

WHAT TO DO WHEN PARENTS OR GUARDIANS ARE UNCOOPERATIVE

No matter how hard you try, parents and guardians will not always be as cooperative as you would like. The best way to avoid this situation is by intervening early, following procedures and rules, maintaining accurate records, presenting yourself as a professional, and keeping parents informed about their child's progress.

If you find yourself in a confrontation with a hostile parent, it is up to you to assume control of the situation. The following steps can help you manage meetings with parents so that the meetings result in productive outcomes instead of heated words.

- Listen to what angry parents or guardians have to say, without trying to interrupt or correct them. Do not try to present your side of the disagreement until they have had an opportunity to express themselves.
- Show your interest by asking questions about specific details. Often, a simple misunderstanding is the cause of the problem.
- Make sure to restate the problem, so that the other person can be reassured that you do understand. Try, "I think you're saying . . . "
- Explain the problem from your viewpoint as objectively as you can. Be specific about what was expected, what the child did that was not appropriate, and how you responded.
- Make it clear throughout the confrontation that you want to work with the parent for the child's welfare.
- Remain calm.
- It will only harm you in the eyes of the parents and your supervisors if you act on your natural desire to justify your actions in a loud tone or to return insults.
- You do not have to accept threats or abuse from a parent. If, after you have sincerely tried to resolve a problem, the parents or guardians remain upset, suggest calling in an administrator to help.
- If you suspect that a parent plans to contact an administrator, you should make the contact first. It is never wise to allow your supervisors to be surprised with bad news. Instead, see an administrator, present your point of view, and ask for assistance.

How to Reach Out to Your Community

Teachers who do not live in the community where they teach often miss an opportunity to bond with their colleagues and their students away from the school setting. While you do not have to live in the same neighborhood as your students, you became part of the life of that community when you signed your contract. As a teacher, you can reach out to the community where your students live in a variety of ways:

- Invite local people to be guest speakers.
- Post a map of the area, and ask students where they live.
- Ask students to tell the class about local events, customs, or activities.
- Spend time driving around and becoming familiar with the area.
- Learn about the community's history, and share it with your students.
- Invite students' families to come to class for special occasions.

Talk It Over

How to Become a Valuable Team Player

You can use the following questions as a springboard for discussions that will help you and your discussion group members grow and develop professionally. Discuss these questions about how to be a valuable team player:

1. Discuss your role as a teacher who is new to your school. What makes you comfortable? What causes you stress? What can you do to improve your role?
2. Given that on-the-job courtesy is a vital component of a productive workplace, what can you conclude about the list of suggestions in this section? How important is workplace courtesy to you? To your colleagues?
3. What do you contribute to your school? Which other staff members seem to make positive contributions? What can you learn from them?
4. Examine the emotions you feel before a parent conference. What choices can you make so that every conference is productive? What suggestions do your colleagues have that can help you make conferences more productive?
5. How diverse is your school? What responsibilities in regard to diversity do you have to your colleagues? What responsibilities in regard to diversity do you have to your students?

6. What are some proactive attitudes that could make the evaluation process easier and more productive for you and your colleagues?
7. What are the qualities of a difficult colleague? What coping skills have worked for you in the past when you have had to deal with difficult people? How can you use them now? How can a new teacher avoid classification as a difficult co-worker?
8. Define your role as a liaison between a student's home and school. How can you present yourself as a friendly, caring teacher to your students and their parents? What suggestions do your co-workers have for you?
9. What do you know about your supervisors' expectations? What can you do to make sure your relationship with each one of your supervisors is positive, professional, and productive?
10. What advice about education have you received? Explore ways in which you apply this in your role as an educator.

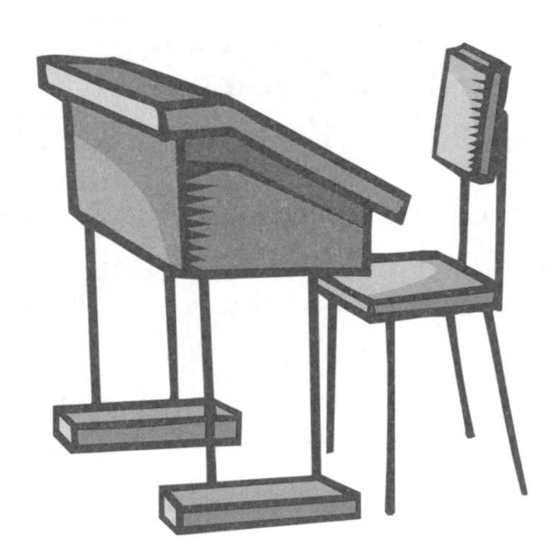

Organize Your Way to a Great Beginning

In this section, you will learn

- ✔ How to organize the time and tasks you will need to manage
- ✔ How to plan for predictable tasks and recurring activities
- ✔ How to arrange your classroom
- ✔ How to welcome students with an inviting classroom
- ✔ How to organize your supplies and materials

You can always tell which teachers are ready for school to begin; their desks are neat, their file cabinets are in order, and their lessons are prepared. They look forward to the day when their students will arrive.

You can be one of those teachers! While it's true that the time before a new school year begins is often challenging and hectic even for experienced teachers, it can also be very satisfying. With careful planning and effort, you can lay the foundation for a successful year before the first day of class arrives.

Lay Your Plans Before School Begins

When you begin to organize your school responsibilities, you should consider how you will manage the tasks you will need to accomplish and the time you have to spend. You should also consider how you will organize your classroom so that it is a welcoming and comfortable place for your students. Self-Assessment 4.1 will help you assess what organizing tasks you need to complete before the term begins, and the time line that follows will help you complete them.

TIME LINE FOR A GREAT BEGINNING

Because there are so many tasks that all teachers must complete in the few weeks and days before the beginning of a school term, it is very easy to be overwhelmed. If you were hired some months before the start of a new term, you have an advantage over teachers who are not as lucky.

If you were offered your position just a few weeks or even a few days before the beginning of school, you will have much to do to catch up. Either way, the time line that follows will help you prioritize your responsibilities and avoid being overwhelmed with too much to do in too little time:

A Month Before the Term Begins

- ☐ Hit the back-to-school sales for supplies.
- ☐ Make sure that your wardrobe reflects your professional status.
- ☐ Order any supplies your district allows.
- ☐ Gather the other supplies you may need.
- ☐ Begin searching the Internet for information about the subjects you will teach.
- ☐ Pick up or download your district's calendar for the school year.
- ☐ Pick up or download your state and district curriculum guides.
- ☐ Pick up teacher's editions and supplementary materials.
- ☐ Begin reading and studying the course materials.
- ☐ Create your professional goals.

Three Weeks Before the Term Begins

- ☐ Create a course overview for the year.
- ☐ Join at least one professional organization.
- ☐ Decide on the resources you will need for each unit of study.
- ☐ Create unit plans.

Two Weeks Before the Term Begins

- ☐ Create a syllabus or planner for your students.
- ☐ Make sure that the equipment in your room works well.

SELF-ASSESSMENT 4.1

What Do You Already Know About Beginning a School Term?

✔ Put a + in the blank beside each item you have already completed as you begin a new term.

✔ Put a – in the blank beside each item you need to complete before you begin a new term.

_____ You have memorized your daily schedule. You know when each class begins and ends and what each bell means. You know what your additional duty assignments are.

_____ You have already written your lesson plans for the next few weeks. You have also scheduled the resources you will need, such as audiovisual equipment or time in the computer lab.

_____ Your handouts for the next few days are ready.

_____ You have checked your calendar against the district one. You have scheduled your lessons around important holidays and other events.

_____ Your folder of information for substitute teachers is complete, including class rosters and seating charts.

_____ You have copies of the forms you will need: attendance forms, discipline forms, and so on.

_____ You have purchased, collected, or picked up the supplies you will need.

_____ You have familiarized yourself with your faculty handbook and other information from workshops and meetings.

_____ You know what to do in an emergency.

_____ You are able to recognize the key people in your building and in the district. You understand what their jobs are and how each one affects you and your class.

_____ You know how to do routine tasks such as entering grades in your grade book, reporting attendance, and scheduling resources.

_____ Your classroom is decorated, all desks are in place, and your own desk is organized.

_____ You have enough copies of the textbook for everyone. You also have the teacher's editions and resource materials you will need.

_____ You know who to turn to for help.

_____ Your personal life is organized so that you can manage your schedule as you adjust to a new term over the next few weeks.

If you have more pluses than minuses, you are well on your way to starting the new school year successfully!

If you have more minuses than pluses, use what you have learned about beginning a school year to guide your preparation.

☐ Brainstorm a list of classroom management strategies and solutions to possible problems.
☐ Create your class rules and procedures.
☐ Put together information for substitute teachers, in case you need them.
☐ Put your classroom in order.
☐ Set up your desk and files.

One Week Before the Term Begins

☐ Obtain the school forms you will need.
☐ Work with a mentor in order to get answers to your procedural questions.
☐ Make sure that you are prepared for emergency drills.
☐ Create a daily routine for attendance, lunch counts, and other student business.
☐ Write a letter to introduce yourself to parents and guardians.
☐ Investigate the Web site you will use to set up your class Web page.
☐ Write out your first three weeks of daily lesson plans.
☐ Study your class rosters in order to familiarize yourself with your students' names.
☐ Create an alphabetical seating chart.

The Day Before School Starts

☐ Finish any last-minute tasks.
☐ Ask any last-minute questions.
☐ Exercise, eat well, and get enough rest.
☐ Make a plan to manage your work-related stress.

Organize Your Time and Tasks

Because teachers control a great deal of the time they have to spend on nonteaching tasks over the course of an entire school year, you can easily organize this part of your school life before school begins. Here's how to get started:

Step 1: Begin with a calendar with large blocks for the days of the week. Block off the time that you must be in direct contact with your students. Because you must put your students first, you can't allot any of this time to other chores.

Step 2: Block off time devoted to standing appointments such as hall duty, faculty meetings, or committee meetings.

Step 3: Now that you have determined the time you have to complete your other tasks, you should figure out how much time each one will take. Write down each task on your calendar as you decide just how long it will take and when you intend to accomplish it.

Step 4: Now, make the commitment to yourself that you will stick to your calendar, and in the future, you will reap the benefits of effective time management.

PREDICTABLE TASKS

Here is a quick list of some of the tasks you should be able to predict and organize successfully. Use it to manage the time you'll need to spend on each one once the school year has begun:

- Checking e-mail
- Phoning parents
- Holding parent conferences
- Checking voice mail
- Checking your mailbox
- Grading papers
- Recording grades
- Filing papers
- Photocopying
- Creating lesson plans

RECURRING ACTIVITIES

In planning to use time wisely and organizing your teaching tasks, it is helpful to think about how you will manage recurring activities. Because these recurring activities happen each day, each week, or each term, you can plan how to use the time you will need for them. As you learn how to complete each task or activity as efficiently as possible, you will see how these recurring tasks give a rhythm to the school year. Here are some of the recurring activities you should plan to master:

Recurring Daily Activities

- Take attendance
- Check and update your class Web page (Section Three)
- File passes, signed forms, and other paperwork (Section Two)
- Report lunch counts and other counts
- Assign and check homework (Section Eleven)
- Begin and end class well (Section Twelve)
- Praise your students as a group and as individuals (Section Ten)

- Reward students (Section Ten)
- Assess how well your students are mastering the lesson (Section Nine)
- Assess how well you present information (Section Eight)
- Adjust schedules and lessons as needed (Section Seven)
- Make sure that every student has an opportunity to read (Section Thirteen)
- Make sure that every student has an opportunity to write (Section Eleven)
- Teach or reinforce a study skill (Section Eleven)
- Review past learning (Section Eight)

Recurring Weekly Activities

- Present at least one active, fun-filled learning experience for your students (Section Ten)
- Look ahead and plan accordingly (Section Seven)
- Plan how you will provide remedial instruction (Section Seven)
- Plan how you will enrich instruction (Section Seven)
- Assess your students' progress at least twice (Section Nine)
- Run off materials for upcoming lessons (Section Two)
- Average all grades for the week (Section Nine)
- Leave your desk clean

Recurring Term Activities

- Create at least one progress report (or more, if possible) for each child (Section Nine)
- Plan for the next term (Section Seven)
- Attend at least one after-school student activity (Section Six)

I think about teaching as a building art form. You make a little progress each day. Some days you need to rebuild.

—Carole Platt,
35 years' experience

Establish Routines and Procedures

All students have some characteristics in common; one of the most significant is the need for structured time. From energetic kindergartners to sophisticated seniors, students need routines in their school day to keep them on track.

While the particulars of these routines will vary from teacher to teacher and from grade level to grade level, adhering to specific "business procedures" for the classroom will give teachers and students the best chance to achieve successful and harmonious learning.

Before school begins, you should decide how to handle the classroom routines and procedures you want your students to follow. If you have these in place before the first day of class, you will be rewarded with a positive classroom environment and successful students. Use Self-Assessment 4.2 to help you begin to formulate your class procedures.

A ROUTINE FOR LUNCH COUNTS AND OTHER COUNTS

Before the school year begins is an excellent time to decide how you will manage to conduct student business such as lunch counts and attendance checks during the school day without losing instructional time. To be successful at multitasking to complete these activities, you should develop efficient routines for conducting student business with a minimum of disruption. Try these steps in order to establish a successful routine:

1. To begin, ask several other teachers in your school how they manage the counts that will be required of you.
2. After you have heard several suggestions, decide on the procedure that will work best for you and your students. Mentally rehearse the procedure in order to anticipate and correct snags.
3. Make sure you have the forms and other materials you will need to complete the task. Carefully think through your procedure, but be prepared to adjust it if you see that it doesn't work as you would like.

ANOTHER ROUTINE TASK: COLLECTING MONEY

Collecting money is another routine task that must be performed accurately and with as little disruption to the learning environment as possible. Again, if you spend time before the term begins deciding how you will carry out this task, your effort will result in less stress for you later. Follow these guidelines in collecting money from your students.

- To reduce opportunities for misbehavior and keep students working productively, plan an assignment for your students to do independently while you collect money.
- Pay attention to your students! Even though you have to collect and count money, your primary responsibility is to teach. You are still responsible for supervising your students.
- Get organized before you begin. Be sure to learn the school procedures you will need to follow as you collect and deposit money. Make sure you have a receipt book, collection envelopes, and other necessary materials or forms ready.
- It is usually not a good idea to allow students to collect or count money because of the possibility of theft and the loss of instructional time.
- If you do decide to allow students to collect or count money, assign two or more students to work together to check each other's work. You should still supervise them closely.

SELF-ASSESSMENT 4.2

Where to Find Help with Establishing Routines and Procedures

Following is a list of essential class routines and procedures. To determine the best course of action to take for each item, will you need to talk with a mentor? Consult the faculty handbook? Brainstorm your own ideas? In the blank beside each item, indicate where you can find information about each one.

Beginning class ______________________________

Ending class ______________________________

Tardies, absences, and make-up work ______________________________

Handing in work ______________________________

Keeping the work area clean ______________________________

Formats for written work ______________________________

Asking questions ______________________________

Emergencies and drills ______________________________

Restroom breaks ______________________________

Materials needed for class ______________________________

Homework ______________________________

Class interruptions ______________________________

Class discussions ______________________________

Coming to attention ______________________________

Tests ______________________________

Other routines and procedures ______________________________

____

____

____

____

____

- Respect the bookkeeper's time. Write receipts legibly and in ink. Place like denominations of bills together. Be accurate and organized.
- If there is a deadline for submitting money to the bookkeeper, respect it.
- You should never leave money in your classroom overnight, even if you lock it in a safe place.

Organize Your Classroom

Before the term begins is the perfect time not only to organize the tasks you'll have to manage all year but also to organize your classroom. You will need to spend time and physical effort to arrange things just the way you want them. If you have friends or family members who can shove desks and hang posters, ask for their help. You will save hours of time, which you can then use to write lesson plans or complete some of the stacks of paperwork that first-year teachers need to finish before the start of school.

In arranging your room, try to minimize any negative conditions that your students will have to overcome. If your room is seriously overcrowded, for example, you will need to arrange desks in such a way that students do not bump into each other while moving around the classroom. Further, you should strive to create an appealing environment in which your students will feel welcomed and able to succeed.

Many Web sites offer first-rate suggestions for teachers who want to arrange their classrooms to be user-friendly. The following three are particularly good.

- **Education Place (www.eduplace.com/rdg/res/classroom.html).** The Houghton Mifflin Company maintains this large site, which features a variety of resources for educators at all grade levels. It offers sound advice on setting up a classroom quickly and efficiently.
- **Scholastic (www.teacher.scholastic.com).** Scholastic, Inc., manages this site, which offers a great deal of helpful information for teachers. Click on "Tools" to learn how to set up a classroom using their interactive template and assistance.
- **4Teachers (http://classroom.4teachers.org).** At this site, you can create a diagram of your room, manipulating an online template to create the best arrangement for your class.

CLEANING ITEMS TO TAKE TO SCHOOL

Although the custodial staff at your school may keep it spotless, it is not their job to clean the inside of your desk or other personal spaces. You may also want to keep some basic cleaning supplies on hand in order to minimize disruptions when an accident occurs. In addition, teachers who keep desktops and other areas clean find that doing so reduces the risk of vandalism. Here are some basic cleaning supplies to take to school:

- Inexpensive broom and dustpan
- Rags or paper towels
- Disinfectant
- Board cleaner
- Desk cleaner

THREE CONSIDERATIONS BEFORE YOU MOVE FURNITURE

When you consider how to arrange your room, think about these three important considerations: the traffic flow, the arrangement of desks, and your personal space.

Traffic Flow

Traffic flow in a classroom is more important than many novice teachers realize. For example, if you place your trash can near the door, the stapler on your desk at the back of the room, and a tray to collect completed work near the front, students will wander all over your room after a test just to throw away scrap paper, staple their papers, and turn in their test. You should think about what students will have to do and put the equipment they will need for each task close together so that they can complete tasks with a minimum of bother.

Carefully consider the routine activities your students will perform before you set up your room, so that you can minimize distractions and interruptions. Some of these routine activities could include

- Entering class
- Checking posted material
- Checking the calendar
- Checking the clock
- Working on the board
- Passing in papers
- Speaking with you privately
- Using a computer
- Picking up supplies
- Disposing of trash
- Sharpening a pencil
- Using a stapler

Arrangement of Desks

Arranging student desks so that your students can focus on their work is important for their success. You will probably change the arrangement of desks several times during the term, to allow your students to work in groups of various sizes. To arrange student desks for an optimum effect, keep these pointers in mind.

- You must be able to see every student's face, and every student should be able to see you with no difficulty.
- Begin the year with desks in traditional rows, if you can. This sends the message that you want your students to focus their attention on you and not on each other.
- You must be able to move freely around the room. You should be able to walk behind every row of desks.
- Keep desks away from attractive graffiti spots such as bulletin boards, window ledges, or walls.
- Avoid placing desks near distractions such as a pencil sharpener or a computer monitor with an interesting screen saver.

Your Personal Space

Your personal space may determine whether you will be comfortable in your classroom or not. Because you will be spending so many of your daylight hours in your room, your personal space should be comfortable as well as businesslike.

- The area you designate as your personal space might include a lockable drawer, your desk and chair, a coat cabinet, a bookshelf, or some other area that is solely for your use and not for your students'.
- Keep the top of your desk as free of clutter as you can. While the items on your desk can reflect your personality, you should keep them businesslike. Here are some of the things you should have on top of your desk:
    - Trays for folders and papers
    - A calendar
    - Pens and pencils
    - Notepads
    - Stapler (labeled "Teacher Use")
    - Paper clips
- Because your desk is a space allotted for your use, you should discourage students from taking items from it. Set up a student work center at a spot near the door. In this area, place a stapler (labeled "Student Use"), a hole punch, a trash can, a recycled paper bin, and a tray for collecting student papers and other work.
- Do not place scissors, knives, correction fluid, tacks, markers, glue, or any sharp object on your desktop. If an item could harm a student or be used as a weapon, it should be stored inside your desk.
- One mistake that many teachers make is putting their desk in the front of the classroom, in front of the board. If your desk is at the back of the room instead, you can

easily monitor your students' activity from there. You can have personal conferences with students without having the entire class as an audience, and you will not block students' view of the board.

- If possible, your file cabinet and other personal storage areas should be set up near your desk, so that you can quickly find what you need. If you have a computer that your students do not use, it should also be in your personal area.
- You will need a safe place to store and lock away your personal belongings. Experienced teachers seldom have credit cards or much cash at school.

Connect with Your Students by Creating an Inviting Classroom

Your students crave approval. They thrive in environments in which teachers take their needs seriously and in which they feel valued. When teachers create classrooms that invite students to join in a learning community, they are reaching out to their students in a tangible way. An inviting classroom sends a clear message to your students that they are important to you—that you approve of them.

One of the best choices for a teacher who wants to create an inviting classroom is to reflect the interests and concerns of the students, not the teacher. Too often, teachers err in decorating their classroom beautifully, but with items that appeal to their own tastes instead of their students'.

Your classroom should be cozy in addition to being well organized. When you have worked out the physical arrangement of the desks so that traffic can flow smoothly, arranged your personal items, and set up the storage areas for supplies, your room will be organized, but not particularly welcoming. The next step is to make your room inviting. Here are some suggestions that will help you get started:

Think outside the box! Go beyond those four blank walls and decorate the entire classroom with items that will enhance your students' school day. Use fishing line or dental floss to hang items from the ceiling, tape messages and reminders to the floor, or use the ceiling to remind students of important facts. You can use the space on the front of your desk, the back of the door, or the sides of file cabinets.

Hang a clothesline under the chalkboard, and pin papers to it. Purchase inexpensive cork squares, and pin student work to them. Your students will delight in your efforts to make their room different from the ordinary classroom box.

Decorate your classroom with students' work. Students feel a sense of ownership and pride in a classroom where their work is displayed. Be sure to display everyone's work. If you hang only the best work, students might feel that you are playing favorites, which, of course, would be harmful to the class environment. You can display all sorts of student work, not just projects or "A" papers. Have students list facts on bright note cards, and then post them near the door as a review. Post drawings, notes, graphic organizers—

anything that shows how much you value your students' efforts. Students will enjoy seeing a changing display of things they have created far more than a purchased poster.

Ask students for their suggestions. You can make creating and then maintaining an inviting classroom a shared concern by soliciting assistance from your students. When you seek their help, you give your students ownership in their environment. Another way to use student input to forge a bond with your class is to offer them a suggestion box. Place a box with a secure lid near the door so that students can slip their suggestions to you with ease. Establish a few ground rules about acceptable topics and language, and then allow your students to connect with you.

Set aside an area for class business. You can keep your students informed and involved by posting items such as assignments, due dates, school announcements, and other shared business. Your students should participate in keeping this area up-to-date, if they are old enough to do so.

Set aside an area for tracking progress. If you have class competitions, students should see the results displayed. For example, if you want to improve the way your students complete homework assignments, create poster-sized bar graphs to record each day's results. Make goalposts, basketball hoops, or racetracks to track good behavior. Making progress visible is a powerful way to keep students on the right path.

Set aside an area for motivation. Have students bring in inspiring posters or display ones they make themselves. Students could illustrate words of wisdom from the Internet, books they have read, or song lyrics. Perhaps a giant graphic organizer full of brainstormed mottoes for success would remind students how much you care about their success.

Create areas where students can work with enrichment materials. Learning centers are not just for young students. Use trays, baskets, large envelopes, or rolling carts to store materials for students to use after they have finished their assignments. In this area, you could include a variety of items that interest your students:

- Books
- Magazines
- Board games
- Pen-and-paper puzzles
- Jigsaw puzzles
- Flash cards
- Art supplies
- Bingo boards

Use bulletin boards to send powerful messages to your students. Take advantage of this space to welcome your students all year long. Try these simple tricks to make the bulletin boards in your classroom effective connection builders:

- ▶ Use inexpensive fabric or wrapping paper as a background. Staple it into place at the start of the term and you will not have to replace it the rest of the year.

- Borders can be as simple as strips of construction paper or more creative. Cut out borders from old newspapers, comics, magazines, wrapping paper, or even maps.
- Go three-dimensional. Consider using Velcro strips to mount CD players or tape players near the bulletin board for audio effects. Or use stuffed animals, objects made of craft foam, or other objects students love, such as balloons.

Many Web sites have great tips for using the bulletin boards in your room to connect with your students. Use the three sites listed here to search for good ideas to adapt for your students.

- **Kathy Schrock's Guide for Educators (http://school.discovery.com/schrockguide).** This site is part of the large Discovery School site. At the home page, use "bulletin board" as a keyword to search for ideas. Schrock's guide offers dozens of links to bulletin board ideas.
- **Kim's Korner (www.kimskorner4teachertalk.com).** Teacher Kim Steele manages this useful site, which provides links to many other sites. Her bulletin board section gives specific links to other sites and offers information about bulletin board topics, trims, and inexpensive materials.
- **The Teacher's Corner (www.theteacherscorner.net/bulletinboards/).** This award-winning site offers many seasonally themed bulletin board ideas as well as bulletin board ideas of general interest.

I think the most important thing is to really enjoy the kids that you work with. If you are having fun, they will have fun learning. Look for crazy moments and things that only kids could say.

—William Leigh, 16 years' experience

Two Special Classroom Situations

In overcrowded schools, many new teachers are not assigned a classroom of their own. Instead, they may "float" or "travel" from room to room, or their classroom may be away from the main building of the school in a portable classroom or mobile unit. In either case, teachers need to be positive, flexible, and proactive in order to turn these classroom assignments into an advantage for students.

Your attitude will determine the attitude of your students. If you see either of these situations as burdens, so will your students. Here are some tips to help you be positive about either type of classroom:

SHARING A CLASSROOM

- When you share a classroom with another teacher, you should begin by introducing yourself to that teacher as soon as possible. Discuss the particulars of sharing the room: how to arrange seats, where to store your personal items, the board space allotted for you, and other details that will make sharing easier.
- One concern that you should be sure to discuss with the teacher with whom you are sharing is whether you are comfortable with that teacher staying in the classroom during your class. If you are not sure that you want this, speak up.
- Because you do not have a dedicated space for your own use in a classroom, you will need an office area with a desk, bookcase, and file cabinet. If this has not been arranged for you, ask for it.
- You will need a sturdy cart large enough to move your teaching materials from room to room. Find one as soon as possible and arrange your belongings on it.
- Use containers to store your belongings on your cart; loose papers and supplies may disappear when you try to navigate crowded hallways.
- Spend time deciding how to move your cart from room to room without losing class time at the start and the end of a class.
- Keep your relationship with the teachers whose rooms you share friendly, respectful, and professional. Respect their classroom rules. Make sure that your students do not leave trash or materials behind.
- Ask your students for help and advice. They can move your cart, gather up materials quickly, and offer other assistance.

TEACHING IN A PORTABLE CLASSROOM

- Make decisions about how you will handle students who are tardy or who take extended breaks when you excuse them from the room. While you do need to be reasonable, you should not be a pushover.
- Learn how to control the temperature of your classroom, if possible. A room that is too cold or too stuffy is not pleasant for anyone.
- Make sure that everyone knows where your mobile unit is located. Bright signs located near the entrance of the school will help students and their parents find your room when you have an event such as an open house. Place another noticeable sign on the door of your classroom.
- Decide how you are going to handle inclement weather. What can you do to help your students stay dry when a sudden downpour threatens?
- Lack of communication with the rest of the school staff is sometimes a problem for teachers in a portable classroom. Work with other teachers to remedy the situation if your classroom does not have a phone, Internet connection, or intercom.
- Pay particular attention to safety issues. Make sure you know what to do during a fire drill, if a student is hurt, or if you need an administrator.

Storage on a Budget

All teachers, regardless of the subjects or grades they teach, need plenty of storage options. Use hints from the following list to create lots of storage in your classroom without spending lots of money.

- **Storage for papers.** Recycled file folders can last for years. Ask office staff, guidance personnel, or other teachers to let you know when they are getting rid of used folders.
- **Storage for files.** If you do not have enough file cabinet space, an excellent alternative is the boxes that reams of photocopier paper come in. Make sure that the boxes you select are sturdy and have fitted tops. Label the front or side of the boxes in large, bold letters.
- **Storage for books.** To create bookshelves in your classroom, use boards and bricks or blocks. Make sure that the shelves you create are extra sturdy so that you do not endanger your students.
- **Storage for other materials.** There is a variety of storage options for the other materials in your classroom. To store objects such as pencils, crayons, scissors, manipulatives, and other small items, consider these:
  - Resealable plastic bags
  - Recycled cans (Be sure there are no sharp edges.)
  - Plastic jugs or bottles (Ask in the cafeteria for large ones.)
  - Shoe boxes
  - Tissue boxes
  - Margarine tubs
  - Cereal boxes
  - Ice cream tubs
  - Sturdy trash bags

TIPS ON ORGANIZING MATERIALS AND SUPPLIES

Before school begins, you have an excellent opportunity to plan how you will organize the materials and supplies your students will need all year. Although the materials and supplies needed in a class vary widely from grade to grade, every teacher needs to devise ways to store them all in an efficient manner.

- ▶ Take the time at the start of the term to clean your file cabinets, closets, and desk. Begin your organizing tasks with a sufficient amount of clean storage space and the materials you will need to keep your supplies in order.
- ▶ To begin the process of getting organized, make sure to have the following basic supplies on hand:

- Cleaning supplies
- Scissors
- Boxes of all sizes
- Rubber bands
- Clips
- Labels
- Tape
- File folders
- Markers
- Cans and other recycled containers
- Plastic bags

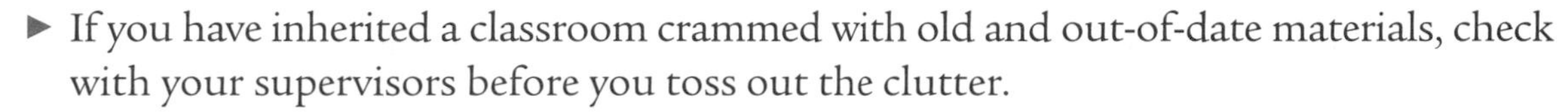

- If you have inherited a classroom crammed with old and out-of-date materials, check with your supervisors before you toss out the clutter.
- Store similar materials together; place paper in one area, crayons in another, oversized books in yet another area, and so forth.
- Set up a color-coded folder or binder for each day of the week. Keep the materials you will need for that day—lesson plans, handouts, and any other resources—in each folder.
- Place a folder, tray, or box on your desk to contain items such as papers to be photocopied that you need to handle during your planning period.
- Make organizing your materials and papers a daily task. Allowing your room to become messy robs you of your peace of mind and sends a negative message to your students.

In addition, you can turn to numerous Web sites for ideas on how to become more organized. A good place to begin is with this site on general organizing strategies:

- **123sortit (www.123sortit.com).** This Web site, managed by two professional organizers, contains resources and information on organizing home and business offices as well as on project management.

YOUR SUPPLY LIST

Even if you teach secondary students, you will need more than just pens and paper to reach your students. Unfortunately, many schools do not provide teachers with enough money to pay for the supplies they need. Teachers everywhere have learned to adjust to tough economics by recycling, asking parents or businesses for help, and making good use of the supplies they have.

Another way that many teachers obtain school supplies is by searching for freebies online. Here are just three of the many sites you can search for items that could benefit you and your students:

- **About.com (www.freebies.about.com).** This Web site is a great place to get started on looking for free materials. In addition to a link just for teachers, this site offers advice on topics such as how to look for freebies, how to recognize fraud, and how to avoid junk mail.
- **CoolFreebieLinks (www.coolfreebielinks.com/Teachers_Freebies/index.html).** This site offers many links to help teachers find items such as rebates, samples, classroom materials, and coupons. It also offers links to freebies that teachers can use at home.
- **Sassy Sue's Freebies (www.sassysue.com).** Sassy Sue's Freebies' offerings include an eclectic selection of samples, materials, coupons, and other free items for home and school.

Following are lists of some of the supplies you may find useful as you go through the school year. Included in this list are plenty of recycled, free, and found items.

Basic Items That All Teachers Need

- Pens—blue and black
- Colored pens for grading
- Pencils
- Calculator
- File folders
- Labels
- Hole punch
- Calculator
- Overhead transparencies
- Overhead pens
- Correction fluid
- Transparent tape
- Computer disks
- An easy-to-find key ring
- Rubber bands
- Pencil sharpener
- Staplers (one for students and one for you)
- Paper clips of all sizes
- Scissors
- Three-ring binders
- Stackable trays
- Board erasers
- Reward stickers
- Mints

Useful Items to Keep on Hand

- Colored pencils
- Baby food jars
- Plastic tubs
- Tissues
- Duct tape
- Boxes, especially cereal boxes and shoeboxes
- Pieces of cardboard
- Display boards from old science fair projects
- Newspapers
- Poster mounting putty
- CD or tape player
- CDs or tapes (check them out from a public library)
- Crayons
- Glue
- Computer paper
- Printer cartridges
- Blank note cards
- Get-well cards
- Thank-you notes
- Envelopes
- A personal first-aid kit
- Index tabs for grade book
- Needle and thread
- Packing peanuts
- Scraps of fabric
- Yarn
- Dental floss or fishing line (great for hanging things from the ceiling)
- Safety pins
- Plastic bags
- Discarded books from libraries
- Cotton from pill bottles
- Board games and puzzles
- Old clothes, hats, sunglasses

Set Up Your File Cabinet

You will need to set up a filing system for the paperwork you will deal with each day. If you have a system in place before the term begins, you will save yourself much frustration and time later. Setting up a file cabinet is not a difficult task, but it does require planning and effort.

1. Once you have a file cabinet, clean it out and lubricate any stuck drawers.
2. Go searching or shopping for file folders. Begin your search by letting it be known that you can use any folders that anyone in your building is about to toss out.
3. If your school has allotted money for you to spend on supplies, be sure to spend some of it for materials for your file cabinet. Purchase hanging file frames and hanging file folders for as many drawers as your budget permits. In addition to hanging files, you will need folders, labels, and permanent markers.
4. Set aside one file drawer for student business. Here you will keep documentation, student information, progress reports, report cards, copies of parent correspondence,

and other paperwork related to students. You should be able to lock this drawer in order to protect confidential records.

5. Set aside another file drawer for general business. Here you will store your folder with information for substitutes, detention forms, and other general paperwork such as memos from the office.
6. In the other drawers, file material such as unit plans, handouts, tests, and paperwork related to your curriculum in alphabetical order.
7. After you have completed the basic steps in setting up your file system, the following refinements will make your system much more efficient and easy to use:
   - Label the front of each drawer in large, bold letters so that you can tell at a glance what is inside.
   - Neatness counts! File material according to subject, in alphabetical order. Make a special effort to maintain orderly files.
   - Label everything. If you can color-code your labels, it will be even easier to find what you need quickly. Even if you cannot color-code the entire file, use a colored dot on the tab to help you group like files together.
   - Stagger the tabbed labels on hanging files and the file folders within them so that you can see what is in the file drawer at a glance.
   - Do not stuff a file drawer so full that it is almost impossible to move files around.

MATERIALS AND PAPERS YOU WILL NEED TO KEEP

During a year when so much of your work experience is new, something as seemingly uncomplicated as knowing what to keep and what to throw away can be frustrating. Use this list to help you make decisions about the materials and papers you should keep.

- If you can store work electronically, you will save paper and space. Be sure to always back up your work.
- Don't throw away any information about curriculum guidelines in your state and local district. Keep it handy, and refer to it often.
- If you give examinations, you should not only keep a master copy and a key, but you should also keep student copies. If a grade is challenged, you will need to produce the test paper. Keep them for a year.
- If you have sent home papers for parents or guardians to sign, keep them on file. This practice applies to progress reports, informal notes, grade sheets, and any other signed paper.
- Keep all attendance records.
- Keep all contact logs.
- Maintain a file of old tests and quizzes to draw from in future terms.

- Don't throw away plans and syllabus information. Unit plans will be particularly useful when you begin to plan new units in future years.
- Keep all papers relating to your observations and evaluations.
- Be sure to hang on to any complimentary notes you have received. They will help remind you on tough days why you are a teacher.

Quick Tips for Creating a Useful Computer File System

Before school begins, you will need to create a way to keep up with all of your new professional passwords, screen names, and voice mail access protocols, to say nothing of the procedures for using all of the technology that is supposed to make your school life easier. Try these quick tips for keeping your computer files organized:

- One efficient way to begin to manage technical information is to create a folder just to store the handouts you will receive on the equipment in your room.
- Make sure that you assign simple, logical names for all of the folders and documents on your computer. Store all documents related to a class or unit of study in their own folder.
- Back up all your computer work. Once you have finished a document, back it up by storing it on a disk, CD, zip drive, or other storage medium. It is less painful to recreate a single document after a computer crash than to lose a semester's worth of work because you had not yet gotten around to saving each document.

Survey Your Classroom

Is your classroom as safe and as inviting as possible? Use Self-Assessment 4.3 to make a final check of your classroom before your students arrive.

SELF-ASSESSMENT 4.3

Is Your Classroom Ready for Students?

Now that your room is finally arranged just the way you want it to be when your students arrive, take a few moments to look around. Use this checklist to make sure you have created the best learning environment possible for your students.

- ☐ Your name and the room number are prominently displayed in the hall.
- ☐ The overall appearance of the room is orderly and attractive.
- ☐ Every student has a desk.
- ☐ Students with physical disabilities have the necessary furniture and equipment.
- ☐ Additional equipment, such as an overhead projector, is in place.
- ☐ Your desk and desk chair are comfortable.
- ☐ Your desktop reflects your personality but is still businesslike.
- ☐ There are two trash cans—one for students and one by your desk.
- ☐ All computers are ready for use.
- ☐ Textbooks and other materials are arranged for easy use.
- ☐ Bulletin boards are attractive and interesting.
- ☐ The room is a safe place for students: all cords are secure; nothing harmful is within reach; fire drill exits are marked; and there is no broken glass or broken equipment.

How to Organize Your Way to a Great Beginning

Use these questions as a springboard for discussions that will help you and your discussion group members grow and develop professionally. Discuss these questions about how to organize for a great beginning to your school year:

1. A well-organized classroom is crucial to beginning a new term successfully. What plans did you make to organize your room and the materials and supplies you will need to use all year? What do you still need to accomplish? How can your colleagues help you?
2. Once your students arrived, you could decorate your classroom by displaying their work. Before they arrived, how did you decorate your room so that it was welcoming? What would you do differently in the future?
3. Correctly organizing your file cabinet and your electronic files is a necessary chore that you will benefit from all year. What techniques did you use to make sure your system is efficient and easy to use?
4. What have you done to make sure your classroom is a safe place for your students? How can your colleagues help you with this?
5. What routines and procedures can you anticipate that are not on the list in this section? How can you plan for them?
6. Brainstorm with your colleagues other ways to make your school calendar a useful tool for teachers.
7. Have you been able to obtain all of the supplies you and your students will need for the term? What can you do to make sure that you will have everything?
8. Which part of setting up a classroom is easiest for you? Which part is the most difficult? How can your colleagues help you with the difficulties you are having?
9. What did you plan before school began that you were not able to accomplish? Brainstorm ways to accomplish each one now.
10. Describe a classroom in your school that is inviting. What qualities make it this way? How can you incorporate some of these qualities in your room?

SECTION FIVE

Have a Fantastic First Day

In this section, you will learn

- ✔ How to create successful seating charts
- ✔ How to create an appealing welcome packet
- ✔ How to provide interesting activities for the first day
- ✔ How to learn your students' names quickly
- ✔ How to give your class a positive identity

The first day of class is exciting and stressful for both students and their teachers, for good reasons. The rest of the year hinges on how well the teacher manages to get students off to a good start.

It is no wonder that many first-year teachers sleep poorly at the beginning of a new term. They spend restless nights worrying whether they will ever be ready for school to begin, pondering what to teach on that first day, wondering whether their students will like them, and thinking about what to do if they don't.

Your first day of class with your new students is one that you will always remember. Every experience will be new and intense. If you are like other teachers, you will be exhausted at the end of the day. With careful planning and attention to detail, however, having a fantastic first day can be one of the easiest tasks you will accomplish all year.

Why the First Day Is Important

The first day of class with your new students is a crucial one for them and for you. There are many reasons to take extra care in preparing for this important time:

- You need to reassure students that they can succeed in your class, setting a positive tone for success. Remember that students may be anxious, too.
- When you give students an idea of the work they will be doing in your class, you need to give them something to look forward to.
- If you let students know that you are confident they will do well in your class, you will win them over.
- You only have one chance to get them off to a good start. Make the day a great one for everyone!

Overcome First-Day Jitters

There are many things you can do to handle the jitters that beginning a new career can cause in even the most self-assured person. To calm yourself, try an assortment of tips and techniques from this list:

- Accept the fact that you will feel nervous and excited on the first day of school. Many veteran teachers do, too. Denying your concerns will not help you deal successfully with them.
- Boost your confidence by dressing well. Teachers traditionally dress up a bit on the first day—even the ones who slouched around in jeans before school started.
- Pack a good lunch, and force yourself to eat it when lunchtime arrives. Avoid having too much caffeine at breakfast.
- Ride to work with a colleague, if you can. Carpooling on the first day will give you a chance to share your fears and provide mutual support.
- Pack your book bag the night before and leave it by the door, so that you can just grab it as you leave.
- Look over the list of your students' names one last time the night before school starts. You will feel better if you can pronounce them correctly.
- Plan more work than you believe your students can possibly accomplish, then plan some more. It is truly terrifying to run out of work for your students on the very first day of school.
- The chances of major behavior disruptions are slim; students tend to be on their very best behavior during the first few days of school. Enjoy the honeymoon.
- Try the video approach to teaching your rules and expectations to students. (Details on creating such a video are given later in this section.)

If you are too nervous to speak well, the video will show a confident and relaxed teacher. Your students will be involved in the assignment, and you will not have to worry about whether you have covered everything.

- Have extra supplies on hand so that every student can complete assignments with no trouble.
- Prepare a seating chart. One easy way to do this is to assign a number to each student on the roster, then place a number on top of the desk or on the seat. As you greet students at the door, ask their name, tell them their number, and direct them to find their seat. You will also match faces to names quickly in this way.
- Smile, even when you feel stressed. Sometimes just acting in a confident manner will help you find the confidence you need.
- Arrive early. You do not have to be so early that you help the custodians unlock the building, but you should be early enough that you do not feel rushed in finishing any last-minute chores.

Keep in mind that the most stressful part of your day will be over sometime in the first half hour of class, when you realize that your students are cooperative and pleasant and depending on you.

Why You Need Seating Charts

No matter what the age of your students may be, seating charts are necessary. Seating charts solve many problems and prevent many more. If you use a seating chart, here's how you and your students will benefit:

- Students from the same neighborhood will not sit next to each other, perhaps creating an obvious ethnic separation.
- Timid students will have the same seating opportunities that aggressive ones do.
- Students will not argue with each other over which desk belongs to whom.
- Unmotivated students can be moved from the back of the room to places where you can more easily engage them in lessons or offer assistance.
- Easily distracted students can be seated in places where it will be easier for them to stay on task.
- Students with special needs can sit in locations where their needs can be met with a minimum of fuss.
- Students with medical problems can be accommodated as necessary.
- Taller students will not block the view of smaller ones.
- Students receive a clear message that you are the person in charge of the class.

How to Create a Seating Chart

Base your first seating chart, which you should make as soon as you receive your class rosters, on the alphabetical order of your students' last names. This is a good way to learn every student's name quickly. In a few days, after you get to know your students, you should make up a permanent seating chart based on other factors. Here's how:

1. Begin by drawing a diagram of your room in which each desk is represented by a rectangle.
2. Using your class roster, pencil the names of your students on your diagram. Begin with the students who must sit in a certain area of the room due to medical issues or the terms of their Individualized Education Plan or 504 Plan.
3. After you have considered students with special needs, move on to the students who misbehave in their current seat. Place them where they can focus on you and their work rather than on having fun with their classmates.
4. Finally, move the rest of your students. Do your best to find each student a seat that will be comfortable for his or her size and temperament.

What to Do on the First Day: Your Priorities

As soon as you have your room set up and your lesson plans in order, you need to give thought to how to convince your students that you are the best teacher they will ever have. Your students are probably concerned that they will not have a good teacher or a good year. Your first-year jitters may be bad, but theirs might be worse!

Because it is so important that the first day of school be an encouraging experience for your students, you must present yourself to your students in as positive a manner as possible. This will be easy for you if you focus your energies on the following five important priorities:

PRIORITY 1: TAKE CHARGE OF YOUR CLASS

- Even if you are overcome with stage fright, you must conquer your personal feelings and pretend to be confident and self-assured. Sometimes, by pretending to be confident, you can begin to convince yourself that you are.
- Have a seating chart ready so that you can show students to their seats and get them started on their opening exercise at once. Have an assignment on the board, or give students a handout as they enter the room.
- Before the term begins, when you have made up your class rules and expectations, have a friend videotape you presenting them. You can really have fun with this if you film your presentation at the beach, on a boat, or even in your own backyard. When school starts, pop in the video and give your students a handout on the class expectations to fill in as they watch and listen.

PRIORITY 2: CALM YOUR STUDENTS' FEARS

> Establish the structure and routines in your classroom on the first day of school. Make sure students know that you mean business, and then you can relax a little.
>
> —*Paige Adcock, 10 years' experience*

- Stand at the door of your classroom and welcome students to your class. Wear a bright name tag. Make sure to prominently display your name and room number so that students and their parents can be sure that they are in the right place.
- Look happy to see every child. Greet each one pleasantly, using his or her name if you can. Assume the best from each one.
- Teach your first lesson as if it is the most important lesson you will teach all year. In many ways, it is. Your students should feel not only that they learned something interesting but that they will continue to learn something in your class every day.

PRIORITY 3: INTRODUCE YOURSELF

- Although it may seem obvious, it is important to introduce yourself to your students on the first day of class. Because you want the first day of class to go well and because you want to control the amount of wild speculation about you, the new teacher, you should introduce yourself. You should be comfortable telling your students
  - How to spell your last name
  - Your title (Mr., Ms., Mrs., Dr.)
  - Where you went to college
  - Where you grew up
  - Why you are looking forward to working with them
  - The positive things you have heard about them
  - The positive things you have heard about the school
  - What your favorite subject was in school
  - Why you chose to be a teacher

PRIORITY 4: ENGAGE YOUR STUDENTS' MINDS

- Design fast-paced instruction that will appeal to students with a variety of learning styles and engage their critical thinking skills.
- Include a brief homework assignment to reinforce the day's work and to get students into the habit of doing homework for your class.

PRIORITY 5: BEGIN TO TEACH CLASS ROUTINES

- Teaching acceptable school behavior is part of what teachers do and is certainly part of what students expect from their teachers. For example, when it is time for students to turn in the day's written assignment, show them the procedure for passing in papers that you will expect them to follow.
- If students lack supplies to do the assignment, lend them what they need for class and gently remind them that they will need to have paper or a pencil in the future.
- Keep any reprimands very low-key. Stick to gentle reminders instead.
- When it is time to dismiss class, spend time showing students how you will dismiss class.

> Do something fun the first day of class. Rules need to be established, but should children do rules all day? If you teach secondary classes, think about what kids will be doing in other classrooms when you prepare your lessons for the first day of class.
>
> *—Stephanie Mahoney, 29 years' experience*

First-Day-of-School Welcome Packet

One of the best ways to get your students off to a good start is to provide each one with a folder containing the many papers they will need on the first day of school. While older students may come to school prepared on the first day, younger students will certainly benefit if you help them by organizing their papers in a folder. Here are some suggestions on how to make that first-day-of-school packet appealing to every student in your class:

- Because you can use these folders all year to organize student information, encourage your students to personalize theirs before they return them. This will also provide you with insight into their interests and skills.
- Sadly, not all students will see their parents after school on the first day of class, yet there will probably be many forms for parents and guardians to sign. If you allow students to return forms during the first few days of school instead of the next day, you will reduce their anxiety about not being able to complete this seemingly simple task.
- One good way to guarantee that students will return all the papers that need to be signed is to offer a reward for those who do it within a few days.
- If you create a spreadsheet with a column for each form that needs to be returned and a row for each student, you will be able to quickly check off the forms as students return them.

- You can also include student inventories in order to learn more about your students.
- Every packet should also include an independent assignment for students to begin as soon as they find their seat. This can be a form to complete, a puzzle, an inventory, or any other activity that will engage their attention while you assist other students.
- You should also include a letter to parents and guardians that
    - Tells a bit about your experience in education
    - Gives information about how they can contact you
    - Requests their support
    - Explains the kinds of work they can expect to see their child doing all year
    - Explains the grading scale
    - Describes the supplies their child will need for class
    - Explains your homework policy
    - States the positive expectations you have for the year ahead

Activities for the First Day

In addition to the lesson and class expectations, your first day of class can include many other activities to engage students in meaningful work. When you are trying to decide just what you want your students to do on the first day, consider some of these activities:

- Fill out forms together. While you are explaining your class expectations, students can fill in the information on a handout instead of just listening passively.
- Photograph students in their new school clothes. This is a good way to begin your class scrapbook.
- Show examples of the supplies they need.
- Pass out colorful paper, and ask students to write on it what they can contribute to make the class a better one for everyone. Display the papers in a giant collage.
- Issue textbooks, and have students skim their new texts, looking for items in a textbook treasure hunt.
- Have students work with a partner, telling that person one thing that they can do well and one thing that they would like to learn how to do. Have partners introduce each other to the class by sharing this information.
- Ask students to write you a note, telling you three things you need to know about them so that you can teach them well.
- Place a large sheet of paper on the wall. Hand students old newspapers or magazines, and have them tear out words and photos that describe their strengths and talents. Focus on what students have in common. Glue the photos and words in place to create an instant piece of art that will interest every student.

- Have students jot down what they already know about the subject you are teaching and then share this information with the class.
- Have students fill out one of the student inventories shown in Section Six.
- Give students handouts with questions directing them to find out what they have in common with their classmates. Some possible areas to explore are hometowns, hobbies, favorite movies, pets, vacations, and sports. Go beyond the obvious and include attitudes for success, goals, or other mental traits.
- Have older students create bookmarks with inspirational messages for younger students.
- Ask older students to recount a memory from their earlier first days of school.
- Put a quotation or unusual word related to the day's lesson on the board, and ask students to tell you what they think about it.
- Have students write exit slips explaining what they learned in class on their first day.

Student Information Records

Ask students to provide you with up-to-date contact information as close to the first day of school as you can. Use Form 5.1, or adapt it to fit your needs. Even young students will be able to fill in many portions of this form. It is also a good idea to ask younger students to take the form home to have adults complete it.

Learn Your Students' Names Quickly

Learning how to correctly pronounce and spell your students' names is one of the most important tasks you will have to master as the school year begins. Being able to call all of your students by name is an important step in getting to know them as people and in assuming control of your class.

The depth of resentment that mispronouncing or misspelling a student's name can cause is often surprising to first-year teachers. Although teachers may think of it as a small mistake, students tend to view teachers who do not call them by the right name as uncaring and insensitive.

How to Get to Know Your Students

Getting to know your students as quickly as you can is extremely important. Although getting to know each child will take time, there are many ways to obtain the background information you need.

One way to get information is to review students' records. Be sure to follow the correct procedures and confidentiality regulations. You may want to jot quick notes on each student as you scan his or her folder.

FORM 5.1

Student Information Form

Your full name: ______________________________

What you want me to call you: ______________________________

Your home phone number: ______________________________

Your cell phone number: ______________________________

Your e-mail address: ______________________________

Your birthday: ______________________________

Your age: ______________ Your student number: ______________

Your brothers' and sisters' names and ages:

____

What are your goals for the future?

____

What hobbies do you have?

____

What sports interest you?

____

Names of your parent(s) or guardian(s):

____

Which parent or guardian would you like me to contact if I need to call home?

____

Mr. Mrs. Ms. Dr. First name Last name

Please tell me the cell phone number, work phone number, and e-mail address of each of your parents or guardians.

Mother:

____

Cell phone Work phone E-mail address

Father:

____

Cell phone Work phone E-mail address

Guardian:

____

Cell phone Work phone E-mail address

Guardian:

____

Cell phone Work phone E-mail address

What is your address?

____

Street address City ZIP Code

Tricks for Matching Names with Faces

Learning all of your students' names on the first or second day of school is not very difficult. These quick tips will make it possible for you to go home on the first day of school confident that you know the students in your class well enough to get the term off to a good start.

- Put in some preliminary work! Organize your seating charts, study class rosters, and prepare name tag materials.
- Make sure that your students sit in their assigned seats for the first few days so that you can more quickly associate names with faces.
- If you have students fill out a student information form, when you read what your students have written, mentally match their faces to the information in front of you.
- While students are working on an opening-day writing assignment, walk quietly around the room, checking the roll.
- Ask each child to say his or her name for you. Repeat it as you study the child's face.
- Mark pronunciation notes for yourself on your roll sheet. Also, make notes to help you match names to students. For example, you can write "big smile" or "very tall" next to a student's name. These little clues will help you when you are struggling to recall a name on the second day of school. Make sure that you pay attention to characteristics that are not likely to change, such as height or hair color.
- When you cannot recall a child's name, admit it, and ask for help. When you hear it again, write it, repeat it, and try again until you can recall it.

When you make a positive phone call to a student's parent, you have a wonderful opportunity to ask the parent about their child. Likewise, when you send home an introductory letter, you can add a section asking parents or guardians to tell you about their child.

You can also learn a great deal about your students from writing assignments in which students write responses to classroom issues.

Your students' previous teachers may be another good source of information. One drawback of this method is that you may sometimes get information that is not completely objective and that may bias your view of a child. Ask for information about students from their previous teachers only if they strike you as fair-minded professionals. If you find yourself listening to unfair horror stories about how much the student misbehaved in previous years, you should excuse yourself from the conversation.

One of the best ways to get to know your students and to help them get to know each other is to use icebreakers. As you watch students interact with each other, you will learn a great deal about them. In addition, icebreakers will give your students an opportunity to learn to value each other's contributions to the class. Try these strategies to get your students off to a good start:

- Have students work in pairs or triads to fill out information forms on each other. Include questions that will cause them to learn interesting and unusual details about each other. For example, having students list their favorite performer or a pet peeve is a good conversation starter.
- Play a chaining game in which students try to recite everyone's last name without having to stop to think. You can even offer a small reward for the first student who is able to do this.
- Pass around a large calendar in order for students to record their birthdays. Also pass around a map and have students mark their birthplace on it.
- Create a class newsletter during the first week of class. Have students share a variety of ideas as they interview each other for articles in the newsletter. You can include almost anything you and your students might enjoy—for example, cartoons, interviews with parents or administrators, advice, predictions, or study skill tips.
- Create a duty roster for the classroom tasks that students can manage well. Sharing tasks will encourage students to work together to take ownership of the class.
- Take photographs of your students and post them. Ask students to bring in photographs from when they were much younger, and post these, too.
- Have each student find a quotation about school success and bring it to class. Post the quotes around your classroom to inspire all of your students.
- Have students create a time capsule about their first day in your class. Have them write a brief description of the first day with you. Ask questions to elicit responses that reveal personal impressions, predictions, and reactions. Gather these and place them in a container that you will keep sealed until a future date, when you will share its contents with students.
- Make it a point to focus on your students' strengths by asking them to reveal what they do well. Share these revelations with the class when appropriate.
- Hand students half sheets of paper and ask them to write three interesting things about themselves without stating their name or obvious characteristics. Have students ball up the sheets before dropping them into a large container. Shake the container to scramble the balled-up sheets. Distribute them randomly to each student. Give students three minutes to try to match their classmates with the information.
- If you have received your class rosters early, use a Web site such as Discovery School (www. puzzlemaker.com) to create a puzzle from your students' names.
- Put students in pairs. Give each pair a blank Venn diagram; have them chart how they are alike and different. After the initial pairs have completed the diagram, each pair should then join another pair and create another Venn diagram that shows how the pairs are alike and different.
- Have each student create a time line of his or her life. If you use large sheets of bulletin board paper and bright markers, you will be able to decorate your classroom with work that students will find fascinating.

Set the table on the first day, so the kids know what's for dinner. A rule set at the beginning of the year should still be in effect in June.

—Sabrina Richardson,
7 years' experience

- Have students group themselves according to birthdays, eye color, favorite sports teams, favorite music, or other common interests.
- Create a blank bingo grid and make copies for all of your students. In addition, print out a list of your students' names and make copies for all students. Ask students to fill in the grids with each other's names in random order. Play several rounds of bingo, choosing names randomly, until your students know each other's names. A variation on this game is to place student interests, hobbies, talents, or other positive student characteristics in the grids.

Analyze Your Students' Readiness for Success in Learning

The analysis of your students that you perform at the start of the school year is different from the assessments of prior knowledge that you will make as you begin new units of study. At the start of a term, you need to learn as much as you can about your students' readiness for success in your class. You can do this in a variety of ways: informal writing assignments, pretests, permanent record checks, or talks with parents and previous teachers. In addition to these useful methods, you can ask the following questions in order to determine your students' readiness at the start of a term.

- Has the student been successful in the past?
- What do his or her parents say about their child?
- Has the student attended other schools? What types of instruction were offered at those schools?
- What deficiencies do you notice right away in the student's general academic and social skills?
- What interests does he or she have?
- How quickly does the student work? Is he or she easily drawn off task?
- What do previous teachers say about this student?
- What does the student say about his or her own readiness for success in your class?

Create a Positive Group Identity

Unless you create a positive identity for your class, students may take your smallest misbehavior correction to mean that you think of them as troublesome. This will happen even more quickly if students in your class have struggled with school in the past. Once a group starts to think of itself in a negative way, it is almost impossible to change the group's self-perception into a positive one.

Sometimes students have been dragging this negativity around for years. If you can eliminate the negative image and give your class a positive self-image, everyone will be rewarded. But this is no easy task. What you must do is make a conscious effort to praise and reinforce your class's positive group attributes. Thus, you will promote the group's desirable behaviors and extinguish their negative ones.

Even difficult classes have positive attributes. If a group is very talkative, for example, you can put a positive twist on it and praise the students for their sociability. Further, focus on students' strengths, rather on what they do poorly. To create a positive group image, you must find and reinforce their positive attributes. Here's how:

Give Your Students a Positive Self-Image in Three Easy Steps

Step One: If you learn that your class has a negative self-image, let students know that you disagree with it.

Step Two: Observe two things about your class: the way the students interact with each other and with you, and the way that they do their work. Find at least one positive attribute that you can reinforce.

Step Three: Begin praising that positive attribute as often as you can. In a few days, you will notice that your students will accept it as truth and will bring it up themselves.

If you have more than one class, think of a positive label or two for each class and use these labels frequently. Each of your classes should believe they have a special place in your heart. Here are a few positive labels your students should hear you use at the start of the year:

- Caring
- Motivated
- Intelligent
- Well prepared
- Successful
- Friendly
- Deep thinkers
- Cooperative
- Polite
- Studious

Achieve Your First-Day-of-School Goals

Because your first meeting with your students is a crucial step in working well with them all year, you should plan and work with purpose in order to be successful. Use Self-Assessment 5.1 to help you set and achieve your first-day-of-school goals.

SELF-ASSESSMENT 5.1

First-Day-of-School Goals

Look at the following list of goals for the first day of school. You will find that the more organized and efficient you are, the more successful your first day of school will be. Plan how to get started by asking yourself how you can work to achieve these goals:

Goal 1: Learn all students' names as quickly as possible.
Steps I can take to achieve this goal:

____

____

____

Goal 2: Establish, teach, and enforce school and classroom rules, routines, and procedures (see Section Fourteen).
Steps I can take to achieve this goal:

____

____

____

Goal 3: Reach out to every child. Make the connection that lets students know they are valued (see Section Six).
Steps I can take to achieve this goal:

____

____

____

Goal 4: Take action to keep discipline concerns from disrupting class (see Section Fourteen).
Steps I can take to achieve this goal:

____

____

____

Goal 5: Assess students' readiness and previous learning.
Steps I can take to achieve this goal:

____

____

____

Talk It Over

How to Have a Fantastic First Day

You can use these questions as a springboard for discussions that will help you and your discussion group members grow and develop professionally. Discuss these questions about how to make your first day of teaching a success:

1. What can you do to make sure the first day of school is productive for you and your students?
2. Brainstorm a list of the words and phrases that characterize the ideal relationship you want with your students. What do these words and phrases reveal about your teaching style? How can you create this ideal relationship?
3. Discuss what you would like your students to say about your class at the end of the first day.
4. Complete this statement: "On the first day of school, I want . . . " How can you make this happen?
5. Discuss with your colleagues the kinds of skills you wish that your students had. What can you do to help them acquire these skills?
6. What do you already know about seating charts? How do you intend to arrange your seating chart at the start of the term? How do you anticipate changing it later?
7. Brainstorm a list of icebreakers with your colleagues. Can you use any of these with your new students?
8. How will you adjust your plan if your students run out of things to do on the first day of class? How will you adjust it if they don't finish?
9. What is your biggest worry about the first day? What can you do about it?
10. What image do you want your students to have of themselves as a class? How will you make this happen?

SECTION SIX

Connect with Your Students

In this section, you will learn

- ✔ How to form a good relationship with students
- ✔ How to earn your students' respect
- ✔ How to be a role model
- ✔ How to let students know you care
- ✔ How to cultivate grace under pressure

School boards everywhere seem to deal with similar problems: teacher shortages, overcrowded classes, and expensive school repairs. As unpleasant as these problems can be, very few teachers leave the profession because of them.

You are far more likely to feel stress caused by the fallout from a poor relationship with your students than you are from any other cause. Many factors can negatively affect this relationship, but only you can make sure it is a viable one. As the adult in the classroom, you are in charge of making sure that each of your students feels connected to you. This connection must be a strong one if you and your students are to have a successful school term.

You will have to be the one who builds the bridge, who reaches out to your students, who inspires them to do their best. A successful relationship with your students will be just like the other meaningful relationships in your life; it will require patience, work, and commitment.

What Your Relationship with Your Students Should Be

As a first-year teacher, you may struggle to determine the relationship you want to have with your students. How friendly should you be? What if your students don't like you? What if they won't listen to you? How strict is too strict?

As a teacher, you are responsible for just about anything that can happen in a class. You will determine the relationship you have with each student. While this is a daunting responsibility, it is also empowering. If the type of relationship you have with your class is under your control, then you can make it a strong bond. This will take deliberate planning on your part.

Inspiring teachers who have positive relationships with their students have characteristics that you should develop as quickly as possible. Here are brief descriptions of five of these characteristics:

You should show that you care about your students. Your students want you to like them and to approve of them, even when they misbehave. Sometimes it is easy to lose sight of this when you have so many demands on your time. It is crucial that your students feel that they are important to you and that you care about their welfare. Get to know them as people as well as pupils you have to instruct. Do not be afraid to let your students know you are interested in how they think and feel.

You should have a thorough knowledge of your subject matter. Knowing your subject matter may not seem to have much to do with developing a successful relationship with your students, but it does. If you are not prepared for class, you will focus on what you do not know instead of what your students need to know. The worst result of a faulty knowledge of your subject matter is that your students will lose respect for you and no longer trust your judgment. Be prepared for class each day.

You should take command of the class. If you do not assume a leadership role in your class, others will. Often there will be a continuing struggle as students try to dominate each other. While you should not be overbearing, you should be in command of the class. You can and should allow your students as many options and as strong a voice in the class as possible, but never lose sight of your role as the classroom leader. Your students won't.

You should act in a mature manner all of the time. This does not mean that you cannot have fun with your students; however, if having fun with your students means indulging in playful insults, then you are not acting in a mature manner. Here are a few of the other immature behaviors that will destroy your relationship with your students:

- Being sarcastic
- Losing your temper
- Being untruthful
- Being unprepared for class
- Ignoring students
- Playing favorites

You should maintain some emotional distance from your students. Being a teacher is much more than being a friend to your students; they have peers for friends. You are a teacher and not a peer. The emotional distance you keep between yourself and your students will enable you to make choices based on what students need instead of what they want.

> Make sure you enter this profession because you want it to be your life's work. Don't enter it as a stopgap measure ("I'm waiting to go to graduate school" or "I don't really know what I want to do with my life yet"). Children deserve more than just a layover in your life.
>
> *—Luann Scott, 31 years' experience*

THE PROBLEM WITH BEING A POPULAR TEACHER

It is natural to want to be liked. It is a wonderful experience to be in a mall or a restaurant and hear a young voice joyfully calling your name or to look out over a classroom full of students who are hanging on your every word. The problem with being a well-liked teacher is that it is sometimes such an exhilarating feeling that you are reluctant to give it up, even when you should.

It is much more pleasant to hear your students cheer when you tell them there will be no homework than to hear their groans when you give a challenging assignment. Choices like this constitute a teacher's day. As a teacher, you should base your decisions not on what your students want at the moment but on what they need for the future. Students can be shortsighted; you should not be.

There are many legitimate reasons for your students to like you. Are your classes interesting? Do you treat everyone with respect? Are you inspiring? Unfortunately, there are many other reasons for your students to like you that are seductive traps; you must avoid these by thinking of your students' needs. If you ever overhear your students make any of the following statements about you, you are becoming popular for the wrong reasons:

- "She's an easy grader."
- "He's just like us."
- "He never calls my parents, no matter what I do."
- "She never makes us do real work in that class."
- "She doesn't make us take notes."
- "She doesn't really care if we swear."
- "He likes to joke around with us."

> **Don't be the students' pal. They've got plenty of those.**
>
> *—Kay Stephenson, 33 years' experience*

WHAT YOUR STUDENTS REALLY WANT

Students who struggle for power or control of the class may intimidate a new teacher. Sometimes these conflicts cause teachers to lose sight of the larger picture of what they want for their students. Worse, teachers may lose sight of what students really want from a teacher.

One effective way to assess how well you are meeting the needs of your students is to ask them for written feedback; a quick survey at the end of class and a suggestion box in the room are both good ways to obtain this information. In general, though, students everywhere want the same things from their teachers. Use the following list to determine how well you are meeting the needs of your students.

Students want a teacher who

- ✔ Listens to all students
- ✔ Enjoys being in the classroom
- ✔ Knows the subject matter
- ✔ Is not too strict but is not a pushover, either
- ✔ Respects them as people as well as students
- ✔ Is understanding when appropriate
- ✔ Makes learning fun
- ✔ Returns papers promptly
- ✔ Helps them learn
- ✔ Doesn't allow harassment
- ✔ Explains the material well
- ✔ Treats everyone fairly
- ✔ Makes the classroom comfortable
- ✔ Doesn't ever embarrass them
- ✔ Does not give too much homework
- ✔ Helps them believe in themselves

Earn Your Students' Respect

One of the challenging responsibilities that novice and experienced teachers alike must take on is the task of earning their students' respect. Respect does not depend on how long you've taught or how much you know. You can plan fascinating lessons and have every procedure in place, but you will be a failure if you don't have the respect of your students.

Although respect is the touchstone of a successful relationship with students, there is no single action that can guarantee every student's respect for you. Respect lies in the small actions you take. It requires that you consistently and successfully manage a delicate balance among the many roles you have at school: disciplinarian, advisor, role model, motivator, and instructor.

When your students respect you, they see that you are not just another friendly adult; you have met their ideal of what a teacher should be.

Many first-year teachers mistake affection for respect. Your students may like you for many reasons, none of which earns their respect. They may think that you do not assign too much work or that you relate well to them on a personal level. This type of affection fades when problems arise or at the end of the term, when students realize that although they enjoyed your class, they did not learn very much.

Despite the distinction between affection and respect, there are many large and small ways to earn your students' respect. Like many other aspects of your new career, earning your students' respect will require time, patience, and persistent effort on your part. You will have to work hard to earn the gift of respect from your students.

Following is a list of questions about practices that are geared to earn students' respect. As you ask yourself these questions, judge yourself as your students would judge you.

- ☐ Do I focus my energies on preventing behavior problems instead of having to deal with the serious consequences caused by misbehavior?
- ☐ Do I make sure that my students know I care about their welfare?
- ☐ Do I know the material I am supposed to teach?
- ☐ Do I respect my students' differences and encourage them to do the same?
- ☐ Am I a good listener who is available to my students on a regular basis?

Mutual Respect, Mutual Courtesy

No one wants to teach a room full of obnoxious children. The goal of most teachers is to work with pleasant students who work together as a community of learners. Your dream of a good relationship with your students should be based on mutual respect and courtesy. Unfortunately, the dream will not happen unless you make it happen.

Teaching courtesy is a task you will have to assume if you want to have a smoothly running classroom. Not only will you have to teach your students the social skills they need to function well in your class, but you will also have to enforce those skills by insisting that they treat each other and you with courtesy.

Your students observe you far more than you can imagine. They want and need your guidance not just in academics but in social skills, too. When you take the time to teach and model life skills such as courtesy, you are teaching your students how to be successful in your classroom and in life.

It is easier to make this effort if you keep in mind that the rewards are great. Your bond with your students will be strong enough to reduce the discipline problems in your classroom. Here are a few suggestions for teaching social skills in your class:

Make sure that everyone understands which behaviors are courteous and which are not. Not all of your students mean to be rude when they shout insults at each other, interrupt, or put their head down on their desk when you are talking. Social rules, particularly those in schools, vary widely. Some teachers tolerate behavior that other teachers find offensive. This confuses children of all ages. Be direct, specific, and clear about what you expect. Do this early in the term so that you can prevent mistakes.

Reward good behavior. Offer little rewards and lavish words of praise when a class has been courteous. This is especially important at the start of a term, when students are still not sure of their boundaries. When you see a student or a group of students being courteous, take notice. Point it out so that everyone else can see what you mean when you talk about being polite.

Exploit the power of peer pressure. You can steer students in the right direction by making sure that everyone in the class is courteous. When this happens, discourteous students will see that there is no peer support for bad behavior. Soon, they will police themselves.

Encourage students to accept each other's differences. Many of the negative behaviors in a class can be eliminated by encouraging students to be tolerant of each other. You can do this by modeling acceptance and respect for each of your students, particularly the ones who struggle with social skills.

Model the respect you want to receive. Rules are useless if you do not model the behavior you want from your students. If you are rude to your students, you can be sure that they will be rude to you. Each day, you have hundreds of opportunities to show your students how to be polite. Take advantage of each one. Being able to show that you are a respectful person is a powerful tool.

You Are a Role Model

We live in a society that values its role models. However, for several decades, social scientists have been concerned about the scarcity of positive role models for young people in the media. Today, all too many children lack the adult support and direction they need to keep themselves safe from harm.

While media heroes may be scarce, for many of your students, you will be a hero whether you want this responsibility or not. It is not always easy to have the right answer, to make the right decision, or to say the right thing, although your students expect all of these from you.

For many students, you may be the only person in their life who routinely stresses the importance of hard work and good character. Depending on the grade you teach, your tasks as a role model may include making sure that your students wash their hands properly, learn about the dangers of using drugs, or get their college applications in the mail on time.

Your actions will influence your students, even when you are not aware that you are having an influence. It can be an overwhelming responsibility, but you have chosen a profession with a profound impact. You can be a positive influence on your students when you

- ✔ Help students manage their anger appropriately
- ✔ Show your appreciation for other staff members
- ✔ Are patient with all students
- ✔ Dress professionally
- ✔ Stay organized
- ✔ Are prompt
- ✔ Show sympathy and concern
- ✔ Handle misbehavior professionally
- ✔ Have high expectations
- ✔ Can laugh at yourself
- ✔ Treat parents and guardians with respect
- ✔ Accept criticism well

CREATE A PROFESSIONAL IMAGE

Just as actors create characters when they are at work, you need to develop an image for yourself as a teacher. This means that you must separate your personal self from your professional self.

Many successful teachers have found ways to cope with the discrepancies between their personal and professional lives. For example, many fearless teachers are too timid to speak publicly outside their classroom. Others drive too fast or stay up too late—both activities they would not encourage in their students.

> **Remember that in the eyes of the community, you are a professional all of the time, even away from school.**
>
> *—Edward Gardner, 36 years' experience*

If you can create a strong image for yourself as a professional educator, your school life will be much easier. You will realize that when your students criticize you, they really do not know you at all. They are only reacting to your professional self—a person who has to set limits and correct mistakes.

Creating a professional image takes deliberate thought and planning. Begin by looking into the future. What would you like your students to say about you ten years from now? How can you achieve this? After you have thought about the long-term effect you want to have on your students, jot down your ideas. Tape your notes in a conspicuous place to help you remember what you want your image to be.

LOOK THE PART

One of the most important ways to establish a satisfying relationship with your students is by paying attention to your appearance at school. You do not have to dress in primary colors or wear ties with the alphabet on them to maintain a professional appearance.

Instead, you should strive to appear as professional as the other teachers in your school. When your appearance is professional, others will take you more seriously. Since different schools have different dress codes, pay careful attention to any information that comes your way about how you should dress. Teachers who insist on extreme individualism in their appearance often find themselves the target of unkind comments from their students and colleagues. The following fashion errors are ones you should avoid at school:

- Smelling like alcohol or tobacco
- Bad breath or unpleasant body odor
- Dirty or unkempt hair
- Distracting makeup, perfume, or jewelry
- Chewing gum
- Dirty or wrinkled clothing
- Missing buttons or broken zippers
- Clothing that does not fit
- Violating the student dress code

"Are You Old Enough to Be a Teacher?"

It is not easy to be a baby-faced teacher. You will have to withstand comments about how you look just like a kid yourself. Teachers on duty will ask you for your hall pass. You will have to deal tactfully with parents who are not certain that you are old enough to teach their children.

You can overcome the problems caused by a youthful appearance without having to wait for wrinkles to appear. You must be as professional and serious at school as you can be. If your conversation and dress are serious, people will soon take you seriously. Let your professionalism rather than your age be what people notice about you.

When parents or colleagues remark that you do not look old enough to be a teacher, accept this as a compliment and laugh about it. Over time, your commitment to your students and to your profession will override the effects of your youthful appearance.

> Sometimes it is an obstacle when students feel that because you look young, you are on the same level that they are. I have had to pull girls and boys to the side and explain to them that I am their teacher and not their peer and that they have to treat me with the same respect that they would any other adult. After I told a few of my students this, they knew I wasn't playing and made a major change for the better.
>
> —*Sabrina Richardson, 7 years' experience*

Handle Student Crushes with Care

Although on a sitcom a student's crush on a teacher is comic, in reality, there is nothing funny about a student who has a crush on a teacher. If you are successful as a teacher, then every student in your class will feel special. However, some students can be confused by the feelings a caring teacher inspires.

Although student crushes are natural and understandable, they are not trivial for the student or the teacher. If you discover that a student has a crush on you, take steps to protect yourself as well as the student's feelings. Never allow yourself to be alone with a student who has a crush on you. If you do, the student may accuse you of serious misconduct, and you will have no defense against the accusation.

If you ever have to confront a student directly about a crush, handle the student's feelings with the utmost sensitivity. Be aware that a scorned student is capable of lashing out at you because of their hurt feelings. If you do not handle the situation with delicacy, a student may accuse you of things you did not do.

Discourage students from acting on their crushes by bringing you gifts or defending you to other students. Tactfully refuse the gifts, if you can. Make sure that students understand that you are clear about your role as a teacher, even if they are not. Your behavior to all students must be fair and friendly, and it must exhibit the emotional distance that your students need from a teacher.

If you find your actions to discourage a crush are not working, then speak with your mentor or a supervisor. Ask for advice. Sometimes inexperienced teachers are reluctant to ask for help in dealing with student crushes, but you should not underestimate the potential for serious problems. If you enlist help from other professionals when you are first aware of the situation, you will have valuable allies should you need more assistance with the student later.

How Much of Yourself Should You Share?

"Do you smoke?" "What kind of beer do you like?" "What's your real hair color?" It is only natural that your students will be curious about you. After the first few days of school, they will become comfortable enough around you to ask personal questions. Because they are young, your students will not always know what is appropriate to ask and what is not.

While you should not answer every personal question your students ask, you do need to handle them with tact. Your response to personal questions will help determine the type of relationship you will have with your students and their families.

In general, your students will only know what you tell them about yourself. To help you determine whether information you are tempted to reveal is appropriate for students to know, ask yourself whether you would be comfortable revealing this information if an administrator or a student's parents were present. If the answer to this question is negative, be prepared with appropriate responses to possible student questions so that you are not taken by surprise. Here are a few other pointers to help you reveal only what you want your students to know:

Plan how you will answer student questions. It is not easy to deflect student interest, so you will have to think carefully about what you want to reveal about your personal life. You can expect to be quizzed on a variety of issues, so be prepared with responses. If you plan what you want to disclose about each topic before your students ask, then you will not be caught off guard. Here are a few areas of your personal life that you can expect your students to be curious about:

- Your social life
- Where you live
- Your living arrangements
- The kind of car you drive
- What you do in your free time
- Your pets
- Your family
- What you think of other teachers

Forestall questions by giving out some information in advance. Your students should see your human side. If you share innocuous information about yourself with your students, you will curb their curiosity, and they will be less tempted to pry. For example, at the beginning of the year, you should tell your students where you went to college and how hard you had to study. Or you can tell them about your family while asking about theirs. By offering information in advance, you can build on your common interests and prevent questions that are too personal at the same time.

Keep students too busy to ask personal questions. Another technique that experienced teachers have found valuable for limiting the information they reveal about themselves is to structure class in such a way that there is little free time for personal questions. If your students are busily engaged in learning all period long, they will not have time to speculate more than necessary about your personal life.

Learn About Your Students

Although you do not want your students to know everything about you, you will prevent many problems by getting to know as much as possible about your students as quickly as you can. In fact, this should be a priority for you during the first few days of school. There are many ways to find out about your students. Two of the traditional ways are to check records and to contact parents.

Another traditional way that many teachers find out about their new students is to ask other teachers about them. However, there are some serious drawbacks to this practice. Students who misbehave for one teacher do not always misbehave for others. Because you are new to the school yourself, it will be difficult for you to determine whether the information you receive from other teachers is accurate. Finally, students do mature, and they deserve a fair chance with you, regardless of their past mistakes.

One way to handle this situation tactfully is to insist that teachers tell you only positive things about your new students. You will still have useful information that you can use to your advantage. For instance, you might tell a student about a positive comment you heard. Your students will be flattered by your interest.

Because excellent opportunities to learn about your students are built into first-day-of-class activities, you can use some of the suggestions in Section Five to get to know your students at the beginning of the term.

Another effective way for you to get to know your students is to observe them as they get to know one another. Do not let them convince you that they know each other already. You will be surprised at how many students do not know something as basic as a classmate's last name. While they are learning about each other, you will have a good opportunity to observe as much as you can about them. Try some of these activities to help you get to know your students:

- **When you have your students fill out a student information form, include a section with questions designed to reveal interesting information.** You could ask students to tell about their hobbies, favorite classes, strengths, weaknesses, goals, or dreams. You could ask them to describe a past success they have had in school or in another activity. You could even ask them to give you advice on how to be the best teacher they will ever have.
- **Ask your students to list ten things they do well.** You will be surprised at how difficult this is for many students; too often, students focus on their weaknesses, not on their strengths.
- **Break the ice by placing students in small groups and handing each group a bag with several common objects in it.** Relate these objects to your discipline, if possible. Ask students to combine these objects in a new way. They can then name their invention and create a marketing plan for it. The point of this exercise is not just to learn about your students but also to have them work together in a way that forces them to think creatively.
- **Group students into teams to create a cartoon panel that illustrates a topic relating to school success.** They can use stick figures to tell the story or generate a story line that uses the members of the group as characters.

> **Get to know your students' dogs, cats, fish, iguanas—anything that can connect you to their whole day.**
>
> *—Sandra Councill, 23 years' experience*

- **Place students in pairs and have them interview each other.** A twist that makes this assignment interesting is to give each student an object and ask what he or she has in common with it. When your students present their findings to the class, you will learn a lot about them as they reveal how they are like paper clips, bookmarks, tissue boxes, or other common classroom objects.

- **Ask students to write descriptive paragraphs about each other.** Photocopy these paragraphs and bind them into booklets for all students. This will be the most intently read document that you will give your students all term.
- **Put your students in pairs and have them determine ten things they have in common.** Insist that they go beyond the obvious to discuss topics such as shared experiences, attitudes, aspirations, or other appealing topics.

STUDENT INVENTORIES

Student inventories are a good way to learn information about your students that you do not have time to learn in any other way. Many teachers ask students to fill out an inventory during the first few days of school. Still others find that if they wait a few days, their students will feel secure enough to reveal more information.

Whenever you decide to use an inventory, be sure to give your students plenty of time to answer thoughtfully. Forms 6.1, 6.2, and 6.3 provide three inventories that you can reproduce for your students.

ADDITIONAL TOPICS FOR STUDENT INVENTORIES

Here are some more inventory items that you can use or adapt to learn more about your students. You can even use these as brief, informal writing assignments at the start or end of a class.

- I am optimistic about . . .
- I am pessimistic about . . .
- I spend my free time . . .
- If I could do anything right now, I would . . .
- If I had ten dollars, I would . . .
- When I do poorly on a test, I . . .
- I tried hard to learn . . .
- If I were five years older, I . . .
- I am most proud of . . .
- I respect these people:
- The hardest thing I ever did was . . .
- At home I have these rules:
- If I were a teacher, I would . . .
- I would like to visit . . .
- Not many people know that I . . .

FORM 6.1

Student Inventory for Elementary Students

Name ______________________ Date ______________________

My birthday is ______________________

My family members are

____

____

____

When I grow up I want to be

____

My favorite things to do at home are

____

My special friends are

____

My favorite things to do at school are

____

The subjects I do best in are

____

The subjects I need help in are

____

If I could change anything about school, it would be

____

This year I am looking forward to learning about

____

I like it when my teachers

____

I would like to know more about

____

I am happiest when I am

____

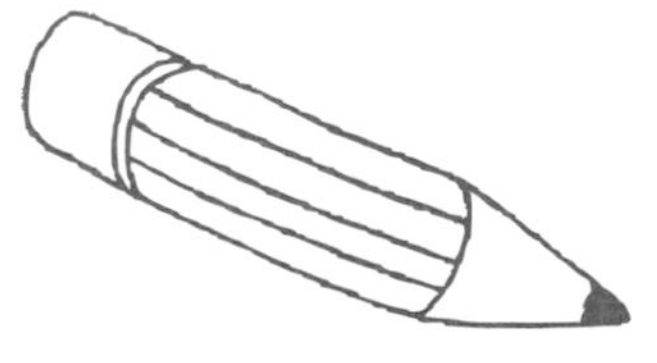

FORM 6.2

Student Inventory for Middle School Students

Name ______________________ Date ______________________

My birthday is ______________________

My family members are

____

____

____

When I grow up, I want to be

____

My closest friends are

____

My favorite things to do are

____

____

Here are my favorites:

Radio stations ______________ Magazines ______________

Sports ______________ Hobbies ______________

Books ______________ Movies ______________

Music ______________ Clothes ______________

One thing people don't know about me is

____

A skill I have is

____

A person I admire is ______________________

because ______________________

Something I would like to learn to do better is

____

I appreciate it when a teacher

____

My previous teachers would tell you this about me:

____

I am proud of myself when I

____

FORM 6.3

Student Inventory for High School Students

Name ______________________ Date ______________________

My birthday is ______________________

My family members are

____

____

____

After graduation I plan to

____

My greatest asset is

____

I am an expert on

____

One thing people don't know about me is

____

My teachers from last year will tell you that I am

____

I have trouble dealing with

____

My favorite class is ______________________

because ______________________

____

The most influential person in my life is ______________________

because ______________________

____

It was difficult for me to learn

____

It was easy for me to learn

____

I want to know more about

____

Three words that describe my personality are

____

One lesson I had to learn the hard way is

____

- I always laugh when . . .
- I wish teachers would . . .
- I deserve a trophy for . . .
- I feel needed when . . .
- Something I value in a friend is . . .
- I like to learn about . . .
- The best advice I've ever received is . . .
- My favorite day of the week is . . .

Let Your Students Know You Care

You can have the most fascinating lesson plan in the world, but it will not work if your students believe you do not care about them. Use what you have learned about your students to show your interest in them by asking them about their activities or relating your lessons to their needs and interests. A good teacher-student connection will make everything in your class run smoothly. Without it, nothing will.

Students of all ages need to feel that their teachers like them and approve of what they do. Fortunately, there are many ways to show that you care about your students:

- Agree with your students as often as you can.
- Set responsible behavior limits for everyone, and be fair when you enforce these limits.
- Use a kind voice when you speak with your students.
- Listen to all of your students. Encourage them to share ideas and opinions.
- If one of your students is in the newspaper for something positive, clip out the article and display it.
- Stress the things that you and your students have in common: goals, dreams, and beliefs.
- When a student speaks to you, stop and listen.
- Maintain a birthday calendar for your students. Celebrate birthdays with birthday messages on the board.
- Attend school events. If your students play a sport or perform in a concert, go and watch them, to show your appreciation for their hard work.
- Use good manners when you deal with your students and insist that they do the same.
- When students confide in you, follow up. For example, if students have told you that they were worried about a test in another class, take the time to ask about how they did.
- Make it very clear to your students that you want to help them achieve their dreams.
- Ask about a student's family. If you know someone is ill, show your concern.

- Show your sense of humor. Laugh when funny things happen in class—especially when they happen to you.
- Speak to every student each day. Leave no one out of class discussions.
- Write notes to your students. Use plenty of stickers, and write positive comments on their papers.
- Pay attention to your students' health. If students need to go to the clinic, send them. When students have to miss several days because of illness, call to see how they are doing, or send a get-well card. Be prompt in sending work to the student's home, if appropriate.
- Use this sentence to convey your concern: "What can I do to help you?"
- Talk with students when you notice a change in their behavior. For example, if a normally serious student is neglecting his or her work, find out why.
- Take the time to tell your students what you like about them.
- Take photographs of your students, and display them.

> **Don't be afraid to share, but don't forget to listen.**
>
> —*Melinda Cummings, 6 years' experience*

Promote Trust

You and your students need to trust each other. Much of what happens at school is based on mutual trust. The following tips will help you and your students make trust a vital part of your relationship.

- Be a model of trustworthiness. Talk about issues such as plagiarism or accurate record keeping, and show how you avoid mistakes in these areas.
- Adopt a "we" attitude. Talk about trust as a mutual responsibility. Make every student feel essential to the smooth functioning of the class, and many of the problems that occur with distrust will vanish.
- Don't promise what you cannot deliver. If a student confides in you, do not promise not to tell anyone else as a condition of the confession. Some things must be shared with counselors and parents.
- Avoid situations that will destroy your students' fragile trust. Do not leave your personal belongings or answer keys where students might be tempted to take them. Situations such as these can destroy months of patient trust building in a few seconds.
- Don't be a pushover. If students see that you believe every false excuse their classmates offer, they will not feel that they can trust you to make good decisions.
- Accept that some students will take a long time to trust you. Be patient and persistent.

WATCH YOUR LANGUAGE

The words you use when you speak with your students are one of the most important ways you have of creating a strong bond with them. Kind words spoken in a gentle voice make it much easier for your students to connect with you. If you say something unkind to a student, it will hurt even more than an insult from a peer because it is from someone the child should be able to count on.

There are very few rules about how you should speak to your students. The age and maturity level of your students will guide how you speak. For example, it is usually a serious offense for a teacher in an elementary classroom to tell students to shut up. In a high school classroom, this phrase is not as serious; it is merely rude. You should avoid using it, however, because there are more effective ways to ask students to stop talking.

The one language mistake you should never make is to swear when you are with your students. When you do this, you cross the line of what is acceptable and what is not. If you are ever tempted to swear around your students, remember that teachers have been fired for swearing at students.

If a word slips out, you should immediately apologize to your students, let them know that you are embarrassed, apologize again, and then continue with instruction. After your class is over, you should speak with a supervisor and explain your side of the situation as soon as you can and certainly before your supervisor hears about it from an angry parent.

While swear words are clearly not something you should say around students, there are other language issues you should also pay attention to. Make sure your own words are ones that help your students and do not hurt them. Never make negative or insulting remarks about any student's

- Race
- Religion
- Family
- Friends
- Gender
- Nationality
- Clothing
- Neighborhood
- Body size
- Sexual orientation
- Disabilities
- Age
- Appearance

USE "I" MESSAGES

"You'd better pay attention!" "You're too noisy." "You're doing that all wrong!" What you say to your students is a key component in building the positive relationship you want to have with each child. One of the best ways to convey a sense of shared concern and caring is to use "I" messages.

"I" messages are statements that use words such as *I, we, us,* or *our* instead of *you.* For example, instead of the harsh "You'd better pay attention," a teacher can say, "I'd like for you to pay attention now." "You're too noisy" becomes "We all need to be quiet so that everyone can hear," and "You're doing that all wrong!" can become "I think I can help you with that." With these simple changes, the statements are no longer accusatory, harsh in tone, or insulting. The language points out a problem but does not put anyone on the defensive.

"I" messages work because they de-escalate conflict, avoid accusatory language, show respect for students, and are nonjudgmental. They state a problem without blaming the child. This, in turn, creates a focus on a solution and not on an error the child has made.

With practice, using "I" messages will become easy. Instead of a harsh accusation, you will find yourself in the pleasant position of working with your students to solve problems instead of merely blaming them for their mistakes.

How You Can Help Students Cope with Negative Peer Pressure

Experienced teachers are aware of the powerful role that peer pressure plays in their classroom. Students of all ages want to fit in, to get along with their classmates, to feel accepted. When this need promotes good behavior, the positive energy it generates is welcome in any classroom.

However, the need for acceptance can be so strong that sometimes it can cause inappropriate behavior in even the best-managed classrooms. Sometimes negative peer pressure can cause students to

- Join a gang
- Experiment with substance abuse
- Lie
- Steal
- Defy authority
- Lose interest in academics
- Bully other students

Although there are many social causes of negative peer pressure, teachers can successfully control a few of them. Here are four causes of negative peer pressure that all teachers can help their students overcome. When you find one of your students responding to the negative influences of his or her peers, look for these causes:

- The child feels isolated from the rest of the class.
- The child does not have clear goals.
- The child has a low sense of self-worth.
- The child struggles to succeed academically.

Start by letting them know you care. Your actions and concern for their success speak volumes.

—Dawn Carroll, 10 years' experience

Based on the possible causes for the self-defeating behaviors you observe, try some of these strategies to help your students cope with the negative effects of peer pressure:

- Teach students how to make good decisions for themselves both in their work habits and in the rest of their life.
- Provide students with an occasional opportunity to reflect on their learning and behavior. This will allow them to clarify their thinking.
- Don't allow students to bully or intimidate each other. Be vigilant, and stop these behaviors as soon as you can.
- Increase your students' self-esteem and confidence by focusing on their success.
- Give your class a positive identity so that they do not create a negative one for themselves (see Section Five).
- Help your students set both long-term and short-term goals for themselves (see Section Ten).
- Work to build a positive relationship with each child. A caring teacher can be a force stronger than peer pressure in a child's life.

Teach Your Students to Believe in Themselves

One of the greatest gifts that teachers can give their students is the gift of self-confidence. Self-confidence helps students cope with negative peer pressure and makes it easier for them to take the risks involved in learning and achievement. When you instill self-belief in your students, you will see them transform into lifelong learners, regardless of their age or ability level.

Every day, you can transmit your belief in the abilities of your students in a variety of ways:

- Post motivational signs, to encourage students to give their best effort. Reward effort as well as achievement.
- Create an environment in which students can risk trying new things without fear of failure or ridicule.

- Tell your students about your confidence in their ability to succeed. Tell them over and over.
- Teach your students how to set measurable goals and how to achieve them. Once they start achieving, students will want to continue.
- Small successes lead to larger ones. Make it a point to arrange opportunities for students to be successful. Soon, your students will be confident in their own ability to achieve.
- At the end of class, occasionally ask students to share what they have learned. Often, they are not aware of how much they have actually achieved.
- Teach your students how to handle the failures that everyone experiences from time to time. Help them understand that they can learn from their mistakes.
- Acknowledge and celebrate your students' successes as often as you can. After all, their successes are your successes.

How to Empower Students and Maintain Control of Your Class

When you give students a say in class decisions, you empower them with your trust and confidence. Many teachers are not comfortable with allowing students a strong voice in the class. They may have tried to allow students to make decisions but found that the choices their students made were not sound.

You can overcome this concern and still empower your students by offering a limited choice. For instance, if you were to ask your students whether they want homework, the answer would certainly be a resounding "no." If you instead ask them whether they would prefer to do the problems on page 6 or page 7 for homework, then everyone wins. You will have the homework your students need to do and your students will have had a voice in a class decision. Even younger students can make simple decisions. For example, should a project be due on Monday or Tuesday? Should there be three or four essay questions on a test?

Your students can make sound choices when you give them the guidance they need to make wise decisions. Be sure to give plenty of guidance, and do not consider allowing students to make decisions that make you uncomfortable.

If you want to experiment with this, begin with small issues. For example, ask students for suggestions on how to handle classroom situations in which they can act independently. Here are some independent activities you could discuss with your students:

- What should you do when you need to sharpen your pencil?
- What should you do when you don't finish an assignment in class?
- What should you do when you finish an assignment early?
- What should you do when you are tardy?
- What should you do when you do not understand the directions for an assignment?

Great Advice: Don't Take It Personally

Sometimes no matter what you do, students misbehave. One of the hardest attitudes for many new teachers to adopt is refusing to take student misbehavior and lack of motivation personally. After a miserable day, negative student attitudes and behavior can sometimes cause even veteran teachers to wonder why they bothered to go to school.

If you were to discuss such a day with an experienced teacher, the chances are good that you would hear, "Don't take it personally." While this is excellent advice, it is one of the hardest things for new teachers to learn to do. However, if you are to thrive in your new profession, it is an attitude that you must embrace. Try these strategies the next time you are tempted to take it personally when your students do not live up to your expectations:

- Remember that students will not always behave well or say the right thing. After all, they are children.
- Part of being a teacher is setting limits and establishing boundaries for your students. While this is necessary, it isn't always easy for you or your students.
- Teaching is a very complicated task. In the course of a school week, you will have to make dozens of decisions. Not all of them will be popular with your students.
- As the adult in the classroom, you have to consider the needs of all students. Often, when a student disagrees with a teacher, it is because that child is only considering what he or she wants instead of what would be good for the group.
- Keep in mind that your students do not really know you. They see only one side of you—the teacher part. They react to that part, not you as a person.

Cultivate Grace Under Pressure

One of the worst mistakes you can make is to lose your temper in front of your students when you are upset. Not only will giving in to the emotion of the moment cause you stress and sway your good judgment, but it may cause irreparable harm to your relationship with your students.

Learning to control your emotions is not an easy task. If you have had a terrible time with one class, you often may not have enough time to recover from the experience before the next class begins. However, taking out your anger or frustrations on innocent students is wrong.

While your students need to see your human side, they do not need to be subjected to your ill temper. When you are tempted to lose your cool in front of your students, restrain yourself.

Students whose teacher loses control may react in various negative ways. Your outbursts may frighten some students and intimidate others. Still other students will react to your anger by losing control themselves. If you raise your voice at a student, you should not be surprised if the student shouts at you in return.

Because you are a role model, your students pay attention to everything you say and do. Learning the fine art of grace under pressure is not easy, but reacting with grace is a powerful tool for any caring teacher.

Seven Strategies for Keeping Cool Under Pressure

There are many things you can do to cultivate grace under pressure. Here are several strategies that other teachers have found useful:

1. Remember that losing control will only make the situation worse.
2. Count to ten before you speak. While you are counting, make your face appear as calm as possible.
3. Instead of shouting, lower your voice to a whisper.
4. If there is a great deal of noise and commotion without a threat of violence, stand quietly and wait for it to subside. Shouting at your students to settle them down will only add to the noise.
5. Talk to your colleagues in order to vent your frustration and plan ways to manage the situation differently.
6. Remember that you determine what happens in your class. If you lose control, you are not working to solve the problem. Channel your energy toward managing the situation in a positive way.
7. Ask your students for help when you are upset. This will redirect their attention toward a productive contribution instead of adding to the problem.

Talk It Over

How to Connect with Your Students

Use these questions as a springboard for discussions that will help you and your discussion group members grow and develop professionally. Discuss these questions about how to connect with your students:

1. Discuss the characteristics of the ideal student. What can you do immediately to help your students come closer to your ideal?
2. What kind of a role model are you? What can you improve? Who can help you with this?
3. Define *inviting classroom.* What are the tangible characteristics of this classroom? What are the intangible characteristics? How does this type of classroom promote a connection between teacher and student?

4. What particular rude behaviors from your students bother you? What can you do to extinguish these behaviors? What can you do to replace them with productive ones?
5. How can teachers show that they care about students while maintaining a respectful emotional distance? Why is this necessary?
6. What have you observed another teacher doing to forge a positive connection with students? What can you do to make sure that your connection with your students is strong and positive?
7. Earning your students' respect takes time and effort. How will you recognize when you are on the right track? What choices can you make to encourage mutual respect in your classroom?
8. Discuss what you did to help your students be successful this week. How did you know they were successful? How did your students react?
9. Complete this statement: "When I have a problem with a student, I . . . " What does it reveal about you?
10. How well do you handle pressure? What can you do to prevent yourself from losing your cool in front of your students?

SECTION SEVEN

Design Effective Lessons

In this section, you will learn

- ✔ How to create course overviews, unit plans, and daily lesson plans
- ✔ How to assess your students' prior knowledge
- ✔ How to build higher-order thinking skills into your lessons
- ✔ How to engage students with technology-based activities
- ✔ How to prepare when you have to be absent

Lesson planning is one of the most important tasks you have as a first-year teacher, as a second-year teacher, as a third-year teacher, and it will be just as important when you are a thirtieth-year teacher. Planning effective lessons is the blueprint for success in your classroom and, ultimately, success in your career. There can be no substitute for this process. Successful teachers plan every lesson every day.

The Benefits of Planning Every Lesson

When you make the decision to plan lessons carefully, you and your students will benefit in many different ways. Here are just some of the benefits you will receive when you make this sound decision:

Don't think that you can wing it. Prepare for class! You will quickly lose credibility with students if you are caught floundering in class.

—Debbie McManaway, 12 years' experience

- You will be more likely to prepare interesting lessons that engage your students' critical thinking skills, leverage their preferred learning styles, and appeal to their interests rather than relying on lackluster routines.
- You will gain confidence from having a clear plan for each lesson. This added confidence will translate into a more successful delivery of material for your students and increased professional credibility for you.
- You will be able to pay attention to the details that will make your lessons successful, such as including technology and real-world assignments.
- You will be able to create a logical progression of learning instead of just presenting bits and pieces of information without a clear purpose.
- Most important, you will be better able to teach the curriculum that your state and district require of you. With well-planned lessons, you can cover the standards that your students need to master.

How Prepared Should You Be?

One of the easiest mistakes for first-year teachers to make is to not prepare adequately. While this is understandable because of the overwhelming newness of each day, it is not a good practice. Put simply, if you are not thoroughly prepared for class, your students will struggle to be successful. While the amount of necessary preparation varies from teacher to teacher, at a minimum, here are some guidelines on how prepared you should be.

At the start of a school year,

- ✔ You must be thoroughly familiar with your state's standards.
- ✔ You must know the material you will be expected to teach each term.
- ✔ You must have a course overview in place as soon as you can.

At the start of a grading period,

- ✔ You must have plans for each unit you intend to teach.
- ✔ You should have daily plans for at least two weeks. Try to have at least two weeks of daily plans prepared at all times. You will probably adjust your plans often, but the basic preparation will remain the same.

How to Find the Time to Plan

One of the excuses teachers give for not writing detailed lesson plans is that the process takes too much time. Whether you choose to create your plans at home or at school, you can master this task. Follow these suggestions to save time as you write lesson plans:

- As soon as you have familiarized yourself with your state's standards, begin reading the text and other materials you will need to cover. If you do this at the start of the term, you will have an understanding of the material you need to teach.
- Create a course overview before you begin unit plans or daily plans. With this in place, you will have a quick reference for all other plans.
- Make lesson planning a priority. Planning lessons should be just as important as photocopying handouts, grading papers, or any of the other tasks that can take up so much of a teacher's day.
- Set aside an uninterrupted block of time to plan. If you plan at the same time each week, it will be easier for you to stick to a routine and to make any necessary adjustments to your plans.
- Be organized. Have texts and other necessary materials ready before you begin.
- Create a template and use a checklist similar to the one later in this section (see Form 7.3) to streamline the planning process.

Begin with Your State's Standards

As part of the No Child Left Behind Act, each state has created standards that indicate what material students must master by the end of the course. As you begin the process of designing a course of study for your students, the foundation of your lesson plans should be your state's standards. You should plan all lessons with mastery of the state standards as your objective because that will be the indicator of your students' success.

Because of the high stakes involved in the NCLB accountability measures, you must familiarize yourself with the standards you will cover as quickly as possible. To learn more about the standards that apply to you and your students, try these tips on potential resources:

- Research your state's department of education Web site.
- Research your local school district's Web site.
- Investigate the ancillary materials that accompany the texts you will teach. Many textbook companies provide excellent support geared to the requirements of individual states.

- Search the Education World Web site (www.education-world.com). Go to the home page and use the term "state standards" to search the site. Education World has a page that helps teachers by providing quick access to the standards for all fifty states and the District of Columbia.

How to Begin Planning Lessons

Successful lesson planning proceeds in an orderly sequence. Here's how to begin:

1. **Create a course overview.** This will give you an idea of the scope of the information your students need to master during the entire term.
2. **Create unit plans.** Divide the material you must teach into smaller units of information, then plan how to teach each one.
3. **Create daily plans.** This final step in the lesson planning process is the most detailed. At this level, you have the most flexibility in determining the activities your students will complete.

Capture the Big Picture with a Course Overview

Before you can write successful daily plans, you must have a clear idea of what your students will have to learn by the end of the school term. You must plan for the entire year before you can plan for each day. Here is how to create a course overview that will serve as a useful guide all term long:

1. **Start with state standards.** You should begin with a review of your state's standards.
2. **Use your district's resources.** Review your local curriculum guidelines; they will be aligned with your state's standards.
3. **Determine the units you need to teach, and prioritize their importance.** Make a list of the units you will have to cover to meet state and district objectives. Prioritize your list into three tiers of importance:
   - Units you absolutely must cover
   - Material you would like to cover if you have time
   - Units you plan to offer to students as enrichment or remedial work

Use Form 7.1 as a template for your course overview.

FORM 7.1

Format for a Course Overview

Essential Units	*Time-Permitting Units*	*Enrichment Units*	*Remediation Units*

Flesh Out Your Course by Creating Unit Plans

Unit plans are the intermediate step between a course overview and daily plans. When you create unit plans, you divide the material into smaller blocks and determine roughly how you will teach it. Use Form 7.2 to guide your planning process and as a template for your written unit plans.

1. **Determine the length of the unit.** To create plans for a unit of study, you must first decide how long the unit will take, from the first objective to the final assessment. The length of time you plan to spend on a unit will determine the activities you need to plan.
2. **Determine essential knowledge.** Using state and district guidelines as well as your text and other materials, identify the essential knowledge that students must learn in order to master the material in the unit.
3. **Determine your students' prior knowledge.** Another crucial step in preparing unit plans is to determine what your students already know about the topic. This, too, will determine the activities you will include.
4. **Brainstorm about activities.** Take time to brainstorm in order to generate activities that will interest your students as you cover the material in the unit. Think of a variety of activities that will interest students, appeal to students with different learning styles, and provide opportunities for them to engage in critical thinking.
5. **Select appropriate activities.** List the activities that you believe would be most useful to your students in the sequence in which you want to present them.
6. **Select materials and resources.** With a time line and prior knowledge firmly established, you can search for the materials you need. While there are many places in which to find interesting materials, it is best to start nearby. Begin with your textbook and the supplementary materials that accompany it. Then, turn your attention to the resources in your building. Are there movies or other resources for you to use? Do your colleagues have materials to share? Finally, turn to other sources such as the Internet and local libraries.
7. **Create assessments.** It may seem strange to create the assessments for a unit of study before you write your daily plans, but if you do this, your daily plans will align with the information you plan to assess.

FORM 7.2

Format for a Unit Plan

Unit Title: ______________________________

Dates: ______________________________

Objectives:

1. ______________________________
2. ______________________________
3. ______________________________

Materials: ______________________________

____

____

____

Essential knowledge for mastery: ______________________________

____

____

____

____

Activities: ______________________________

____

____

____

____

____

____

Assessment types and dates: ______________________________

____

____

____

Create Daily Plans That Work for You and Your Students

Good classes do not just happen. A course overview and unit plans will form the basis of your curriculum planning, and your daily plans will make lessons come to life for your students.

Your daily plans should follow a standard format. Your school district may have a format that you will be expected to use. If not, then you should create a format that you can use with ease. Many teachers design their own planning templates and photocopy them, so that they just have to pencil in information for each section. If you have access to a computer at school, you can also create an electronic template that you can adjust as you see fit. If you use a computer-generated template, you will need to print out a copy to refer to during the day.

> **Do not lecture for the entire block. You'll bore yourself.**
>
> —*Kay Stephenson, 33 years' experience*

With your format decision under control, keep these pointers in mind to make sure that the lessons you plan are not just effective but easy to manage.

- **Make each day's lesson a gem.** Your goal is not to just make it through a class but to make sure that every student leaves your classroom having learned something new.
- **While you should vary your lessons, routines will keep students on track.** Establish some routines, so that students can predict what their days will be like. For example, your routine could include a quiz every Thursday, a review game every Monday, or no homework on Tuesday nights.
- **You should not expect to cover every element on a lesson plan template every day.** Different activities take different amounts of time, and it is impossible to fit them all in.
- **No matter what you have planned to do each day, you must include two vital lesson elements.** First, you must have an exciting anticipatory set that will encourage your students to recall what they did in your class during the last meeting and to look ahead to the current lesson. Second, you must also include a satisfying closure to your lesson. This will help your students recall what they learned and reinforce their knowledge as they review the day's material.
- **Your lesson plans should be written for your own use.** Even though your supervisors will probably want to see your plans from time to time, you should plan for your own benefit. Learning to write useful plans will take time. If you are in doubt about how much to write, writing detailed plans may give you a needed boost of confidence.

You can also use Form 7.3 to create your lesson plans, or customize it to fit your needs.

What to Include in Your Lesson Plans

The following list will help you as you begin to write your daily lesson plans. While there may be other items that you find useful to include, these will constitute a good beginning:

Objectives. Objectives indicate what the result of a lesson will be, not what activities students will complete. The objectives for a lesson should be stated in specific terms and must follow state and district guidelines. For example, an objective for students in a geography course might be "Learners will be able to identify forty-five of the fifty state capitals."

Necessary materials and equipment. You should determine what resources you need to teach innovative and interesting lessons.

Prior knowledge assessment. You must assess your students' prior knowledge before you begin teaching a lesson to determine exactly what you need to review or introduce. How to do this will be discussed in more detail later in this section.

Anticipatory set. Creating anticipation in your students should be an integral part of the opening exercise in your class each day. An anticipatory set allows students to shift gears mentally from what they were doing before class began to the lesson they are about to begin. More information on anticipatory sets will be given in Section Eight.

Explanation or teacher input. Your input is necessary for a successful lesson. Carefully plan what you are going to do or say to make your points.

Student activities. Use a wide range of independent and guided practice activities that will appeal to students with a variety of learning styles. Be careful to include critical thinking activities.

Alternative activities. Allow for differences in students' ability and speed of mastery by preparing alternative activities that provide enrichment or remediation.

Closure. Close each class with an activity designed to reinforce learning. Allowing students to drift from one class to another without formal closure fails to make use of students' tendency to recall the beginning and ending of a lesson with clarity.

Homework. Homework assignments should arise naturally from the lesson. Because they are part of what you teach, you should record specific assignments in your plans.

Assessments. You should include a variety of assessments in each unit of study. Plan several small assessments before a test so that you do not have to deal with students who failed because they were not prepared.

Notes. Leave space in your daily plans to record your successes, failures, or any other information that will allow you to teach this lesson more successfully in the future.

FORM 7.3

An Easy-to-Use Format for Daily Lesson Plans

Lesson Topic: ______________________________

Date: ______________

Objectives: ______________________________

____

Materials, Equipment, or Textbook Pages: ______________________________

____

Prior Knowledge Assessment:

____

Anticipatory Set:

____

Teacher Input:

____

____

Student Activities:

____

____

Guided Practice:

____

____

Independent Practice:

____

____

Alternative Assignments:

____

Assessment:

____

Closure:

____

Homework:

____

Notes:

Common Planning Problems

While it is true that all teachers may have occasional problems with planning effective lessons, some problems seem to be especially prevalent during the first few years of teaching. The biggest disadvantage you have in creating lesson plans is that novice teachers do not have a storehouse of tried and true materials. Every lesson plan you write in your first year is an experiment. No matter how much effort you put into your plans, a lesson can fail simply because it has unforeseen drawbacks. You can reduce the likelihood of an unsuccessful lesson by paying attention to some of the incorrect ideas you might have about writing your plans. Here are a few of the problems concerning lesson plans that many first-year teachers encounter:

- Ignoring state and district standards and guidelines
- Rushing to cover material instead of teaching students
- Failing to connect current learning to previous learning
- Spending a disproportionate amount of time on one unit
- Failing to include activities to engage critical thinking skills
- Not allowing for differences in learning styles
- Failing to assess students' prior knowledge before starting new instruction
- Neglecting to provide an anticipatory set for each day's lesson
- Neglecting to provide closure for each day's lesson
- Testing students on material they have not adequately mastered
- Failing to provide the correct amount of practice
- Failing to provide enough "checkpoint" assessments before a final test
- Mistaking a list of activities for a lesson plan
- Failing to write a course overview, unit plans, and daily plans

> **Even after you've planned out a lesson, add a few activities. It's amazing how fast that time can pass. You don't want to end up with 30 minutes and nothing to do.**
>
> —*Patty Muth, 14 years' experience*

Some Internet Lesson Plan Resources

Thousands of Internet sites offer lesson plans at all grade levels and for all subjects. Many of these sites are designed by teachers and contain a wealth of practical information on planning lessons.

A good place to start designing lesson plans is your state's department of education Web page. At this site, you should be able to download curriculum standards, pacing guides, and lesson plan resources for your subject and grade level. Your school district may also have a Web page that provides curriculum guidelines. Another excellent place to search for lesson plan ideas is on the Web sites maintained by the authors or publishers of the textbooks your students use.

After you have researched the official state and district sites available to you, you should begin to research other sites for helpful information. Try some of the following sites for fresh ideas and helpful solutions to the planning problems you may be experiencing. Here is a partial list of some of the major sites containing general lesson plan information and links to specific topics, subjects, and grade levels:

- **EdScope (www.lessonplanspage.com).** At this extensive site, you will find over three thousand lesson plans covering topics for teachers of the full range of grades from preschool to high school.
- **Educators Network (www.lessonplans4teachers.com).** This site contains over two hundred pages of Web resources, a wide-ranging lesson plan directory with links to many major lesson plan sites, lesson plan guidelines, templates, and much more.
- **A to Z Teacher Stuff (www.atozteacherstuff.com).** Here you can search the large lesson plan section by grade level, topic, or thematic unit. The lessons cover every grade and every subject.
- **AT&T Knowledge Ventures' Blue Web'n (www.bluewebn.com).** At Blue Web'n, lesson plans and other resources are divided by content, subject matter, and grade level. This site also offers many links to other resources.

How to Sequence Instruction

On Thursday, I'm giving a quiz; on Friday, we're watching a movie. Oh, and we've got a trip to the computer lab on . . . what day was that? I think I signed up for Thursday. But that's my quiz day . . .

This scenario presents itself when teachers try to fit in all of the activities they have planned for their students. Sometimes the activities that teachers plan for their students don't follow a systematic plan; the result is instruction without a logical sequence.

The preceding scenario is common because it can so easily happen to a teacher—especially one who does not spend enough time planning lessons. By using the following simple tips, you can be sure to avoid this common problem.

- **Be aware of how activities fit together.** Check your plans for a logical sequence. The activities you have planned must arise naturally from the material in the previous day's learning.
- **Follow your state's standards.** Let the standards be your guide as you develop your course overview.

- **Teach to your objectives!** Too often, poor planning results in a list of activities that have little relationship to the serious business of mastering the information and skills in your objectives.
- **Pay attention to your course overview and unit plans.** If you have these in place, then you should find it easier to avoid hodgepodge instructional practices.
- **Create assessments when you plan units.** If you plan and write your assessments as you create unit plans, you will have a clear idea of not just the essential knowledge your students must have in order to master the material but the order in which you must present it.

Tap Your Students' Prior Knowledge

Experienced teachers know that their students' prior knowledge is a gift that students bring to class each day. Before you decide what you are going to teach, you first need to determine what your students already know.

Determining your students' prior knowledge is crucial because it determines the approach you will take with a unit of study. For example, if most of your students understand a concept, then you may wish to only review it briefly as a springboard to studying the next concept. On the other hand, if most of your students are unfamiliar with information you assumed they would already know, your approach will need to be more comprehensive.

You can use what you learn about your students' prior knowledge in many different ways. For instance, if you discover that one student understands a concept and can explain it to the rest of the class, that student's success will motivate the others to succeed.

One of the unexpected bonuses of tapping your students' prior knowledge is the intrinsic motivational appeal of these activities. Try adapting some of the following techniques to assess what your students already know about a topic.

- Ask students to write out a quick list of three facts they already know or think they know about a topic. After they have passed their responses to you, read some of them aloud (without revealing the author) and ask the entire class to judge their veracity.
- Ask students to write a brief description of what they have already been taught about the topic you are about to study. You could even ask them to tell you when and how they learned the information.
- Create a brief sampling of some of the questions you plan to include on a quiz or test later in the unit. Ask students to predict the correct answers.
- Divide your students into small groups and ask them to share everything they know about the topic under study. Set a time limit. After the time limit is up, have a representative from each group share the group's knowledge with the rest of the class.
- List the main points of the unit you are about to teach, and ask students to write what they already know about each one. Share their answers with the entire group.

- List the key terms that students will study. Have students write what they believe each term means based on what they already know about the topic. They should share their answers with the entire group.
- Ask students to work in pairs, and hand each pair a transparency or a sheet of poster paper. Have each pair brainstorm, listing everything they know about the topic. Share the lists with the class, or display them.
- Offer a puzzling scenario, and ask students to solve it, using what they already know about the topic. Have students keep their responses in order to verify their knowledge as they progress in their study.
- Show students a photograph, cartoon, diagram, quotation, or brief article related to the topic you are about to study. Ask them to share their reactions.
- Ask your students to create a Know/Want to Know/Learned (KWL) chart. The first two sections of the chart will give you a good summary of their previous learning.

Perfect Your Pacing

Good pacing means providing the right mixture of activities at the right speed, so that students can learn at the optimum rate for mastery. Correctly pacing a lesson takes practice. It usually takes a few weeks of getting to know your students, a few months of designing instruction, and a few years of general teaching experience before you can be confident that you have mastered the art of pacing. Although pacing takes experience and practice, you can master the rudiments quickly in your first few weeks as a teacher.

An important facet of perfecting your pacing skills involves getting maximum value from your class time. Be sure to include a variety of activities in each class, to keep students focused and working purposefully. If you divide your class into small blocks of time, you will find success with almost every student at any grade level, whether you teach on a traditional schedule or a variation of a block schedule.

Even though it takes time to get control of the fine points of correctly pacing a lesson, there are several things you can do in your first year of teaching to get on the right track with this teaching skill. Start with these suggestions:

- **Be as flexible as you can.** The biggest problem you will experience with pacing is that the work may take longer than you expect. You might have allotted a week for a unit but find that you need to spend an extra day to cover missing background information first. You also may be surprised at how long it takes your students to complete assignments. Be ready to add or drop activities as needed. In addition, focus on essential units of knowledge first and add enrichment material later.
- **Plan too much work for your students.** If your students finish a day's work early, you should always have one more activity you can offer, to keep them learning. Do not make students do busywork when you need an extra activity. Design purposeful work that will truly help your students learn.

- **Plan homework assignments that will add to your students' learning.** Used correctly, homework time is a valuable commodity that can increase the rate at which your students learn.

Change activities every 30–45 minutes, depending on the level of students. Honors kids can work longer; slower kids may need to take a break every 20 minutes. If your activities need to be long, give the kids a thirty-second or one-minute break so they can stand and stretch.

—Charlene Herrala, 24 years' experience

Include Opportunities for Critical Thinking

Information bombards us each day. On the Internet, anyone can review scientific data from the Arctic, check the weather in Japan, or skim "news" stories about products that produce instant weight loss. Because of this glut of information and misinformation, it is more important than ever for students to learn to think critically.

Critical thinking skills are thought processes involving activities such as logical reasoning, problem solving, and reflective thought. To develop these skills, students need sufficient daily practice. When teachers offer opportunities for critical thinking, watching students become absorbed in their work is only one of the rewards. Critical thinking activities also promote active learning and increased retention.

When you plan lessons that involve critical thinking, students must first have some awareness of the material so that they have information to draw on. If you plan carefully, the activities that involve critical thinking will arise from the lesson itself. Offer your students games, puzzles, real-world problems, or other exercises to stimulate their thinking about a lesson.

As you can see, creating activities to encourage high-level thinking is an enjoyable aspect of designing effective instruction. To incorporate critical thinking in your lessons, you can ask students to complete activities such as these:

- Give reasons for their answers
- Generate problems
- Generate multiple solutions
- Give extended answers
- Make predictions based on evidence
- Relate the lesson to their lives

- Solve brainteasers
- Relate the lesson to other classes
- Trace the origins of their thinking
- Compare and contrast information
- Collaborate on responses
- Determine causes and effects
- Combine ideas from widely differing sources
- Classify items in various ways
- Evaluate each other's work

GIVE DIRECTIONS THAT ENCOURAGE CRITICAL THINKING

Another way to include critical thinking opportunities in your instruction is to change the language you use to give directions. Instead of using broad terms such as *understand* or *complete,* give students instructions that require them to examine the material in more depth.

For example, if you ask students to retell a story, you are only asking them to demonstrate that they comprehend the events in the story. If you ask students to classify those same events according to whether they are causes or effects, you are requiring students not only to comprehend the story but to analyze it.

The following lists of verbs or verb phrases apply to the six areas of Bloom's Taxonomy. Use them to involve your students in meaningful activities.

Knowledge

The knowledge level of Bloom's taxonomy involves the identification and recall of information. The following verbs will lead students to recall and recognize.

Label
Select
Recall
Identify
Describe
List
Outline
Diagram
Define
Recite
Enumerate
Match
Cite
Draw

Comprehension

The comprehension level of Bloom's taxonomy involves the organization and selection of facts and ideas. The following verbs will lead students to interpret, explain, and demonstrate.

Associate
Estimate
Infer
Distinguish
Compare
Clarify
Approximate
Discuss
Characterize
Determine
Add
Demonstrate
Explain
Classify

Application

The application level of Bloom's taxonomy involves the use of facts and principles in new situations. The following verbs will lead students to construct and solve problems.

Sequence
Solve
Compute
Customize
Project
Transcribe
Classify
Judge
Sketch
Construct
Change
Apply
Predict
Adapt

Analysis

The analysis level of Bloom's taxonomy involves the separation of a whole into component parts. The following verbs will lead students to dissect, uncover, and list.

Analyze
Dissect
Summarize
Outline
Classify
Separate
Simplify
Categorize
Prioritize
Optimize
Inventory
Infer
Experiment
Characterize

Synthesis

The synthesis level of Bloom's taxonomy involves the combination of ideas to form a new whole. The following verbs will lead students to discuss, relate, and generalize.

Blend
Arrange
Modify
Reorganize
Rearrange
Compose
Construct
Integrate
Invent
Propose
Combine
Specify
Organize
Generalize

Evaluation

The evaluation level of Bloom's taxonomy involves the development of opinions or judgments. The following verbs will lead students to debate, judge, and form opinions.

Appraise
Verify
Assess
Compare
Debate
Critique
Evaluate
Contrast
Recommend
Judge
Select
Rate
Justify

Offer Your Students Options

If your students' success is your primary concern when planning lessons, you will find that offering options or alternative assignments is a reasonable thing to do. When you offer alternative assignments, you are not offering students a choice of whether or not to do the work. Instead, you are giving each student the opportunity to engage more fully in an assignment.

If you have ever purchased an automobile from a successful salesperson, you have probably experienced the high art of offering options. For example, instead of asking how you intended to scrape up the money on your teacher's salary, the salesperson probably asked if you wanted to finance the car through a bank or through the car dealership.

In this situation, the salesperson offered attractive options that had the same objective: to encourage you to purchase a car. Similarly, you can make a lesson attractive to students by offering a choice of activities.

Sometimes, a lesson doesn't lend itself to options, but many times, offering alternative lessons just makes sense. Consider offering alternative assignments when you and your students experience any of these situations:

- The assignment for the day turns out to be too much work for students to accomplish at one time.
- Students are successfully completing the day's work much faster than you had planned for them to do.
- The work proves to be too difficult for many students.
- Students are increasingly restless and off task.
- Many of your students lack the background preparation to master the material without more support from you.

Review the following suggestions when you want to offer students attractive and effective options. Not all of them will be appropriate for your students, but you can adapt them and create options of your own.

- Allow students to choose between the even and the odd questions when they have a long practice assignment.
- List the day's tasks on the board and allow students to decide on the order in which they will complete them.
- Allow students leeway in the length of writing assignments. Instead of saying, "Write a one-half page response," tell your students to write a response that is "at least one-half page long and as long as three pages."
- When assigning reading for class discussion, allow students to choose from a variety of articles you have selected.
- Allow students to skip directly to enrichment assignments as soon as they demonstrate mastery of the lesson's objective.

How to Adjust a Lesson

It is not uncommon for students to feel frustrated or to have trouble staying on task. When such behavior seems to be the norm rather than a temporary situation, you must be prepared to adjust your lesson plans to meet your students' needs.

While the methods of adjusting your plan will vary from class to class, you can quickly correct most situations by taking specific actions. The following tips will help you turn a frustrating lesson into a successful one as quickly as possible.

- Resist the temptation to give in to your own frustration by reprimanding your students. Think about why they are off task, and solve that problem instead.
- Often just switching to another learning modality will engage students enough so that they will work harder to overcome any small frustrations.
- Either reduce the amount of drill and practice you have assigned or make it more palatable by allowing students to tackle it in pairs or small groups.
- Call a stop to the lesson, and assess the situation. Determine what your students already know, to avoid needlessly repeating information or leaving them behind by moving to a subject they are not ready to process.

Always Have a Backup Plan

Few situations in a classroom are more dismaying than realizing that your students have nothing constructive to do. In situations like this, you must have a backup plan ready.

The ideal backup plan would extend the material that students are currently learning. When you write your daily plans, you can often jot down ideas that would be useful as a backup plan. However, this is not always possible. Experienced teachers have found two good solutions to this problem that you can adopt.

First, you can brainstorm a lengthy list of interesting activities that are related to the general topic under study and will last anywhere from ten to thirty minutes. When you see the need to use your backup plan, you can quickly scan your list to select an appropriate activity.

Still other teachers keep an eye out for good backup plans all year long. They maintain collections of reading passages, games, and other learning activities. You can begin with a few simple puzzles or other high-interest activities that will provide your students with opportunities for a constructive use of their time.

Successful Learning When Your Class Is on a Nontraditional Schedule

An innovative national trend in recent years is nontraditional scheduling. There are countless versions of nontraditional schedules. For example, some classes may meet every day for an extended period for half the school year; some classes may meet every other day for the entire year; still others may meet for varying lengths of time a few days a week for only one grading period. Many districts are also trying year-round school schedules or modified summer schedules.

While nontraditional schedules have many benefits, they can also create drawbacks. In particular, it can be difficult to cover all the material the curriculum requires in the allotted time. If students need enrichment or remediation, it is even more difficult.

Student absenteeism during a nontraditional schedule is another serious matter. When students miss a class, they may be missing the equivalent of at least two classes, depending on the type of nontraditional schedule.

It is also easy for teachers to waste class time while on a nontraditional schedule because many nontraditional schedules have longer class periods. While wasting the end of class is a poor use of a student's time when classes are on a traditional schedule, it becomes a more serious misuse of a student's time when a nontraditional schedule is in effect, given the compressed time frames for each class. Because a nontraditional schedule is likely to have fewer sessions for each class, instructional time in each must be maximized.

Despite these problems, many school districts have moved to nontraditional schedules to take advantage of the many benefits that such schedules offer:

- With longer class periods, students can finish lengthy assignments such as experiments or projects before the end of class.
- With less hall traffic, there are fewer opportunities for discipline problems.
- Teachers benefit from having fewer students in a semester. This translates into fewer papers to grade and a greater opportunity to connect with all students.

Nontraditional schedules have disadvantages and advantages, just as traditional school schedules do; in both cases, you must learn to use the time you have with your students as fully as possible. Here are some strategies that may assist you as you work to master the challenges of a nontraditional schedule:

- ▶ Divide the class period you have with students into smaller blocks as you plan. Vary the activities in each of these smaller blocks, to keep students alert and interested in working.
- ▶ Expect your students to work independently for at least part of the period. Very few teachers are able to lecture for a sustained period and keep the interest of a room full of restless students who are used to a fast-paced world.
- ▶ Plan the entire term carefully. You have a limited amount of time to cover the material your students need to know. You must keep your students on track if you are to succeed.
- ▶ Plan each day carefully. Always have backup plans in order to avoid running out of things for students to do. One of the worst mistakes that teachers new to nontraditional schedules make is telling students to study or start their homework at the end of class. Too often, students just waste this time because they are restless.

- Make connections for your students. Spend time at the start of class reviewing the previous day's learning and the last few minutes of each class reinforcing the material that students have just learned.
- Take advantage of innovative activities that require extended periods of time, such as simulations, debates, seminars, or online learning games. Take advantage of the extra time.

Set up lesson plans that are interspersed with individual work, teacher lecture, and, certainly, hands-on work. Teachers must incorporate all different learning styles when teaching in extended blocks of time.

—Carolyn Marks Bickham, 16 years' experience

Using Technology to Teach

On days when you finally unfreeze the computer only to find the server down again, using technology in the classroom can create chaos. Everyone who uses computers, software, or other technology will experience problems from time to time, but a teacher's problems are unique:

- There will seldom be enough functioning equipment for every student.
- Finding the best ways to help students use the technological resources available to them is a constant challenge.
- Teachers must become proficient at a variety of technological tasks related to instruction.
- Students do not always have the knowledge, resources, or skills to complete assignments successfully.

While many problems can arise with technology in the classroom, fortunately, there are also many solutions. If you are resourceful and determined, you can overcome technology problems. For example, a common problem is a shortage of equipment. Try some of these solutions:

- Have students work in teams.
- Stagger deadlines.
- Have students rotate among tasks.
- Involve the PTA, parents, and the community in finding ways to acquire more equipment.
- Allow students to work on home computers.
- Have students work before or after school.
- Collaborate with teachers in other grades or disciplines on shared projects, so that you can use each other's equipment.

As a new teacher, you should be comfortable with the technology you do have. Start small and gradually add to your repertoire of skills. There are many ways to use technology in your classroom; however, designing lessons that combine students and technology requires some special considerations. These tips can help you overcome many obstacles.

- Have a clear purpose for using technology; communicate this purpose to your students.
- Make sure that the equipment is working and that you know what to do if it is not. Have a backup plan in case of equipment failure.
- Try the activity yourself to see just how difficult it will be for students.
- Monitor students carefully. For example, if you have students researching a topic on the Internet, make sure that everyone is on task and that no one is checking e-mail or visiting sites that are off-limits.
- Show students how to research efficiently. If you show them how to narrow and define a topic before exploring, you will avoid behavior problems arising from students who are frustrated when they cannot immediately find the information they need.
- Use technology to engage students in real-life applications of their learning. Students who engage in activities that take them beyond the boundaries of their classroom are likely to find their learning relevant to their needs and interests.
- Make sure the lesson has an end product so that you can keep students on task. If they have to hand you a report or a disk, students are more likely to stay focused.
- Set clear rules and expectations for your students when they are working with computers or other equipment. Make sure that students know how they are supposed to behave.
- If students will be printing documents, make sure that the printer is working and that you have enough paper and time for everyone to finish printing.
- The primary concern when designing lessons that incorporate technology should be the content of the lesson, not the use of technology.

WEBQUESTS

Pioneers in outer space? Exploring sea caves? Field trips inside your own body? These are just a few of the exciting topics that you and your students can explore when you use WebQuests in your class. WebQuests include everything that is right in modern education; they are student-centered, discovery-based, open-ended, conducive to higher-order thinking, and, best of all, appealing to even the most disengaged student.

A WebQuest is just what its name implies: a search for information on the Internet. However, it is much more than an exercise in finding a fact or two. A WebQuest is a way for your students to explore the Web and then integrate the information they find through their search into a creative product that stimulates them to think deeply about a topic that interests them. For example, instead of just having students discuss a short story they have read, you could have them first research the geographic region in the story and then draw

Ideas for Using Technology in Class

There are many, many different ways to integrate technology into your lessons. In the following list, you will find some suggestions on how to incorporate computers and other technology into your lessons. Use these, or adapt them to suit the needs of your students.

Ask students to

- Create a slide presentation
- Find a Web site of the week or of the day
- E-mail pen pals
- Play instructional games
- Complete drill or review activities
- Create documents, using word processing software
- Create graphs
- Create spreadsheets
- Produce a class newsletter
- Draw an illustration of a vocabulary definition
- Reproduce digital photos
- Play music
- Take tests online
- Chat with a discussion group
- Practice problem-solving activities
- Research vocabulary words
- Create graphic organizers
- Create and maintain a class Web site
- Simulate a situation, using games or educational software
- Create puzzles
- Solve puzzles
- Check the weather
- Check the news
- Access online databases

conclusions about how the geography in the setting affected the outcome of the plot. Your students will learn some geographic facts, but in addition, they will apply their new knowledge to determine cause and effect.

To begin working on a WebQuest with your students, start with your state's standards. What topics can your students learn better from the information on the Internet than from their textbook? Once you have determined what you want to teach, you can begin designing your own WebQuest.

Before you begin, however, you should educate yourself further, using the enormous and fast-growing wealth of information on the Internet about successful WebQuests. The resources for this new approach to learning are user-friendly and interesting. Try these sites in order to learn more about this exciting and effective strategy.

- **BestWebQuests (http://bestwebquests.com).** Tom March, a WebQuest guru, maintains this excellent Web site. Here you will find links to articles and online training as well as to other useful resources.
- **Kathy Schrock's Guide for Educators (http://school.discovery.com/schrockguide/webquest/webquest.html).** Kathy Schrock's guide on the Discovery School Web site has links to a slide show of information on WebQuests, rubrics, tutorials, examples and models, advice, and more links to other resources.
- **The Education Technology Department at San Diego State University (http://webquest.sdsu.edu).** Here you can access training materials and hundreds of WebQuests, as well as articles and other information to help you design innovative Internet activities for your students.

Effective Lesson Plans When You Are Absent: What to Do When You Have to Miss School

If you strive for perfect attendance, you and your students will benefit. You will avoid having to make lesson plans that you can only hope a substitute teacher will be able to follow, and your students will not miss instructional time because you are absent. While you should not attend school if you are ill, there are plenty of times when you may be tempted to miss a day of school when you are not really sick, just as you were when you were a student yourself.

Be careful not to abuse your district's leave policy. If nothing else, you can never be sure when you will need to use the sick days you should have saved. A serious illness or an accident can erode years of banked leave time. Try to save those days for when you really need them.

If you do have to miss school, there are several things you must do. Some of these will probably be required by your school district, and others are just common-sense ways to make sure the day goes smoothly. Here are the steps you should take when you need to miss a day of school:

INFORM THE RIGHT PEOPLE

- Contact the people who are responsible for hiring a substitute teacher for you. Try to do this as quickly as you can so that they can hire the most competent sub for you.
- Call a colleague and ask for assistance. Ask that person to look in on your class during the day and make sure the substitute knows what to do.
- Contact an administrator. Ask the administrator to look in on your classes from time to time throughout the day.
- If you think your students will not take advantage of the situation, you should tell them that you are going to be out. Use this time to ask for their cooperation and to talk about any problems that may arise with a substitute teacher. Stress the importance of maintaining the daily routine even when you are not there.

LEAVE GOOD LESSON PLANS

- You should not ask a substitute teacher to interpret lesson plans from your plan book. Instead, give a class-by-class description of what you want your students to do.
- Base your plans on written work that your students can do independently. Write out clear directions on the work itself so that students can complete it without having to talk with others or ask the substitute to interpret.
- Don't ask a substitute teacher to show movies or take your students to the library or to a computer lab.
- Don't assign group work when there is a substitute teacher in charge.
- Students should not use computers when you are not there to supervise them.
- Let your students know that they are not just doing busywork. Make sure they know that the sub will collect the work at the end of class and that you intend to grade it.
- If the work involves handouts, photocopy them in advance and label them so the substitute can find them quickly. Don't ask a substitute to photocopy for you.
- A common complaint that substitute teachers have is that teachers do not leave enough work for students to do. You should plan more work for your students than you would expect them to do if you were there.

HANDLE BEHAVIOR PROBLEMS WHEN YOU RETURN

Let your students know you expect good behavior from them while you are absent. However, if your students have misbehaved while you were out, don't rush to punish. First, have students write out their version of the events of the class. Read these, and think about what you are going to do before you punish an entire class based on what a substitute teacher has told you. If you then have to deal with misbehavior problems after you have gathered the facts from the sub and from your students, strive to be fair.

Provide Essential Information for Your Substitute

In addition to lesson plans, you should leave a folder of information for your sub. Because most of this information is not as apt to change as your daily plans, you should make up this folder early in the year and update it as often as necessary. Your sub folder should include the following items:

- An updated seating chart for each class
- A class roster
- Attendance procedures
- Your daily schedule
- The names of helpful students
- The names and room numbers of helpful colleagues
- A notepad and pen
- Class rules
- Class routines and procedures
- Where to find supplies and extra texts
- A map of the school
- Your phone number
- Fire drill or other emergency information
- Information about students with special needs
- Referral notices and information
- Extra work for students to do if they finish everything else

Talk It Over

How to Design Effective Lessons

Use these questions as a springboard for discussions that will help you and your discussion group members grow and develop professionally. Discuss these questions about how to designing effective lessons:

1. How can you improve the way you plan lessons? What can you do to make planning effective lessons easier? What suggestions do your colleagues have?

2. Beginning and ending class with a structured format is an important element in successful lessons as well as in effective classroom management, and your lesson plans should reflect this. Discuss the techniques you have used to generate ideas for anticipatory sets and reviews. How can you make these routines interesting and useful?
3. How can you tell when your lessons are stimulating for your students? What specific factors can you include to make sure that your lessons are interesting and challenging?
4. What steps can you take to ensure that you cover all the material in your state's standards that your students need to know?
5. Brainstorm a list of real-life experiences you could include in your lessons to capture your students' attention. How can you use this information? Who can help you with this?
6. One of the worst nightmares for any teacher is teaching a lesson that is not working. What plans can you make now for use if this happens to you? Share techniques that can be used to adjust a lesson and not lose valuable class time.
7. What does *learning* mean to you? How would your students define it? How can you make sure that learning happens in your room all class long?
8. Critical thinking opportunities are not only enjoyable for students but also effective for improving long-term recall of material. What daily activities can you use to help your students develop their critical thinking skills?
9. Describe a time when your students learned an unexpected lesson. What knowledge or understanding can you gain from this experience?
10. What assessments do you use at the start of a unit of study to assess your students' prior knowledge and level of readiness? How do you differentiate instruction to meet the needs of every student in your class? How can you find out more about how to do this?

SECTION EIGHT

Deliver Effective Instruction

In this section, you will learn

- ✔ How to improve your classroom charisma
- ✔ How to conduct productive classroom discussions
- ✔ How to ask engaging, productive questions
- ✔ How to give effective verbal and written directions
- ✔ How to conduct effective practice and review

Even the best-prepared teachers can have unsuccessful students. A teacher may have the most detailed lesson plans in an entire school, but if he or she does not deliver instruction effectively, students just will not be able to learn. On the other hand, when a lesson is delivered skillfully, a cycle of success gains momentum. Confident teachers inspire their students. Successful students, in turn, create confident teachers. This cycle is one of the most satisfying reasons to teach.

What is effective delivery, and how does it give a teacher control? Many teachers believe that effective delivery of instruction means speaking well in front of students. Although a teacher does need outstanding speaking skills, those are only one part of delivering instruction well. Other components of a good lesson can include class discussions, questioning sessions, frequent reviews, and innovative activities, just to name a few. Best of all is the result of putting all of these elements together; when teachers know that students have learned the

> **Be ENTHUSIASTIC about your subject! If you enjoy yourself at your job, your students will embrace what you're showing them.**
>
> —*Kay Stephenson, 33 years' experience*

material in a lesson, they can feel that they are having a positive impact on the success of their students.

Let Your Enthusiasm Show

If you want your students to be interested in a lesson, one of the most important things you can do is project a keen interest in the topic. If you doubt how important it is to be enthusiastic about every lesson, consider this: if you let students see your enthusiasm, they will probably like the lesson, too. On the other hand, if you are bored with a topic, your students will certainly be bored also.

Guidelines for Improving Your Classroom Charisma

If you look back on your own student days, you can easily recall the teachers who made learning fun; you wanted to be in their classes.

What makes certain teachers exceptional? Charisma—the elusive quality that makes ordinary people into leaders—is the key. Fortunately for many of us, classroom charisma can be learned. You should begin to cultivate your charismatic appeal on the very first day you step to the front of a class, and you will still be working on it on the very last day you teach.

Here are some general guidelines to help you become a charismatic teacher. Begin by selecting the steps you know you can manage with ease, and then move on to the ones that will require a more determined effort.

- **Your class should be about your students and their work.** Make them the focus of your attention. Some inexperienced teachers make the mistake of talking about their own lives too often while ignoring students, who are quietly tuning out.
- **Smile at your students.** No one likes a grouch. A teacher with a pleasant demeanor has half of the charisma battle won. What if you don't feel like smiling? Do it anyway. You owe it to your students. Remember that your difficult students are the very ones who most need your smiling support.
- **Stand at the door to greet your students as they come into the classroom.** You should greet your students to convey the message that you are glad to see them.
- **Overlook what you can.** Although it is certainly OK to be strict with your students, there is a fine distinction between a strict teacher and a too-strict teacher. If you spend your day quibbling over minor problems with your students, you will not have enough time to attend to larger issues.
- **Early in the term, establish the procedures and routines your students should follow, and then stick to them as much as reasonably possible.** Students who

know what they are supposed to do and how they are supposed to do it are much more comfortable than those who are uncertain about what you expect.

- **Laugh at yourself.** While you should not be the focus of the class—your students and their work should be—you should let your students know that you have enough confidence to not take yourself too seriously.
- **Make sure to eliminate distracting personal habits that might annoy students.** Some of the most obvious behaviors that interfere with classroom charisma are a monotone voice, poor eye contact, sloppy speech patterns, and distracting gestures.
- **Use multiple modes of learning to make sure that your lessons are as dynamic and exciting as possible.** Include visual aids, technology, music, and other active learning strategies to involve every student in every lesson every day.
- **Charismatic teachers talk less than their students do.** Ask questions that will encourage students to share their ideas with you.

Self-Assessment 8.1 will help you assess the effectiveness of your instructional delivery.

Avoid Pitfalls That Plague Too Many Teachers

Many factors can interfere with a teacher's delivery of instruction. Teachers who are stressed, too tired to plan appealing lessons, or not quite in tune with the needs and interests of their students are likely to lack a smooth flow of instruction. Happily, you can avoid most of these pitfalls with just a bit of awareness, common sense, and planning. Here is a list of considerations that will help you avoid mistakes when you deliver instruction:

Whose voice is heard?

Don't talk more than your students do.

Do design activities that encourage your students to speak to each other and to you.

Who does the work?

Don't create lessons that allow your students to be passive.

Do skip the worksheets that require only recollection by rote, and ask students to solve puzzles, highlight notes, debate points, or engage in other open-ended thinking activities.

Are you letting teaching opportunities go by?

Don't let the national push for accountability intimidate you into neglecting to use those serendipitous moments that sometimes arise in every classroom.

Do turn any occasion into a learning event in your classroom. Seize every opportunity, and capitalize on current events and student interests whenever you can.

SELF-ASSESSMENT 8.1

Is Your Delivery Effective?

Rate yourself, assigning yourself a letter grade for each area.

A = Excellent; B = Good; C = Satisfactory; D = Needs work

_____ 1. My voice is loud enough for all of my students to hear me.

_____ 2. I vary the expression in my voice.

_____ 3. I sound respectful and serious when I speak to my students.

_____ 4. I have eliminated fill-in expressions such as "like" and "you know."

_____ 5. I use a vocabulary appropriate for my students' age.

_____ 6. My posture projects enthusiasm and confidence.

_____ 7. I move around during the class period.

_____ 8. I politely wait until I have everyone's attention before I begin.

_____ 9. I use eye contact effectively.

_____ 10. Class discussions in my room include every student.

How much material can you teach in one class?

Don't allow yourself to drift when it comes to finding the correct pace for the delivery of instruction. This takes practice, organization, and planning.

Do make sure to plan alternate lessons in case the pace you initially set for a lesson needs adjustment.

How much time do you really need to teach the material?

Don't allow your students to sit around with nothing important to do while they wait for class to begin or end or for their classmates to finish an assignment.

Do follow this practical advice from veteran teachers: plan more work than you think your students will be able to accomplish.

How will your students know what to do?

Don't confuse your students by giving hurried or unclear directions.

Do be sure to deliver a combination of written and oral directions and to check for students' understanding of directions.

Set the Stage

Before you begin an oral presentation, set the stage for a successful presentation by previewing the topic in such a way that students will want to know more about what you have to say. If you begin a lecture or presentation in a traditional, dull way, many of your students will quickly tune out. However, if you incorporate one or more of these preview techniques, your students will be motivated to pay attention.

- Post a motto, slogan, or other catchy phrase related to the lesson in a conspicuous spot, and ask students to comment on it.
- Display and talk about an unusual object related to the lesson.
- Make a provocative statement, and ask students to respond to it.
- Read part of a passage to the class. Be sure to stop reading at an exciting part of the text. Finish the passage in your lecture.
- Tell students what new skill or knowledge they will have after the presentation is over. Show them how the lecture will benefit them.
- Pass out a handout with missing parts. Your students can fill in the missing information as they listen.
- Give students part of a scenario before the presentation. Stop and discuss it. Finish the scenario during the presentation.
- Have students enact a brief scene related to the topic under study.
- Do a demonstration, then ask students to explain what they observed.
- Play a game related to the topic of your lesson.
- Take a poll of your students on some aspect of the topic.
- Pose a problem for students to decipher. Use the presentation to solve the problem.

Use Body Language to Motivate Your Listeners

Your students can tell right away when they have your full attention. They can also tell when you like them, when you find a lesson interesting, and when you are reaching the limits of your patience. The nonverbal language you use in your classroom can be a powerful way to capture your students' attention and motivate them to work.

First, you must learn to use it effectively. You have to make sure that the body language signals you send match the verbal ones. For example, if you try not to laugh when you are trying to scold a student who has misbehaved in a way you find funny, no one will take you seriously. If you frown unconsciously while praising your class, you will confuse your students. To avoid sending mixed signals such as these, review this list of confusing or negative body language cues:

- Pointing at your students
- Standing with your hands on your hips
- Putting your hands too close to a student's face
- Speaking too loudly or in a monotone
- Jabbing a finger at a student's chest to make a point
- Tapping your fingers to show impatience
- Leaning away from students
- Snapping your fingers at students
- Laughing while delivering a serious message
- Rolling your eyes as if in disgust
- Ignoring a student who is upset
- Slamming doors or books

The Power of Positive Body Language

Nonverbal language is a powerful way to give your instruction a confident and caring tone. Use the following signals to send positive messages to your students.

- Leaning forward to indicate that you are interested
- Extending your hand toward students, palm facing the ceiling
- Making eye contact
- Nodding your head
- Lightly touching a student on the arm
- Smiling
- Giving a thumbs-up signal

Pay Attention to Your Audience

Establish an atmosphere of mutual respect. This is a day-to-day process that involves thoughtful work with every student in your class. Begin by being careful that your body language and tone of voice convey your respect for your students.

Good speakers pay attention to nonverbal cues from their audience. You need to add some pizzazz to your delivery if you notice that your students are doing any of the following:

- Watching the clock
- Looking confused
- Flipping through their notebooks
- Staring off into space
- Talking to someone sitting nearby
- Refusing to look at you
- Putting their heads down on their desks to sleep
- Doing homework for another class
- Asking to go to their locker, the restroom, the nurse, the phone
- Tying and retying their shoes
- Sighing loudly and rolling their eyes

> Teachers must be aware of the level of understanding of their students and prepare accordingly. This requires a great deal of effort on the part of the teacher. I am convinced that all students want to learn, but not at the expense of failing in the presence of their peers.
>
> —*William N. Owen, 43 years' experience*

Use Toys to Capture Attention

Rubber ducks in math class? Spinning tops in history class? Not only do toys capture the attention of children of all ages, but the intrinsic contrast of a toy and an academic setting is enormously appealing to almost every audience. Successful teachers who want their students to enjoy a lesson know that few things are as useful in capturing their students' attention as toys.

Depending on your imagination, the lesson, and the age of your students, toys can be used in many different ways before, during, and after a presentation. Try some of these activities to help your students relate the toy to the information in your instruction.

Ask students to

- Describe the toy
- Tell how the toy works
- Relate it to the lesson
- Research the history of the toy
- Give other uses for it
- Brainstorm a list of reasons why it is appealing
- Create other names for it
- Share memories about similar toys
- Take it apart, to . . .
- Find out where the raw materials for it are from
- Estimate information such as its weight, length, origin . . .
- Use it to illustrate a point

Make learning fun! Engaging students in fun activities allows them to learn without stress. It's kind of like a sneak attack. They are having so much fun in class that they don't realize they are mastering a difficult chunk of information until the close of the lesson.

—Debbie McManaway, 12 years' experience

Make a Point That Students Will Remember

Although there are endless creative techniques to help your students remember the main points of your presentation, you will have to plan and prepare to make each technique successful. Successful teachers often experiment with a variety of new approaches to help their students find success.

The following techniques are some you can use to help your students stay alert and interested in a lesson. Do not be afraid to modify, adapt, or combine these ideas to get your points across to every student.

- **Help your students make a personal connection to the lesson.** They should be able to identify with the material under study. One easy way to do this is to include the names, interests, hobbies, experiences, or cultures of your students when creating worksheets or questions.
- **Present a slide show.** Using yours as a model, have your students prepare and present a slide show of their own.
- **Invite guest speakers to talk to your students as part of a unit of study.** Hearing a community leader talk about the importance of local government, for example, will reinforce any point you are trying to make about this topic.
- **Use plenty of models or examples and a variety of media when you demonstrate how to do something.** Try these: newspapers, advertisements, T-shirt slogans, cartoons, movies, art, computers, television, magazines, videos, or music.
- **Hide items related to the lesson in a large box.** Ask students to guess what the items could be. As they open the box, have students explain or predict the significance of each item.
- **Play music that fits the lesson of the day.** As you play parts of songs, ask students to tell how each relates to the lesson.
- **Hand out blindfolds and have your students put them on.** Give them objects related to the information you want them to recall and have them identify them without peeking.
- **Display a statement that you want your students to recall.** Guarantee that they will do so by immediately playing a video clip that supports it.
- **Surprise students with a bit of theater.** This will not only make your lesson enjoyable but will also make it one your students will recall for a long time. Try some of the following ideas to develop your dramatic flair.
  - Say something outrageously startling and interesting.
  - Stage a reenactment.
  - Videotape your students as they work.
  - Wear a costume, or have your students wear costumes.

Help Students Stay on Track During a Lecture

Few classroom proceedings are as discouraging as preparing a fascinating lecture for a roomful of students who don't listen. Sometimes teachers assume that their students are paying attention only to find out later that the entire class missed the fine points of a presentation. Through planning and preparation, you can avoid this disappointment. Here are some suggestions on how to help your students stay on track during a lecture:

- Tell students a specific number of facts they will learn during the course of the presentation. As you cover each one, mark it off, resulting in a countdown of the facts.

- Give students a handout to fill in as you talk. It will be even more interesting if they fill it in for a partner.
- Tell students that you only have a certain amount of time to lecture. Set a timer to make students aware of the passage of time as you speak.
- Give students an outline of the lecture to copy. Or give them a skeleton outline to fill in.
- Stop periodically to review notes by calling on students to share a fact. Keep at it until all the points have been mentioned.
- Announce that there will be an open-note quiz after the lecture is over.
- Stop and ask students to share their notes with a partner so they can fill in any missing information.
- Hand students two sets of cards. On one set, have the first part of a fact from the presentation. On the other set, have the second part of the fact. As the lecture progresses, students can match the cards from the two sets, based on the information they are learning.
- Ask students to complete a graphic organizer as they listen.
- Stop and ask for a quick recap.
- Have students mark off items on a checklist.
- Give students a word bank of key words, dates, or other items to use in their notes.
- If the lecture involves events in a particular order, give students a handout with the events in scrambled order, and ask them to rearrange the events in the correct order.
- Put ten words from the lecture on a handout. Ask students to mark them off as you speak. Tell them that you will discuss nine of the words and that they are responsible for telling you which one was not in the lecture.

Improve Your Oral Presentations

One of the most important things to remember about speaking to a potentially bored group of students is that you need to practice what you are going to say and how you are going to say it. Rehearse, and then rehearse some more. In a few years, you may be comfortable enough to teach without rehearsals, but for now, consider rehearsing an important part of your lesson preparation.

In addition to practice, there are several other activities you can use to improve the way you speak in front of a class. Try these exercises in order to make your oral presentations as interesting as possible.

VIDEOTAPE YOURSELF

One of the most effective ways to evaluate your delivery of instruction is to videotape yourself several times during the term. If you tape yourself several times, you will see how you have improved and which weaknesses still exist. Of course, it is not enough to just videotape and then watch. To assess your presentation, consider these questions:

- What annoying verbal and nonverbal tics do I have?
- Is my voice loud enough for all students to hear?
- Do I include all of my students by calling on them?
- Do I project enthusiasm, authority, and confidence?
- Do I command my students' attention when I speak?
- What messages am I conveying through my body language?

THE ART OF THE PAUSE

Practice the art of the pause by training yourself to restrain from enthusiastically "walking over" student responses. When a student speaks, mentally count to three before speaking or allowing others to jump in. Similarly, when students are slow to respond to a question, do not rush to save them from an awkward silence. Pause long enough to allow your students to think.

EYE CONTACT

Another important skill you must refine is eye contact. As you speak with your students, refrain from looking at the wall or even the floor. Focus your attention on every student by making it a point to keep your eyes focused on two or three for a few seconds and then move on to another group.

It can be especially difficult to maintain eye contact while writing on the board. The trick to this is to not face the board at all but to almost face the class by turning to the side while writing and continuing to talk. Students will feel you have spoken directly to each of them if you maintain direct eye contact throughout class.

Meet the Needs of Students with Diverse Learning Styles

Imagine this scene in a typical classroom: An enthusiastic teacher explains the material in the day's lesson to attentive students. When students ask questions, the teacher carefully reteaches the material. When test time comes, some students do well, some show partial mastery of the material, and some fail. Their discouraged teacher tells a colleague: "I told them over and over how to do the work. Why didn't they learn?"

Unfortunately, it is true that even the best-intentioned teachers will fail if they ignore students' learning needs. Due to the scholarly attention focused on this issue in recent decades, educators now know a great deal about how different students learn and what teachers need to do to reach every child.

There is a great deal of online information about learning styles; the following two Web sites provide current, easy-to access information.

- **Learning-Styles-Online.Com (www.learning-styles-online.com).** Here you will find a free learning styles inventory, an excellent overview of learning styles, and comprehensive information on various learning styles.
- **LD Pride (www.ldpride.net).** LD Pride offers free learning styles inventories, information on multiple intelligences, and practical tips on how to work with differences in learning styles.

The glut of information on learning styles, some of it conflicting, can be overwhelming, making it difficult to decide which learning needs to address first. A good way to start is with the basic needs of the pupils in your class. Students can often be grouped according to these three learning preferences:

1. **Visual learners.** These students prefer to take in material through activities based on reading, writing, and learning material visually.
2. **Auditory learners.** These students prefer activities that involve listening, speaking, and reorganizing material orally.
3. **Kinesthetic or tactile learners.** These students prefer activities allowing them to interact physically with the material through touch or actions.

It is tempting to believe all people can be grouped into one of these three categories; however, this is a simplistic view. Although many individuals have a preferred learning style, most seem to operate best with a combination of learning preferences. With this in mind, it is prudent to pack all three modes of instruction into as many assignments as possible.

Here is an example of an assignment that has been revamped to include activities that meet all three learning preferences:

Original Assignment

"Finish reading pages 17–21 of Chapter One, and answer the questions at the end. You will be tested on the material in pages 13–21."

Here is the same assignment presented in a manner that incorporates the learning preferences of all students in the class. Note that although there are many more steps for students to follow, each one is brief. Students should be able to complete this work in roughly the same time as the original assignment.

Revised Assignment

- ☐ Look at the illustrations on pages 14 and 16, and jot down two unusual things you notice about each one. (visual)

- ☐ Read the chapter subsection title and key ideas. List them in your notes. (visual)
- ☐ Take turns reading pages 17–20 aloud with your study partner. Write the key words from each subsection in your notes. (auditory, visual)
- ☐ Create an idea map of the information on page 19. (kinesthetic/tactile)
- ☐ Share your map with your partner, and combine ideas. (auditory, visual)
- ☐ When you and your partner are finished, move to a computer to record your answers to the questions on page 21. One of you should read the answers aloud as the other types. (auditory, kinesthetic/tactile)
- ☐ Correct your answers by checking the video display on the television monitor in the back of the room. (visual)

> The students' assignment was to do research reports on inventors and their inventions. Rather than just assign the inventors, I put names into a bowl, and the students made their selection. I then provided poster board, Magic Markers, and other materials for these projects to be done in the classroom. Their posters were displayed for all to enjoy. It was fun, they learned, and they did the work.
>
> *—Marlene M. Stanton, 23 years' experience*

Activities That Accommodate Each Learning Style

Here are some brief lists of suggested activities for each modality. Some of these activities are interchangeable because they depend on whether you ask students to complete them verbally (auditory mode), by sight (visual mode), or by moving (kinesthetic/tactile mode).

Auditory learners are comfortable when you ask them to

- Interview
- Read aloud
- Listen
- Retell
- Talk over a process
- Restate
- Recite
- Discuss

- Listen to music
- Fill in the blanks while listening

Visual learners are comfortable when you ask them to

- Make a flow chart
- Outline
- Survey
- Diagram
- Illustrate
- Graph
- Read and compare
- Study maps
- Look at illustrations
- View a video

Kinesthetic or tactile learners are comfortable when you ask them to

- Draw
- Role play
- Build
- Finger spell
- Play a board game
- Create a diorama
- Construct
- Make a bookmark
- Make a model
- Dissect

The following activities offer a combination of learning styles.

- Make a sketchbook
- Stage a talk show
- Write a letter
- Draw a comic strip
- Teach a class
- Demonstrate a skill
- Publish a tabloid
- Make a flag

- Conduct a survey
- Invent something new
- Form an investigative panel
- Brainstorm ideas
- Edit a paper
- Practice taking rapid notes
- Fake a crime scene
- Interview someone
- Celebrate an unusual holiday
- Vote on an issue
- Invent a dialogue
- Create a wall of fame

Conduct Class Discussions That Engage Every Student

If you have fond memories of classes in which everyone seemed to be involved in discussing a topic of burning importance, you probably want to help your students have that experience, too. Remember how you left the room exhilarated, still debating your points, and in full possession of strong opinions that you did not hold when class began?

Class discussions are an excellent way to deliver instruction that students will remember long after the class is over. Best of all, class discussions create active learners who are perfecting their thinking skills while expanding their knowledge of a topic.

What role should you take in a class discussion? First, envision yourself as the facilitator of the discussion. Your job is to plan the discussion, keep things running smoothly, and wrap up at the end. Think about your role in making this a successful and stimulating method of delivering instruction in three easy steps: what to do to prepare for the discussion, what to do during the discussion, and what to do after the discussion is over.

Before the Discussion

- ▶ **Post procedures in a prominent place in the classroom.** You should consider how you want your students to relate to each other and to you. Here are some guidelines you could establish:
  - Wait until the moderator recognizes you before you speak.
  - You may not speak after you have reached your limit of speaking opportunities.
  - Treat other people's opinions with tolerance and respect.
  - Listen more than you speak.
- ▶ **Determine the purpose of the discussion.** What outcome do you want? Do you want students to analyze an issue? Combine information in a new way? Brainstorm new ideas? You should convey the purpose of the discussion, to focus the conversation.

- **Create the questions your students will discuss.** Successful questions for class discussions require higher-order thinking skills. For the first discussion session, prepare ten thought-provoking questions. Use the reactions of your students to gauge how many to prepare for future sessions. When appropriate, give students advance copies of questions so that they can prepare.
- **Move the chairs.** Set up chairs so students can see each other's faces. Taking time to arrange the seating as you wish the first time will establish how you want it done in the future.

During the Discussion

- **Enforce procedures.** As the discussion gets under way, remind students of the importance of the conduct procedures for class discussions. Be steadfast in enforcing them. It may be difficult for your students to adjust to them at first, but with persistence, you will succeed in having productive class discussions.
- **Introduce the topics of discussion.** You can display questions using an overhead projector, write them on the board, or ask students to review their advance copy of the questions.
- **Teach your students the importance of supporting their opinions.** When someone makes a point, keep probing until enough support has been presented. Students need to realize that it is not enough to express their opinion; they must also be able to defend and support it.
- **Encourage deeper thinking.** Elicit thoughtful responses by trying these techniques: invite a student to comment on someone else's response, ask for elaboration, ask another student to refute, or ask for a restatement.
- **Allow everyone to participate.** Keep outgoing students who want to express themselves at the expense of everyone else in check. One easy way to do this is to give all students the same number of slips of paper. Each time someone speaks, he or she has to give up one of the slips. When a student is out of slips, he or she is out of opportunities to speak.
- **Recognize speakers.** To determine who gets to speak, have an unbreakable object such as a book or stuffed toy for students to hand to each other as they take turns speaking.
- **Encourage risk taking.** Make it easy and nonthreatening for all students to risk answering. Encourage and validate answers when you can.
- **Step back.** Refrain from dominating the discussion. A class discussion works best when all students are prepared and when all students join in.

After the Discussion

- **Have students reflect.** Ask students to reflect on the discussion by asking for
  - Written or oral feedback on what went well
  - Suggestions for improvement

- A retelling of the important points
- A written summary

Strategies for Asking Engaging Questions

Asking engaging questions is a skill that will take you some time to perfect, but that one skill can guarantee an exciting and beneficial lesson. Regardless of your experience, you can learn to ask just the right question in just the right way at just the right time. The following steps will help you develop the skill of asking questions that will draw your students into a lesson and make them eager to participate.

Plan your questions. The first step you must take is to plan questions that will generate the answers you want from your students. There are two types of questions you can use. *Recall questions* require a response based on facts that your students have learned prior to the questioning session. *Thought questions* require a more in-depth response and are often open-ended.

Establish a routine. The next step is to teach the routines you want students to follow during class questioning sessions. Even if you have created fascinating questions, your effort will be useless if students shout out answers at random or are not respectful of each other's answers. Teaching these routines will take more than just one or two attempts, but it will be worth the effort. Some simple rules you should consider include these:

- Don't talk while others are talking.
- Don't speak without raising your hand.
- Treat other students' answers with respect.
- Listen to the questions without interrupting.

HOW TO HELP ALL STUDENTS BENEFIT FROM QUESTION-AND-ANSWER SESSIONS

Question-and-answer sessions are fast-paced drills that can engage all students in active learning. With practice and planning, you can make sure that question-and-answer sessions in your class benefit every student. Try to incorporate as many of these strategies as you can, to involve every student in productive learning.

Have students write responses before speaking. One strategy that will absolutely guarantee success in a questioning session is to have students write out responses to your questions as you ask them. You can hold responses until you have asked every question, or you can check after you have asked a few questions to see if students are on the right track.

Wait for a response. A common mistake that teachers make in asking questions is not allowing sufficient time for students to respond. You must learn to allow your students enough time to formulate a response before you call for an answer. This technique will also require you to teach your students not to blurt out answers but to wait for you to call on them instead.

Ask the question before you call on students by name. It is important to ask the question first and then wait for a response. If you call out a student's name before posing the question ("John, can you solve the next problem?), you send a message to the rest of the class that only John has to think about the question.

Hold students accountable for answering all questions. If a student refuses to answer a question you have asked of the entire group, there are many possible reasons for this refusal. One way to hold students accountable for participating in the session without embarrassing them is to say, "I'll come back to you." With these words, you are pleasant but firm in your expectation that students will participate.

Avoid large group shouting matches. It will be impossible to hear your students if they all shout out responses at once. If some of your less-interested students see that you are not listening, they will grab the opportunity to tune out. Refuse to allow this kind of disorder; teach your students to raise their hands and be recognized before they speak.

Don't follow a pattern. When students observe that you are following a pattern in calling on them, they may tune out until it is their turn or count to see which question they will be asked. There are several ways to avoid following a pattern. One is to create a spreadsheet of your roster or to photocopy your grade book. Use the list to mark off your students' names as you call on them. Another method that works for many teachers is making a note card for each student at the beginning of the term. If you have note cards, you can flip through them while you are questioning, and place a mark on each student's card as you call on him or her.

Establish simple signals. If you are reviewing questions that require a simple yes-or-no response, there are many signals you can invent to let your students express their thoughts. For example, you could make up response cards in advance with "Yes" on one side and "No" on the other. If you are asking students to classify information, you could have cards with a category heading on each side. You could also use gestures such as thumbs up or thumbs down. The possibilities are endless.

Provide a safe environment. Your students must be allowed to risk mistakes. Never be sarcastic with a student who has risked an incorrect answer. Do not allow students to laugh at each other's responses. Instead, encourage teamwork by asking, "Who can help with this answer?"

Emphasize listening and speaking skills. Try to avoid repeating your question or a student's response. If someone has not understood your question, ask another student to rephrase it for the class. If a student is so soft-spoken that most of the class cannot hear, ask that student to repeat instead of restating the response for the class yourself.

Respond to every answer. While it is easy to become involved in classroom dynamics and in anticipating the next question, you must take time to respond to each student's answer. Don't just nod or grimace. If a response is correct, affirm it. When it is not, say so but keep your reaction neutral. If part of a response is correct, acknowledge that part and continue probing until you have an entirely correct answer. Here are some helpful responses you may want to use during question-and-answer sessions:

- "That's correct. How did you arrive at that answer?"
- "Mike, can you help Joseph with that answer?"
- "Jessica, do you agree with Rachel's answer?"
- "What do you think about that?"
- "Nice try. Part of your answer is correct. Would you like to add more?"

Ask only one question at a time. If you bombard your students with several questions, they will not be able to keep up.

Find the correct pace. Finding the best pace at which to question your students can be a challenge. If your pace is too slow, many will tune out. If your pace is too quick, then just as many others will tune out because they will stop trying to keep up. Be sensitive to the pace of your questions, and work to keep as many students engaged as possible.

Go beyond simple answers. After you have become reasonably confident that you can successfully manage simple question-and-answer sessions, move on to questions requiring thoughtful responses. When you move beyond recall questions, you encourage students to think, take risks, and become involved.

Promote student interaction. One way to involve every student is to set up "cross fire" situations in which you ask students to comment on each other's responses. This will guarantee that your lesson will be a lively event for your students.

Ask for a recap or a poll. Here are two excellent ways to end a questioning session: The first is to ask students to recap the session. You can do this orally, by having students take turns stating information, or you can ask students to write down some facts from the session. A second way to end a question-and-answer session is to poll your students. This will force them to take a stand on an issue you have just discussed. Giving students the opportunity to express their opinion rather than passively absorb information will involve them fully.

Use Essential Questions to Stimulate Critical Thinking

"What does it mean when teachers are advised to not smile before Thanksgiving? How have teachers in the past found this advice useful? What can you predict about the effect this advice would have on your students?"

This example of essential questions for first-year teachers illustrates one of the most intriguing concepts in education in recent years: asking questions that develop higher-order thinking skills when students are engaged in efforts to understand material that may be difficult for them.

Instead of questions that ask students to just recall information by rote, essential questions ask students to develop or invent their own answers to complex, open-ended problems. Essential questions ask for insight and understanding as well as knowledge.

Essential questions

- Can arise from curriculum standards
- Often lead to other questions

- Are open-ended
- Can be controversial
- Can be revisited repeatedly during the course of a term
- Can draw on personal, community, school, and technological resources
- Are relevant to students' real-life interests and concerns
- Can provide authentic motivation for learning

How to Formulate Essential Questions with Your Students

To begin using essential questions in your class, follow these steps:

1. Begin with a thematic unit or a strong interest your students may have. For example, your state's standards may dictate that you teach a unit on weather.
2. Work with students to brainstorm questions that appeal to them about this topic. Focus on general, open-ended questions rather than detail-specific ones—for example, "How do changing weather patterns affect our lives?"
3. Use the six classic questions that expand investigations:
   - *Who* is affected by weather?
   - *What* changes are happening now?
   - *When* will the changing weather patterns improve or grow worse?
   - *Where* will citizens be safe from weather disasters?
   - *Why* are weather patterns changing?
   - *How* are we coping with these changes?
4. Work with your students to plan strategies for investigating answers to these questions. Help them create predictions, use planning tools, and select and evaluate materials, resources, and information.
5. As your students gather information and decide how to synthesize it, you should decide how you want them to present their work.

How to Publish Student Work

Students will usually work with greater purpose when they know that someone other than their teacher will see their efforts. Before you publish a student's work, however, consider how it will be received. If the work goes beyond the boundaries of your classroom, will any errors in it embarrass the student? Be sensitive to the needs and wishes of your students before you publish their work.

Many teachers have found that publishing work on the Web is an effective motivational tool for many students. While there are hundreds of sites available for this purpose, you must be careful to have written permission from the student and the student's parents or guardians before you do this. You should also inform your principal, to make sure that you do not violate a school or district policy regarding student privacy.

Publishing student work on the Web is just one possibility; teachers who want to provide an audience for their students have several other options. Consider some of the following choices for your students.

- Display work on a bulletin board dedicated to this purpose.
- Post student work on your class Web page. Again, you should have permission from the student, the student's parents or guardians, and your principal.
- Include the work in a class newsletter.
- Create a booklet of student work for your students to share.

Use Graphic Organizers to Help Students Reach Mastery

Can you imagine how hard it would be to make up a seating chart without the chart? You would have to write sentence after sentence explaining who would sit where. Instead of writing it out, you save time by using a learning tool called a *graphic organizer.*

Graphic organizers are more than visual representations of material. They are composed of both diagrams and words. Students like them for their nonlinguistic appeal. Teachers like them because they work.

Graphic organizers not only help students decode, process, and understand material, but they do so in a way that helps students retain information. Graphic organizers can also help students solve problems and comprehend material quickly. When students create graphic organizers, they can see the relationship among the important elements in the assignment. Moreover, students of all ages and ability levels can use them successfully for a variety of purposes:

- To take notes on lectures and reading
- To describe people, places, events, ideas, or objects
- To compare and contrast
- To determine the validity of assumptions
- To classify and categorize information
- To determine effective details
- To see how parts make up a whole
- To solve problems
- To predict outcomes
- To plan reading and writing activities
- To understand cause and effect

- To support arguments
- To organize concepts into key components
- To analyze vocabulary words
- To organize text material

You will find that there are several common patterns for graphic organizers. Here is a very brief list of some of these patterns, descriptions of what they can be used for, and the names of some of the graphic organizers that could be associated with each one:

Pattern 1: Concept maps. These allow students to understand the attributes of a concept. Some examples include

- Herringbone maps
- Venn diagrams
- Spider maps
- Network trees
- Outlines
- Novel or story matrices
- Hierarchy maps

Pattern 2: Description maps. These allow students to comprehend the facts that describe a person, place, thing, idea, or event. Some examples include

- Characterization maps
- Family trees
- Clustering
- Webbing
- Episode maps

Pattern 3: Time sequence maps. These allow students to put items in chronological order. Some examples include

- Time lines
- Continuum maps
- Circle story cycles
- Story boards
- Story maps
- Chain of events maps
- Cycle diagrams

Pattern 4: Cause-and-effect maps. These allow students to see the relationships that result when one event causes another. Some examples include

- Flowcharts
- Stepladder charts
- Problem/solution charts

If you would like to read more about graphic organizers, two useful books are *Visual Tools for Constructing Knowledge* (1996) and *A Field Guide to Using Visual Tools* (2000). Both are by David Hyerle, and both were published by the Association for Supervision and Curriculum Development in Alexandria, Virginia.

Web resources for graphic organizers are not only comprehensive but also easy to find and use. To find graphic organizers that are already designed for you and your students, try these sites:

- **Teachnology (http://www.teach-nology.com).** At the home page, click on "Teacher Tools" and then on "Graphic Organizers" to access dozens of free and easy-to-use organizers for students of all ages.
- **Kathy Schrock's Guide for Educators (http://school.discovery.com/schrockguide).** This site has useful organizers as well as links to other sites for organizers and even (at the time of publication) a video of a teacher using a graphic organizer with students.
- **Scholastic (http://www.scholastic.com).** Scholastic's site offers excellent graphic organizers of all sorts. On the home page, use "Graphic Organizers" as your search term.
- **Houghton Mifflin's Education Place (http://www.eduplace.com/graphicorganizer/index.html).** Here you will find more than three dozen useful graphic organizers to download.

If you want to create your own organizers or have your students create their own, two software products that many teachers have found to be invaluable classroom tools are *Inspiration* for older students and *Kidspiration* for K–5 students (both available at http://inspiration.com). If your school has these programs installed on its computers, you and your students can enjoy using them to generate graphic analysis of information for a limitless number of purposes. Although neither program is free, the Inspiration company generously allows a ninety-day download for teachers.

Create Learning Centers for All Types of Students

A learning center is an area of a classroom set aside for specific student activities. Although most teachers and students think of learning centers as suitable for younger students, they are appropriate for all classrooms. When students are finished with the day's assignment, instead of waiting aimlessly for the bell to ring, they can move to a learning center. While there are limitless variations, learning centers all share some features:

- Students can work individually, in pairs, or in groups, depending on the activity.
- Students can develop skills as well as learn concepts, depending on the center.
- Students can learn self-discipline through on-task, self-directed behavior.

The learning centers you create in your classroom should appeal to your students and fulfill a specific need. If your students are old enough, you can even enlist their advice and help in establishing centers that appeal to them. Here is a brief list of some types of learning centers that you can adapt for your classroom:

- A center for independent reading
- A center based on news, periodicals, and current events
- A center that involves a current interest of your students, such as a sport or hobby
- A center where students can review and prepare for standardized tests
- A center for vocabulary enrichment
- A center for math review or enrichment
- A center with audio books
- A center where students can work online
- A center where students can review the current lesson
- A center for remediation work
- A center for enrichment work

Teach Your Students to Follow Directions

Teachers expect their students to follow complicated directions with ease, even though many students just cannot do this. Why? Part of the problem lies in our students' impatience with reading long sets of directions (more than three steps) or listening to what they perceive to be a long explanation (more than three seconds).

Following directions well is an important skill that is neither hard nor time-consuming to learn. Teach your students this skill early in the school year, and your efforts will be rewarded daily. Here are some tips to get you started:

- **Make following directions well a part of the culture of your classroom.** Talk about it every day. Work on it until your students see that following directions is not just something their teacher thinks is important but a necessary life skill.
- **Expect and command attention.** When you are ready to go over written or oral directions, expect your students to stop what they are doing and pay attention to you from the beginning of your explanation to the end.
- **Seek clarification.** Ask students to rephrase directions until you are sure everyone knows what to do.

- **Give students practice in step-by-step sequences.** One way to raise your students' awareness of the importance of following directions in a certain order is to give them a paragraph consisting of a jumble of directions and ask them to sort it into manageable steps in the correct sequence.
- **Play a silly game.** To help your students practice following oral directions, try a modified game of Simon Says. Ask your students to do such silly things as placing both hands over their ears, standing by their desk, nodding three times, or holding up one thumb and three fingers.
- **Teach your students origami.** Following even basic origami instructions will not only be fun for your students but also increase their ability to follow written directions. You can find directions for simple figures in library books as well as on the Internet. To begin, try the Web site sponsored by OrigamiUSA, a national educational and cultural arts organization. The site (www.origami-usa.org) has general information and resources about origami as well as many different diagrams for your students to follow.
- **Ask students to focus when you read test directions.** When you are giving a test, teach students to read the directions on the test with you. They should not be trying to complete the first page as you explain the directions on the last page.
- **Be alert to impatient, anxious students.** Don't be fooled by students who inform you that they know what to do. These impatient students just want to get started; they do not always have a clear understanding of the assignment.

To learn more about how to teach students to follow directions, begin with Education World's Web site (www.education-world.com), where you can find excellent lesson plans and activities for teaching the skill of following both written and verbal directions. Browse the lesson plan archive to find the activities that meet your needs.

HOW TO GIVE VERBAL DIRECTIONS THAT ALL STUDENTS CAN FOLLOW

Giving clear verbal directions is a key element in delivering effective instruction. Imagine students' frustration at hearing a teacher say something such as "Turn to page 167 in your books and begin reading all of Section 18. Then answer questions 1 to 9 and 11 to 17 at the end. You have 45 minutes to complete this."

While this teacher is giving directions, two students slip in tardy, three rummage in their book bag, two more realize their book is in their locker, and no one really knows what to do.

How can you avoid the mistakes that this teacher made? It will not be hard if you remember these simple guidelines:

- Don't rely only on your voice to convey your message.
- Don't present your students with a maze of steps to follow.
- Don't begin to give directions until you have everyone's attention.

How to Give Written Directions That All Students Can Follow

Many teachers find it puzzling that some students cannot follow brief directions for written assignments. One of the problems, of course, is that students do not always see the importance of following school directions. Sensible teachers take care to build relevance into every assignment. Here are some other ideas on how to help your students succeed in following written directions:

- Divide large tasks into manageable smaller ones.
- Express directions in the form of logical steps that students should accomplish in order to complete the assignment. List and number the steps in the order you want your students to complete them.
- Don't arrange directions in paragraph style. Instead, separate each step, using a list format.
- Pay attention to the verbs you use. Be as clear and as specific as possible. For example, "Look over page 17" is not a clear direction. Telling students to "Read to the bottom of the first column on page 17" is more specific.
- Keep each statement brief. For example, try "Write your answers on your test paper" instead of "Be sure to put all the notebook paper on your desk away because I want you to just write on the test."
- Provide concrete examples to help your students understand what to do. It is better to give too many examples than too few.
- One of the most successful ways to give directions for a long assignment is to use a checklist for students to mark as they go.
- If the various parts of an assignment are worth different amounts of points, be sure to indicate the point values.
- Take the time to go over directions orally with students. This is especially important on tests that have several sections, each with different directions.
- If you want to call attention to an item, try a bold font, underlining, capital letters, or other eye-catching strategies.
- Check for understanding by asking students to restate or clarify the directions and by monitoring students' work after they begin the assignment.

Here are some strategies to guarantee that every student in your class understands your oral instructions:

Before Class

- Write the instructions where students can read them as you review them orally: on the board, on slips of paper for each student, on a transparency sheet, on a computer display, or on a large piece of bulletin board paper.
- Divide the instructions into small, numbered steps so students know the sequence they should follow to complete the assignment.
- Word each step simply and positively. For example, "Turn to page 117" is a well-expressed direction. "Turn to page 117 and begin about halfway down the page; you don't need to read the top of the page" is not as easy to follow.

During Your Presentation

- Call for your students' attention by using the same signal every time. Something as simple as "May I have your attention, please?" is enough to let your students know to listen to you.
- Stand in the same spot every time you give oral directions. Wait until all students have stopped what they are doing and can look at you. Take as long as you need to ensure that students are focused on you and are no longer opening their books, rummaging in their book bags, or trying to borrow a pen.
- Speak clearly, loudly, and seriously.
- Use the written instructions you have prepared in advance to reinforce what you say.
- Check for understanding by asking a student to restate the directions. If necessary, ask students to clarify and explain until everyone is clear about what to do.
- Consider having students clear their desks in order to listen or take notes as you speak.

> **Don't be ambiguous with directions. Most students want to do well in class and will work to the best of their ability if they know what is expected of them.**
>
> —*Debbie McManaway, 12 years' experience*

After You Have Given Instructions

- Stay on your feet and monitor students to see that they are starting the work correctly. Circulate in order to answer questions or provide encouragement.
- If you see that several students are having trouble with one of the steps, do not hesitate to stop class and clarify it for everyone.

Make Seatwork Appealing

Dull worksheets have no place in today's classroom. While students do need to complete work at their desks, that work does not have to be tedious. Instead, you can make seatwork engaging and interesting as well as productive.

To give seatwork pizzazz, think of what would delight your students as they sit down to work. Do your students like bright colors? Political cartoons? Clever graphics? Options? You should take advantage of your students' preferences to make their work agreeable. Consider the following suggestions to make seatwork a pleasant learning experience in your class.

- Personalize handouts with the names of your students, local places, or interests of your students. Be sensitive about how you use personal facts, to avoid inadvertently embarrassing a student.
- Provide access to a key so that students can check their progress on drill work.
- Provide scrambled facts, words, terms, or other items for students to unscramble.
- If the seatwork has several sections, create a small bar graph for students to fill in as they finish each section. This allows them to see their progress.
- Students of all ages enjoy matching exercises.
- Offer optional work. When students finish an assignment, they may opt for another activity.
- Allow students to use colored paper, crayons, and colored pencils or ink when appropriate.
- Puzzles hold built-in appeal for students. Even a brief puzzle or riddle at the bottom of a page will be interesting to your students.
- Allow students to work with a partner or to have access to a study buddy when a question arises.
- Offer choices within the seatwork itself. For example, offer two sections, and allow students to choose which one they would like to tackle.
- Ask students to create potential test questions with answers.
- Reward students for working well or for completing seatwork on time.
- Allow students to be creative. Even simple activities such as making up their own problems or drawing to illustrate a point will please many students.
- Ask students to give their opinions or to respond to questions in a personal way.
- Make all handouts as attractive as possible. Use a readable font and clear organization, and add clip art when appropriate.

Practice: The Neglected Success Strategy

"An 'F'? How could I have an 'F'? I did my work!" Too many teachers hear this plaintive cry when students receive graded papers. Somehow, students have ignored their teacher's advice to study and have paid for this with failing grades. Students are sincere when they say they do not understand why they failed. They equate the effort they expend in doing the work their teacher requires with success.

In addition, many students do not understand that mindlessly completing an assignment is not the same as learning. For example, many students can look up complicated definitions for a list of vocabulary words while watching television and, at the end of this task, be unable to recall even one of the definitions.

A teacher's task is to help students understand that they must work with attention to learning and that just completing assignments is not enough. One of the most effective ways to make this connection is through practice.

Practice is the ongoing systematic review of knowledge until students master the material. When students practice, their confidence rises with each successful review of the material. They begin to see the connection between their efforts and what they have learned. Practice does not require large amounts of time, but it does require frequent application in order to be successful.

How can you begin to incorporate practice techniques into your lessons? Start by taking a two-minute break from an assignment to review the material that students have just learned. Ask students quick questions about the material. If you do this several times in a class period, your students will have a better grasp of the subject than if you expect them to comprehend it through their own efforts. The key to successful practice is to make it brief, repetitious, and frequent.

Help Students Practice What They Have Learned

Here are some general practice activities that you can adapt for your students:

Have students

- Write a fact from the lesson on a scrap of paper and share it with the rest of the class
- List every important fact from a section of the reading
- Make a quick outline of their notes
- Summarize the reasons why an event happened
- Create a mnemonic device
- Match terms to definitions
- Share a fact from the lesson with classmates, who then write it into their notes
- Write a key word on a scrap of paper and pass it to a classmate, who then has one minute to tell five things about it
- Use flash cards to practice with a partner for three minutes
- Participate in a rapid-fire drill of the facts in a lesson

Using Class Time to Review

"But I read them the test! How could they all fail? I wish my teachers had told me the test and the answers when I was in school." At first glance, this strategy for reviewing for a test would seem likely to be effective; after all, the guesswork has been removed from the process. However, because the students were passive receivers of the information, they did not learn it.

If you want to improve the way you deliver instruction, you should treat review time as an integral aspect of instruction. Reviewing is not something you should force your students to do immediately before a test. It should be part of the daily fabric of the lessons in your class. If you think of lessons as layers of information that your students need to know instead of as large units, it will be easier for you to find ways to incorporate review into each day's work. When you assume responsibility for creating daily review opportunities, your students will be able to build their knowledge.

When is the best time to review instructional material with your students? Each day offers time for brief mini-sessions. Research studies identify the beginning and the end of a class as optimum times for increasing student recall.

If you use the small moments of time that are available each day instead of waiting until right before a test, you will not overwhelm your students with too much information. Here is a list of review activities that can enliven your class and reinforce what your students have recently learned:

- Use a few minutes to teach just one quick and interesting word, fact, or concept about the lesson your students have just learned. Relate it to the earlier lesson in such a way that students will leave your class with something new and interesting to think about.
- Have students predict five possible quiz questions. Ask each student to share one with the class and discuss the answer. To extend this lesson, ask students to share how they made the prediction. This technique will not just review facts; it will enhance students' test preparation skills.
- Hold a rapid-fire drill covering some of the facts you have taught recently. You could do this daily, keeping a running tally of the scores for your students or classes and transforming your review routine into a contest or tournament of knowledge.
- Students of all ages love to play board games. Design a giant one for the chalkboard or the wall. Divide your class into teams and allow them to roll dice to move their team's token along the board if they can answer drill questions correctly.
- Read a brief passage related to the day's topic to your students, and then ask for their reactions. An interesting twist on this idea is to read a passage that does not seem to be related to the topic and ask your students to explain how the two might be connected.

- Divide students into review teams of three or four. Hand each team a transparency and a transparency marker. Allow three minutes for students to write as many review facts as they can on the transparency. The real review occurs when students share their facts with the class.
- Use the last few minutes of class to review the underlying principles of the material in the day's lesson. Reviewing principles in this way on a regular basis will help students focus not just on detailed facts but also on the big concepts in their lessons.
- Have students write three difficult questions and their answers, based on the lesson. Have them select one question to read aloud in order to stump their classmates.
- Use a computer, an overhead projector, or a wall chart to reveal a graphic organizer that will help your students study the material in a new way. If you have been using an outline format, a Venn diagram or cluster web might be an effective way to reorganize and reinforce your students' learning.
- Have students go through their notes and list the key words. This will be much easier for students to do if you have them take notes in the double-column style—that is, if students leave a wide left margin so that there will be space for them to write key words or other comments about the material.
- Have students link ideas and facts in a knowledge chain. Begin by asking one student to state a fact from the lesson. Next, select another student to repeat the first student's fact and add another fact to it. That student, in turn, repeats both facts and adds a third. The chain can go on until you run out of facts, students, or class time.
- Give students a crossword or word search puzzle in which just a few major words or concepts are hidden.
- Teach students to review their notes by underlining, circling, or highlighting the most important terms, using colored pencils or pens.
- Review important information by making flash cards for your students. You can involve students even more thoroughly by having them create their own flash cards to share with the rest of the class.

Talk It Over

How to Deliver Effective Instruction

Use these questions as a springboard for discussions that will help you and your discussion group members grow and develop professionally. Discuss these questions on how to deliver effective lessons:

1. Rate your instructional delivery with the inventory in Self-Assessment 8.1. Discuss what you can do to avoid having your students tune out. How can you use your strengths as a speaker to improve your delivery of instruction?
2. How can you assess your students' learning styles? What can you do to include activities that appeal to varied learning styles in every lesson?
3. If your students were to compare you to a celebrity, to whom would they choose to compare you? What can you learn from this? How can you improve your classroom charisma?
4. When delivering instruction, what student behaviors should teachers overlook? What can a speaker do to hold students' attention and prevent misbehavior? How can your colleagues help you with this?
5. Complete this statement: "When I give oral directions to a class I tend to . . . " What did you learn from this? What can your colleagues suggest to help you?
6. When you conduct question-and-answer sessions, what student behaviors do you want to see? What behaviors let you know that not everyone is engaged in the lesson? What can you do to maximize the effectiveness of these sessions?
7. What can you do to make sure class discussions are valuable and enjoyable learning experiences for your students? What do you need to teach your students about their role in class discussions? What do you need to do to prepare for a successful class discussion? What suggestions do your colleagues have about conducting discussions?
8. What is your own preferred learning style? How does this preference affect how you teach?
9. How well do you give directions? What can you do to make sure all of your students know what to do at any given moment? What steps can you take to evaluate yourself on this skill?
10. What activities do your students enjoy for practice sessions? What activities are most helpful as well as enjoyable? How do you keep the practice activities in your class fresh and interesting?

SECTION NINE

Evaluate Your Students' Progress

In this section, you will learn

- ✔ How to prepare students for standardized tests
- ✔ How to create effective tests and quizzes
- ✔ How to prevent students from cheating
- ✔ How to use alternative assessments
- ✔ How to manage student grade records

One of the most important tasks you will have as a first-year teacher is learning how to evaluate your students' progress in a fair and accurate manner. During this time, you will learn to design tests, quizzes, and other instruments to evaluate what your students have learned. You will also have to do this in the midst of one of the most widely publicized debates in the history of education: the controversy over high-stakes testing brought about by the No Child Left Behind Act.

The stakes are indeed high. School districts have much to lose if their students do not perform well on standardized tests. In some localities, students who fail standardized tests are not promoted to the next grade or allowed to graduate. Test results are also part of the public record. Scores are published by school district, by school, and sometimes even by teacher's name. Thus, the pressure to have students do well on these tests is intense. Regardless of the final resolution of the high-stakes debate, assessments will not only help you evaluate your students' progress but also give you information on how well you are teaching.

Prepare Your Class for Success on Standardized Tests

It is highly likely that your students will have to take at least one standardized test this year. Under the No Child Left Behind Act, school districts rely on standardized tests to assess not only the performance of individual students but also the performance of schools and how well teachers are achieving the goals of the school district.

> **Preparation for standardized tests begins with practice. Students should work with multiple-choice or essay questions similar to those on the test. Strategies to eliminate answers and decipher what the question is asking are valuable skills.**
>
> —*Melinda Cummings, 6 years' experience*

Because standardized tests have serious implications for everyone involved, the test administrators in your district will give teachers a great deal of information about the specific tests that students will have to take. Take this information seriously.

Teachers are often asked to sign an acknowledgment that they have received information about the particular tests that their students will be taking. When you sign such an acknowledgment, you are indicating that you understand the kind of help that you will be allowed to offer your students before and during the testing time.

In addition to taking a professional approach to administering standardized tests, you can help your students by teaching them skills that will be useful in taking standardized tests. The following tips can help you teach important test-taking skills.

- Teach students to take the time to listen as the test examiner reads the instructions, even if they believe that they are familiar with the directions. They should also reread the instructions for themselves as they work through the test.
- When your students practice taking the test, show them how to pace themselves. Make sure they know where to find a clock at the testing site.
- Many mistakes happen because students do not read the questions carefully. Practice reading test items together and analyzing what information the answers require.
- Students often become bogged down in a difficult reading passage and just skim the questions. Teach them to read the questions carefully first and then skim the passage, looking for the answers.
- When students have passages to read, teach them to underline the parts of the passage that are covered in the questions. They can also circle key words or write notes to themselves in the margins.
- Teach the process of elimination in regard to answer choices. Students should practice eliminating the answers that are obviously not correct until they arrive at a reasonable answer.
- Because marking a bubble sheet during a test can be stressful for many students, give your students lots of opportunities to practice marking their answers on a bubble sheet.

- Students must learn to go back and check their work. If the test is a very long one or if it is timed, teach students to check the questions they are unsure of first and then check the ones they are sure of as time permits. When students have math problems to check, teach them to use another method to solve the problem when they check the accuracy of their answers. For example, instead of adding numbers in an addition problem again, students can check the answer by subtracting.
- Teach students how to proofread their answer sheets to make sure that the test item numbers on the answer sheet match the items in the test booklet.

Take advantage of materials provided by textbook companies that are patterned after state tests. Textbook companies know what the states are doing, so they market their materials to be helpful. Use them! If tests are online, give kids plenty of practice online, to improve reading from a computer screen; it's often an awkward new ballgame when they are used to being tested with paper and pencil and then are given the standardized test on a computer.

—Charlene Herrala, 24 years' experience

How to Design Effective Tests and Quizzes

Tests and quizzes are the chief tools that many teachers use to assess their students' progress. While tests and quizzes offer many advantages, using these instruments has a few disadvantages. Too often tests and quizzes focus on low-level thinking skills and offer question formats that do not appeal to the learning styles of all students. However, you can successfully handle these problems and design effective assessments to evaluate your students' progress. The following strategies offer ways to design tests and quizzes that will be fair and valid.

- For a test to be considered valid, it must accurately measure what it was designed to measure. Aim for validity by making sure that the test or quiz covers the content you want to assess. One way to do this is to create the test when you plan each unit of study. Focus first on the objectives for your course and then on the smaller objectives for each unit.
- Include a variety of question types on each test or quiz. Objective questions do not always give an accurate assessment of your students' thinking. Striking a balance between objective questions and essay questions will provide a better assessment of your students than either type will by itself. Vary the types of objective questions to provide more success opportunities for students who may not excel at one particular type.

- Write questions that require students to think beyond the recall level of learning. You can still use an objective format if you model your questions on the format used on many standardized tests. These tests often offer a reading passage followed by questions that require students to apply their knowledge, judge the validity of a statement in the passage, or use another high-level thinking skill.
- Prevent problems with cheating by presenting different versions of the same test to your students. Give different tests within the same class, or give each class a different test. You should also plan to give future students different versions from this year's tests.
- Make your tests and quizzes easy to follow by grouping similar question types together.
- Place the point value for each section beside the directions for that section so that your students can judge their own progress.
- Share tests with your colleagues. If you and another teacher cover the same material, you can save time by using the best questions from each other's assessments.
- Begin any test or quiz with simple questions that your students will find easy. This will help them over their initial anxiety. Make sure to give clear directions that are easy to follow. When you change question types, you must give new directions even if the procedure seems obvious to you.
- Number each page so that students can stay on track.
- Humanize your tests and quizzes with encouragement, hints, and advice. Suggest how long a section should take to complete, underline key words, or even wish students good luck.
- If you type your tests, make sure to use a plain font that is large enough for students to read easily. If you write tests by hand, make sure that your writing is extremely neat.
- Avoid vague questions that are difficult for students to comprehend easily.
- Don't make your assessments so long that your students will not be able to finish them. To judge the length of your test, take it yourself, and then allow two or three times that amount of time for your students to complete it.
- Save your questions electronically so that you will have ready access to them. Experienced teachers create banks of test questions that they can use again in a different format or on future tests.

Quizzes are similar to tests in that they require the same careful attention to fairness and validity. With a few exceptions, you should follow the same guidelines for designing quizzes that you use for tests. Here are some suggestions on how to make sure that the quizzes you design will be accurate assessments of your students' progress:

- Design quizzes to last thirty minutes or less. Because they are less comprehensive than tests, quizzes should be much briefer.

- Use quizzes to lead up to a longer assessment. If you give your students several quizzes before you give them a test, you will have a more accurate measurement of their test readiness than you will if you only offer one quiz.
- It is fair to warn your students when you are planning to give a quiz. Students tend to regard pop quizzes as vengeful.
- Give students quizzes on paper instead of using an overhead projector or a television monitor; some students may have difficulty reading a screen or monitor.
- Oral quizzes are very difficult for students who have trouble processing auditory information.
- One of the chief benefits of giving quizzes is that they offer immediate feedback to your students. Grade and return them promptly—ideally, by the next day.

CREATE USEFUL OBJECTIVE QUESTIONS

Objective questions have many advantages for teachers and students. While it can take a very long time to construct valid objective questions, they are very easy to grade. Also, objective questions are not subject to the grader's subjectivity, as essay questions are. Use the following tips to create useful objective questions that allow you to assess your students' knowledge and understanding accurately.

True or False Statements

- Remember that this type of question is less useful than others because students can guess the answer.
- Make sure that the answers don't follow a pattern.
- Avoid ambiguous statements.
- Avoid giving away the answers with words or phrases such as *not, none, at no time, never, all of the time,* or *always.*
- If you would like to increase the thinking skills required on a test with true or false statements, ask students to explain or rewrite the answers they find false.

Matching Questions

- Involve high-level thinking skills by asking students to do more than just recall information. For example, instead of asking students to match a character with the title of a short story, ask them to match a character with a type of conflict the character may have experienced.
- Make sure that the answers don't follow a pattern.
- Be sure to work out the answers before you give a test so that you can find any words that may inadvertently be spelled with your answers.

- Allow students to cross out answer choices as they use them.
- Offer more answer choices than questions.
- Give several short lists of ten to fifteen items rather than a longer list that students will find difficult to follow.
- Arrange matching questions to fit on the same page so that students will not be confused by having to flip back and forth.

Short-Answer Questions

- Keep in mind that while it does not take long to create short-answer questions, it does take longer to grade them.
- Use short-answer questions to see how well your students write and how well they think.
- Provide opportunities for high-level thinking by using short-answer questions; answers are not predetermined, so students have to think more in order to supply their own.
- Design short-answer questions to yield responses that can be a word, a phrase, or even a paragraph in length.
- Avoid giving clues such as "a" or "an" to indicate the answer. Instead, use "a/an" to give your students a full range of choices for their answers. For example, your quiz might read, "A wheelwright is a/an ______________________________.
- When you ask questions that require brief answers, make all the blanks the same length; otherwise, many students will interpret the length of the line as a clue to the answer.

Multiple-Choice Questions

- Use multiple-choice questions to measure your students' mastery of both simple and complex concepts.
- Don't allow your answers to follow a pattern.
- Avoid overusing one letter by making up the answer pattern in advance and arranging the questions so that the answers conform to that pattern.
- Provide answer choices that are all roughly the same length, to avoid giving away the answer.
- Make every answer choice a possibility by not including options that students can immediately eliminate as possible answers. For example, if your science test includes a question about who discovered DNA, don't give George Washington as one of the answer choices.

ESSAY TESTS AREN'T JUST FOR ENGLISH CLASSES

Essay tests are frequently a source of anxiety for students. They are not alone; educators who teach disciplines other than English may be intimidated by the prospect of administering and grading an essay test. However, essay tests offer many benefits:

- Essay tests allow you to judge high-level thinking skills because they enable students to use their own words to integrate and interpret knowledge from a variety of sources.
- Essay tests focus on bigger issues and not merely on details; therefore, students have to study more extensively for them. This extra preparation usually results in better performance.
- The nature of an essay test requires that you relate to your students in a more personal way. You will be able to comment and give positive feedback on their thinking, their writing, and their grasp of the material.

Despite these benefits, two reasonable concerns can keep teachers from using essay tests: the difficulty of asking the right questions and the length of time that it takes to grade the tests. With careful attention to test construction, you can manage both of these concerns.

The difficulty of asking the right essay questions is a legitimate concern. If you ask the right questions, you will have a very clear assessment of what your students do and do not know. If your questions are too vague to yield the information that you want to assess, then you and your students will be frustrated.

Here are two suggestions to help you write useful essay questions:

Teach your students with confidence. Instill the confidence in them that they will be prepared. Don't let your anxiety about tests transfer to students.

—Luann Scott, 31 years' experience

- Focus first on the large objectives for the subject that you teach. Use these as a springboard to formulate questions about the larger issues that the material covers.
- Use Bloom's Taxonomy of thinking skills to help you create questions that will require students to go beyond the knowledge level of thinking. (See Section Seven for more information on Bloom's Taxonomy.)

PITFALLS TO AVOID WHEN CREATING ASSESSMENTS

Whether it is a third-grade quiz on multiplication tables or a senior final exam, your students need teacher-made assessments that are fair and accurate. To be sure that your assessments serve your students well, avoid using assessment instruments that

- Are too long to complete in the allotted time
- Don't assess what you have taught
- Use a format that is hard to follow
- Don't list point values
- Ignore high-level thinking skills
- Contain poorly worded directions
- Don't match your objectives
- Don't meet the needs of all learners
- Contain trick questions
- Don't match the test-taking skills of your students

Teach Your Students Successful Test-Taking Strategies

Many students have never been taught how to take a test. Without this skill, even good students will fail the tests you construct for them. Even if you design tests that are fair and valid, if your students do not know how to take a test intelligently, the picture you have of their progress will not be accurate. You can overcome this problem by telling students these things:

- Make sure you have your teacher's permission to mark on a test first, but when you can, circle the questions you are unsure of, so that you can return to them if you have time. You should also underline key words to help you focus on them. As you work your way through a matching section, neatly mark through the choices you have used.
- Read all the way through a test before you begin answering questions. Use what you learn as you read to plan your strategy for taking the test.
- Before you begin answering questions, you should estimate how long each section should take. Watch the clock as you work through a test.
- You do not have to answer questions in the order they appear on the test. Answer the questions you are sure of first.
- Pay attention to point values. Spend more time on questions with higher point values.
- Neatness counts. If your teacher cannot read an answer, it will probably be counted as incorrect. If you need to erase, make sure that your erasures are clean.
- When you have an essay question, read all of it, and answer every part.
- As you take a test, carefully reread the directions for each section before you begin the questions in that section.
- If you do not know the answer to an objective question, make an educated guess. If you leave a question blank, you have no chance for a correct answer.
- Double-check your work right before you turn it in. You can catch many careless errors this way.

Rules of Student Conduct for Quizzes and Tests

When your students take quizzes and tests, they should not cheat and they should not disturb others who may be struggling with an answer. You can prevent both of these from invalidating an assignment by teaching and enforcing rules for your students to follow while taking a quiz or test. These rules will make it easier for you to give quizzes and tests.

- Don't allow students a few minutes to study before a test. Ill-prepared students may take advantage of this opportunity to write cheat notes.
- Use scrap paper to provide students with a cover sheet that will allow them to keep their answers hidden from other students seated near them. Have students turn in their cover sheet with their paper. Some teachers encourage recycling by having students use the same cover sheet all term.
- Limit the materials on students' desks to the minimum of necessary paper and one or two writing utensils. Students who are allowed to have extra paper might use it to hide cheat notes. If students want to pad their paper because the surface of their desk is uneven, allow them to fold their paper in half.
- Before giving an assignment, have students neatly stow their belongings under their desk and not beside it. All notes and loose papers should be inside a binder. If your students have cell phones, remind them to turn their phones off. Check to make sure that materials are ready before you begin.
- Require students to sit facing the front with their knees and feet under the front of their desk. Allowing students to sit sideways during a quiz or test increases the chances that cheating will occur.
- If students need extra paper, pens, or pencils while they have a test paper, require them to ask permission before searching their book bag.
- Monitor your students carefully until all papers are in. If students have a question, teach them to raise their hand and wait for you to come to them. Do not allow them to walk to you.
- Do not allow any talking until all students turn in their test paper. If you allow talking, other students could be disturbed and you will find it impossible to control cheating.
- Once students turn in their work, don't allow them to retrieve their paper to add answers.
- Set a reasonable but firm time limit. Students who take much longer than others to take a test have more opportunities to cheat and may cause the rest of the class to become restless while waiting for them to finish.
- Take time to check for cheat notes on your students' hands, desk, clothing, and shoes. Students who know you will check will be less apt to attempt cheating.
- Be sure to erase the board cleanly, to remove any information that will be on the test.
- Make sure that you do not leave an answer key where students can see it.

What to Do When You Suspect a Student of Cheating

When you suspect a student of cheating, be certain you have enough evidence before you speak to the student. Begin by speaking privately with the child. Do not be confrontational; instead, remain calm as you present your point of view.

If, after talking with the student, you are still sure that cheating has taken place, you must follow your school's guidelines for handling cheating incidents. The guidelines will likely direct you to contact the child's parents, inform an administrator, and withhold credit for the assignment.

If you suspect that several students are involved in a single incident of cheating, you still need to speak to students individually and handle the problem one student at a time. In such a case, it is important to involve an administrator early in the process because you will need support in order to deal with all of the students involved.

Write Useful Comments on Student Papers

You should think of grading papers not just as an exercise in finding incorrect answers but also as an opportunity to help your students focus on what they did well and how they can continue with that success.

Giving useful advice is crucial if you want students to improve, but how much advice should you give? When you write comments on your students' papers, focus on one or two incorrect items and one or two accurate items. The key is to balance negative and positive comments, regardless of the student's grade.

Tips on Grading Objective Questions

One of the chief advantages of using objective questions is ease and speed of grading. Here are some tips to make this task even easier:

- Group similar items together. For example, place all true-or-false questions together and all short-answer questions together.
- Place questions with the same point values together so that you don't have to keep checking the value of each question.
- Keep the number of total points at 100 so that you will be able to quickly add up the missed points and subtract them from 100 to determine the percentage.
- If you ask students to write short answers, provide lines for their answers. They will find it easier to write on the lines, and you will not have to decipher answers that slant off the page.
- If the test is long, create a blank answer form on a separate sheet that students must use to record their answers.

25 Ways to Give Positive Feedback

It is not always easy to find a fresh way to tell students that their work is good and that they are on the right track. Use these quick comments to let your students know when they are doing well:

1. Commendable work!
2. First-rate work!
3. Your best work yet!
4. A world-class product of your effort!
5. Keep up the good work!
6. This shows your brain at work!
7. You deserve kudos!
8. A superior accomplishment!
9. This shows a great deal of work!
10. Superb insights!
11. You're improving!
12. Distinguished effort!
13. A powerful masterpiece!
14. A first-rate accomplishment!
15. I commend your outstanding work!
16. You catch on quickly!
17. Remarkable work!
18. A superior piece of work!
19. Nice wording!
20. Laudable effort!
21. A superlative achievement!
22. Insightful points!
23. You are on the right track!
24. Your determination has paid off!
25. Show this to your parents!

- Teach students to use a plus sign for "true" and a minus sign for "false," allowing you to grade true-or-false questions very quickly. It is not always easy to distinguish students' answers when they use "T" and "F."
- If a student leaves an answer blank, draw a straight line through where the answer would have been instead of an "X" to prevent students from cheating by adding answers when you go over the graded papers together.
- Ask your students to use dark ink to take a test (when appropriate). Dark ink makes the answers easy for you to read.

- Grade all of the same pages at once instead of grading each test separately. For example, grade all of the first pages, then go back and grade all of the second pages.

Grading Essay Questions Made Easy

Many teachers do not like to grade essay questions because the task can be time-consuming and tedious. It will be even more onerous if students are not successful. With a bit of attention to the construction of test questions and how you will mark responses, you will be able to grade essays quickly. To make your work easier, try these techniques:

- Decide on the basic information you want from your students for each question, and list it on a note card or sheet of paper that you can refer to as you grade a set of papers.
- Assign a point value for each topic you want your students to include in an answer. This will make grading less subjective.
- Teach your students to use the first sentence of an essay response to list the main points of the answer in the order that they will appear. You will be able to check this sentence first to see if any of the basic points that you expect are missing. Then you can check the answer to see how thoroughly the student explained each point.
- Be sure to prepare your students by showing them models of good essay answers and by pointing out how they can write answers similar to the models.
- Don't try to write correct answers for your students. Instead, give them the information they need to revise their own answers.
- Find a balance between negative and positive comments. Students learn more from constructive criticism than from hastily written negative comments.
- Teach your students the importance of neat handwriting in an essay answer.
- Separate essay papers into several stacks so that you can take a break between stacks.

When I have students come to me after a test and they are all excited about how far they have come and they want to thank me for it, I get all happy inside, knowing that I helped at least one student.

—Julie Savoy, 3 years' experience

How to Use Assessment Data

While you will probably receive useful data from the standardized tests that your students have taken in the past and any that they may take while in your class, every assessment that you give will also provide much valuable information. All assessments, even final exams, can yield important information that will help you become a better teacher. The feedback from tests, quizzes, and other assessments can also help you raise the achievement levels of your students if you take the time to analyze it. For example, if a number of students missed the same question, take a closer look. Ask yourself these questions:

- Did I adequately cover the material covered by the question?
- Did I word the question poorly?
- Did I provide enough practice or review?
- Do students need to change the way they prepare?
- How can I improve the way I taught this material?
- How can I improve the way I assess my students' knowledge?

Teachers should never assume that all students are experts at a particular skill just because it seems easy for some.

—Sabrina Richardson,
7 years' experience

In addition, you can also ask your students questions about assessments. Consider asking students to write explanations of why they missed the questions they did, how they prepared, and how the lessons leading to the assessment could have been more helpful. With this feedback, you can improve their learning and your teaching.

What to Do If Many of Your Students Fail a Test

Few things are as discouraging as having a number of students fail a test. When this happens, there are three possible causes: the test itself is flawed, students did not prepare for the test, or you did not sufficiently help students master the material before giving the assessment. Here are some suggestions on how to handle each problem:

PROBLEM: THE TEST IS FLAWED.

Suggestions: Look at the test. Is the format easy for students to follow? Are the point values logical? Do the questions match the way you taught the material? You can correct this situation by designing another test and using the one that students failed as a pretest and study guide.

PROBLEM: STUDENTS DID NOT PREPARE FOR THE TEST.

Suggestions: Determine the reasons why your students did not prepare for the test. Ask them to describe how they studied and why they did not study more. Teach students how you want them to review. You can also correct this problem by designing a new test and using the one that students failed as a pretest or a study guide.

PROBLEM: YOU DID NOT SUFFICIENTLY HELP STUDENTS MASTER THE MATERIAL.

Suggestions: Sometimes teachers underestimate their students' readiness to take a test. When this happens, learn from your mistake and help students master the material better before the next test. You can correct this problem by using the failed test as a review guide to help students determine what they don't know. Remedy the situation by providing additional instruction and then retesting.

How to Encourage Students to Correct Their Errors

It happens every day in classrooms everywhere: a teacher returns papers he or she has spent hours carefully grading, only to have students glance at the grade and toss the paper aside. You can prevent this from happening in your class if you teach students that their learning does not stop when they finish a test.

You can help students learn from their mistakes by teaching them to correct the errors they make on assessments. Here are some suggestions for making error correction an integral part of assessment in your class:

- Hold students accountable for correcting errors by making it a graded assignment.
- Consider devoting class time to making sure that students know how to make the kinds of corrections you want from them.
- Be consistent in expecting students to correct their errors after every test or quiz. Once it is part of the routine, students will be inclined to do it.
- Don't allow students to just copy a correct answer from another student. They should explain why the answer is correct or why they missed it.
- If students know that their corrections will be graded before you actually go over the answers with them, they will pay closer attention.
- Consider asking students to explain how they can avoid making similar errors in the future.

Alternative Assessments

Alternative assessments are evaluation instruments you can use in addition to traditional tests and quizzes to measure student achievement. Alternative assessments have become popular in the last few years as educators realize that traditional methods do not always meet the needs of all learners.

Students who do not read or write well struggle with tests and quizzes, even though they may know the material as well as students with stronger verbal skills. Recognizing the need for a variety of assessments, educators have developed a wide variety of evaluation instruments to measure what their students know.

Begin slowly, choosing alternative assessments that are easy to manage. As you grow in confidence and as you get to know your students' strengths and weaknesses, you can incorporate assessments that are more extensive. When you make up your next assessment, consider using some of the following assessments in addition to traditional measurements.

- Oral reports
- Research projects
- Creative projects
- Posters
- Work contracts
- Models
- Booklets
- Online assessments
- Class Web pages
- Self-evaluations
- Peer evaluations

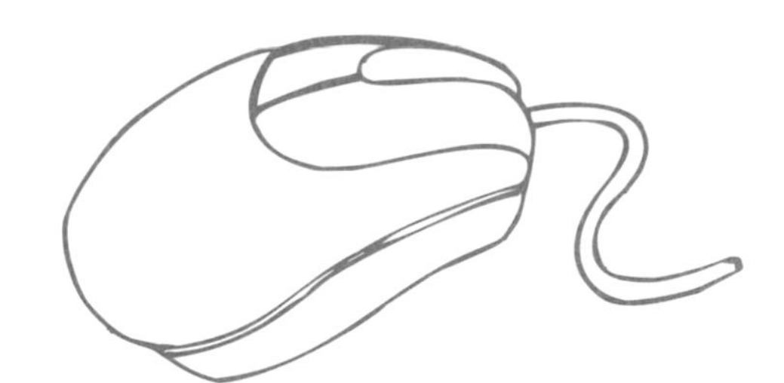

How can you determine whether an alternative assessment will be successful with your students? Follow these suggestions:

- ▶ Make sure to align the assessment very closely with the material. For example, asking students to demonstrate a process is an appropriate assessment after you have taught them the steps of the process.
- ▶ Give scoring information to students when you make the initial assignment. No matter which method of assessment you use, your students need to know the criteria for success as they begin their work.

The following paragraphs provide more information on some alternative assessments you might wish to try during the school year. The list begins with some that you may find particularly easy to incorporate into your lessons.

OPEN-ENDED QUESTIONS

When answering open-ended questions, students can reveal what they know about a topic without the constraints of fixed-answer responses. Skillfully worded open-ended questions can elicit a great deal more information about a topic than objective questions can. If you use open-ended questions based on real-world situations, you will elicit meaningful responses that require students to use high-level thinking skills. Here are some examples of open-ended questions:

- How did pioneer settlers in 1825 experience hardships similar to the ones you and your classmates experience?
- Predict the changes that the main character will have to go through before the end of the book, and tell whether each one is positive or negative.
- How do you think Thomas Jefferson would feel about the laws on illegal immigration today? Explain your answer.
- Describe several ways that you can learn about another country. If you were planning a trip, which one would you prefer? Why?

VARIATIONS ON TRADITIONAL TESTS

There are many variations on traditional tests that can help you assess your students' knowledge. Use one or more of the following:

- **Group tests:** Students work as a group to answer questions.
- **Pairs tests:** Students work in pairs to answer questions.
- **Take-home tests:** Students work out the answers to the test at home.
- **Open-book or open-note tests:** Students can refer to their book or their notes when answering questions.

PERFORMANCE ASSESSMENTS

Instead of asking students to write answers, you can give them a task to perform in order to elicit the information you need to measure. Some examples of activities suitable for this type of assessment include these:

- Science experiments
- Oral reports
- Skits
- Demonstrations
- Book talks
- Projects

JOURNALS AND LEARNING LOGS

Journals and learning logs are particularly useful as alternative assessments because they allow students to reflect on their learning.

Learning logs are different from traditional journal assignments because they do not focus on diary-style entries. Although they are frequently grouped together as writing tasks, journals and learning logs are used for different purposes. When students write a journal entry, they react to the material under study in a personal, subjective way, expressing their opinions. When students write a learning log entry, they write a response that is factual, objective, and more impersonal than a journal entry. In both types of writing, students write about what they have learned and how they learn the material. Both of these assessments are particularly easy to adapt to students of all ages and abilities.

INTERACTIVE RESPONSE SYSTEMS

One of the most exciting new alternatives to traditional assessments is interactive response systems, automated assessments that allow students to use a software program, computers, and handheld response pads to answer questions. When using interactive response systems, students usually read questions on a shared monitor or projector screen and record their answers by clicking buttons on individual response pads. Because the feedback is immediate, students learn quickly. The advantages of interactive response systems are immediate feedback and highly motivated students. Although such a system is too expensive for you to purchase by yourself, your school may already have a system. If so, your students will enjoy the opportunity to assess their knowledge with a clicker. To learn more about how to use an interactive response system to assess your students, try searching these Web sites:

- **eInstruction Corporation (www.einstruction.com).** Over a million students have used eInstruction's user-friendly response system, which was launched in 2000. To learn more about how to use the innovative Classroom Performance System, visit the eInstruction site and explore with a video tour.
- **Qwizdom (www.qwizdom.com).** This site offers a great deal of information about Qwizdom's various software products, which were created to help teachers create lively presentations and interactive quizzes. Using Qwizdom's versatile site and online tutorials, you can easily access a great deal of useful material about interactive response systems.

> Some students learn better by reading the text from cover to cover, others by watching a video about the material; still others listen well and absorb every word from your mouth, and then there are those who will create a poster, diorama, shoebox display, or needlecraft rendition of the material. Include all or most of these different venues in your teaching style.
>
> *—Marlene M. Stanton, 23 years' experience*

RUBRICS

A rubric is a sophisticated assessment tool that more and more teachers are using to evaluate what their students understand. Like other good ideas, rubrics began simply and have grown in usefulness as more teachers have learned to adapt them.

Both students and teachers use rubrics. Students use them to complete assignments, while teachers use them to assess student performance. Although rubrics save teachers time in grading student work, the success of rubrics lies mainly in the clarity they provide about what is expected when students complete assignments.

Goals are very clear when students receive a rubric before they begin an assignment. Because students know what to do, their work is usually of higher quality than it is with traditional assessments. An added benefit of rubrics is that they force students to critique and reflect on their own work. Rubrics often help students find and correct mistakes before their teacher has to subtract points for errors.

How can you use rubrics in your class? While it takes practice and patience to learn how to develop a clearly expressed rubric, you can begin with these steps:

1. Determine the criteria by which you will grade an assignment.
2. Decide on the levels of mastery you want in an assignment. Begin by determining the best and the worst levels, and then determine the levels in between. Although you can use a scale with only three or four levels of quality, it will be easier for you to assign a final grade if you use a scale that matches the traditional A–F scale.
3. Create your own rubric, using a chart format similar to the one in the sample rubric that follows. Using a chart makes it easier for students to see the relationships among the various assessment items.
4. Show students models of acceptable and unacceptable assignments. Demonstrate how you would evaluate each assignment, using the rubric.
5. Encourage students to practice using a rubric with several model assignments before you move them to self-assessments.

Web Resources for Rubrics

Many Web sites are devoted to the various types of rubrics. To begin refining your knowledge and to access free models, try these three outstanding sites:

- **4Teachers (www.4teachers.org).** At this helpful site, you will find RubiStar, a tool that allows you to create customized rubrics for all grade levels, in English and in Spanish. You can save the rubrics you create online, and modify them whenever you need to.
- **Kathy Schrock's Guide for Educators (http://school.discovery.com/schrockguide/assess.html).** This site has dozens of rubric articles, along with examples and instruc-

Sample Rubric

Here is a sample rubric that students could use with an assignment requiring them to create a map of the United States.

	Criterion			
Qualities	Excellent "A"	Above Average "B"	Average "C"	Needs Work "D" or "F"
Neatness	Lettering is very neat. States are colored.	Lettering is neat. States are colored.	States are colored. Lettering is sloppy.	States are not colored.
Accuracy	All capitals, states, and features are correct.	Almost all elements are correct.	More than 75% of the elements are correct.	Less than 75% of the elements are correct.
Details	States, capitals, cities, and all major features are shown.	States, capitals, cities, and some major features are shown.	States, capitals, cities, and few major features are shown.	States, capitals, cities, and no major features are shown.

tions for specific types. You can learn how to create useful rubrics and modify existing ones, how to use rubrics in your classroom, or even how to guide students in creating their own rubrics.

- **The Educator's Network (www.rubrics4teachers.com).** This excellent site offers free rubrics on a wide range of topics. It also offers information on how to create effective rubrics, many models of rubrics, and advice on how to use them with a variety of students, grade levels, and subjects.

PORTFOLIO ASSESSMENTS

On a basic level, portfolio assessments are collections of student work over a period of time. However, portfolios can play a much more complex and useful role in your class as you learn to guide your students in developing their portfolio. When you begin to use this type of assessment, you will see that there are several advantages:

- Portfolio assessments allow students to see a relationship among various assignments.
- Students present a full picture of their work and their progress at one time, so you can see the development of skills and knowledge. More important, students assess their own growth.

- The portfolio process requires students to engage in high-level thinking skills. Students have to reflect on the quality of their work as they decide what to include in a portfolio.
- The flexibility of portfolio assessments allows you to accommodate the different learning styles of your students. When students are comfortable with how they present material, their self-confidence can boost the quality of their work.

To integrate portfolio assessments into your class, follow these steps:

1. Ask students to collect their assignments in a working portfolio. There are many ways to collect this material, depending on the type of assignments they will need to save. Students can use boxes, folders, binders, or other ways to store their work products.
2. Select work products for students to include in their presentation portfolio. With guidance, your students can also select some of the products they would like to include.
3. Ask students to evaluate each item in their portfolio. Students can use an assortment of criteria for this self-evaluation—for example, quality, relationship to other items, accuracy, neatness, or others.
4. Assess the portfolios according to the criteria you established for your students when you gave the initial assignment.

Three Types of Portfolios to Try

Because portfolios are so flexible, there are many types from which to choose. Here are three commonly used ones:

- A collection of student work over a period of time—for example, a portfolio of a student's best work over a marking period or semester
- A collection of work relating to a unit of study—for example, a portfolio of assignments relating to a set of skills or concepts
- A collection of work relating to the steps in a process—for example, a portfolio of the material a student has created to complete the steps in a project, demonstration, or experiment

Web Resource on Using Student Portfolios

Although there are many Web sites concerned with student portfolios, the Family Education Network site (www. teachervision.com) has excellent general information to get you off to a good start in using a portfolio assessment. At this site, you will find an introduction to portfolios, tips on how to implement them, and information on specific types of portfolios for various grades and subjects. At the home page, click on the "Lesson Plans" tab and then select "Assessment."

Keeping Track of Grades

Although you hope it will not happen to you, many teachers have had to produce their grade book as evidence in court. Because your grade book is a legal document, you must maintain it meticulously throughout the year. Your school district will have strict policies about how you are to keep student grade records, and you should follow them precisely.

There are three ways you can record student grades: record all grades electronically, record all grades on paper, or use a combination of paper and electronic record keeping.

The combination approach is currently the most common way that teachers maintain grade records. Here's why:

- Electronic grade systems can fail.
- You can lose a paper grade book.
- A paper grade book is usually more portable than an electronic grade book.
- One method can serve as a backup for the other.

To manage both types of grade books successfully, you will have to be very organized. Following are some tips for success in managing student grade books.

GENERAL INFORMATION ON GRADE MANAGEMENT

- You should perform a variety of assessments during a marking period, to provide balance in the types of grades that your students earn. For example, if you use grades from class work, quizzes, projects, portfolios, and tests to determine a student's average, you will have a more accurate assessment of what a student knows than if you rely only on test and quiz grades.
- You should collect several grades each week so that you can have an accurate idea of each student's progress.
- You should determine how you will weight your grades before school begins. In general, you should have a greater percentage of objective measurements (as opposed to subjective ones).
- You must inform your students of how you will weight their grades. Many teachers post this information in a conspicuous place and also send it home in a letter to parents and guardians at the start of the term.
- You should plan the assessments you are going to use during a marking period before it begins. While you do not have to know what every small assignment will be, you should know what your basic plan is—for example, "Students will keep a portfolio" or "There will be ten quizzes and four tests."

- When you plan your grades, you must also plan how you are going to handle missing work, make-up work, and assignments for students who are homebound.
- Students' grades are confidential; the Family Educational Rights and Privacy Act protects them. By law, you should never announce grades, post grades, tell a student's grade to a classmate, or allow students to look at your grade book.

PAPER GRADE BOOKS

- Never leave your grade book where a student can take it. Keep track of your grade book by keeping it in the same place each day. You should either lock it away securely at night or take it home with you.
- Use black ink in your grade book whenever you can. Be very neat.
- Record your students' names in alphabetical order. You should also include student identification numbers if you will be required to use them during the term.
- You should record the dates when your class will meet at the top of each column if you will be maintaining attendance records in your grade book.
- At the bottom of each column, you should record the specific names of assignments. For example, write "Quiz on Chapter 1," "Fractions Test," or "Homework, page 17" rather than "quiz," "test," and "homework" so that you can quickly identify the assignment later in the term.
- When you record grades, place a line under the box where a student's grade will be if the student is absent and needs to make up an assignment. Convert this line to a circle when the student makes up the work. This will be very useful when you need to transfer your paper grades to an electronic program or when you have to average grades by hand. You will know whether a student has made up the work, and it will make it easier to take the missing grade into account when you input or average grades because you will be able to easily find the spot on the page.

ELECTRONIC GRADE BOOKS

- Schedule a set amount of time each week to update your electronic grade book. Trying to record hundreds of grades the day before you are supposed to give report cards to students is almost impossible.
- Save your grades in several places. Be very careful to keep all copies secure, however.
- Be aware that students can read the screen when you record grades while they are present. Place your classroom computer in a spot where you can maintain confidentiality.
- One good reason to print grades for students often is so your students can help you correct errors. To maintain your students' privacy, keep the printouts of their grades in a secure place, just as you would a paper grade book.

- If your school district requires you to keep electronic grades, you should use a password to protect them.
- If your school district does not require all teachers to use the same electronic grade book program, there are several good ones that you can purchase. Here are some grade books that other teachers have found easy to use:
  - **Learner Profile (www.learnerprofile.com).** This grade book not only records grades but tracks Adequate Yearly Progress information and allows users to access test objectives for Houghton Mifflin reading tests.
  - **MyGradeBook (www.mygradebook.com).** This grade book by Pearson Education offers grade and attendance management on an online site, allowing teachers to access it from home as well as at school.
  - **Microsoft Excel (www.microsoft.com/education/ManagingGrades.mspx).** You can use an online tutorial to learn how to manage student grades with Excel 2002. It can be customized to fit your needs and to help you organize and analyze student grades.
  - **GradeBookWizard (www.gradebookwizard.com).** This grade book allows teachers to access their grade and attendance information online. It also offers a class Web site feature that teachers can use to post other information about their class.

How to Personalize a Grade Report

One of the best ways to send home meaningful grade reports is to personalize them. There are two types of information that you can place on a report: general information intended for all parents or guardians and information that is specific to each child.

Many types of general information can be included on a grade report. Parents and guardians will appreciate a notice of upcoming events such as science fairs, project due dates, or parent conference days. You can also include your contact information, in case parents or guardians want to discuss the grade report with you.

In addition to the general information on a grade report, you should include information that is specific to the student. Here you can explain matters such as the due dates for any missing work or why the grade is what it is; if appropriate, you can write a brief note thanking parents and guardians for their support. You should also be sure to make a positive comment about the child on each grade report. If you have trouble thinking of fresh ways to write comments about students, you can get ideas from other teachers who have had this problem and shared their solutions with others. For hundreds of comments that you can use on grade reports, try these terrific Web sites:

- **Teach Net (www.teachnet.com).** At this site's home page, click first on "Power Tools" and then on "How To," "End of Year," and "Report Card Comments" to bring up many useful comments.

- **Teachers Network (www.teachersnetwork.org).** At this site, click first on the "How-To's" tab and then on "Report Card Comments" to find great ideas for constructive grade report comments.

What to Do When a Student Challenges a Grade

It is only natural for students to challenge their grades throughout the term. If you do not handle their challenges well, the resulting problems may cause long-term resentment. Here are suggestions for dealing with student challenges in a way that benefits everyone involved:

- **Take a proactive attitude.** Anticipate that some of your students will challenge their grades, and prevent as many problems as you can by being proactive. Here's how:
  - Make sure that your assessments and the weights for each one are in keeping with your district's policies.
  - Publish the grading scale for your class so that students know just how much weight a particular assignment will have.
  - Be careful to have many assessments for your students and to vary the types of assignments you use so that your students will have many different opportunities for success.
- **Do not take the challenge personally.** Focus on the complaint and not on the fact that a student is questioning your judgment.
- **Listen to students.** Their complaints, even if they are not legitimate, are often the result of confusion. Take what students have to say seriously, and use their complaints to improve your teaching.
- **Expect challenges to daily or weekly assignments.** When you go over a graded assignment with students, tell them that you could have made mistakes. Ask them to let you know about mistakes you have made by putting a large question mark beside any item they would like you to look at again. They should also write a note to let you know why they are challenging the grade. Collect those papers and look at them again. By doing so, you are letting your students know that you will address their concerns. You will also benefit because you won't have a group of students shouting at you.
- **Expect challenges to progress reports or report cards.** You can preempt many of these challenges by letting students know their averages more often than when progress reports and report cards are distributed. If you use an electronic grading program, print copies of averages frequently. Another advantage of this practice is that students can help you correct errors you may have made in recording grades.
- **Sometimes students are mistaken.** When a student challenges a grade and is mistaken, take care to explain the error completely. Thank the student for checking with you, and encourage him or her to continue to be concerned about the work.

Talk It Over

How to Evaluate Your Students' Progress

Use these questions as a springboard for discussions that will help you and your discussion group members grow and develop professionally. Discuss these questions about how to evaluate your students' progress:

1. Discuss the problems you and your colleagues can anticipate that your students will have with traditional assessments. How can you solve these problems?
2. Think back to a time when you performed poorly on a test. How did you feel? How did you react? How can you use this experience to be a better teacher?
3. Which types of assessments do your students prefer? Why? Which types of assessments should you use most often? Why? How can you explore ways to make your assessments more useful?
4. Traditional tests and quizzes can be useful tools for evaluation. How can you maximize their effectiveness? How can your colleagues help you with this?
5. What are some of the flaws associated with objective test questions such as true-false or matching items? What are some of the benefits of such questions? How can you make sure that the objective questions in your class are fair indicators of your students' knowledge?
6. Asking students to write essay questions is a task that too many teachers avoid. Discuss how you can use essay questions in your class and not spend hours grading papers.
7. Discuss what you should do if many of your students fail a test. Who can help you learn about your school's policy on student failures? What can you do to prevent this from happening (or happening again)?
8. How have you prepared your students for the standardized tests they will take this term? What test-taking skills are important for them to know? How have you taught those skills? Where can you find more information on how to prepare students for standardized tests?
9. What kinds of alternative assessments would work well in your class? Discuss how you can incorporate these assessments into your lessons.
10. What plans have you made in order to manage your students' grades in an organized way? What does your school district expect of you? What tips can other professionals in your building share with you to help make this workload easier?

SECTION TEN

Motivate Your Students to Succeed

In this section, you will learn

- ✔ How to include motivation techniques in every lesson
- ✔ How to help students set and achieve goals
- ✔ How to manage successful group work
- ✔ How to use games in your classroom
- ✔ How to use positive reinforcement

If your students are so engaged in their work that they groan when the bell rings to end class, you know you have been successful in motivating them to succeed. If you have not been successful in motivating them, even beautifully planned lessons and a flawless presentation will be in vain, because your students will not be interested.

The Self-Fulfilling Prophecy

You have enormous power over the lives of your students. In fact, you can make the children in your classroom into successful students or you can make those same children into failures. Your beliefs about your students form a self-fulfilling prophecy.

The self-fulfilling prophecy begins with the expectations you have about your students. These expectations are your unconscious as well as your conscious attitudes about your students' ability to succeed. You communicate those expectations to your students in many subtle ways—for example, through your body language, by the assignments you make, in the language you use, and through how much time you spend with individual students.

Because humans tend to behave as they are treated, your students will react to the way that you communicate your expectations to them. If you think highly of your students, they will tend to behave better for you than they do for teachers who obviously do not enjoy being with them.

If you believe that the students in your class are capable of good behavior and academic success, then your students are highly likely to behave well and strive for success. When you begin to think about how you will motivate your students to succeed, don't disregard the remarkable power of the self-fulfilling prophecy. After all, somewhere along the way, a teacher had faith in you and empowered you through that faith.

Ways to Motivate Your Students

To motivate your students, include the following ten practices in your repertoire of teaching skills:

1. **Call on every student every day.** Students who know they will not be held accountable for answering a homework question or responding in a class discussion are not going to try as hard as students who know you are going to call on them.
2. **Ask students to evaluate themselves.** If students know in advance that they will have an opportunity to assess how well they accomplished their goals, they will work harder to meet those goals. Evaluating assignments as a group or with a partner has a similar effect of encouraging students to have a serious attitude toward their work.
3. **Employ cooperative assignments.** Students usually enjoy the process and excitement of being in a group. Working in groups encourages responsibility, and the division of labor and mutual encouragement make students' workload easier to manage.
4. **Provide audiences for student work.** If you are the only audience that your students will have all year, they are missing many opportunities. If your students know that their work will be placed on display, published, read aloud, or shared over the school public address system, they will take it more seriously than if you are the only person who will see it. (See Section Eight for more advice on publishing student work.)
5. **Ask open-ended questions.** Posing open-ended questions gives students the opportunity to employ high-level thinking skills and creative approaches to problems and reduces the risk of failure. Many students who hesitate to answer objective questions will welcome the challenge of open-ended questions.
6. **Make sure that your expectations are high.** If students believe that you do not think them capable of hard work, they will not deliver it. Students are often more capable than their teachers believe them to be. Motivate your students to do their best, and they will strive to live up to your expectations.

7. **Arouse students' curiosity.** If you do things such as ask provocative questions, show an odd painting, or even hold up a large box and ask students to tell you what's inside, you'll get their attention and make them want to learn more.
8. **Allow student input whenever you can.** Your students should be involved in planning some of the assignments they have to do. Students who have choices will be more involved than students who are just passive receivers of information. Allow them to adjust deadlines, suggest projects, and offer other suggestions whenever possible.
9. **Let your own enthusiasm show.** If you are interested in a subject that you are teaching, you should let that enthusiasm show. Students may not always be interested in every topic that you teach, but they will never be interested in a topic that you do not teach with enthusiasm.
10. **Offer in-depth assignments.** It is better to cover less material well than to try to cover everything in the textbook as fast as you can. While you do need to meet your objectives, you do not have to assign every problem or question at the end of a chapter. Spend enough time so that your students can do independent, challenging assignments that stretch their imagination.

Teaching gave me the chance to share the love for my subject with new minds. I learned a good deal about my subject and life, even, from my students.

—Carole Platt,
35 years' experience

TIPS FOR USING VISUAL AIDS EFFECTIVELY

If you are like many teachers, you already use visual aids to motivate students to do well. You post information on the bulletin board, write on the overheard, make computer presentations, use maps, and draw diagrams on the board. You can expand how you use visual aids in your class in order to motivate your students to learn. Follow these guidelines for making sure that your visual presentations are effective:

- Use visual aids as often as you can. Many of your students are visual learners, and even the ones who are not will appreciate them.
- Make sure your visual aids are eye-catching and colorful but not cluttered with too many graphics or too many different fonts.
- When you hold up objects for students to see, hold them high enough for everyone to see them clearly. If necessary, pass them around after you have finished discussing them.
- When you demonstrate how to do something in front of your class, be sure that everyone can see you work. If you have a handout for students to follow as they watch the demonstration, they will find it easier to learn what you are teaching them to do.

- When you write or draw on the board, write large enough and neatly enough so that students sitting in the back can read what you have written. Erase cleanly. Be sure to allow space between columns or groups of words so that students will not be overwhelmed with a completely covered board.
- Students like to watch movies. They especially like to see movies they have created themselves.
- When you use an overhead projector, project the image onto a wall or screen that all students can see easily. Use a large, plain font. Create a transparency that all students, including those sitting at the back of the room, will be able to read comfortably.
- Use graphic organizers to help students interpret text. A graphic organizer enables students to quickly understand how the most important points relate to each another.

TIPS FOR USING MODELS EFFECTIVELY

When you use a model to show your students how to do a task, you eliminate the confusion that many students feel when learning new material or skills. You should use models at the beginning of an assignment to show what the final product should be like. Models are effective motivational tools because they show students how to do their work well. Make sure you select models that serve this purpose. Some types of effective models include successful art projects, well-drawn maps, correctly done math problems, and well-written essays or reports. Follow these guidelines for making sure that the models you use are effective:

- If you display a model a week or two before you actually teach the material, you will stimulate curiosity and increase motivation.
- When you use models at the beginning of an assignment, be sure you leave them out where students can refer to them throughout the time they work on the assignment.
- Use several different models, to prevent students from slavishly copying from one instead of adapting the information for their own work.
- Spend plenty of time going over a model, explaining its strengths and weaknesses thoroughly so that students can grasp the concepts you are promoting.
- If you want to use models created by students, be sure to ask their permission before you use their work.
- Never embarrass a student by using his or her work as an example of poor work.
- When you use a model with your students, you can increase its effectiveness by pairing it with a checklist so that students can see the key features of the model as you demonstrate it.

Teach Your Students How to Set and Achieve Goals

Students need many positive messages from the adults in their lives in order to succeed in school. One of the most powerful messages we can send our students is that they can achieve

15 Ways to Get Students Involved with Learning

Fortunately for busy teachers, many simple techniques for motivating student interest are available. Try these techniques to find the ones that appeal to your students.

1. Help students set goals so that they can work with a purpose.
2. Use hands-on activities whenever you can.
3. Include high-level thinking skills in every lesson.
4. Give sincere praise.
5. Encourage students to collaborate.
6. Design activities to allow your students to do more talking than you do.
7. Use tangible rewards.
8. Show students how they can use their learning in other classes.
9. Use a variety of media, such as music or art.
10. Send home positive notes.
11. Display, post, or publish student work.
12. Display inspirational banners, posters, and quotations.
13. Give students real-life problems to solve.
14. Make sure that your expectations are high.
15. Play frequent learning games.

their dreams. We send this message to students when we give them a solid reason to study: to achieve a dream by setting worthwhile goals and working consistently toward them.

When students work toward a goal, they work with purpose. They achieve more than students who just appear at school. When students set and achieve goals, they can begin to see the relationship between the actions they take now and their future. Another benefit of teaching students to set goals is that students who work to achieve goals learn how to be successful. They learn to take responsibility for their own actions instead of waiting for others to intervene in their lives.

To begin to help your students set and achieve goals, follow these steps:

1. Hold a brainstorming session in which students discuss the qualities of successful people. Help students see that success is something that happens not by chance but through careful goal setting.
2. Help students determine what strengths and interests they already possess that could help them achieve their goals.
3. Work with students to visualize what they would like their life to be like in the future. What steps do they need to take in order to reach those goals?
4. Use Student Worksheet 10.1 to help your students set goals for themselves and determine how they will achieve them.

5. As students develop their goals, check to make sure that their goals are specific, realistic, attainable, and worthwhile.
6. When students have set their goals, set aside a regular time to work with them in order to examine their progress and make suggestions on how to achieve success.
7. As students begin to see that achieving their goals is possible, continue to help them develop strategies for meeting their goals. Use class discussions and individual conferences as appropriate.

"Why Do We Have to Learn This?"

If your students ask this question, you have failed in one of your most important tasks: making students aware of the benefits of their instruction. Students often do not automatically understand the connection between sitting for hours at an uncomfortable desk and the successful life they envision for themselves when they are adults. You must help them to make these connections. Preempt their questions by teaching your students why they need to know what you are teaching them. Here's how:

- Put the benefits of the lesson on the board so that students will know them right away. Tell students how their lives will be better when they know the material you intend to teach.
- Begin a unit by connecting it to previous learning, so that students can see a progression of knowledge and skills in their schooling.
- Be very specific. Say, "At the end of class today you will be able to ________________. You need to know this because ________________."
- Take time every now and then to ask students to tell you why they need to know the information you are presenting. Make a list of their ideas and post it in a conspicuous spot.
- Focus on why students need to know the information right now as well as why they will need it in the future.
- Draw connections between what your students are doing now in your class and what they will be doing later in the term in your class.

The following answers are ones you should not give when students ask, "Why do we have to learn this?"

- You need it for your test next week.
- Your teachers next year will expect you to know it.
- You will need it for college.
- Because I told you so.

STUDENT WORKSHEET 10.1

Setting and Achieving Goals

Goal 1: ____________________

Date when I expect to achieve this goal: ____________________

Steps I need to take in order to achieve my goal:

1. ____________________
2. ____________________
3. ____________________

One problem I will have to solve in order to achieve my goal:

____

____

Goal 2: ____________________

Date when I expect to achieve this goal: ____________________

Steps I need to take in order to achieve my goal:

1. ____________________
2. ____________________
3. ____________________

One problem I will have to solve in order to achieve my goal:

____

____

Goal 3: ____________________

Date when I expect to achieve this goal: ____________________

Steps I need to take in order to achieve my goal:

1. ____________________
2. ____________________
3. ____________________

One problem I will have to solve in order to achieve my goal:

____

____

Bumping into students a few years after graduation and hearing that they have a job will always put a smile on my face. They almost always tell me they wish they were back in school or wish they had worked harder in school to do better.

—Charlene Herrala, 24 years' experience

Design Lessons to Maximize Intrinsic Motivation

Intrinsic motivation is the incentive to work that is built into an assignment that is satisfying in itself. Although praise and tangible rewards can be effective in boosting students' self-confidence and their desire to do well, intrinsic motivation is the most effective way to promote a fundamental change in student effort and achievement. Intrinsic motivation is always present, even when there is no tangible reward; therefore, its effects last longer than those of tangible rewards.

There are many ways to harness the power of intrinsic motivation in every assignment. Many effective teachers do this automatically when they offer a variety of activities, arouse curiosity, and play games with their students. You can increase intrinsic motivation by including one or more of these ten techniques in each lesson:

1. Help students make a personal connection to the material they are studying. Show them how the material is relevant to their concerns. Try one of these ways:
   - Use students' names in examples and questions.
   - Ask students to write a response before giving them the opportunity to engage in a discussion. This will automatically involve all students in thinking about a response instead of just listening to their classmates.
   - Ask students to draw comparisons between what they are studying and their own life.
   - Have students explain material in their own words.
2. Incorporate your students' interests, backgrounds, and concerns into lessons as often as you can. When students solve real-life problems, they are more interested because they can see the value of their work.
3. Challenge your students to beat their personal best on a test or other assignment.
4. Open class with an anticipatory set that will help students recall their previous knowledge about a subject. This will add interest to the new information you are about to present.
5. Show students how to work to achieve their goals by accomplishing a series of smaller goals.

6. Make an assignment dependent on the successful completion of an earlier one. Help students recognize that in order to understand the next topic they will have to know the current material.
7. Involve parents and guardians in class activities. Keep them advised of due dates and other information that will help them encourage students to stay on task.
8. Combat students' piecemeal approach to their education by using a course outline or a syllabus. Too often, students are not aware of the big picture and don't understand how one assignment will lead to the next.
9. Include opportunities for discussion in your class. Encourage students to debate topics of interest and to share their mastery of a lesson. In a math class, for example, you can have teams of students solve a problem and then explain to the class how they derived their answer.
10. Encourage your students to be open-minded and tolerant of ambiguities so that they will not be afraid to take intellectual risks. Often, students are not motivated to attempt their work because they are afraid of failure.

To motivate students, use daily examples of individuals who have overcome failures—athletes, musicians, and others.

—Nancy Parker,
31 years' experience

Add Interest to Assignments

Many educators complain that they find it difficult to compete with the fast-paced entertainment that consumes so much of their students' time. Although your role is not to entertain your students, you do need to make your lessons as lively, interesting, and appealing as possible.

If students enjoy an assignment, they will take it much more seriously. Listening to a lecture for one hour is not intrinsically interesting to many students. Working in a group to solve a problem or playing a simulation game are likely to be much more effective modes of learning for your students.

Making assignments enjoyable is an important part of your teaching duties. One method is to add creative touches to each unit of study. Here is an example that will help you see how you can modify assignments to increase their motivational potential:

Topic: A seventh-grade history unit on the 1920s

Original assignment: In one week, students will read the chapter, take notes, listen to a class discussion, and answer the questions at the end of the chapter.

Modified assignment: In one week, students will read the chapter on the 1920s and prepare a four-minute researched report accompanied by a project. All students are expected to take notes on each other's projects and to review the content of the chapter.

Time line for modified assignment:

Monday: Students read the chapter aloud in class. They receive a list of the project topics for their reports on Friday. Each student chooses a topic to research. Students review the chapter by completing a homework worksheet.

Tuesday: Students check homework and begin their projects and reports.

Wednesday: Students work on projects and reports.

Thursday: Students continue to work on projects and reports.

Friday: Students present reports to the class.

Report topics for students' independent research:

- The life of one of the presidents during this era
- The life of one of the First Ladies of this era
- Reasons for the stock market crash
- The relationship among ethnic groups in different areas of the United States
- Sporting events
- Medical discoveries
- Newsworthy events of the era in the town where their school is located
- Popular music
- What schools were like in the 1920s
- Leisure activities of children
- Fads and fashions
- Nobel prize winners
- Transportation
- Notable crimes

Suggestions for projects: Students are to create one of these projects to accompany their four-minute report:

- Postage stamp
- Sketch
- Poster
- Map
- Overhead transparency
- Photo collage
- Computer presentation
- Flip chart
- Comic strip
- Banner
- Diorama

Points to note:

- Each student has to master the major concepts of the chapter.
- Students have a choice of topics.
- Each report is very brief.
- Students are expected to take notes on each other's reports.
- The projects are not time-consuming.
- The time frames of both assignments are the same.
- The modified assignment will involve students fully because
    - Students will have choices.
    - The topics are engaging.
    - The topics will enhance the general knowledge that students gained by reading the chapter.
    - Students have an audience other than the teacher.
    - The projects are hands-on.

Help Students Learn Through Working in Groups

Group work is one of the most enjoyable activities you can assign for your students. Because of its popularity and because it allows students to share ideas, group work is a motivational tool that is well worth the effort it requires. Teachers who plan carefully can eliminate many of the problems of group work. Conversely, teachers who allow group work but take little time to plan work activities carefully are likely to experience many problems: high noise levels, off-task behaviors, and confused students.

Using group work to advantage in your classroom requires that you spend time planning what your role will be, creating groups, getting groups started well, designing general strategies, fostering team spirit, managing noise levels, and evaluating groups fairly.

> You can really learn when you teach someone else something. Have your students work together. When students jump in and help each other, I just stand back and watch in amazement at what they can learn that way.
>
> *—Carole Platt, 35 years' experience*

YOUR ROLE IN GROUP WORK

- When you create the assignments for each group, make sure your students have clear and measurable objectives for each activity so that they will stay on task and benefit from working together.
- Group work often requires special resources or adaptation of existing materials. For example, you will need to prepare individual handouts for an activity in which students work on separate sections of a larger assignment.
- You will have to show students how to work well together. If they are to work as an effective team, they need to learn how to divide tasks, how to remind each other to stay on task, and how to signal for assistance.
- Plan to coach and actively monitor your students throughout the time they are working together so that you can help them stay on track.
- You will have to quickly resolve problems that group members cannot resolve for themselves. One of the most common problems requiring your intervention will be students who are reluctant to assume responsibility for their part of the work. Here are some suggestions for how you can handle this problem successfully:
    - Offer support and affirm that you know that the student can do the work well
    - Break large tasks into manageable activities
    - Assist students in resolving their differences
    - Contact parents
    - Remove the offending student and allow the rest of the group to work without distraction
    - Don't lower the grade of other group members because of one member's misbehavior

> **I tell students that I won't give up on them, and I ask them not to give up on me.**
>
> —*Yann Pirrone, 15 years' experience*

CREATING GROUPS

- Although students will insist that they are the best judges of how they should be grouped, you should take an active role in selecting which students will work together. Taking time to explain that you want them to be teammates and not playmates will help students accept your grouping decisions.
- Some teachers use random selection to create groups that will work together for only a brief time. Some ways of randomly grouping students include categorizing them according to their birthday months, counting off, or pulling numbered slips of paper from a hat.

- While random selection is acceptable for very brief activities, when grouping students for extended assignments, you should spend time planning more successful group configurations based on factors such as compatibility, learning styles, work ethic, and ability.
- You will find that a mixture of ability levels and interpersonal skills is the most productive combination for maximum learning. It is usually best to start with teams of pairs and triads so that you can monitor their activities closely and so that they can learn to work well together. When you have gained confidence in your students' ability to work together, you can create larger groups. The task, students' interpersonal skills, students' age and maturity, and the length of time involved are important factors to consider in determining the ideal size for a group.

GETTING GROUPS OFF TO A GOOD START

After you have notified students of their groups and gotten them settled in place, check to make sure that your students know

- How to get your attention
- Exactly what they are supposed to do
- How long they will have to complete the assignment
- What the final product will be
- What their responsibilities are
- How much noise is acceptable
- What to do when they are finished

GENERAL STRATEGIES FOR FACILITATING GROUP WORK

- Plan solutions to any concerns you have about group work before you ask your students to work together. Some areas you may want to consider include ways to increase student responsibility, how to control noise levels, how to increase time on task, and group evaluation.
- Teach your students the interpersonal skills they will need to work well together:
  - Listening to each other
  - Asking questions
  - Staying on task
  - Remaining open-minded
  - Assuming responsibility for group success
- A brief successful activity once or twice a week is preferable to an extended unsuccessful group collaboration.

- Have clear objectives for group activities, and take time to ensure that your students are clear about how they are to achieve the objectives. One way to do this is to have students explain the assignment to one another after you have presented it to the group.
- Design activities that will encourage your students to collaborate, not just divide the workload.
- Establish a few ground rules for group work. The following are some rules that other teachers have found effective:
  - Stay seated.
  - Listen to each other.
  - Face each other.
  - Don't talk to other groups.
  - Ask questions of each other before requesting outside help.
- Teach students how you want them to manage their questions or concerns, so that they do not lose valuable time. One technique is to have students write their questions or concerns on the board for you to address later. You could also have them take a number or place a sign on their desk with "Okay" on one side and "Need Help" on another.
- Avoid assignments that require too much of the work to be done outside of class. This often results in an uneven division of labor. If students are working in class, you can take an active role in supervising them and making sure that all students are participating.
- After students have worked together on an assignment, have them reflect how they worked as a group. They should assess their strengths and weaknesses and how they can work together more efficiently in the future.

WAYS TO FOSTER TEAM SPIRIT

- Take photographs of students working in groups, and display the photos.
- Allow students to name their own group.
- Celebrate small achievements and successes. Establish checkpoint times for rewards.
- At the end of a group session, ask students to share what they have learned from each other during the session.
- Provide each group with certificates, stickers, or other tangible prizes to award to each other for categories such as best communicator, most on-task team member, hardest worker, or best contributor.
- Assign specific roles to each person in the group so that every person has an important task.
- Have a team reporter write a brief report on team successes to share with the entire class at the end of the assignment.

MANAGING NOISE LEVELS

- Managing noise must be everyone's responsibility, not just yours. Select a team member to monitor the noise from a group and alert teammates when the group is too loud.
- Spread groups out in your classroom whenever you can, to discourage them from talking with students in other groups.
- Be consistent about enforcing acceptable noise levels.
- Before you begin an activity, explain what the acceptable noise level is and ask students to share suggestions for controlling noise. (See Section Seventeen for more information about controlling excessive noise.)
- Establish signals for letting your students know when they are too noisy. You will have to devise signals that will not require shouting to be heard.
- Have students move their chairs close together so they don't have to talk loudly.
- Teach students to listen carefully to members of their group to avoid needless repetition and raised voices.

EVALUATING GROUPS FAIRLY

- Assign individual grades, not one grade to the whole group.
- Do not penalize an entire group for one student's poor contribution.
- If you use rubrics to structure and assess group assignments, make sure that students are aware of how you intend to grade their contribution to the group.

Pair Students for Maximum Learning

Many teachers who have trouble tackling the problems of group work can find success by using another method of collaborative learning: putting students in pairs. When you have students work in pairs, they tend to stay focused on their work. Further, a student who is having difficulty with an assignment can often get help from a partner. Working in partners allows students to work out their problems with understanding the material while they are still minor and builds the confidence of less able students because their problems remain manageable.

Be sure to select the pairs yourself; otherwise, students are likely to choose their friends. Although working with a friend is pleasant for students, it does not always make for an optimal learning partnership. Get to know your students well, and then spend time working out pairs whose strengths and weaknesses complement each other.

After you have announced the pairs, have students move in order to sit near their partner. Be sure to have a structured activity for them to complete. If you tell students simply to study together, they will not be as focused as they would be with a specific assignment.

Finally, the pairs you establish should not outlive their purpose. Once you see that a particular pair is no longer positive or productive, switch partners. You may also consider switching pairs at established time intervals. The following are just a few of the many partner activities that work well:

- Check your partner's homework
- Confirm that your partner understands how to do the assignment correctly
- Have your partner check over an assignment before turning it in
- Ask for help from your partner before turning to the teacher
- Listen as your partner explains information
- Share the workload when there are many questions or problems to do
- Share resources on a project
- Combine ideas on a paper, project, or other assignment
- Take turns reading the assignment aloud
- Brainstorm facts to determine prior knowledge
- Preview a reading assignment together
- Take a pretest together
- Generate lists of study questions as a review

Introduce Peer Tutoring for High Involvement

Peer tutoring motivates students because it is highly interesting and because it encourages successful learning. When students work together to help each other learn, both the person learning the material and the tutor can benefit.

There are two types of peer tutoring: informal sessions and formal sessions. Informal sessions are generally spontaneous, whereas formal sessions are often planned to occur after school. Make either type of peer tutoring an effective motivational tool for your class by implementing some of these pointers:

- Carefully monitor two or more students studying together to ensure that they stay on task. It is easy for students' conversation to stray to topics other than the one they're studying, so you must be careful to let them know that you are aware of what they are doing when they work together.
- Peer tutoring will be most efficient when students have specific information to cover in a session. For example, instead of reviewing material for a unit test, students should focus on particular areas of weakness within that material.
- Before you encourage students to work together, discuss with them what peer tutoring is and the behaviors you want from them while they are working together. You should encourage them to stay on task, keep their voices down, and be respectful of each other.
- Limit the time that students work together to sessions of fifteen minutes or less during class and about thirty minutes after school. If you allow longer sessions, students will find it too easy to wander off task.

- One of the most successful uses of peer tutoring is engaging struggling students as tutors. Students who have to work hard to learn the material can grow more self-confident by teaching what they know to others.
- Be careful not to allow students in your class who are quick to understand the work to spend too much time tutoring their classmates. Although it is acceptable to ask your more able students to help their classmates on occasion, tutoring is not the best use of a student's time if it is used too often. If you have several students who complete assignments significantly before the rest of the class, you should involve them in more challenging work and in enrichment activities.

Use Games to Encourage Learning

Your students love to play games. You can capitalize on this natural interest by playing games often in your classroom. Games are positive learning experiences because they provide opportunities for interaction, offer immediate feedback, make the work relevant, allow plenty of practice, and motivate students to collaborate on higher-order learning tasks. Consider arranging team games to help students review, teach each other information, or simply work together in a structured fashion.

Before your students engage in a classroom game, you must establish ground rules so that the activity will be a successful one for everyone. Here are some suggestions for managing games in your classroom:

- Consider the geography of your room before you begin. Move furniture, put breakable items in a safe place, and plan how you will put the room back in order at the end of the game.
- Teach good sportsmanship in advance of the game day. Be very clear with your students about what behaviors you expect from them and what behaviors are not acceptable.
- Make sure there is a sound educational purpose for each game and that you are not simply using it as a pleasant way to pass time.
- Pay attention to safety. If you see that students are so excited that the competition is becoming too intense, stop play at once.
- You should select the team members, so that no one will be left out. Allow students to make decisions about scoring procedures and rules of sportsmanship.
- Keep a container of numbers or other markers on hand for students to draw from in order to determine who goes first or makes other decisions.
- While you don't really need prizes for class games, you could offer ribbons, stickers, trinkets, or bookmarks.
- Your students will find it easier to get into the spirit of the game if you add realistic touches like music or other props.
- Have students assume the roles of scorekeeper, timekeeper, and master of ceremonies so that you can monitor activities.

- Prepare to move your class to a location where they won't disturb other students if the game gets noisy.
- After a game is over, ask your students to tell you what they learned.

GAMES YOUR STUDENTS WILL ENJOY

There are hundreds of ways to incorporate games into your lessons. The first way you can find games that will interest your students is to ask them to tell you about games they already enjoy. Another useful place to find game ideas is on the Internet. Begin your Internet search with these sites:

- **Boardgames.com (www.boardgames.com).** This commercial site offers a large variety of handheld, electronic, and traditional board games at reasonable prices.
- **Dave's ESL Café (www.eslcafe.com).** Dave Sperling's site lists dozens of classroom games, along with rules and suggestions. Click on the "Stuff for Teachers" tab and then the "Games" tab to access the large list. This site has many other resources for teachers, too.
- **Discovery School (http://school.discovery.com/brainboosters).** This page on the Discovery School site offers dozens of brain twister puzzles, activities, and games for all ages and ability levels of students.
- **Out of the Box Games (www.otb-games.com).** This is also a commercial site with a large assortment of games for sale. You can find classic board games, dice games, and word games, as well as newer games.

In addition, you can always adapt games you enjoyed as a child. To give you some ideas as you begin your adaptations, here are some suggestions:

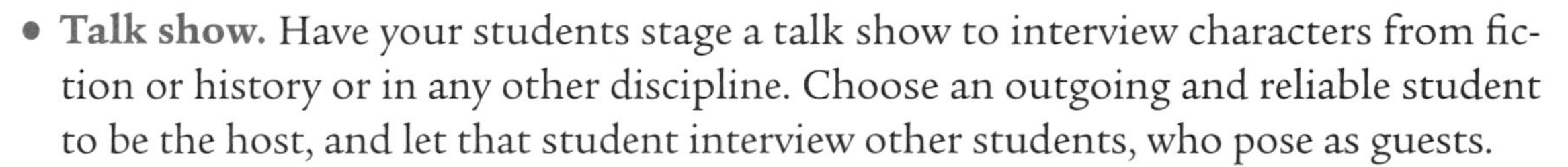

- **Talk show.** Have your students stage a talk show to interview characters from fiction or history or in any other discipline. Choose an outgoing and reliable student to be the host, and let that student interview other students, who pose as guests.
- **Storytellers.** Have students sit in a circle. To play, one student begins a story, stops after a few sentences, and then points to another student, who continues the story. You can adapt this activity to teach vocabulary, order of events, facts, or other information.
- **Quiz Bowl.** Set up a tournament of quick questions and answers involving as many of your students as possible. To add interest, vary the level of difficulty, rules of play, way of scoring, and incentives.
- **Board games.** Design your own board game to fit your topic. You can make small boards and photocopy them for students to use in a small group, or you can make a large board for the entire class to use. The tasks you assign your students in a board game can range from simply answering questions to solving problems. Students also enjoy creating and playing their own board games.

- **Twenty Questions.** Write an answer on a slip of paper, then have students take turns asking a question each until they guess the answer. Keep track of the number of questions that they have to ask in order to guess correctly. In this game, the lowest number of questions wins.
- **Name That Person, [Battle, City, or other item].** This game is similar to Twenty Questions in that students try to guess answers with as few clues as possible. You should make up the clues in advance. On game day, you'll call them out one at a time until someone can name the targeted person, battle, city, or other item.
- **Ball toss.** Line up your students in two teams facing each other. As soon as a student correctly answers a question you ask, that student tosses a soft foam ball to a student on the other team. That student has to answer the next question.
- **Chain making.** This is an educational version of the old alphabet game that small children play. One player begins thinking of an object relating to the unit of study and beginning with the letter A. The next student has to repeat that clue and add an object with the letter B. The game continues until students are stumped or until they reach the end of the alphabet.
- **Bingo.** Many teachers use this game to review vocabulary words. Photocopy a game board with sixteen or twenty-five blocks. Give students a list of words to place in the blanks. They can use bits of paper to cover the words when you call out definitions.
- **Hangman.** In the traditional version, students guess letters in a word or phrase to keep the figure "alive." In other versions, students can give correct answers to short-answer questions or define vocabulary terms.
- **Sporting events.** Divide your students into teams, and use the chalkboard to play games of football, soccer, or whatever sport currently interests your students. Students advance by correctly answering questions or completing assigned tasks.

Use Positive Reinforcement to Motivate Your Students

Positive reinforcement is a much more powerful motivational tool than punishment. Even though it may seem that you should take a firm stand and punish students for misbehaving, you will have more success in getting students to behave by encouraging and praising their good behavior instead. If you want students to act in a certain way, you should reinforce that action.

> **Calling home for a good reason is motivation for students who normally get the bad phone calls.**
>
> —*Melinda Cummings, 6 years' experience*

One of the reasons that positive reinforcement works well with students is that many of them are so accustomed to negative reinforcement that it no longer motivates them to improve. Positive reinforcement, on the other hand, sets a supportive tone that allows students to see the connection between their efforts and the results. Positive reinforcement is also effective because it can move students away from failure and toward the intrinsic motivation necessary for self-discipline.

USING PRAISE EFFECTIVELY

Regardless of their age, students like to be recognized for doing well, and they respond positively to praise when it is given in a sincere manner. Encourage your students by using praise in the following ways:

- Communicate your high expectations to your students. Students whose teachers expect a great deal from them will soon be students who are confident that they can accomplish a great deal.
- Make it clear to your students when you praise them that you are commenting on their work or their behavior and not on their worth as a person. For example, you should replace "You are such a neat kid!" with "Your work is very neat!" This will place emphasis on the activity and will encourage them to continue their good work.
- Do not overpraise students for behavior that is only minimally acceptable; such excessive praise communicates to them that you do not believe they are able to accomplish much and may erode their confidence in your judgment.
- When you praise a student, be careful not to overdo it. If you are overly dramatic, your students will find your praise insincere and you will risk embarrassing sensitive students.
- Be aware of the connection between your body language and the praise you give your students. Let your expression and the tone of your voice express approval along with your words.
- Praise individual students whenever possible, and vary what you say to each one so that they will know that you see them as individuals. Also, occasionally follow up your praise with a positive note or phone call home.
- Be careful to reach out to every student. Some teachers unconsciously favor some students. Be positive with every student at least once during every class.
- Identify specific actions when you praise students. For example, instead of "Good work," say, "Thorough and insightful analysis," and instead of "You behaved well today," say, "I was proud of the way you continued to work quietly while I spoke with our visitor." Knowing exactly what they did well will enable and encourage students to repeat the action.
- Be sensitive to whether students prefer public or private recognition. Some of your students may prefer not to be in the limelight for any reason. If you want your encouragement to be effective, be careful to consider their preferences.

> **Make positive phone calls within the first week of school, or send a positive note home.**
>
> *—Yann Pirrone, 15 years' experience*

- Point out the progress that students have made over a period of time. When you acknowledge their progress, you not only reward students for their current work but show them how their efforts in the past have influenced the present. Everyone benefits when students can see that they are making progress.
- Encourage effort. If you have students who are struggling, encourage them to persevere by praising their efforts. Also, boost their confidence by praising their successes along the way.

REWARDING STUDENTS FOR APPROPRIATE BEHAVIOR

Rewarding students for excellent work or appropriate behavior can be satisfying if the result is students who work for the intrinsic satisfaction of performing the assignment rather than students who work just for a reward. It follows, then, that you should not offer homework passes. These rewards are popular because they allow students to skip homework assignments, but they send the wrong message about homework, implying that it is an onerous task rather than a satisfying one. Instead, offer a pass that allows a student to delay homework for a night.

What choices do you have other than homework passes? One is to offer trinkets and prizes. A good source of inexpensive items that appeal to a variety of ages is the Oriental Trading Company (www.orientaltrading.com). On their Web site, you can find value-priced toys, school supplies, and even a special section just for teachers. Another way to obtain prizes is to enlist the assistance of local businesses by asking them to donate gift certificates or coupons. Many businesses budget for educational donations and are prepared to help you.

You can also create certificates for your students whenever you want to reinforce positive behaviors. Try these free Web sites that will help you create your own certificates:

- **Dyetub Media (www.dyetub.com/certificates).** This site offers many different types of certificates for you to customize.
- **Teachnology (www.teach-nology.com).** From the home page of this Web site, click on the "Teacher Tools" tab and then on the "Award Certificate Maker" to create your certificates.
- **Kids Store (www.certificatemaker.com).** This site also offers free and easy-to-use templates for a variety of certificates that your students will enjoy.

Some of the Best Rewards Are Free

You do not have to spend a fortune on rewards for your students. The most effective rewards are activities that students enjoy. Instead of going shopping for stickers or other prizes, offer students some of these free rewards:

- Extra time on the computer
- An educational computer game
- Being team captain
- Time to work on a puzzle
- Bookmarks made by other students
- Extra credit points
- A walk for the entire class
- A bulletin board featuring their work
- Having their name displayed on a wall of fame
- Having their work displayed
- Watching a film
- Using the library during free time
- Time to do homework for another class
- Being on a class honor roll
- Being the Student of the Week
- Participation in a paper airplane contest
- Extra time to complete an assignment
- Borrowing a book from the classroom library
- Time for independent reading
- Encouraging notes on their work
- A free pass to a school sporting event
- A positive note from you to take home
- Having you call their parent or guardian with a positive message
- Having their photograph in a class newsletter

WHY YOU SHOULD NOT USE FOOD AS A REWARD

For many years, educators used candy, snacks, and other sweet treats to encourage students to do their work and behave well. These edible rewards were fun not only for students but for their teachers, too.

Recently, however, educators have begun to realize that using food as a reward is not a sound practice. Here's why you should not offer sweet treats to your students:

- Childhood obesity is a national epidemic. As caring adult role models, teachers have a responsibility to help students stay healthy.
- Using food as a reward contradicts the information about fitness that students learn in health or nutrition classes.
- When teachers offer candy and other snacks to students, they make life more difficult for students who do not want to overeat.
- You may have students with serious medical conditions such as diabetes or food allergies.
- When you reward students with food, you establish a connection between food and behavior that can lead to problems later in life.
- Parents often object to food as a reward because it may undermine the values about nutrition that they are trying to teach their children.

Talk It Over

How to Motivate Your Students to Succeed

Use these questions as a springboard for discussions that will help you and your discussion group members grow and develop professionally. Discuss these questions about how to motivate your students to succeed:

1. Brainstorm ways that you can arouse your students' curiosity about a lesson. How can you use these motivation techniques when you plan other lessons?
2. How high are your expectations for your students? How do you convey your belief that they are capable learners?
3. What are the benefits of using games in your classroom? What are some games that your students would enjoy? Where can you find more games to use with your classes?
4. What can you do to activate intrinsic motivation in every lesson? What do you find intrinsically motivating? How can you use this knowledge about yourself to help your students?
5. How can you praise your students effectively? Which students need it most? What mistakes in praising students have you observed in the past? How can you avoid those mistakes?
6. Brainstorm a list of tangible rewards that would appeal to your students. How can you find other rewards to motivate your students?

7. When students work together, much can go right and much can go wrong. Predict some of the problems your students will have with group work. How can you prevent these problems?
8. A highly motivated class is often a noisy and active class. How can you make sure that the noise and activities in your classroom are productive?
9. How can you make every lesson relevant to the needs, concerns, and interests of your students? How can you determine those needs and interests? How can your colleagues help you with this?
10. Students of all ages benefit from teachers who frequently use visual aids and models when presenting material. How can you motivate your students in this way? What problems should you take care to avoid?

SECTION ELEVEN

Help Your Students Become Successful Learners

In this section, you will learn

- ✔ How to help your students learn to study effectively
- ✔ How to help students with notes and notebooks
- ✔ How to create a homework partnership
- ✔ How to help students make up missing work
- ✔ How to assist students with projects

Many teachers make the mistake of assuming that someone else has taught their students how to study. However, few teachers teach this important skill, even in school districts that stress the acquisition of study skills. All of the students in your class need your help in learning how to do their work successfully.

The rewards for teachers who teach their students how to learn are satisfying ones; confident pupils are a pleasure to teach. Conversely, failing students are a constant drain on the emotional and physical energy of every person in the class. When you teach your students how to study efficiently, you prevent years of frustration and failure and create successful, self-directed learners instead.

Teaching students how to be successful in their learning is the job of every teacher at every level of instruction. If you want to create a roomful of lifelong learners, teach them the tools they need to unlock their potential.

Habits of Mind to Encourage

Just what is a successful student? Successful students everywhere share similar mental traits that create their academic achievements. Experienced teachers have found that promoting these positive mental habits tends to enhance success. Here is a brief list of mental habits that are appropriate for students of all ages and that you should encourage.

> **I have the opportunity every day to make a lasting impression on each and every young person I come in contact with.**
>
> —*William N. Owen, 43 years' experience*

Students should

- Be confident enough to take risks and not be afraid to experiment
- Be self-disciplined and self-directed
- Take an organized approach to their work and to their materials
- Be open-minded
- Set goals for themselves so that they work with purpose
- Be keenly curious about the world
- Be willing to accept constructive criticism
- Be logical and clear in their thinking
- Be persistent—that is, willing to work until a task is complete

Incorporate Study Skills in Every Lesson

Instead of taking the approach that students need a separate course in study skills, incorporate study skills into every lesson. Here are some uncomplicated ways to make learning study skills part of your daily classroom routines:

- Incorporating study skills into your class will not be difficult if you choose one or two useful skills to focus on in each lesson. For example, if you are going to lecture, begin by teaching students how to take notes while listening.
- When you assign work, ask students to estimate how long it should take them to complete it. With practice, your students will become proficient at estimating the length of any assignment.
- Use a checklist for daily assignments so that students can prioritize their work. List the assignments for the day in the order that students should complete them. When you go over the checklist with students, discuss how long each assignment should take.
- Have your students set goals for themselves and work toward those goals. (See Section Ten for more information on how to teach students about goal setting.)

- Be a good role model for your students when doing your own work. When you distribute handouts, for example, explain how you had to proofread them to make sure they were correct. By talking about your own work habits and consistently modeling them, you will raise your students' awareness of how to improve the quality of their work.

> **Teaching has made me a lifelong learner.**
>
> —*Nancy Parker, 31 years' experience*

- Thousands of Web sites provide suggestions for teaching study skills to students of all ages; you can often find up-to-date tips at sites maintained by colleges or universities. Another good Web resource is How to Study (www.how-to-study.com), a site that offers a large menu of strategies arranged by categories such as test preparation, flash cards, and reading improvement.
- Put a study skill on the board each day for students to record and discuss. You can even hand over the task of researching good study habits to your students by having them contribute a new study skill each day.

STUDY SKILLS TO TEACH YOUR STUDENTS

Use these study skill tips to begin your collection of quick strategies that you can post on the board each day.

- Attend class. Students who are in class do better than those who are absent.
- Prioritize your time. You'll have to make choices about all of your activities if you want to do well in school.
- Focus your attention in class and while you are studying. Concentration is an acquired skill; make it yours.
- Plan your work as far in advance as you can. Learn to use a calendar or a planner and allow plenty of time for projects that may take longer than you think they should.
- Be an active learner when you study your notes. Don't just look them over; underline or circle key points.
- Pack your book bag at night and leave it by the door so that all you have to do is grab it on your way out in the morning.
- At the end of class, don't just sit and watch the clock; instead, try to fit in one more problem or read one more page.
- Allow enough time to study. For example, if you have homework in three subjects on the same night, you will need to spend more time than on nights when you have homework in only one subject.
- Homework isn't something you should do when you have the time. It's something you must do.

- Set up a comfortable study area at home where you can store your supplies and work without interruptions.
- Limit phone calls, text messages, and instant messages on school nights. Make other arrangements with your friends so that you can communicate with them and get your work done, too.
- Find a friend with whom you can study. You'll both benefit from the encouragement you give each other.
- Take notes in pencil or erasable pen so that they will remain neat.
- When you have to read a selection and then answer questions about it, read the questions first so that you can read the selection with purpose.
- Make sure you have the supplies you need for projects and for class. This will save you trips to the store the night before a project is due or having to borrow pens and paper.
- When you pack up at the end of a class, don't just shove papers into your book bag or notebook. Spend thirty seconds stowing your work in an organized way so that you can find it quickly.
- Write down your homework assignments so that you won't have to waste time phoning around to find out what they are or worrying about whether you did the right ones.
- Use your class time wisely. It will save you time at home if you learn the material in class.
- Work with a purpose in mind. If you do this instead of daydreaming, you will cut down on the time it takes to do homework.
- Reward yourself for staying on task for a week or even for a day if you had to struggle to do it.
- Develop a few abbreviations for some of the words you use most often in your notes.
- Don't give in to the temptation to stay up too late on school nights. You need to have enough rest so you won't be sleepy in class.
- Take a break from your homework about every fifteen or twenty minutes. Make it a short break, but get up and move around. Stay away from the television and the phone.
- When you have facts to look up and learn, concentrate on learning them as you look them up. It will take you longer to master the material if you have to memorize them later.
- Always label your work and your notes with the date, subject, and page number so that you can find information quickly when you need to review.
- Try to study at a time of day when you are alert. Most people are more alert during daylight hours.

- Review your class notes before you start your homework. A quick review will refresh your memory and make doing homework much easier.
- At the end of a homework assignment, ask yourself what you could do to learn just one more fact in the assigned work.
- When you find that your locker, book bag, or notebooks are getting messy, take a few minutes to clean them out. Staying organized is an important part of being an efficient student.
- While you want your work to be accurate and neat, don't be a perfectionist. It's not sensible to waste time picking over mistakes that only you notice.
- Take the time to do each assignment correctly the first time so that you don't have to redo it.
- Figure out what learning style you prefer, and use it when you review on your own for tests.
- Study the most difficult or boring subjects first. You will find it easier to do them well when you are not tired.
- Make a list of your goals and the reasons you want to do well in school. This will help you stay on track when you are tempted not to give your best effort.
- Set aside a set amount of time each night to study. If you don't have any written assignments, read or review your notes for an upcoming test.
- If you need help, don't be afraid to admit it. Asking for help when you need it is one of the best ways to be a successful student.

> **Don't be afraid to admit that you don't know an answer. Ask for students' help in finding the correct answer.**
>
> *—Edward Gardner, 36 years' experience*

Have your students fill out Student Worksheet 11.1 in order to assess their study skills. After they have filled it out, you can use the results to help students improve their study habits.

STUDENT WORKSHEET 11.1

How Well Do You Study?

Evaluate each statement as it applies to you, and write the appropriate number in the blank beside each excellent study strategy. If you can't mark "Always" beside a strategy, it is one you can improve!

4 = Always; 3 = Sometimes; 2 = Seldom; 1 = Never

I use these study strategies:

______ Take planned study breaks

______ Have a quiet place to study at home

______ Focus my attention in class

______ Take time to proofread

______ Rewrite notes in my own words

______ Make up missing work on time

______ Spend enough time studying

______ Plan what I need to study

______ Finish my homework

______ Create my own study guides

______ Have someone quiz me

______ Have enough supplies

______ Use a planner to schedule my work

______ Do difficult homework first

______ Ask for help

______ Take good notes

______ Have a plan for taking tests

______ Skim material before reading

______ Work toward a goal

______ Keep an organized notebook

Teach Your Students How to Organize a Notebook

Students who can find their homework papers on the day they are due find school easier than students whose work is less orderly. Don't assume that your students know how to take notes or keep their papers organized. No matter their age, your students may never have been taught how to keep their notes and papers in order. Adopt some of the following strategies to teach your students how to organize their notebook.

- Explain to your students how keeping an organized binder or notebook will benefit them in all their classes.
- Take time at the beginning of the term to make sure that students are getting off to a good start with organizing their notebook. After this initial organization, spend a few minutes each week to make sure that your students know how to keep their papers in order.
- Teach your students to organize their papers by date. This will make it easier for them to find the work they need when reviewing for a test.
- Encourage your students to use three-ring binders instead of paper folders. They are worth the extra money because they can be used for years. Have a three-hole punch available for students' use, making it much easier for them to file the papers you want them to keep.
- Require students to label the front of their notebook with their name and room number so that misplaced notebooks can be returned.
- Show students how reinforcing and protecting the edges of a notebook with sturdy tape will extend its life.
- Students with more than one notebook should color-code them by subject.
- Encourage your students to use reclosable pouches to store pens, flash cards, and other small objects.
- Have students label every assignment so they can quickly find their work.

Teach Your Students to Think on Paper

From Congressional vetoes to fishing licenses to birth certificates, people keep important information on paper. Not only do people have the important events of their lives recorded in writing, but many people use pen and paper for everyday tasks such as planning their day, making a shopping list, or leaving an important phone number for the baby-sitter. Somewhere in their school years, adults learn to do this. A teacher showed them how to plan, how to organize information—how to think on paper.

If you would like this important skill to be part of the culture of your classroom, there are several ways to make it happen. Try some of the following techniques when you want to teach your students how to think on paper.

- Whenever you ask a question in a class discussion, instead of having a few students blurt out answers, ask everyone to jot down their answers first. Wait until you see that everyone has had a chance to finish writing before you ask students to share their answers.
- Ask students to analyze a subject by writing out their thoughts in a quick response. For example, you can ask students to write out the steps of the procedure they used to solve a math problem.
- Ask students to predict what information will be in a unit of study by writing out what they already know or what they would like to know.
- Ask students to write out a plan for accomplishing an assignment or completing a project.
- Teach your students how to take notes. When you show students how to outline a chapter or take notes from a lecture, you are teaching them how to organize their thoughts on paper. To find a template that will make note taking easier for your students, try Incompetech (www.incompetech.com). This ugly Web site with brilliant content allows you to download various templates such as graph paper, writing paper, and calendars, among others.

STRATEGIES FOR TEACHING STUDENTS HOW TO TAKE NOTES

Help your students learn to take good notes, regardless of their age or the subject you are teaching. To get an idea of how to begin instructing your students in the art of note taking, ask them to tell you what they already know about it.

Teach students to come to class or to approach their homework prepared to take notes. At a minimum, they will need paper and a pen. Also, teach students that although there is a difference between the way they will take notes as they read and how they will take notes as they listen, both types of notes involve three steps: paying attention, writing notes, and reviewing the information.

Paying Attention

- If you want to have a successful class, never lecture on cold material. Have students preview the material in their text or in a preliminary handout before you begin the day's lecture.
- When you give notes, put an outline on the board or give students the key points in advance so that they can stay on track.
- Before you begin a lecture, have a brief review session on previous material to help students connect the key points to prior knowledge.

Writing Notes

- Teach students how to use outlines and other methods of organization instead of taking notes in paragraph form.

- Work with your students to develop a bank of common abbreviations and symbols.
- When students need to take notes on a reading assignment, spend time showing them how to use text information such as boldface type or captions.
- Have students take practice notes as they listen to you read a very brief human interest article from the newspaper. Spending just a brief amount of time on this skill each day for a few days will teach students how to identify key points.
- Teach students the Cornell system of double-column note taking. There are many versions of this technique, but the basics are simple:
  - Students divide their page into two parts by drawing a vertical line all the way down the page, dividing it into sections of one-third and two-thirds.
  - As they hear or read the information, students should take notes in the larger section.
  - After students finish taking notes, they should record the key points of the material in the smaller section.

Reviewing

- Work with your students to help them understand that just writing notes is not enough. Students need to learn the material in their notes in order to be successful. Many students, especially younger ones, fail to realize this.
- Teach your students that just looking over their notes is a waste of time and that studying with a pencil is a better way to learn. Teach them to highlight key words, underline or circle important points, and use other symbols to call attention to significant points.
- Students should review their notes within twenty-four hours. Don't assume that your students will do this on their own until you have taught them the benefits of this practice and gotten them in the habit.

Help Students Become Good Listeners

Because listening is the primary way that humans communicate with each other, good listening skills are crucial for academic success. Listening well is a skill anyone can learn over time and with practice. Fortunately, students of all ages can practice their listening skills in many ways. For example, you could read aloud from a short news article each day and then quiz your students about what they heard. Or you could have students enact a real-life scenario, such as making a complaint, and then ask the student audience to recount what they heard.

The key is to offer many practice opportunities appropriate to the age and interests of your students. An excellent Web site for teachers who want to help their students improve listening skills is Many Teaching Ideas (www.teachingideas.co.uk). A British primary school teacher, Mark Werner, manages this site. Although many of the ideas are for younger children, the site has hundreds of useful games, activities, and teaching suggestions for all teachers.

How to Teach Active Listening Skills

You can help your students become good listeners by teaching what it means to be an active listener who pays attention. Here are some tips to help you teach active listening:

- Talk with your students about the importance of maintaining an open mind when someone is speaking. They should listen closely to their teachers and not quit listening when they disagree with what they hear.
- Teach students to listen for the key topics under discussion, an important skill for students who take an active role in their learning.
- Teach your students to generate questions as they listen to you but to hold their questions until you call for them.
- If students are not sure whether they have understood the main points of a presentation, ask whether they can summarize it. If they can summarize what they've heard, then they are competent in active listening.

Teach Students to Speak in Front of the Class

Many people fear speaking in front of a group of people. For students, this often translates into a fear of speaking in front of their classmates. Even chatty students who are not afraid to shout across the room to friends may be overcome with stage fright when asked to present a report to the entire class.

As a caring teacher, you can do a great deal to help your students learn to speak well in front of their classmates. Here are some suggestions on how to help your students become confident speakers:

- As early in the year as you can, give your students opportunities to speak to small groups. It will not be as intimidating for them to speak to a group of four or five classmates.
- Another way to painlessly habituate your students to public speaking is to call on every student every day. You should sometimes ask students to stand by their desks while speaking.
- Students find it easier to be in front of the class when they are part of a group of students. When several students stand together to present various parts of a report, mutual support reduces their stage fright.
- When you expect students to speak formally in front of the class, you must prepare the audience. Explain why good listening habits are important. Be very specific about the behaviors you expect from students as members of the audience.
- When you assign projects that students are expected to present orally, be very clear about what they are supposed to do and set a reasonable time limit.

- Allow students to have some say in the order in which they present their work. Some students genuinely prefer to be the first or the last speaker.
- Allow students to use note cards, visual aids, or other props whenever you can. Having props will lessen their fears about forgetting what they have to say.
- Teach techniques for controlling stage fright—for example, taking deep breaths before speaking to help control anxiety.
- Encourage sufficient practice. Students who are fully prepared tend to perform better than students who are not.

Teach Students How to Memorize

Memorization has earned an undeserved bad reputation. Memorizing facts just for the sake of memorizing them is not a practical use of instructional time, but learning important information is. You can help your students learn to memorize material quickly and retain it. If you make developing and strengthening their memory a part of your classroom business, you are helping your students learn. Follow these guidelines in order to help your students develop their memory.

- Provide students with frequent review opportunities. Students who review frequently and at short intervals tend to do better than students who try to learn too much information at one sitting.
- Make memory practice meaningful. Your students will not enjoy memorizing something just for the sake of memorizing it. They will enjoy real-life applications, competitions, games, and intrinsic rewards for the memory practice they do in your class.
- Allow students enough time to memorize material. Students will find it difficult to memorize when they are stressed or rushed to get an assignment completed on time.
- Structure the assignment so that students can learn a small part first, then piggyback another part on that one, then another and another, until the entire assignment is completely mastered.
- Teach your students to use visual organizers to help them memorize material. They can use diagrams, charts, or even silly sketches to help them recall the important parts of an assignment.
- Show your students how to use more than one modality in their learning. For example, if they make flash cards and make an audio recording of the same material, they will be using both sight and sound and will be far more likely to retain the information than they would if they used only one or the other.
- Remember how you used mnemonic devices such as the acronym HOMES to recall the names of the Great Lakes or a rhyming verse to recall the number of days in each month? Teach your students to make and use their own mnemonic devices for the information you want them to learn.

- Show students how easy it is to learn something when they make a rhyme about it. This is the reason that most of us find it easy to recall song lyrics. Your students can make rhymes on almost any subject if you encourage them to do so. You could even enliven an assignment by asking students to perform their rhymes in a rap contest.
- Teach your students the importance of actively listening in class. They should hear you say "focus" and "concentrate" often as you help them memorize new material.
- Teach your students to study in intense brief bursts of time. Students who actively work at memorizing information for fifteen minutes will be more successful than those who contrive to look busy for thirty minutes but daydream through most of that time.
- Among the dozens of Web sites with examples of mnemonic devices, The Word Play Web Site (www.fun-with-words.com) is particularly easy to use. Select the "Mnemonics" tab for information, examples, resources, and suggestions for teachers and students.

Help Students Improve Their Writing Skills

In the last two decades, many research studies have traced the effectiveness of writing as a learning tool in all subjects and in all grade levels. The result of this work is clear: every teacher teaches English. All teachers teach English by modeling the language that professionals use when speaking with their students, when writing for students, and when asking them to write.

Along with modeling good language skills, you should teach writing skills and hold students accountable for their writing. You don't have to be an English teacher, a grammar expert, or even a veteran teacher to teach your students to write well. Following are some ways to help your students become effective writers:

- Keep a dictionary on your desk, and let students see you using it often.
- Encourage your students to use a dictionary and a thesaurus. If your school doesn't provide a set of these books for each teacher, then borrow a few from other teachers.
- When students ask, "Does spelling count?" say, "Yes. How can I help you spell a word?"
- Encourage students to use the writing process whenever possible. When you ask students to write even brief essays for you, encourage them to plan or prewrite their answers, write a rough draft, edit and revise that draft, and create a final copy to turn in to you.
- Encourage students to catch your errors. When you make a mistake, acknowledge it and correct yourself, showing students that correctness is not something that ends when English class is over.
- Don't be sarcastic when correcting student papers. Sometimes students will make ridiculous or very funny errors. Be kind, and save your frustration and amusement for later. The purpose of marking a paper is to help students learn.

- Circle obvious errors on papers. You don't need to circle every one or use elaborate editing marks. You should not correct the mistake yourself; instead, just make students aware of a mistake by circling it and asking them to make a correction.
- Because students tend to write the way they talk, speak Standard English around your students and expect them to speak it, too.
- Model good writing for your students. Proofread your own work.
- Offer lots of writing opportunities for your students. You can do this on tests and quizzes as well as in daily informal assignments and projects such as reports.

NEATNESS AND ACCURACY COUNT

While some teachers may ask students to recopy papers with only one misspelled word, other teachers happily accept crumpled or ripped papers. Although neatness and accuracy are very important, you need to strike a balance. Having requirements that are too strict will discourage students; on the other hand, allowing students to turn in poorly done papers sends the message that you do not expect much from your students.

What should you do when a student turns in a paper that is obviously not acceptable? Speak privately to the student. Ask, "Do you want me to grade this paper that you have handed in?" If the student says yes, say, "I'll be glad to grade this paper, but you must rewrite it so that it is neat and accurate. Would you like some help so that you know just what to do for it to be acceptable?" With such a fair and reasonable approach, students should be willing to redo their work. If you have a student who refuses to redo a paper, consider speaking with the child's parent or guardian about the problem.

Although there will be times when you will have to ask students to redo their work, some preventive measures will go a long way to reducing such occasions. Start by making sure that all your students know exactly how to do their work well. Then make neatness and accuracy a strong component of the culture of excellence in your class by applying the following guidelines:

- Talk with your students about why accuracy is important, not just on papers for school but in other parts of life as well. One way to open this discussion is to ask them how their lives would be different if doctors, architects, or pharmacists were not concerned with accuracy. How would they react if you consistently miscalculated their grades?
- Your school may have a standard manuscript format for students. This is a standard way of heading papers, creating margins, and other preparation concerns. If such guidelines are not available, ask other teachers how they handle this issue or create your own. Guidelines should address the following areas:
  - Where should students write their name?
  - Where should students write the date?
  - How should students label or title their paper?

- Should students write on the front only?
- Can students use a pen or pencil?
- What kind of margins do you prefer?
- How many misspelled words are acceptable?

Use Exit Slips to Develop Metacognition

When students think about how they learn, they practice metacognition—thinking about thinking. Metacognition activities help students become self-directed, self-disciplined learners. Teachers who encourage students to be aware of how they learn best are teaching an important life skill.

While metacognition activities are essential for high-achieving students, they do not have to be time-consuming or complicated. One of the easiest ways to give students an opportunity for metacognition is by using exit slips.

Begin by giving each student a note card or a half sheet of paper near the end of class. Have students write a brief, informal response to an open-ended question about the day's lesson and turn it in as they exit. Have your students complete statements such as these:

- Today, I learned . . .
- I am not sure about . . .
- I need to know more about . . .
- I can use today's information to . . .
- Today, I did well on . . .
- In today's class, I enjoyed . . .
- I still have questions about . . .

Stop the Futile Cycle of Delayed Learning

Perhaps you can recall from your own school days the satisfaction you felt when you successfully finished writing definitions for a list of vocabulary words. That feeling may have vanished the next day when you realized that you had only defined the words, whereas your teacher expected you to have learned them. This scenario occurs daily in schools everywhere; students do their work without thinking about what they are doing. The futility of this cycle of delayed learning has serious consequences for student success. Students who just go through the motions of doing their work never learn enough to do well on tests. Their delay in learning is simply too great to be overcome.

You can do a great deal to prevent your students from delaying their learning. First, you can make your students aware of the value of learning their work when it is assigned. Teach them the difference between just completing an assignment and actually learning the information in it. Stress the importance of learning information the first time they see it.

Another strategy you can use to engage students in continual learning is to extend assignments. Instead of just asking students to read a chapter, ask them to complete such activities as completing graphic organizers, outlining, or making flash cards. All of these activities will motivate students to become more fully engaged with the material.

You can also prevent the tendency to delay studying until just before a test by including frequent checkpoints early in the unit. If students prepare for a daily quiz three days in a row, being prepared for a test at the end of the week will be more manageable. Hold students accountable for their learning every day, not just on test days.

A final way to stop delayed learning is to increase student awareness of the importance of concentration while working. Many students daydream in class but still appear to be on task because they are not disturbing others. Help them break this bad habit by making efficient learning an open topic of conversation in your class. Your students can succeed if you teach them how critical it is that they take an active role in their learning. Just doing the work should not be enough to get by in any classroom. Expect your students to engage in real learning.

The reward of teaching is the light in a child's eyes when the comprehension of something thought to be difficult has been reached.

—Melinda Cummings,
6 years' experience

Help Students Manage Their Stress

Sadly, students are just as apt to be stressed about school matters as their teachers are. Anxious students struggle to achieve the same success as their classmates who are not as stressed.

While you certainly want students to feel challenged, their anxiety needs to remain manageable. Unfortunately, many students have never been taught how to keep their stress level under control. The result is unhappy students who dread school. You can help students manage their anxiety.

Pay attention to your students' reactions throughout the school day. When you make homework assignments, when you plan tests or projects, or even when you assign practice work, you have an excellent opportunity to observe their reactions and to modify the work if it seems unmanageable for many students.

Help Students Meet Deadlines

Prepare yourself! Terrible things can happen to homework assignments after students complete them. Here are some of the excuses for missing homework that you can expect to hear about this year:

"I left it at home."

"I left it in my locker."

Strategies for Teaching Stress Management

You can help students keep their stress levels under control in many ways. Try these strategies:

- Teach students to expect setbacks from time to time; a perfect academic record is unattainable.
- Encourage students to prepare thoroughly. Attending class without sufficiently studying for a test or completing homework can heighten a student's stress level.
- Help students learn to monitor their own stress and to seek assistance when necessary. Offer your support, and be prepared to involve a school counselor if the need arises.
- Teach students to be mindful of the positive and negative consequences of their actions. If they pay attention in class, for example, they will feel more confident of their mastery of the material. If they neglect to study for a quiz, they will probably feel stressed.
- While you should not accept shabby excuses, be careful to listen before reacting when a student asks for an adjustment in an assignment. If you can reduce student stress by remaining flexible and supportive, do so whenever you can.
- Make sure that your class is a place where students do not cause each other stress by harassing each other. (See Section Fifteen for more information about stopping harassment.)

"Another teacher took it by mistake."

"Our printer is out of ink."

"My baby brother hid it."

"The power was out."

While students never seem to understand that their teachers are not gullible, it can be hard to know what to do when an earnest student offers a plausible excuse for missing work. It's hard to know where to draw the line between being inflexible and being a pushover.

You can avoid many problems if you help your students meet their deadlines. Here are some strategies for helping your students become responsible about meeting deadlines:

- Have students use a planning calendar for long-term projects so that they remain aware of what they have to do each day.
- Write assignments in a conspicuous spot, and expect your students to record them, too.
- Create a policy for late work, and make sure that your students know about it. Out of fairness to the students who do their work on time, you should take off points for

work that is late, except when students speak to you about problems well in advance of the due date or bring a note from home asking for your assistance.

- Break large projects into smaller, manageable units of work so that all students can stay on target. Make sure each smaller unit has a reasonable due date.
- Encourage older students to set due dates for themselves earlier than the ones you establish. This is also an excellent way to promote self-discipline.
- Post a countdown of days on the board. For example, if a project is due in ten days, students will be aware of the passage of time if you tell them when there are nine days before it is due, and then eight, and so forth, down to one.
- Call the student's home if you believe that a student has a problem with meeting deadlines. Your call will alert parents or guardians about any grade penalties for missed work.
- Print small labels for students to use in their planning calendars as reminders of their due dates.
- Make sure that you clearly post the due dates for projects, tests, and other assignments on the board, near the clock, by the door, or in other obvious places.

Create a Homework Partnership

The tension created between students and teachers, teachers and parents, and parents and students over homework has grown in recent years into a national debate. For decades, the issue of homework and its impact on home life has been a concern for families and schools. Although the pendulum of the debate seems to swing with the social climate, homework has remained a staple of education despite the problems associated with it.

Teachers at all levels of experience are judged by their homework assignments. If you assign too much, you are too strict. If you assign too little, you are too lenient. The parents of your students may also represent two extremes: parents who take an active role in homework and parents who resent the demands of homework assignments. One thing is clear: teachers cannot please everyone.

You can overcome many homework hassles by creating a strong partnership with students and families. The best way is to communicate your expectations in a letter and be consistent in adhering to your plan.

If you teach young students, consider a homework folder. Many teachers have found that this is a convenient way to contact parents. These teachers laminate a folder for each child to take home each night with returned papers and the day's homework assignment tucked safely inside.

Many school districts now provide better communication opportunities for teachers and parents by using homework hot lines or voice mail for homework questions. Many teachers also have school e-mail accounts that parents can use to clarify homework questions. If you create a class Web page (see Section Three), students and their families can access homework information at home.

Students and their families can also get help with homework by going online for support. Many Internet sites are dedicated to homework help. While some sites are limited to a specific content area or grade level, many are not. You can help families by checking out a few sites and then recommending the ones you feel would work best for your students. You might wish to begin your investigation with some of these sites:

- **B. J.'s Homework Helper (http://school.discovery.com/homeworkhelp/bjpinchbeck).** The moderator of B. J.'s Homework Helper is B. J. Pinchbeck, who offers more than seven hundred links to sites that students can access for homework help.
- **Pearson Education (www.factmonster.com).** This user-friendly site offers many categories of information that students can search when they need information for reports or other homework assignments.
- **Homework Center (www.infoplease.com/homework).** At the Pearson Education's Homework Center, students can find information on core subjects as well as skill builders and online reference sites.
- **National Geographic (www.nationalgeographic.com/homework).** National Geographic offers a student-friendly site with topic categories such as animals, history, culture, or science.
- **Hotmath (www.hotmath.com).** For a fee, this site offers tutorial assistance and solutions to the odd-numbered problems of many different math textbooks.

Develop a Homework Policy

Experienced teachers know that homework success does not just happen; it requires the same degree of planning and preparation as other assignments. Remember, you will avoid many of the problems associated with homework if you involve parents and guardians early in the year, communicate with them frequently, alert them promptly if a problem arises, and are organized about homework. One way to begin is by developing a homework policy for your class.

Start by finding out whether there is a formal policy for your school district or your school. If there is no formal policy, then you should find out how the other teachers in your school handle homework.

Next, you will have to determine how you want to handle each one of these concerns:

- What is the purpose of homework in your class?
- How much weight will you assign to homework grades?
- How long should each homework assignment take?
- When will you assign homework? When will your students not have homework?
- How will students know what their assignments are?
- What types of homework will you assign?

Ten Homework Strategies to Boost Student Interest and Motivation

When students don't do their homework, it becomes more than just an assignment; it becomes a headache for parents, students, and teachers. Here are ten homework preparation strategies you can use to avoid homework headaches and to help your students find success:

1. **Ask your students their opinion about homework assignments.** Go beyond the initial complaints to discover the types of assignments that students feel they can learn from and still find enjoyable.
2. **Allow your students as many choices as you can.** For example, you can let students choose the even or the odd problems in their textbook or one of several essay questions.
3. **Consider designating some nights as homework-free nights.** This is a good way to dispel some of the complaints about too much homework. If you leave weekends free of new homework assignments, your students can use that time to read for pleasure or to catch up on long-term projects and other work.
4. **Be careful to balance the amount of homework you assign with other work that students have.** Typically, you should assign more homework to older students than to younger ones. Work with other teachers to stagger the due dates for major projects.
5. **Show plenty of examples and models.** Students need to have a clear idea of what the final product should be in order to work with assurance.
6. **Make the work as interesting as possible.** Use real-life examples, television shows, actual student names, sports, or other eye-catching details to engage students.
7. **Assign work for many different audiences.** For example, have students write letters to a pen pal or give oral reports.
8. **Allow students to consult each other when they all have the same assignment.** You should expect that your students will help each other on homework assignments, even ones that you want them to do independently. Build in collaboration when you can to help your students avoid the temptation to cheat.
9. **Never assign homework as punishment.** Giving homework as a punishment encourages students to perceive homework as a burdensome task.
10. **Have a clear purpose for each assignment, and make sure that your students understand it.** Acceptable purposes for homework include reviewing material, applying learning, practicing, and previewing new material.

- How will you communicate with parents and guardians when problems arise?
- How will you grade homework?
- What will you do when students turn in late homework?
- What will you do when students do not do their homework?

Following is an example of a letter to parents outlining a homework policy.

Sample Letter for Parents on Homework Policy

Dear Parent or Guardian of ______________________________ :

Homework is a powerful tool for learning and a necessary part of any student's successful mastery of skills and knowledge. You can expect that your child will have homework on Monday through Thursday nights. These assignments will usually take no longer than thirty minutes to complete. On weekends, I will make no formal assignments, but students can use this time to read, research, and work on projects.

Homework due dates will be given on the day it is assigned. I expect students to turn work in on time. If there is a problem, please send a note to let me know so that I can help your child. The first time an assignment is not completed, I will speak with your child to see if I can help. After that, I will contact you when assignments are not completed on time.

I will make sure that my students write their assignments down each day. I will also record the assignment on my voice mail, which you can reach at ______________________ and on our class Web page www.______________________ .

You can help your child do well on homework assignments by setting aside a study time each night, encouraging good work habits, and contacting me if there is a problem we can solve together.

Please discuss these points with your child. Please sign below and return the bottom portion of this letter to school with your child. Keep the part above the dotted line for your reference.

Sincerely,
Julia G. Thompson

....

I have read this homework policy and discussed it with my child.

______________________________ ______________________________

Parent or Guardian's Signature Student's Signature

Steps to Follow When Assigning Homework

Giving effective homework assignments can be broken into three steps: before, during, and after the assignment. Use the following information to make homework a successful experience for you and your students:

Before the Assignment

- Follow your district's homework policy, or make sure that your own policy is in line with that of other teachers in your school.
- Teach study skills so that your students can complete their work with little or no anxiety.
- Allow students to design their own homework assignments when appropriate. If they did not finish an assignment in class, they should have the option of completing it for homework, for example. If students are working in a group, they should plan the work they need to complete each night.
- Have a well-structured schedule for homework so that students can anticipate assignments.

While Presenting the Assignment

- Spend enough time going over the assignment and checking for understanding so that students know you are serious about it. Give plenty of models and examples, letting students know what the final product should be.
- Don't wait until the last few minutes of class to assign homework. If you want students to take it seriously, it should not be a last-minute item.
- Write the homework assignment in the same spot on the board each day. Write it on the board even if you also give your students a syllabus, post it online, and record it on your voice mail.
- Ask students to estimate how long it will take them to do the assignment so that they can set aside the time to do it.

After the Assignment

- A note or phone call home when a student does not complete an assignment will often correct the problem of missing work. If nothing else, it alerts parents or guardians to be more vigilant about checking on their child's homework.
- Offer help to students who may need extra assistance in doing their work. A bit of extra time with you after school will often clear up problems and give students a boost of confidence.
- Be reasonable if a student brings in a note from home requesting an extension. Sometimes unforeseen events can cause even the most conscientious child to not complete homework on time.
- Check homework at the start of class on the day it is due. If you do not take homework assignments seriously enough to provide feedback, then your students won't, either.
- If a student does not submit homework on time, consider asking that student to write out the reason for not doing the work and a phone number where parents or guardians can be reached.

- Grading homework can be overwhelming! Follow these tips to make giving prompt feedback a manageable task:
  - Collect and grade only some assignments yourself.
  - Go over the work together as a class. Give a grade for completion.
  - Go over the work with your class, and then give a quiz on it.
  - Check the work every day. Have students slip their assignments into a weekly portfolio and then select their best work for you to assess.
  - Have students work in small groups to discuss their answers.

Help Students Make Up Missed Work

When a student asks you, "Did we do anything when I was out?" resist the urge to respond sarcastically. Your student is only asking for a chance to make up work.

Attendance problems occur at every grade level. Very few students have perfect attendance for even one year of school, so helping students make up missed work is a responsibility you will have to undertake almost every day.

Helping students make up missed work will not be difficult if you establish a policy, make sure that your students understand it, and enforce the policy consistently. Here are some guidelines that will help you:

Establish a Policy

- Learn your school's policy on making up missing work, and align your policy with it. If there is no formal policy at your school, ask if there is one for your department or grade level.
- A workable policy for making up work should include the due date of the assignment, how much and what kind of help a student may receive from others, when you are available to help students make up work, the point at which you will contact parents or guardians, and the penalty for late work.
- Inform parents and guardians of this policy in the letter that you send home at the beginning of the term to introduce yourself.
- If you use a syllabus, encourage absent students to follow it as closely as they can so that they will find it easy to catch up when they return.

Make Sure That Students Understand What to Do

- At the beginning of the term and at subsequent intervals, discuss the issue of making up missed work in class. Making up missing work should not be a hidden policy in your classroom.
- Divide your students into study teams early in the term. Within each team, students can help each other make up missing assignments by calling absent members, shar-

ing notes, collecting handouts, and reviewing the difficult parts of the assignment. Even very young children can help each other by being part of a study team.

- Consider having students rotate the task of recording class events and assignments on a large calendar, on your class Web page, or even in a binder each day. When students return from an absence, they can check the class record or logbook to see what they missed and what work they need to do.
- Keep all papers to be returned and new handouts in a special folder so that students can pick up missing papers when they return.
- Set aside time before or after school each week to meet with students and help them make up work. Post your hours, and be sure to inform parents and guardians about them.
- If a parent asks you to send work home to a student, be prompt and very specific. Give details that will enable the child to complete the work at home. Write a note, offering extra help. Such a gesture is not just professional but courteous.

Enforce Your Policy Consistently

- Although allowing students to make up missed work during class time is certainly convenient, it allows students to miss yet more work. It is better to have students make up their work before or after school rather than miss more class.
- Make time to speak about missing work with each student who has been absent. Make sure that the child knows what is due and when it is due. Document the conversation.
- If a due date is approaching and the student has made no effort to make up the missing work, call the student's parent or guardian. This sends a clear message that you are serious about students' making up their work.
- Be flexible. Inevitably, some situations will require you to alter your policy, using your best judgment. For example, if a student is absent because of a serious illness or because of a death in the family, you should respond with compassion. You will need to adjust the make-up work and the amount of support you offer a child in such a situation.

Extra Credit Dilemmas and Solutions

Extra credit is often a controversial topic for teachers. Some teachers are adamant about its usefulness, while others believe that offering extra credit encourages poor study habits. Either way, offering extra credit can be a trap for the unwary first-year teacher. When you are trying to establish a workable extra credit policy for your students, follow these guidelines:

- Before you give in to student pressure for extra credit, decide on your expectations. Don't give in on the spur of the moment because students want extra points.

- Make sure that your plan for extra credit is in line with your school's policy. If the policy is not in your faculty manual, check with several colleagues in order to learn what other teachers do.
- Be aware of just how easy it is to skew grades with extra credit points. If you assign extra work without considering the impact it will have on grades, you may devalue the work you have assigned throughout the grading period.
- If you do offer extra credit, do so at the beginning of a marking period and assign a clear due date and point value. If you don't do this, you will find yourself grading too many papers at the end of the term.
- Extra credit assignments should have rubrics, just as other assignments do. Grade them on the quality of the work, not just on effort.
- You should offer extra credit to every student in your class, not just to students who request it. If you don't offer it to everyone, you can legitimately be accused of favoritism.
- Don't offer extra credit for activities that require your students to spend money. For example, don't give students an extra credit assignment of going to see a local play. Some students will not be able to afford the admission fee, no matter how small it might be.
- If you offer bonus questions on a test, make sure they are not worth as much as the other questions. The purpose of such questions is to encourage students to stretch their minds, not earn easy points to make up for what they did not know.

Help Students Complete Long-Term Projects

In recent years, teachers have begun assigning more long-term projects to students at all grade levels. Even very young students have been assigned a wide range of projects: oral reports, dramatic presentations, science fair experiments, and researched or creative booklets and reports.

Few teachers have been able to avoid the sinking feeling that occurs when a project looks terrific in the lesson plan stage but fails miserably in practice. The length of most projects and their impact on students' grades compounds the problem. If nightly homework assignments can cause stress for teachers, students, and parents, the potential for trouble from long-term projects is even greater.

You can avoid problems by teaching your students how to plan and carry out each stage of a project successfully. With a bit of planning and a bit of instruction in the skills that students will need, these projects can become the enjoyable and productive learning processes that you intend them to be.

TEACHING PROJECT SKILLS

Although your students may have had to complete projects before, don't assume they have been taught the skills needed for success on long-term projects. Apply the following steps in order to teach your students how to complete a project.

Project Planning

To increase your students' success in completing long-term projects, follow these guidelines:

- Choose a topic and a format that your students will enjoy. Remember that real-life situations have intrinsic appeal and that students who choose their own topics tend to be more motivated and successful than those who have no choices.
- Think of a long-term project as a series of smaller steps. Each step should have a separate due date and grade. This step-by-step process will give students and their parents early warning about any concerns you may have about their work.
- Your students will need plenty of models and examples for each step in the process, not just the final project. You should also include checklists, flowcharts, or other visual aids that allow your students to see when each part is due and how it fits into the entire project.
- Be careful to schedule enough time for students to complete their work successfully. If you miscalculate, you will have to either deal with frustrated students or extend the due date.
- Not all students can afford resources such as art supplies or multiple trips to a public library. Be sensitive to expenses that your students may incur while working on a project for your class.
- Schedule times for your students to meet in pairs or small groups to review each other's work and times for them to meet with you to make sure they are on the right track.

- Before you assign a project, brainstorm a list of the skills your students will need to complete it satisfactorily. Plan how you will teach each one.
- Teach students how to plan their projects themselves. Have students write proposals telling you about the materials they will need, the time they will have to spend on each part, and what they want to accomplish. You can help students solve problems before those problems become serious.
- It is never too early to teach your students about plagiarism and how to avoid it. An excellent Web site for educating students about plagiarism is iParadigms' Plagiarism.org (www.plagiarism.org), which offers information and assistance for teachers and students, as well as a link to its popular anti-plagiarism site, Turnitin (www.turnitin.com).
- Emphasize the value of good work habits as students work on projects. Establish high standards for each step of the project process, and help your students turn in excellent work. One way to communicate your standards is to show examples of excellent work for each step of the project.

- Ask students to assess their project and to reflect on how well they completed each step. This type of closure provides meaning and insight for your students and for you.

Talk It Over

How to Help Your Students Become Successful Learners

Use these questions as a springboard for discussions that will help you and your discussion group members grow and develop professionally. Discuss these questions about how to help your students become successful learners:

1. What problems can you predict that your students will have with homework? How can you handle these problems? How do other teachers in your school deal successfully with homework issues?
2. What is your school's policy on making up work? What problems can you foresee with implementing this policy? How can you solve these problems?
3. What is your plan for teaching students how to keep their work in order? Why is this important? What tips do your colleagues have to share with you about student organizational skills? Where can you find out more information on this topic?
4. What can you do to help students who always seem disorganized? What causes their lack of organizational skills?
5. How well do your students listen to you? To each other? What causes them to tune out? How can you improve their listening skills? Where can you find out more information about this topic?
6. Brainstorm on what you already know about teaching students how to take notes. How can you evaluate your students' note-taking skills? How can you help them improve how they take notes as they read? As they listen to an oral presentation? What advice can your colleagues offer?
7. What experiences in your past have given you insight into the difficulties that students have with study habits? Share your experiences and insights with your colleagues.
8. What can your students teach you about study skills? What can they teach each other? How can you make learning about study skills a part of your class culture?
9. How can you teach your students to do neat and accurate work? Why is this important? What do other teachers in your school do to promote neat and accurate work?
10. What are your students' worst study habits? Ask your colleagues as well as your students to suggest ways to help your students rid themselves of these bad habits.

SECTION TWELVE

Make the Most of Your Instructional Time

In this section, you will learn

- ✔ How to use instructional time efficiently
- ✔ How to apply the principles of good class time management
- ✔ How to begin and end class productively
- ✔ How to manage interruptions
- ✔ How to handle requests to leave class

Teachers can't control many of the more challenging aspects of their profession, but there is one important factor that they can control: class time. You have door-to-door control over how your students use the all-too-few hours they spend in your classroom. You can choose whether to engage students in meaningful and interesting learning activities or condemn them to boredom and missed opportunities.

You Control the Time Your Students Have with You

You control whether your class's time is wasted or productive. Unavoidable disruptions and interruptions will inevitably cause some class time to be wasted, but you should strive to minimize this loss. You can allow students to waste much of the time they spend with you on unproductive activities, or you can make sure that your students are engaged in a variety of learning tasks while developing a positive, productive attitude about their academic responsibilities.

Sometimes it will seem that interruptions such as intercom announcements, commotion in the halls, or unruly students disrupt your class much too routinely. Just as other teachers do, you will have to find ways to cope successfully with these obvious disturbances as well as with many more subtle disruptions of your class routine.

You may be tempted to believe that your day is so consumed by interruptions and distractions that these circumstances regulate what happens in your class, but this is not true. While there are certainly many things you can't change about your school situation, you do have control over the way your students spend their time while they are with you.

If you do not control the use of time in your classroom, what are the consequences? If you waste only two minutes of your students' day—a few seconds at the opening of class, a distraction or two, a lost handout, maybe even a minute of free time at the end of class—over the course of a typical school year, those two minutes a day will add up to more than six hours of lost instruction. That's an entire school day.

The results of misused instructional time can be grim. Teachers who do not use class time wisely experience far more discipline problems than teachers who make use of every minute. Students who waste class time are less able to succeed academically. Discipline problems and academic failures not only make a teacher's workday unpleasant but can eventually lead to burnout.

What can you do to avoid the hazards of wasted class time? Start by making a commitment to yourself and to your students that you will teach them during every minute that they are with you. Resolve to make good use of the time that your students are in your class.

How Teachers Waste Time

One of the best ways to use class time to the best advantage is to be aware of how easy it is to waste it. Some of the ways that teachers misuse class time include the following:

- Teaching lessons that are not relevant or interesting to students
- Not using the first few minutes of class effectively
- Allowing students to goof off for the last few minutes of class
- Not intervening quickly enough to keep problems manageable
- Confusing digressions from their topic with teachable moments
- Not establishing routines for daily classroom procedures
- Calling roll instead of checking attendance with a seating chart
- Not enforcing a reasonable policy for leaving the classroom
- Not providing assistance for students without materials
- Allowing students to decide when class is over
- Not determining students' prior knowledge of new material
- Assigning an inappropriate amount of work
- Giving confusing directions

- Making poor transitions between activities
- Giving homework that is only busywork

Principles of Effective Classroom Time Management

Learning to use class time wisely is a skill that will take time, patience, and practice to acquire; however, the rewards are well worth the effort. You and your students will benefit every day from classes that run smoothly. You will eventually get many tips from your colleagues and learn much from your own classroom experiences; until then, you can start with these general principles for using class time wisely:

- **Reduce distractions.** The old image of restless students staring dreamily out of the window has much truth in it. Students of all ages are always able to entertain themselves by paying attention to distractions in the classroom rather than focusing on the teacher. Look around your classroom for things that might distract your students. Some obvious sources of distractions might be windows, desks too close together, doorways, pencil sharpeners, trash cans, screen savers, too many posters or banners, graffiti, or—the most enticing one of all—other students.
- **Raise student awareness.** Your students need to learn that time is important in your class. This doesn't mean that you should rush them through their tasks, but you should discuss the importance of using class time wisely, making sure that your students understand that you expect them to work productively while they are in your class.
- **Establish routines.** If you have routines for daily activities in your class, your students will save minutes each day and hours each week instead of wasting time because they don't know what to do.
- **Monitor constantly.** Monitoring your students is of primary importance for the smooth running of your class for a variety of reasons, not just for efficient time use. Staying on your feet instead of sitting at your desk will allow you to help students while their problems are still manageable.
- **Be very organized.** If your students have to wait while you find your textbook or a handout, that is a poor use of their time. Make it a point to be so organized that you will be able to keep yourself and your students on task.
- **Have a backup plan.** If a lesson isn't working, if a guest speaker cancels, or if the equipment you need to use isn't working, you will need an alternative way to teach the material you planned to cover. Have a backup plan in place so that you can quickly shift gears if your first plan doesn't work out.
- **Take a door-to-door approach.** Engage students in learning from the time they enter your classroom until the time they leave. Many teachers make the mistake of thinking that students need a few minutes of free time at the start of class and at the end of class to relax. Although students do need time at both ends of class to make effective transitions, they do not need free time to do this. Instead, give them interesting activities that relate to the day's lesson.

- **Use small blocks of time.** Just as you can accomplish many of your own tasks with brief bits of concentrated effort, so can your students. If you only have five minutes until dismissal, don't allow students to do nothing because it will take too long to get them working on a new assignment. Instead, use this time and other snippets of time in a class to review or to teach a new fact.
- **Teach to an objective.** If you teach a subject that you enjoy personally, it is tempting to spend more time on it than the curriculum dictates. Stick to your plan so that your students won't be shortchanged on other topics. In addition, keep the purpose of the work that you are asking your students to do clearly in mind and communicate the purpose to them. If you are unclear about why your work together is important, your students will also be unclear, and you will have trouble keeping them on task.
- **Give enough work.** If students finish a task, there should be another waiting for them. For example, students who sit around after a test waiting for others to finish before going on to the next activity are obviously wasting time. Always make sure that your students know what they are supposed to do after they finish their current assignment.

Raising Your Students' Awareness of Time

You are not the only person in your class who is concerned about how your students spend their time. Your students are, too. They want to spend their days successfully doing the work that you ask them to do—and to have fun while doing it.

When you have to deal with a series of petty misbehaviors, it is easy to forget that your students want to do well in school and that they want to spend their time doing interesting and useful work. You can take this natural interest and use it to help your students learn to become efficient at their classroom tasks. Obviously, you cannot manage this feat by yourself; it makes sense to enlist the support of the people you are trying to help.

A good way to make your students aware of how they spend their time is to discuss it with them. When students see that you are not just nagging or rushing them through their work, they will be more willing to work well with you. Discuss the intangible rewards they enjoy when they use class time well.

Teach your students key word signals such as "Focus" or "Concentrate" so that they know exactly what to do when they hear you say these words. Make concentration an expected behavior in your classroom so that students will be aware when they are not as attentive as they should be. Offer to teach your students study skills and show them how to achieve good grades without having to spend hours on their work (see Section Eleven).

Display constant reminders of the importance of using time well. Use some of the study tips from Section Eleven to create banners and posters that address the issue. You can also use your own tips, ask students to share their tips, or find quotations about time management.

Another technique that will help students become aware of how they spend class time is completing a questionnaire such as the one in Student Worksheet 12.1. This exercise will allow students to think honestly about how they use and misuse class time. Reflecting on the questions might be particularly effective after a day when students have been off task more than usual.

STUDENT WORKSHEET 12.1

Track How You Use Time

Name ______________________ Date ______________________

Think back over class today and answer these questions as accurately as you can. The more thorough your answers, the easier it will be for you to improve how you use your time in class.

1. Class is __________ minutes long.
2. Of the __________ available minutes in class today, I estimate that I did NOT use __________ of them wisely.
3. Put a checkmark in the box next to each item that applies to you.

I was off task during the . . .

- ☐ first five minutes
- ☐ first ten minutes
- ☐ last ten minutes
- ☐ written assignment
- ☐ reading selection
- ☐ class discussion
- ☐ listening section

4. I used class time well today when I ______________________________
____
____
5. I am easily distracted when ______________________________
____
____
6. The most productive part of class was ______________________________
____
____
7. A suggestion I have for my teacher is ______________________________
____
____
8. I can improve the way I use class time by ______________________________
____
____

The First Ten Minutes of Class

Too often, teachers overlook the potential power of the opening minutes of class. They watch as students drift into class, visit with their classmates, and leisurely rummage around to find last night's homework. After they find their materials, students are frequently content to just sit and wait to be told what to do. Often, if they are quiet enough and if there are many pressing demands on a teacher's time at that moment, more than ten minutes can vanish before class starts. It's no wonder that students are tardy to class; they have little reason to be on time.

You can use the first ten minutes to get your class off to a great start, or you can choose to waste it. The first minutes set the tone for the rest of the class. If you are prepared for class and have taught your students an opening routine, they can use this brief time to make mental and emotional transitions from the last class or subject and prepare to focus on learning new material.

You should establish a comfortable and predictable routine for the opening of class. Here is a simple opening routine that many teachers follow and that you can adapt to meet the needs of your class:

The teacher greets each student as he or she enters the class. You can hand out any papers you need to distribute at this time. You can also answer questions, collect attendance notes, and check the emotional states of your students. Your students will appreciate that you care enough to stand at the door to greet them.

Students go immediately to their seats. You will avoid many problems if you strictly enforce this part of the routine. Students who wander around the room while you are busy at the door can cause problems that will last throughout class. Furthermore, students will often carry problems from earlier in the day to your room. By insisting that your students take a seat right away, you will help focus their energies on your class and on learning.

Students check the board for a predictable organizing exercise. The organizing exercise gives them time to settle down, organize their materials, and shift mental gears to what is going to happen in class. Your message on the board might include directions such as these:

Today's Tasks

1. Open your textbook to page 23.
2. Please get out a pen and paper. Head your paper for today's class work.
3. Copy tonight's homework assignment into your notebook.
4. Place last night's homework on your desk.
5. Read the objectives for today's class work.

Students complete an anticipatory set. The anticipatory set should arouse curiosity and relate the day's new learning to previous knowledge. It should be interesting yet simple enough for students to complete independently. The activity will thus increase their confidence, so that they are even more interested in the day's lesson.

Inviting Ways to Open Class

Use your creativity to design activities that your students will enjoy as they look forward to the day's lesson. For example, ask students to do one of the following activities or modify one to suit your students' needs.

- Complete or create a graphic organizer. (You can download dozens of samples from Houghton Mifflin's Education Place at www.eduplace.com/graphicorganizer.)
- Use stick figures to illustrate a concept or event.
- Select two or three objects from a box containing many items and then predict how they will relate to the lesson.
- Write a rhyme to help recall information.
- List what they already know about the day's lesson.
- Skim the day's reading material and predict what they will learn.
- Create or study flash cards with a partner.
- Solve a brainteaser. (Brain Bashers [www.brainbashers.com] is an excellent site to search for brainteasers. Managed by a British mathematician, Kevin Stone, it features thousands of games, riddles, puzzles, and illusions.)
- List three reasons to study the day's topic.
- Read a news article and summarize the information in it. (Imagine how your students will react when they read an article from a newspaper in a country they are studying in class! To find newspaper articles from all over the world, try searching NewsDirectory [www.ecola.com].)
- Combine information from their notes with another student.
- Listen to a recorded audio message and respond in writing.
- Watch a video clip and write about it. (You can find thousands of short audio or video versions of historical events as well as clips from movies and television broadcasts at American Rhetoric [www.americanrhetoric.com].)
- Brainstorm ideas with a partner about an assignment.
- Complete a prewriting exercise for an essay.
- Label or draw a map. (A helpful Internet source for free maps of all types and interactive activities to go along with them is Magellan Geographix at www.maps.com.)
- Look at odd objects from the past and predict what they were used for. (Game pieces, kitchen gadgets, and old tools are all intriguing puzzlers.)
- Write a response to a quotation. (Quoteland [www.quoteland.com] is an easy-to-use Internet source offering quotations suitable for students of all ages.)
- Tell about any problems they had with the last homework assignment.

Accommodating Students Who Work at Different Speeds

Your students are working quietly on an assignment that should take about ten more minutes for them all to finish. One student finishes early and asks to be excused to the restroom. Because the student has finished, you allow him to go. Another student finishes and asks to leave, and then a third. There's still a little time left until the rest of the class will be finished, so you let them go. Some other students who have finished early are doing homework for other classes, while others are just sitting quietly staring off into space. The less able students are working frantically to finish their work before you call for it.

Both types of students—the ones who finished quickly and had nothing to do and the ones who struggled to complete the work on time—lost in this situation. The problem with such a lesson plan is that it supposes that all students will work at the same speed. This rarely happens.

When you design a lesson, pay attention to three levels of students in your class: those who will finish quickly; those who will finish their work in the time you have allotted (the majority of your students); and those who will take longer to complete the work. You can begin to use every minute of class time wisely if you keep these points in mind:

- Plan enrichment activities that will benefit students and that are interesting enough so that students will want to complete their regular work. Enrichment activities should be intellectually stimulating, not just more work for students to plow though.
- Consider posting a list of activities for students who finish their work early. Suggested activities might include starting homework early, working at a learning center, using a computer for a game or for review, reading a library book, working with another student on an extra project, or organizing a notebook. Post the instructions for the day's work on the board or on a handout for students. If you use a checklist format, students will be able to check off items as they finish them and work at their own pace, without having to wait for other students.

I learned early in my first year that if I have several tasks for my students, I should do the things that we will complete together first so that I can control the length and speed of a lesson. I save the independent work for the last part of class because I don't want to interrupt students when they have settled down to work. They find it too frustrating.

—Yann Pirrone, 15 years' experience

Productive Transitions

Because your students are accustomed to the fast-paced action of modern life, they may lose interest in a lesson that seems to last too long. Experienced teachers create a positive learning environment by designing lessons around several brief activities. While having several activities is sensible, it requires transitions that encourage students to be productive between activities.

Transitions are difficult to manage well because they require students to do three things in a very brief amount of time: mentally close out one task, prepare for the next one, and refocus their mental energy on a new topic. Fortunately, a wise first-year teacher can do several things to help students handle transitions effectively:

- Design activities that flow naturally from one to the next, requiring a minimum of large-group instruction from you. Sequencing instruction in this way encourages students to manage their own learning.
- Try using a kitchen timer to set a time limit for a change in activities. When students know that they have only a minute or two to switch from one activity to another, they are more likely to move quickly.
- Make transitions productive by providing your students with activities that will convert useless waiting time into learning opportunities. Using small blocks of time to engage your students in active thinking and learning can be enjoyable for both you and your students.
- Such small activities (called *sponges* because they soak up class time that would otherwise be lost) can add interest and new information to a lesson. Though these activities are brief, their impact on productivity in your classroom can be significant. Adapt, adjust, or add information to the following activities to create other activities that will keep your students involved in productive learning throughout class.

A TREASURE TROVE OF TRANSITION ACTIVITIES

Ask students to

- Justify the rules for . . .
- Apply the information in the lesson to a real-life situation
- Defend a position
- Write the definition of an unusual word
- Match words and meanings
- Unscramble vocabulary words
- Create a to-do list for a project or other activity
- Explain the correct procedure for . . .
- Complete a word sort

- Modify a procedure so that it is more efficient
- Modify a tool so that it is more efficient
- Explain what they learned in the lesson
- Read a brief newspaper article and respond to it
- Create a time line of . . .
- Explain what to do in an emergency involving . . .
- Create a brief outline of . . .
- Fill in the blanks in a brief outline
- Brainstorm as many ____________ as they can
- Read a brief Internet article and respond to it
- Put a series of events in chronological order
- Read a catalogue to find . . .
- Practice the process of elimination on the answers to some sample standardized test questions
- Paraphrase information
- Respond to a political cartoon
- Respond to a humorous cartoon
- Respond to a picture
- Respond to an advertisement
- Review information with a partner
- List important facts from the last few days of class
- Explain why the day's lesson is useful
- Recall facts from the last lesson
- Predict the outcome of a story
- Predict an outcome that can be inferred from information in the chapter under study
- Explain why it is important to use time wisely
- Use two of the key terms from the lesson in a sentence
- Answer trivia questions related to the lesson
- Find places on a map
- Draw a map
- Color a map
- Write a key term on a scrap of paper and pass that scrap to a classmate, who has to explain it
- Circle or highlight key words in their notes or reading
- Play a game of Hangman to review vocabulary words
- Make quick flash cards to review vocabulary

- Proofread a paragraph containing many grammatical errors
- Proofread a paragraph containing many factual errors
- Read the opening paragraphs from the lesson and tell a partner what they learned from the reading
- Brainstorm a list of key words from the lesson
- Offer solutions to a variety of problems
- Create a mnemonic
- Brainstorm a list of ten important concepts from the lesson
- Brainstorm a list of ideas for a creative project based on the lesson
- Explain the day's objectives
- Explain a study skill
- Write a time line of a current event
- Brainstorm the causes of a current event
- Brainstorm about the effects of a current event
- Summarize the lesson orally with a partner
- Describe an object in the room in twenty-five words
- Draw a concept from the lesson
- Use stick figures to draw idioms
- Make up a true-or-false quiz on the lesson
- Take a true-or-false quiz on the lesson
- Time a classmate as he or she reviews the main point of the lesson
- Scan the text to find . . .
- Complete a logic puzzle or brainteaser
- Copy and define the word of the day
- Read a newspaper article and respond
- Complete a brief cloze exercise
- Go to a learning center and . . .
- Complete analogies
- Put words in alphabetical order
- Explain what they learned in another class that they can use now
- Explain what they learned in this class that they can use in another class
- Classify groups of words
- State the reasons for . . .
- Create a brief word search puzzle for a classmate to solve tomorrow
- Create test questions (with answers)
- Create relationships among the vocabulary terms in the lesson

- Practice math problems
- Help a friend drill math facts
- Complete a math word problem
- Make up a math word problem
- Make up math problems for review
- Quiz themselves on the words on a word wall (see Section Thirteen)
- Brainstorm a list of the similarities between themselves and the people in the lesson
- Define some of the words on standardized tests that trouble students: *imply, infer* . . .
- Follow directions in order to create a simple origami figure
- Brainstorm a list of people who epitomize words such as *politician, healer, explorer*
- Follow specific directions to star, underline, or circle certain words in a passage
- Create a cause-and-effect web about an event in the lesson
- Complete a Mad Lib with a partner. (Mad Libs are word games in which one partner prompts another for a set of words to use in a story. Because the person supplying the words does not know the story, the result is often comical as well as engaging. To find out more about Mad Libs, go to TeacherVision's Web site: www.teachervision.com. From the home page, use "Mad Libs" as a search word in order to access activities that your students will enjoy.)
- Make a Venn diagram illustrating a concept or a relationship in the lesson
- Write about the meaning of a quotation
- Write a question about the lesson they will study tomorrow
- Find as many synonyms as they can for a word
- Clean out their book bags
- Clean out or organize their binders
- Finish famous proverbs such as "The early bird gets the ____________"
- Decide how and when they will complete their homework assignment
- Find three dissimilar objects and describe what they have in common
- Explain a favorite line from a song

Keep students engaged. If students are allowed free time, they will often abuse it and get out of hand. If you have even a few minutes at the end of class, allow the kids to pack up and spend those few minutes reviewing vocabulary, spelling, or content orally.

—Charlene Herrala, 24 years' experience

How to Handle Interruptions

Class interruptions are stressful for any teacher. Many teachers feel frustrated when their carefully planned lesson is interrupted by a fire drill, a class visitor, or even too many students who need to sharpen their pencil.

Interruptions destroy instructional time not just because they distract you but also because they tend to distract every child in your class. The best defense you have against losing instructional time to interruptions is to deliver an interesting lesson. Students who are fully engaged in meaningful and interesting work would rather stay on task than pay attention to yet another classmate sharpening a pencil.

You can minimize the negative effects of interruptions by meeting three goals:

Goal 1: Prevent as many interruptions as you can. Some teachers find that putting signs such as "Learning in Progress. Please Do Not Disturb" on the door serve as a gentle reminder to those whose business may not be urgent. Others work with colleagues whose classrooms are nearby so that one teacher does not schedule a noisy class activity on the same day that another has planned a test or other quiet activity. Still others have talked with their principal about poorly timed intercom announcements. Work with your colleagues in a similar fashion to solve problems when you can.

Goal 2: Minimize the disruption caused by an interruption. While you can prevent many interruptions during your school day, some are unavoidable. For example, you cannot prevent the interruption caused by a message from the office requesting a student for an early dismissal. In such situations, your goal must be to keep the other students on task. If you remind yourself that your goal is to minimize the disturbance, you are likely to create a solution to the problem.

Goal 3: Prepare for predictable interruptions. Have a plan in place for unavoidable interruptions. Having a plan will give you confidence, and your students will behave better because you will know what to do in almost any situation. When you make your plans for predictable interruptions, keep your solutions simple so that your students will be able to respond appropriately when the interruptions occur. Here is a list of some of the predictable interruptions that teachers have to handle successfully. Plan how you will manage each one.

- A student has no paper, pencil, or pen.
- Students ask to leave the class to use the restroom, see the nurse, or go to their locker.
- Students need to listen to intercom announcements.
- A visitor asks to speak with you.
- Students leave class early or arrive late.
- The class needs to rearrange desks for group work.
- Students need to sharpen pencils, staple papers, or dispose of trash.
- A student from another class asks to speak with one of your students.
- There is a commotion in the hallway or another classroom.

How to Handle Requests to Leave the Classroom

"Can I go to the restroom?" "Can I go to my locker?" "Can I take this lunch money to my brother?" Sometimes it may seem that you are the only person who does not want to leave the room.

Learning how to manage student requests to leave class will save you lots of time and trouble. The time you spend in planning how to cope successfully with these requests will be rewarded when students develop the self-discipline to manage such requests themselves.

In handling student requests to leave class, you first need to determine whether students are being truthful about why they need to leave class. If your hall pass has places for the signatures of other professionals such as the nurse or the media specialist, check the signature when students return, to ensure that they went where they told you they needed to go.

Where do your students want to go when they leave your class? Here is a list of some of the places that students at all levels of schooling ask to go to when they leave class, along with suggestions for how to effectively handle each type of request.

Library. You can allow students to go to the library, because they will have adult supervision there. If you are sending more than one or two students, you should check with the librarian first. Make sure that your students have a specific task there and that they know when you expect them to return.

Clinic. You can also send students to the school nurse's office without worry, because there is adult supervision there. If a student asks to go to the clinic too often, check with the nurse to see whether the requests are genuine. If a student is gone too long, make sure that you check to see whether there is a problem. Also, if a student is obviously ill, consider sending another student along to assist the ill child.

Another classroom. Sometimes a student will ask to go to another teacher's class; for example, cheerleaders may want to make posters for the big game or drama students may want to rehearse. These requests should not come from students. If another teacher wants you to release students from your class, then that teacher should contact you about it; you have no other way of knowing whether the requests are legitimate. Speak to the other teacher before you send students to another class. You should also refuse to be pressured into letting students leave if you do not believe that they can make up the work that they will miss in your class.

Locker. If you have a bank of shared supplies for students to use and if you allow students to turn in any assignments they have left in their locker immediately after class without a penalty, you will eliminate some requests. You can determine the validity of other requests on a case-by-case basis. At times, you can allow students to go to their locker, but you must also avoid giving the impression that students can use such requests whenever they feel like taking a little break from class.

Parking lot or car. Never send a student out of the building without checking with an administrator first. If a student has something that needs to be turned in during class, offer to accept it after school with no penalty rather than send a student to the parking lot.

Phone. Your school probably has a policy about student use of pay phones or office phones during class time. Unless it is an emergency, tell your students to use the phone between classes or at other times when they are not supposed to be in class.

Guidance office. Before you send a student to the guidance office, make sure that a counselor will be able to see the student. Students have been known to wait patiently for a counselor for hours rather than attend class.

Office. If a student asks to see an administrator, make sure that the administrator is available and willing to see the student before you honor the request.

To see another student. Sometimes, in the middle of your class, students will remember that they have the lunch money for their sibling or a note excusing a younger family member's tardiness. Do not allow students to leave your class to attend to this non-emergency business. Instead, allow students to take care of it between classes or during a break.

Water fountain. Unless a student is coughing or obviously in need of a drink of water, say no. Students use this request as a way to stretch their legs and break up a monotonous class. Make sure that you design your class so that you break up the monotony caused by sitting too long and that you encourage students to stretch their legs at appropriate intervals. Even older students periodically need a "wiggle break."

Restroom. You should never refuse a student's request to use the restroom. If you do and the student is ill, you may make the situation worse. Instead of saying no outright, you can say, "Have you finished your work? Can you please wait a few minutes?" If the student insists, then honor the request.

GUIDELINES FOR HANDLING STUDENT REQUESTS TO LEAVE CLASS

Making good decisions about whether to allow a student to leave the classroom is not always easy, no matter how much teaching experience you have. Consider the following guidelines as you begin to formulate your policy on students' leaving class:

- Do not allow more than one or two students to leave at one time.
- Do not refuse to allow students to go to the restroom or to the clinic. Use your best judgment about other requests.
- If a student seems to be making too many requests to leave the classroom, speak privately with him or her about the problem. If this does not work, call a parent or guardian. If there is a problem, the parent or guardian can apprise you. If there is not a problem, enlist that person's help in keeping the student focused and in class. Often, just knowing that you take the problem seriously enough to call their home will convince students to make fewer requests.
- You can prevent too many requests to leave the room by presenting fast-paced and interesting lessons that keep your students so engaged that they will not want to miss anything exciting.

- When you send students out of the room, whenever possible, make sure that an adult will supervise them. You are responsible for your students until that responsibility is assumed by another adult.
- Never allow students to leave the building without contacting an administrator first. Older students may wish to retrieve items that they have left in their car, but studies show that school parking lots provide opportunities for violence and other misbehaviors.
- Make sure to keep all used hall passes (if you do not use a generic one). File them in the folder that you maintain for each student; you may need to show them to an administrator or parent later in the term. You will also be able to keep better track of how many times a student has left class.
- Some teachers use laminated passes for each student. At the beginning of the year, you can photograph students and then use the photographs to make individual hall passes. Individual hall passes are useful because they allow supervisors on hall duty to quickly identify students who are not in class.
- If you intend to keep track of how often a student leaves class, you will need to devise a workable system. Some teachers use a sign-out sheet, some make notes on a class roster, and others issue a certain number of personalized hall passes per marking period and reward students who do not use all of them.
- There are many ways to refuse a request in a polite but firm manner. Instead of brusquely refusing, try one of these:
  - "Can you wait a few minutes?"
  - "Have you finished your work?"
  - "Let me check to see whether ____________ is in the ____________ office."
  - "Our school policy prohibits students from ____________ during class."
  - "Can you do that right after class?"

KEEPING TRACK OF STUDENTS WHO LEAVE THE CLASSROOM

Because you will need to keep track of who is out of your class, you should have a sign-out sheet as well as hall passes. A sign-out sheet can take many forms. You can post a sheet for students to fill out as they leave, have them sign out on a computer, or maintain a class logbook. If you are fortunate enough to teach in a school that is very small or peaceful, a generic hall pass may be acceptable. If you don't use a generic hall pass, your school probably has a hall pass form for you to use. You will need to keep plenty of these forms on hand.

The Last Ten Minutes of Class

You have two goals for the end of class: to have students who are reluctant to leave and to have students retain the information you have just taught them. The last ten minutes of class are the ideal time to accomplish both goals.

Things to Consider When Creating a Policy for Requests to Leave Class

You will need to establish and enforce a fair policy about leaving the classroom. Ask your mentor or a colleague whether there is a school policy or how other teachers handle this matter. If there is no formal school policy, consider these issues when creating your own policy:

- How often is it acceptable for a student to leave your class during a grading period?
- Where will you allow students to go without first consulting another adult?
- How can students ask permission so that the interruption is minimal?
- How will you maintain records of which students have left your class?
- Where will students sign out?
- When students return to class, where will they put their hall passes for you to keep?
- How will you enforce your policy? What consequences will your students face if they do not comply?

The routine you create for the end of class should be predictable, but also one that students can look forward to. Here is a simple two-step plan for the ending of class that you can follow in order to make sure that the last few minutes of your class are as productive as all the rest.

Step 1: Eight-minute closing exercise. Use this brief period to help students retain information by reviewing what you have just taught and by helping students look ahead to what they will be learning next. Here are some activities that you can adopt or adapt to end your class on a positive note:

- Have students list several things that they have just learned. Have them share this list with a classmate or with the entire group.
- Ask students to predict what they will learn next.
- Ask students to predict the meaning of the key terms for the next part of the unit.
- Have students write a quick explanation of the most interesting aspect of the day's lesson.
- Hold a quick review, vocabulary practice, or spelling bee.
- Ask students to explain the directions for their homework. Be sure to ask them to estimate how long it should take them to complete the assignment successfully.
- Unveil a final thought for the day that you have hidden under a sheet of paper that was taped to the board earlier in the day.

- Give your students a brief reading passage and ask them to comment on it.
- Show a cartoon or relevant illustration on the overhead projector.
- Assign an exit slip activity. (For information on exit slips, see Section Eleven.)

Step 2: Two-minute dismissal. After the closing exercise, you should allow two minutes for your students to prepare to be dismissed at your signal. During this time, they should have a routine to follow. This should include the following activities:

- Disposing of trash
- Stowing away books and materials
- Checking to make sure they don't leave anything behind

Do not let the end of your block disintegrate into a "do your homework" half hour. In doing so, you will have forfeited a significant amount of your instructional time.

—Luann Scott, 31 years' experience

During the last two minutes of class, you should move to the door so that you can speak to students as they leave. This will prevent any last-minute misbehaviors and show your students that they have a teacher who cares about them. You should not allow students to congregate at the door or jump up and bolt when the bell rings. Insist that you will dismiss class and that they should wait for your signal. You should not detain students after the bell has rung.

Talk It Over

How to Make the Most of Your Instructional Time

Use these questions as a springboard for discussions that will help you and your discussion group members grow and develop professionally. Discuss these questions about how to make effective use of instructional time:

1. Use Student Worksheet 12.1 to test your students' knowledge of how to use class time well. Discuss what you learned from this assessment.
2. Discuss the ways that teachers unintentionally waste their students' time. What can you do to avoid misuse of instructional time?
3. What does the expression *door to door* mean when applied to class time management? How do your colleagues use their time from door to door? What have you observed other teachers doing that made class time more productive?
4. One way to use time wisely is to give students enough work to do. What steps can you take to make sure you provide enough work? Who can help you with this?
5. What is your policy concerning students leaving the room? What is your school's policy? If you had to adjust it, what would you change?
6. Ask your colleagues to list the distractions they observe in your classroom. How can you minimize the disruptions caused by distractions?
7. Which of the anticipatory sets in this section would work well with your students? Brainstorm about other activities you can use to relate new learning to your students' previous learning.
8. The beginning and ending of class are times you can use to your students' advantage. What routines have you planned in order to open and close class on a positive and productive note?
9. How did you waste time when you were in school? How does this affect how you manage your own classroom? What do your colleagues have to share about this topic? How does this information help you?
10. When do your students tend to waste time most often? How can you help them be more productive at these moments?

SECTION THIRTEEN

Help Struggling Readers Find Success

In this section, you will learn

- ✔ How to avoid the most common mistakes in reading instruction
- ✔ How to use a balanced approach to help struggling readers
- ✔ How to use comprehension activities to help students master content
- ✔ How to enrich your students' vocabulary
- ✔ How to provide opportunities for your students to practice reading

Millions of students in our country struggle in school because they can't read well enough to keep up with their classmates. Eventually, many of these students drop out rather than continue the painful cycle of failure. When students are young, the situation is serious. When students are older, their struggles are heartbreaking. The problem is severe and widespread.

While illiteracy is receiving more attention than ever as reading experts develop strategies to address the situation, the challenges presented by struggling readers are very real, affecting almost every classroom teacher. No longer is reading the sole responsibility

It is *not* the responsibility of English teachers to direct the instruction of reading. It is the responsibility of everyone in the school.

—Sabrina Richardson, 7 years' experience

of instructors who teach reading, language arts, or English. If we want to eliminate illiteracy and reach all of our students in time to keep them from failing once more, all teachers must teach reading skills.

Time after time, studies show that students improve when teachers intervene to help them learn to read. And although it is more difficult to intervene with older students, when their teachers help them with reading, they show improvements, too.

Factors That Contribute to the Literacy Problem in Our Schools

Here is a brief list of some of the contributing factors that may have affected your students' reading development:

- Not all students are alike. Each student who struggles is unique in his or her reading problems and in what solutions to those problems will work best.
- Students who are poor readers usually do not want to read. Students who do not read do not improve their skills; they remain poor readers in a downward spiral of failure.
- All teachers will have to go beyond what is expected of them as classroom teachers if they wish to help students learn to read. They will have to commit themselves and their time to helping students build a foundation in reading, no matter what subject they teach.
- Few teachers are trained to teach reading, especially to struggling older readers.
- Finding materials that students want to read is often a problem. If a student is fifteen years old and reads at a third-grade level, it is not easy to find an engaging book that will appeal to a teenager.
- Some students are so used to a chaotic time schedule that they have trouble sustaining attention for more than a few minutes.
- If students come from a family that speaks nonstandard English or doesn't speak English at all, then it is unlikely that they will be able to understand what they read if it is written in Standard English, not to mention academic English.
- Many older readers who struggle with reading are so ashamed that they become adept at hiding their deficiency with behavior problems in order to avoid ridicule.
- Students may not have enough background information to understand what a passage is about even when they understand each word. Limited life experience causes many students to miss important facts that others may take for granted.
- Students who struggle with reading may not have access to the technology that makes it easier for successful students to read well. If students do not have access to computers outside class, it is harder for them to engage in meaningful real-life experiences that others can access from their home computer.
- Students who are used to failure are not easily convinced that they can improve with effort, instruction, and practice. They must be taught to believe in themselves in order to learn to read well.

Effective Reading Is Important for All Students

Even though you may teach older students or a subject, such as advanced math, in which reading for pleasure is not as frequent as it is in an elementary classroom, it is still your responsibility to work with your students to help them become better readers. If reading is, indeed, the primary learning tool for all students, then working to increase your students' reading skills is a responsibility you cannot ignore.

If you choose to accept the challenge of making your students more literate, your work will go far beyond the confines of your classroom. You will have a profound effect on your students' lives. While this is a daunting task, it does not have to be an impossible one. In the following list, you will find strategies to help students improve their reading skills regardless of their age or the content of the course.

- Teachers should use appropriate motivational techniques to interest students in learning to read well. Reading should not be an unpleasant chore for students; rather, it should be a gateway to learning.
- Teachers should observe their students as they read, to determine their strengths and weaknesses.
- Teachers should also learn as much as possible about their students' lives at home and in the community, to determine the levels of support available to help struggling readers.
- Teachers should use a variety of activities to teach reading skills. Appealing to students' learning preferences is essential, regardless of their age.
- Before reading a passage, teachers should activate any prior knowledge their students may have or provide enough background information for students to make connections between the material and their own experiences.
- Teachers should use real-life, informational texts in their classes when appropriate. Reading aloud to students as they follow along in a text is a powerful tool that teachers should use daily. Poor readers often are not exposed to rich oral language at home.
- Teachers should provide time each day for students to read independently. Providing a text-rich environment for students in every classroom would do much to help them become better readers.
- Teachers should prepare students for successful reading of an assignment with activities before, during, and after the assignment.
- Teachers should work with the families of students who struggle with reading. Many times, parents and other family members are willing to be supportive but do not know what to do. A partnership between classroom and home is an important source of support for inexperienced readers.
- Teachers should train students to determine the purpose of assigned reading and to adapt their rate and method of reading accordingly.

- Teachers should engage students in metacognitive strategies such as reflection, questioning, and problem solving. Students who are aware of how they read are more likely to be skillful readers than students who are not aware.
- Teachers should take time for vocabulary enrichment. Many different activities can help students increase their word recognition if teachers take the time to build them into their lessons.
- Teachers should include activities to help students comprehend the information in the text. Using a variety of techniques such as graphic organizers and collaboration with peers will help students derive meaning from their assignments.
- Teachers should not give up on their struggling readers. In time, with increased instruction and support from all teachers, students can improve their reading skills. Work with a steady heart, knowing that improved readers will be the result of your effort.

> As a reading intervention teacher with experience in middle school and elementary school settings, I would say that one important thing for all teachers to keep in mind is that it is never too late to teach students to read and write.
>
> —*Paige Adcock, 10 years' experience*

What Are the Most Important Reading Skills to Teach?

Reading experts have spent decades in the "reading wars" that have shaped our national reading programs in various ways, for better and for worse. While some reading specialists believed that students learn best from phonics instruction, others believed that the whole-language approach was more effective. In recent years, however, many reading experts have come to agree on an important guideline for teaching reading skills: a balanced approach is best.

Students, especially those who are beginning to learn to read, need instruction in phonics. Trained reading teachers usually perform this instruction. Older students benefit from instruction in the other aspects of reading: comprehension of text, vocabulary acquisition and improvement, and fluency development. Any teacher, even one who works with older students in specific content areas, can and should work with students to improve these three areas.

A Dozen Mistakes to Avoid When Teaching Literacy Skills

1. Don't ask students to read aloud in front of other students if doing so makes them uncomfortable or if they are such poor readers that other students will ridicule them.
2. Don't neglect to teach students how to pronounce words. If they are to integrate a word into their vocabulary, they need to know how to say it.
3. Don't embarrass a student who can't read. Work to help students, not humiliate them.
4. Don't expect other teachers to teach your students how to read. You need to teach your students the skills they need to tackle the texts and language of your content area or grade level.
5. Don't neglect to introduce new words before students read a passage. When they can make the connection between the words in the new material and what they already know, students can learn more quickly.
6. Don't forget to use activities to help students understand the material before, during, and after they read.
7. Don't neglect opportunities to involve your students in selecting the material they will read. When students have choices in reading, they tend to read with more intensity.
8. Don't disregard the importance of reading every day. Students need to read every day in order to improve their skills.
9. Don't neglect to include a variety of reading materials in your lessons. Students need to read more than just the text if they are to become accomplished readers.
10. Don't ignore the importance of a rich oral language when you work with students' reading levels. Include auditory experiences such as reading aloud, listening to audio books, and other oral activities to enrich the language your students bring to what they read.
11. Don't forget to include plenty of authentic reading experiences for your students. When students are reading to solve real-life problems, they read with more interest than when they are reading just to get to the end of an assignment.
12. Don't complain about your students' lack of reading skills. It is up to you to help them. Do so with confidence in the knowledge that they will be better readers when they leave your class.

I feel strongly that teaching a child to read is the most important skill we can teach. It is the foundation on which we build. Just like a house must have a strong foundation to support the first and second floor, reading provides that foundation for math, science, history, English, and so on.

—William N. Owen, 43 years' experience

Helping Students Comprehend What They Read

Helping students improve their comprehension of what they read is something that almost every teacher already does to some degree; after all, students have been performing activities—such as answering the questions at the end of a textbook chapter or reading a word problem aloud—for years.

One of the biggest problems that students who have poor reading skills face is that because they are likely to be behind in all of their learning, it is hard for them to catch up with their peers. Reading comprehension is the key to all of their learning in school. The work you do to help them with reading skills will be amply rewarded as they reverse the cycle of falling behind and begin a cycle of successful comprehension of what they read.

There are many reasons that students do not comprehend what they read. The language of the text, their lack of prior knowledge, and insufficient guidance from their teachers are just a few. Teaching reading is a complex issue, but here is one simple thing for a first-year teacher to remember: you must help students comprehend what they read by giving them assignments and activities before they read, while they read, and after they have completed reading.

ACTIVITIES FOR STUDENTS BEFORE THEY READ AN ASSIGNMENT

Pre-reading activities can benefit students of all ages. Pre-reading activities have several purposes. An important one is to activate students' prior knowledge so they can connect the new information in the text to previous learning. Another purpose is to make sure that students have the vocabulary they need to understand the concepts in the text. You should also use pre-reading activities to motivate students to learn more about the topic and to read independently. Finally, pre-reading activities give your students the confidence they need to read with interest, purpose, and intensity. Use the following pre-reading activities, or adapt them for your students and their needs.

- Show students a photograph or a video clip that is related to the content of the text. The images will help students engage with the reading and visualize the action or material.
- Use a Know/Want to Know/Learned (KWL) chart to help students recall what they already know and anticipate what they will learn. The benefits of a KWL chart are that it helps activate prior knowledge, engages students in the reading, and allows an opportunity for reflection.
- Create an anticipation activity in which students can predict what they will learn. Try different formats; for example,
  - A true-or-false exercise in which students respond to facts that will be in the text
  - A scrambled list of events to put in order
  - A list of statements for students to agree or disagree with

- A list of people and places to match with information about them
- A cause-and-effect chart

▶ Ask students to skim the text, looking at the headings, boldface type, illustrations, and other textual elements. When they have done this, ask them to write notes on topics such as these:

- Questions they have for you
- Questions they want classmates to answer
- Questions they believe the text will answer
- Anything that appears confusing before reading
- How long it will take them to read the selection
- The information they already know
- Unusual words they notice
- Which illustrations are most interesting

▶ Give students a set of questions that they will answer as they read the text. Discuss the questions before they read, in order to see what information they already have. Help them see how the questions are aligned with the text and how they should answer them.

▶ Discuss the best ways for students to read the text. Should they read it all at once? Read part of the way through and then answer questions? Scan for information?

▶ Give students a checklist of the key points to watch for so that they can check them off as they find them while reading.

▶ If there are questions at the end of the selection in a textbook, ask students to read them first so that they can find that information as they read.

▶ Give students an incomplete chart of facts or key terms from the text and ask them to predict the missing information.

From the math teacher: problem solving is all about interpretation and analysis. Most people think you can do math without good reading skills—not so.

—Kay Stephenson, 33 years' experience

▶ To prevent students from jumping into reading without preparation, time them as they skim and scan the text. Insist that they cannot begin reading until a predetermined amount of time has passed. This bit of reverse psychology works surprisingly well to motivate even the most sophisticated learners.

▶ Give students a concept map, web, or other graphic organizer to allow them to anticipate what they will be learning about as they read.

▶ Provide students with a summary of the information they will read. This technique is surprisingly successful because it lets students read with confidence.

- Give students a summary of what they will read in which some of the information is missing. This technique is successful because students will read to find the missing material.
- Ask students to brainstorm what they already know about what they are going to read. If you ask them to do this by themselves for a few minutes, then combine their information with a partner's, and then share that information with the entire group, your students should have a good background for understanding the reading.
- Give students a problem similar to a situation in the text and ask them to solve it. Later, they can come back to this problem with new knowledge and analyze their solution.

ACTIVITIES FOR STUDENTS WHILE THEY ARE READING AN ASSIGNMENT

Activities that you ask students to complete during an assignment should motivate them to continue reading, to learn the content you want them to know, and to interact with the text in a meaningful way.

Don't hesitate to break up the reading into manageable segments so that you can monitor for comprehension early in the process. When you help students divide their reading into manageable amounts, they are less likely to be overwhelmed by the volume of information they need to master.

Other successful general strategies include making sure that students think with a pen as they read. When students read and write, they master the content much more efficiently than they do when they just read mindlessly.

Students may also benefit from reading with a partner or with a group. When students work together, they can share ideas and solve problems quickly. Students can work with each other in a group to discuss topics such as what they have learned, problems they are having, or aspects such as what parts of the material they enjoy.

The following list of activities is just a brief inventory of some of the ideas that other teachers have found to be successful with their students. Consider the needs of your own students as you adapt them for your class.

- Create questions for your students to answer as they read. You can make this process pleasant for your students by building in choices or activities such as allowing them to answer only some of the questions or ask a friend for help when the passage is difficult.
- Have students formulate their own questions as they read. An interesting twist on this assignment is to have students write their questions on self-sticking notes that they can store in their books.
- Hand students a blank strip of paper similar in shape to a bookmark. Ask them to write their notes on it as they read. Because poor readers are often uncertain about how to take notes, the limited size of this paper allows them to work with greater

ease. You can vary this technique by printing key terms, an outline, or other helpful information on the bookmark.

- Have students time themselves periodically to see how fast they read. Students who read quickly tend to comprehend more than students who read and reread a passage.
- Give students a partial outline of the material and ask them to complete it. Or show students how to outline the basic parts of the text themselves.
- Have students complete graphic organizers similar to the ones they used as a pre-reading assignment, filling them in with information from the text instead of their own previous knowledge. Many Web resources can be searched for graphic organizers to help your students comprehend what they read. Begin your search with these:
    - **Teachnology (http://www.teach-nology.com).** At the home page, click on "Teacher Tools" and then on "Graphic Organizer Makers" to access dozens of free and easy-to-use organizers for students of all ages.
    - **Scholastic (http://www.scholastic.com).** Scholastic's Web site has many excellent graphic organizers devoted to reading comprehension. At the home page, use "Graphic Organizers for Reading Comprehension" as your search term.
    - **Houghton Mifflin's Education Place (http://www.eduplace.com/graphic organizer/index.html).** Here you will find more than three dozen useful graphic organizers to download.
- Ask students to find the main idea and the supporting ideas in sections of the reading.
- Have any photos or other visual representations that you presented before students began reading available for them to look at as they read.
- Have students highlight important information, if the text is one they can mark.
- If the selection contains events or facts in a specific order, scramble them and ask students to put them in the correct order.
- Stop students periodically and ask, "What have you learned so far?"
- Have students read together in order to answer each other's questions as they arise.
- Have students take notes in a column style such as the Cornell system (see Section Eleven). If they work together in pairs to do this, both partners will benefit. Once they have each taken notes, they can then compare them to make sure that their understanding of the text is accurate.
- Provide students with a reader's checklist of suggested strategies that they can use to help them understand the text—for example, find topic sentences, look for supporting details, or formulate questions.

- Ask students to make a statement of fact from the text, then ask them to support their statement with evidence from the text.
- Ask students to describe what they are reading, to help them visualize the material.
- Provide students with drawings or photographs of people or other items in the selection and ask them to match them with items from a list of terms or other descriptors.

- If you can play appropriate music to enhance the tone of the selection, you should.
- Many students benefit from listening to an audiotape of the material. It tends to motivate them to keep reading while it focuses their attention.
- Many of the activities you introduced to your students as pre-reading activities can be continued as activities that will help them during the reading phase of their assignment. Work with students to continue or complete those activities as they read.

ACTIVITIES FOR STUDENTS AFTER THEY HAVE READ AN ASSIGNMENT

The third component of reading comprehension instruction involves the activities that students do after they have read a selection. The pre-reading activities set a purpose for reading; the activities while students are reading guide them through the assignment; and the activities afterward encourage them to use the information they have just learned.

After students have read an assignment, many of the same types of activities you have used with them earlier are still appropriate: concept maps, brainstorming, or working with vocabulary, for example. The difference is that after students have read, their focus should be on analyzing, synthesizing, evaluating, and reflecting on information from the content they have just studied. The following activities will help them interpret their learning in a new way so that their understanding as well as their knowledge is broader than before they encountered the material.

- Ask students to skim the passage again, looking for specific information or details they did not look for earlier.
- Quiz students in a variety of nonthreatening ways, to check their knowledge. Or have them quiz each other.
- Give students a checklist of information in the passage that others have found to be significant. Ask them to find details pertaining to the information or to use the checklist to make sure that a partner has mastered the information.
- Ask students who have made predictions as part of a pre-reading assignment to check the accuracy of those predictions. In fact, when students have completed any sort of anticipation activity, such as a KWL chart, now is the time to check it, verify it, or complete it.
- Have students write a summary of what they have read. Or have students do their summary orally, using group members to assist them.
- In groups, have students discuss the parts of the text that they found confusing, interesting, or significant.
- Have students brainstorm ways they can use this information in other aspects of their school life.
- Have students interpret the material in a new, creative way by making a poster, a diorama, or some other imaginative project.

- Give students a new example, scenario, or problem to solve based on the information in the text.
- Ask students to evaluate how well they achieved their purpose for reading the text.
- Ask students to tell you the most significant information they learned from the passage.
- Check the answers to questions that students formulated, that you used as a reading guide, or that students may still have about the material.
- Give students a provocative statement from the text and ask them to respond to it, using their new knowledge.
- Ask students to find quotations from the text that they find interesting, thoughtful, or confusing.
- Give students some lines from the text and ask them to put these lines in order.
- Ask students to go back through the selection and examine the textual elements again. Can they suggest changes or improvements—for example, different headings or illustrations?

Not every child has the same problem with reading. The problem must be identified before instruction is done. There may be a child who stumbles over every other word, indicating a problem with fluency. However, there may be one who is a fluent reader but has no clue what was read, which indicates problem with comprehension. You must have a starting point; you can't just dive into it!

—Sabrina Richardson, 7 years' experience

Enriching Students' Vocabulary

The second aspect of improving your students' reading proficiency is helping them with vocabulary acquisition. For all students, from emergent readers to graduating seniors, vocabulary acquisition is an important skill. In fact, it is a lifelong process for all of us. However, it is not enough to expect students to memorize the terms associated with the unit they are studying, as so many teachers in the past have done.

Poor readers do not have the background to understand most of these textbook words and the concepts associated with them. It is up to their teachers to help them make the connection between the words on the page and their meanings. You can teach students new words and their concepts in many different ways, which can be divided into two main categories.

The first way that many students learn new words is through new experiences. When you take your students on field trips, show them a video clip, sing a silly song with them, or involve them in other activities that are new and different, you enlarge their language skills.

Activities such as these broaden their world and give them a real-life context in which to understand what they read.

The second significant way that students learn new words is through reading. The more reading experiences a child has, the more language he or she will acquire. However, if students are not capable or independent readers functioning at grade level, it will be very difficult for them to acquire new words from reading without help. Therefore, their teachers need to assist them in learning new words. Here are some basic actions that every teacher should take when teaching students new vocabulary words:

- Teach students to associate words with other material. Build connections between words they are studying in your class and words or concepts they have learned previously or in other contexts.
- Present the words many times and in different ways. Present vocabulary words before you teach a lesson so that students can understand them and, in turn, comprehend the text. As your students study the material, take care to go over the words again. Finally, at the end of a unit of study, review the vocabulary so that students can lock in their learning.
- Make connections with other content areas. If students can take words from your class and use them in other classes, you have been successful. Help students make this connection by asking them how they could use a word or a form of the word you are studying in other ways.
- Take the tedium out of finding meanings. Derive meanings together. When students formulate their own definitions, they tend to remember those meanings far better than the ones they look up in a dictionary. Here are some quick tips for you to adapt:
    - When you present a list of words before a lesson, ask students to anticipate what the words might mean in the context of the lesson.
    - Allow students to work in groups to restate textbook definitions.
    - Have students match vocabulary words to photographs that illustrate the meanings.
    - Have students brainstorm other meanings for a word under study.
    - Put a list of words in one column with a scrambled list of definitions in another column for students to try to match before they begin studying the unit.
- Students need to hear the words. Always spend time pronouncing the words under study with students. This technique is particularly helpful to auditory learners, and it helps everyone make the words part of their spoken vocabulary.
- Show students how to use context clues. For example, you could ask students to read a passage and find three words that have the same definition. You could also have a mini-discussion in which you ask students how they figured out a word's meaning from the text.
- Expose students to a variety of words. It is not enough for poor readers to just see and hear the words in a textbook if they are going to improve their reading skills.

They need to see and hear the words associated with real-life occupations, technology, academics, current events, and other aspects of everyday life. Often, students who are poor readers are not exposed to these words at home.

- Raise your students' awareness of the words around them. Use games, activities, discussions, varied readings, and other strategies to help your students pay attention to the words they encounter each day.
- Model good vocabulary skills. Let students see you looking up words in a dictionary or taking care to use the correct synonym when you write sentences on the board, setting a powerful example for all of your students. When you teach students whose families are not educated, whose families do not speak English as a first language, or who live in poverty, it is especially important to model good vocabulary attack skills often.

HOW TO MAKE YOUR CLASSROOM RICH IN WORDS

If you want to increase your students' oral and reading vocabularies, common sense will tell you that you must expose them to words. Some students do not read well because the language they are exposed to at home and away from school is not content-rich or varied enough to enable them to advance their reading skills. Fortunately, there are many, many ways for teachers at all grade levels to help their students learn new words. Customize some of the following strategies to make your classroom a place where students see and hear interesting words in a variety of ways.

- Each day, present a word of the day. This word can be from your content area or from the academic language of school, or it can be just an interesting word from the news or daily life. Your students can learn many words painlessly in this way. Write the word on the board or on an overhead transparency, say it, post it near the clock or a window, have it as your screen saver, or do whatever else it takes to make students aware of this new word.
- Have a student version of the word of the day. All but very young students can take a turn at bringing in a word for the day. Combine this word activity with the teacher's word of the day, and your students can learn two new words each day with little effort.
- Use the opening and ending exercises of your lesson to make students aware of words associated with the lesson. If you hold up flash cards, write vocabulary words on the board, have students play word games, give a quick little puzzle, or ask students to sketch the definitions of the words in the day's lesson, you are making vocabulary important to your students.
- Display large graphic organizers. Ask students to complete or create a web, chart, or other visual representation of some of the words in the lesson. Not only will students learn by completing the graphic organizer, but they will also benefit again when you display them.

- Make a word wall. Although this is a popular activity with young students, it can be easily adapted to the needs of older students. Before you begin a unit of study, list the key terms that students will be learning on a large sheet of paper. Throughout the unit, the words remain on the wall, reinforcing key concepts that students should know. Variations on this idea include having students bring in words for the word wall, having students create individual word walls, and making the lists unique by adding examples and illustrations.
- Have students make personal dictionaries. The format does not have to be elaborate in order for students to benefit from them. A personal dictionary is a record of the words a student has learned throughout a unit of study. It can be housed in a separate folder or in a section of a student's notebook.
- Have plenty of text-rich materials on hand for students to use in class or to browse. Because many less capable readers have not been exposed to many print media, they need to see the written word in your classroom. Newspapers, magazines, catalogues (yes, those you classify as junk mail), telephone directories, cookbooks, comic books, and books are all essential. If you have a computer for students to use, you can also use it as a source of text for students. Here are some ways to add more reading materials to your class:
    - Ask students to bring in old magazines, papers, or books.
    - Shop at yard sales.
    - Purchase books at book sales held by public libraries.
    - Ask local businesses for donations.
    - Seek support and donations from your school's parent-teacher association.
    - Try the Gutenberg Project (www.gutenberg.org), a Web resource for free e-books. At this site, there are thousands of free books available for downloading. Read the copyright information on the site to make sure that you can use a particular downloaded book in class.
- Have reference materials handy. As soon as they are able to use them, students should have access to dictionaries, thesauri, instruction booklets, atlases, old textbooks, charts and graphs of all kinds, maps, and other reference materials. Even out-of-date encyclopedias from yard sales will enrich your students' word usage. Students can use them for a variety of activities such as browsing, reading for pleasure, looking for new words, finding facts, or writing essays or responses to questions.
- Have oral language materials available for students as well. Audio books, Library of Congress recordings, and other oral materials that allow students to hear words that they do not usually hear spoken will enrich their vocabulary. Have students read aloud to each other in small groups. Reading aloud to your students every day will also enrich their world.

I've found that vocabulary is a great obstacle for students who read at low levels. When explaining content vocabulary, keep in mind that a low student's vocabulary is usually quite low. Don't assume that a student knows even basic concepts. Take a moment to explain.

—*Dawn Carroll, 10 years' experience*

ACTIVITIES THAT MAKE LEARNING VOCABULARY WORDS ENJOYABLE AND SUCCESSFUL

Direct instruction is one of the most effective ways to increase your students' vocabulary. In the past, direct instruction meant making students look up a tedious list of words and attempt to memorize them for a weekly test. Today, educators realize that learning words out of context or from isolated lists in a textbook is not an effective method of learning. Here are some ideas to spark interesting vocabulary activities in your classroom:

- Have students complete or create puzzles. Use one of the many online puzzle sites to create a crossword, word search, or other type of puzzle for your students to solve as they master the meaning of the vocabulary terms associated with a unit of study. Students of all ages also enjoy talking over words as they complete a puzzle as part of a team effort.
- Have students categorize words. There are many ways for students to learn to classify words. A simple one is to give students a list of words to place on a chart with column headings that you have created. For example, if your students were studying weather, you could give them a list of thirty words to place on a chart with the column headings "Cloud Types," "Types of Precipitation," and "Heat Wave Words." Another way to have students categorize words is to ask them to brainstorm as many words as they can about a certain topic. Or you can ask them to predict a classification of words before beginning a unit of study or to classify words according to their connotation or association—positive or negative words, for example.
- Learn other forms of words. For example, if your class is studying a concept such as "expert," then a quick side lesson into various forms of the word itself may help less able readers. If they learn that *expertise* and *expertly* are related to the original word, your students have increased their vocabulary.
- Play word games with your students. A simple game that many teachers have found successful is played like this: Divide students into two teams. Have a representative from each team sit in the front of the room, facing the class. Write a word on the board behind them. Have team members take turns giving one-word clues until one of the students guesses the word. Or play Hangman, Scrabble, or any of the hundreds of other games that can be adapted for vocabulary learning.

- Use flash cards. Students benefit from the repetition and reinforcement provided by flash cards. Flash cards have many other benefits, too. They offer a kinesthetic element, because students create them and then manipulate them while studying. When students study together with flash cards, they are no longer mindlessly looking over their work. To add interest to flash cards, have students use photographs or drawings, colored ink, or even mnemonic devices when making them. Students can store their flash cards in plastic bags in their notebooks.
- Discuss words with your students. After students read a passage from a textbook, ask each of them to write down a word that interests them. Have some students share their word with the class. Or find a word with an interesting history and tell students a quick anecdote about its origin. Talk about the connotations of words and why some words have the power they do.
- Appeal to students' imagination. Choose an ordinary word for an object, such as *chair* or *pencil*. Ask students to use their imagination to see how many uses the object could have other than its intended original one. Have them share their responses in various ways, depending on their age and skill level. If your students ask for a thesaurus to look up other meanings for verbs associated with the object, then you will know that your students are having fun and are engaged in expanding their vocabulary.
- Get students moving. Using a large font, print out the vocabulary words and meanings that your class is studying. Cut the words apart, forming individual squares, and do the same with the definitions. Pass out the squares to your students. Have them mingle until they match the words with their definitions.
- Reuse the words in original sentences. Divide students into teams and give each team the same word to use in a sentence. Ask students to write their sentences on the board, read them aloud, or otherwise share their sentences so that the class can decide which one is the best sentence. Or ask students to select an important sentence from the reading assignment in the lesson and rephrase it.

Increasing Reading Fluency

Fluency in reading can be defined in several different ways. Here is one definition that may be relevant for many first-year teachers: fluency is effortless application of the skills needed to comprehend the text being read. When all of the parts of the reading process come together, students can be considered fluent readers. Fluent readers understand what they read because they understand the words in the context in which the author used them.

Becoming a fluent reader is a multifaceted, complicated task for readers who function at grade level. It is even more complex for students who struggle to read. As a concerned teacher, there is much that you can do to help your students become fluent readers.

One of the most significant steps you can take is to educate yourself. To learn more about the complex issues of reading fluency and reading instruction in general, take advantage of the many, many sources available to you. Begin your search for current and useful information with these outstanding Web sites:

- **Educational Development Center (http://www.literacymatters.org).** Here you can learn much about how to help students in middle and secondary grades learn to read with greater skill. This useful site has extensive links to the latest information on reading and literacy for adolescent readers.
- **Center for the Study of Reading (http://csr.ed.uiuc.edu/Index.htm).** The Center for the Study of Reading conducts research and provides much useful information about reading practices for educators on its Web site.

Web Resources to Help You Improve Your Students' Vocabulary Skills

Many useful Internet sites are available to help teachers who want to make vocabulary study an important part of their class. You can learn many innovative ways to teach words and word study, and your students can use many of these sites independently. Try these sites:

- **Vocabulary University (http://www.vocabulary.com).** Jan and Carey Cook, creators of nationally syndicated word puzzles, maintain this word-rich site. Your students will enjoy the interactive puzzles and activities, and you will find helpful activities for your class.
- **ProTeacher (http://www.proteacher.com).** Here you will find many links and activities that have been tested by other elementary teachers. Use "Vocabulary" as a search word to access the wealth of materials you will find at this excellent site.
- **Teachnology (http://www.teach-nology.com).** Search on the word "Vocabulary" to link to other useful sites as well as to access strategies, activities, and lesson plans. This site is useful for teachers of students of all ages.
- **Wordsmith (http://wordsmith.org).** At the home page for Wordsmith, you and your students can search for the word of the day. You can also search for previous words of the day or even submit a word.
- **Merriam-Webster (http://www.wordcentral.com).** Here students can build their own dictionary online, use a student dictionary, access a daily buzzword, and link to other resources related to dictionaries and words.
- **Interactive Wordplays (http://www.wordplays.com).** At this site, your students will be able to play dozens of interactive word games such as anagrams, puzzles, Boggle, and many more.
- **AOL Study-Buddies (http://homework-help.aol.com).** Although this is a site geared toward helping students with homework, there are over a hundred word games for students here. You can click on the "Games" tab to access them. You can also search a large library of lesson plans for vocabulary activities.

- **International Reading Association (http://www.reading.org).** The International Reading Association is an influential organization of literacy professionals. At their Web site, you will find extensive information about literacy issues. You will also find specific links to resources devoted to reading and reading issues at all grade levels.
- **Reading Is Fundamental (http://www.rif.org).** This organization focuses on young children. It offers advice, tips, lesson plans, book-based activities, Web resources, and daily activities for young readers.
- **International Reading Association/National Council of Teachers of English (http://www.readwritethink.org).** Here two powerful organizations involved with school literacy have joined to offer thousands of links to resources for teachers who want to help their students improve their literacy skills.

It doesn't matter what they read, as long as it is reading.

—*Nancy Parker,*
31 years' experience

There are no easy solutions for students who are not fluent readers. All of the skills involved in successful reading must come together in order for fluency to occur. Because they are not good readers, many students who struggle to read do not want to practice until they become proficient. Without practice, students do not increase speed, develop comprehension, or acquire vocabulary. However, many students do overcome their lack of fluency to become proficient readers; your students can, too.

HOW TO BUILD FLUENCY THROUGH SUSTAINED SILENT READING

For decades, sustained silent reading has been used in American education in various formats ranging from a schoolwide endeavor to an occasional practice used only by language arts or other interested teachers. Despite its irregular history, sustained silent reading is a method many teachers today use to improve their students' fluency.

Sustained silent reading is just what it says: students reading silently for a sustained period of time. Students practice their reading skills when they do sustained silent reading. Why is a formal program needed? Many students do very little reading when they are not in school. Moreover, many students do not read even while they are in class.

Design and implement a program for sustained silent reading in your classroom; your students will benefit. Vary the activities and strategies you use to make it a positive, engaging, and useful period for your students. To create a sustained silent reading program in your class, consider some of these ideas:

- Sustained silent reading should happen every day.
- The length of the time allotted for sustained silent reading will vary from classroom to classroom and with the age and nature of your students.

Four Strategies for Building Reading Fluency

Here are some simple strategies you can use right now to help your students become more fluent readers:

1. **Students should know the words that occur most frequently on sight.** These high-frequency words make up much of the text that we read. When students can recognize these words quickly and easily, they are on their way to fluency. Don't be misled by the age of your students. You may assume incorrectly that middle school or secondary students are already familiar with these words. For a variety of reasons, they may not be. To learn more about the *sight words* your students need to learn, try visiting Literacy Connections (http://literacyconnections.com). At this site, you will find more information about sight words and other aspects of literacy that you can use in your class, no matter how old or young your students are.
2. **Provide plenty of oral reading opportunities for your students.** When students listen to an audiotape of their textbook, a story, or even their teacher reading to them as they follow along in the text, they gain from the experience. They learn how to express themselves, how to follow punctuation and other clues, and how to pronounce words. Even older students who struggle to read fluently will benefit when their teachers model how to read a passage aloud.
3. **Discuss the use of clues such as punctuation with students.** Poor readers often do not catch meanings because they overlook punctuation. When you read aloud to students as they follow along in a text, they learn the significance of punctuation and other clues such as headings, titles, and captions.
4. **Expose your students to a wide range of reading materials.** Students who see a variety of words or the same words in different contexts read better than students who do not.

- Students should read for the entire time allotted for this activity. They should not be allowed to do homework or unfinished work.
- Students must already have selected a book when the time to begin reading starts. Otherwise, some reluctant readers will take the entire time to select their reading material.
- Students should not be allowed to talk, disturb others, or leave the room if sustained silent reading is to be a serious endeavor in your classroom.
- Many teachers allow students to read whatever they want as long as it is not work for another class. If your classroom is rich in text materials, your students will have plenty of reading material.
- If students want to change the book or other item they are reading, it is usually best to do so after the day's reading period is over.

- You should devise a structured way for students to respond to their reading. Whether through a book talk, a journal entry, a quick exit slip, a discussion with you, or in some other way, students need to reflect on what they have read. They should be held accountable for this work.
- Work with your students to devise rewards, set class and individual goals, and maintain the integrity of this time.
- You and your students need to work together to make this a pleasant activity. Ask their opinions about how to make it so.
- You will send a powerful message to your students if you model good reading strategies by reading with them.

> **When students are in a higher grade than their reading level shows, don't dwell on how it has happened. Identify students with needs and address those needs.**
>
> —*Dawn Carroll, 10 years' experience*

Talk It Over

How to Help Struggling Readers Find Success

Use these questions as a springboard for discussions that will help you and your discussion group members grow and develop professionally. Discuss these questions about how to help your struggling readers find success:

1. What strategies will you use to include independent reading time for students in your class? What do your colleagues suggest?
2. Which of the reading strategies in this section are you already using in your class? Which can you implement right away? Which will you need help from others to implement?
3. Discuss with your colleagues some of the strategies they use to introduce reading material and vocabulary words at the start of a lesson.
4. What reading problems do your students have? What can you do to help them with these problems? Who can help you find solutions?
5. What can you do to make your classroom a print-rich environment? What can you and your colleagues do to make your school a place where reading materials are easily accessible to all students?

6. What types of materials do your students like to read? How do you know this? What can you do to capitalize on this interest?
7. How can you increase the support your students have for their reading from the community and at home? How can you connect with family and community members to enlist their support? Brainstorm ways to include parents and families in the process of improving your students' reading skills.
8. How can you raise your students' awareness of the importance of improving their reading skills? What suggestions do your colleagues have on how to motivate students to learn to read better?
9. How will you know when your efforts to improve your students' reading skills have been successful? What steps will you take to capitalize on this success?
10. What can you do to improve the oral language skills of your students? What issues pertaining to your students' oral language are sensitive ones? What will you need to do to manage these issues successfully?

SECTION FOURTEEN

Manage Your Classroom Through Early Intervention

In this section, you will learn

- ✔ How to avoid punishing students and promote self-discipline
- ✔ How to use early intervention strategies
- ✔ How to create and enforce classroom rules
- ✔ How to monitor students successfully
- ✔ How to be consistent in preventing discipline problems

Most new teachers report that their biggest fear is one that also plagues experienced teachers: not being able to control their class. Unfortunately, this fear is legitimate. Many educators leave teaching because the lack of respect and basic social skills among their students is so discouraging.

You do not have to be one of those teachers who gives up on the profession. You can learn the classroom management skills you need to control your class and enjoy your students. While classroom management can be a daunting concern, it is also one of the essential aspects of your new career.

Can you recall a teacher who was able to control a class effortlessly? It is never effortless; skillful teachers only make it seem that way. *Every teacher has discipline problems.* These problems can involve simple issues such as the best way to manage the traffic flow in a classroom as well as serious concerns such as what to do when a student becomes violent.

Experienced teachers will tell you that it is far easier and more productive to prevent discipline problems than to deal with their aftermath. While you can learn to prevent behavior problems from disrupting your classroom by taking a proactive approach when they do occur, successful classroom management also includes strategies such as motivating your students to be self-disciplined, teaching and enforcing behavior expectations, and maintaining a caring relationship with your students. With all of these elements in place, you will experience very few serious discipline problems.

Why Punishment Is Not the Answer

Punishment as a behavior management technique has been around for hundreds of years. Even though educators know that harsh punishments will not transform troublemakers into well-behaved students, threats of punishment, fear of punishment, and punishment itself are still common methods of making children of all ages behave.

There are several problems with using punishment as a means of crowd control. Punishment is a short-term solution that actually creates long-term problems. Adults cannot simply bully students into lasting good behavior. If you use punishment techniques often enough, you can expect a backlash. If you do succeed in making your students afraid of you, then you can expect to have students refuse to work, talk back to you, or worse.

Punishment is ineffective because it does not effect a permanent change in your students. A class controlled by a tyrant quickly falls apart if there is a substitute teacher in the room. Students who are punished frequently do not grow into self-disciplined learners who take control of their own behavior.

Another reason not to use punishment is that, sadly, some of your students are probably accustomed to cruelty and harsh behavior. It is highly likely that at least some of your students have such a chaotic home life that a cruel teacher would be just another adult who is unkind to them. Wouldn't it be better to make an impression on your students by offering a safe haven from violence rather than inflicting more misery?

Finally, it is important not to rely on punishment to motivate students because of the effect it will have on you. Did you really become a teacher to play the part of a prison warden? Teachers who try to rule their class with an iron fist will burn out as soon as they see that this strategy does far more harm than good.

Punishment is a behavioral management practice that has outlived its dubious usefulness. When you create a positive behavior management plan for your students, you minimize the role that punishment will play in your class and maximize the importance of the positive strategies at your disposal.

While, as a new teacher, you may be unsure of which discipline practices are effective, you should definitely avoid these:

- Commanding students to comply with your directives
- Accepting excuses or being a pushover

- Making bargains with students to coerce them into obedience
- Making fun of students
- Allowing students to make fun of each other
- Raising your voice
- Bribing students
- Assigning work as punishment
- Throwing students out of class
- Nagging
- Allowing students to sleep in class
- Being confrontational
- Ignoring serious misbehavior
- Being sarcastic
- Embarrassing students
- Being a poor role model
- Losing your temper

Teachers can prevent behavior problems by knowing their students. Talking to students and finding out their situations, likes, dislikes, and difficulties allows the teacher to see changes and see when students need to take a time-out.

—Melinda Cummings, 6 years' experience

Self-Discipline Is the Answer

If punishment is not the answer to classroom management problems, then what is? The ultimate goal of spending energy to prevent discipline problems is to have students who are self-directed. Teachers strive to create self-disciplined students who are happy, cooperative, and productive. After all, who wants to teach students who behave only because the teacher is bigger or meaner than they are?

Unfortunately, just when teachers think that their discipline techniques have been successful, something will happen to remind them that students still need help to stay on a successful path. As a first-year teacher, you should work steadily and consistently with your students to teach them self-discipline. Even very young children can learn to control themselves when their teachers encourage them to do the right thing at the right time.

By modeling the behavior you want, maintaining high standards, and motivating students to work, you will help your students learn to manage their own behavior. Be as positive and encouraging as you can; make it clear to your students that you have confidence in them and their ability to succeed. When all of these elements are working together, success and self-directed learning will be the order of the day in your classroom.

Your Goal: A Positive Classroom Culture

The goal of classroom management is to create a culture so positive that all of your students can achieve their fullest potential. The encouraging atmosphere in such a class is what makes it so different from classrooms where teachers and students engage in scholastic warfare. How will you know when you have reached your goal of having a positive class culture? Here are some of the traits that your management policies should be geared to produce:

- ✔ Students are on task throughout class.
- ✔ Student work is on display.
- ✔ The business of the class is everyone's business.
- ✔ There is a clear expectation of success.
- ✔ Lessons are well planned and engaging.
- ✔ Routines and procedures provide a structure for behavior.
- ✔ Classroom rules are posted, enforced, and observed.
- ✔ Students are aware of the objectives for the day's lesson.
- ✔ The pace of class work is appropriate for all students.
- ✔ Mutual respect is evident.
- ✔ Disruptions and interruptions are managed with a minimal loss of instructional time.
- ✔ Students work on real-life assignments.
- ✔ The conversational tone is positive.
- ✔ Students collaborate with each other and with their teacher.
- ✔ Students and teacher exhibit courtesy.
- ✔ Students and teacher enjoy their work and each other's company.
- ✔ Everyone works with a purpose.

Early Intervention Strategies

Preventing misbehavior is much easier and more productive than having to cope with discipline problems once they have already disrupted your class. Unfortunately, no single strategy will prevent behavior problems. Instead, preventing misbehavior relies on many factors that work together to create the harmonious classroom you want for your students.

Because all teachers want to prevent discipline problems from disrupting their class, thousands of Web sites address the subject. Some sites are more helpful than others; the following three offer excellent suggestions, tips, and strategies.

- **Behavior Advisor (www.behavioradvisor.com).** Thousands of teachers from all over the world have visited this site, which is maintained by Tom McIntyre, a professor of special education at Hunter College. Here you will find terrific advice from other teachers, thousands of practical tips, and instructions on how to manage even the toughest discipline problems.
- **ProTeacher Directory (www.proteacher.com).** P–8 teachers can access ProTeacher's archive, which contains thousands of suggestions, strategies, and tips submitted by teachers. An ongoing discussion board helps teachers find even more solutions to discipline problems.
- **Master Teacher (www.masterteacher.com).** This outstanding site offers extensive support on an assortment of topics for all teachers. One of the best resources is the "You Can Handle Them All" section, which offers an insightful four-step intervention plan for 117 common classroom misbehaviors.

In addition to the interventions and other strategies that you will learn about in this section, others that teachers have found successful in preventing discipline problems are discussed in depth in other sections of this book, including the following:

- **Engage students in meaningful work during your entire class (Section Twelve).** You already know that students who are busy learning will not have time to misbehave; however, it is easy to underestimate the length of time that students will need to finish an assignment. If you engage students in meaningful, interesting work from the beginning of class until the end, you will prevent many of the problems that will occur when students do not have enough to do.
- **Create a sense of community in your class (Sections Six and Ten).** Students who feel that they are a respected and valuable part of the group will hesitate before letting their classmates down by misbehaving. When students are actively involved in class, they have fewer reasons to disrupt and everyone benefits.

> **Be flexible. Overplan and have a backup. Always remember: you can't demand respect; you have to earn it. Be firm and consistent.**
>
> —*Dawn Carroll, 10 years' experience*

- **Reward your students when they are successful (Section Ten).** Rewarding good behavior successfully prevents bad behavior for two reasons: (1) it lets students know which behaviors are acceptable, and (2) it encourages them to choose those productive behaviors.
- **Seek support from other adults in a child's life (Section Three).** Students who know that the significant adults in their life are working together for their benefit are far less likely to misbehave than students who feel that no one cares about them.

From phoning a student's home to talking with another teacher, there are many ways for you to tap into sources of support.

- **Establish and teach classroom routines (Sections Four and Twelve).** When students know how to act in predictable situations such as a fire drill or the first few minutes of class, they will behave much better than students who are waiting for their teacher to tell them what to do.
- **Talk with a student when you see a problem beginning to develop (Section Fifteen).** You can forestall many behavior problems by talking directly with a child who is beginning to misbehave. When you know the reason for misbehavior and can act on that knowledge, you can work with the student to keep the problem minor.

Use Self-Assessment 14.1 to assess your classroom management skills.

TEN QUICK TIPS FOR PROMOTING ON-TASK BEHAVIOR

1. Design instruction that encourages student engagement.
2. Closely monitor students' activities to help them stay on task.
3. Give clear and easy-to-follow directions for all assignments.
4. Make sure that school rules and class rules, routines, and procedures are well established.
5. Don't allow down time in which students have nothing to do.
6. Offer a variety of challenging, interesting learning activities.
7. Make sure that students have the materials they need to do their work.
8. Motivate students to be confident, self-disciplined, active learners.
9. Communicate your high expectations, and encourage student success.
10. Encourage students to reflect on their learning while you reflect on your teaching.

> **Don't tell them what they can't do. Tell them what they *can* do!**
>
> —*Sabrina Richardson, 7 years' experience*

How to Set Up a Shared Supplies Bank

Off-task behavior and discipline problems are just two of the things that can go wrong when students come to class unprepared. Keeping extra supplies on hand will help you avoid many problems.

Try to have extra textbooks on hand to lend to students if they forget theirs. When you lend a book to a student, make sure that the student writes his or her name on the board or in another safe place so that you have a record of where the books are. You could also assign a responsible student to be in charge of issuing and collecting borrowed texts.

SELF-ASSESSMENT 14.1

How Effective Are You at Preventing Problems?

Read each of these positive management practices and grade yourself on each one. Use a traditional letter scale:

A = Excellent; B = Very good; C = Average; D = Needs improvement; F = Failing

_____ I have a set of positively stated rules posted in my classroom.

_____ I use a friendly but firm voice when I ask students to do something.

_____ I make sure to build relevance and interest into every lesson.

_____ I make sure that all my students know that I care about them.

_____ I have taught my students the routines, procedures, and rules that will make class run smoothly.

_____ I use nonverbal interventions to keep misbehavior manageable.

_____ I consistently enforce my classroom rules.

_____ I consistently enforce school rules.

_____ I design lessons that will engage my students throughout the class period.

_____ I contact students' parents or guardians in order to keep problems manageable.

_____ I praise my students more than I criticize them.

_____ I monitor my students constantly.

_____ I refuse to nag or bribe students into good behavior.

_____ I respect the dignity of all of my students.

_____ I accept responsibility for what happens in my class.

If missing pens or pencils are a problem, set up a shared bank of supplies that students can borrow from. Here's how:

1. Select one or two students to be in charge of the supplies bank.
2. Ask every student to donate a new pen or pencil.
3. Mark each pen and pencil with a number.
4. When a student needs to borrow a pen or pencil, the students who are in charge of the bank record the number of the item and the name of the student who borrowed it.
5. The students who distribute the supplies are also the ones who should remind the borrowers to return them at the end of class.

Create a Safe Environment for Your Students

A safe and orderly environment should be one of the fundamental components of any school. Few children can thrive in an environment where violence threatens students and their teachers. Despite the increase in violent behaviors at all grade levels, school safety practices are not always described clearly in faculty manuals. It is possible that you will have to learn about school safety by observing other teachers, asking questions, and using your common sense.

You can prevent many discipline problems by paying attention to your school and classroom environment. Here are some proactive measures you can take to prevent discipline problems caused by an unsafe school environment:

- If you suspect that a student has guns or weapons, report it immediately. Do what you can to make it easy for students to report their suspicions to you.
- Educate yourself about gangs in your area. Report suspected gang activity to an administrator or your school's security officer. A visit to the Web site of the U.S. Department of Justice (www.usdoj.gov) can help you learn more about gangs. At the home page, search using the word "Gangs." The site provides many useful, up-to-date statistics and resources on gang violence.
- Become a part of your community; know the neighborhoods where your students live. Learning about their lives outside of school will make it easier for you to keep students safe in school.
- Familiarize yourself with your school's rules, and enforce them.
- When you have a duty assignment such as monitoring the cafeteria, be on time to your duty location, and take your responsibilities seriously.
- Be alert to students who may be under the influence of illegal substances. If you suspect that a student is intoxicated or in possession of illegal drugs, report your suspicions to an administrator.
- If you hear rumors of a potential fight, contact an administrator promptly.

- Never allow a student to torment another one, even in jest. Report suspected bullies to an administrator or counselor.
- Consider putting a suggestion box near your classroom door so that students can communicate anonymously with you about conflicts they are having with other students or about other safety issues.
- Keep your classroom locked when it is not in use.
- Never leave your students unsupervised.
- When you permit your students to leave your room, you are still responsible for their safety. Pay attention to where your students go and how long they are out of your room (see Section Twelve).
- Send students who say they do not feel well to the school nurse as quickly as you can. Pay attention to notes from a doctor or parent about potentially dangerous medical conditions.
- Return phone calls from parents quickly. Not only is replying promptly the professional thing to do, but it is also prudent, for the parent may have a concern that you should address at once. When there is a close relationship between home and school, everyone benefits.
- Keep matches, scissors, teacher's editions of textbooks, money, and your personal belongings in your desk or in another secure place. Teach students not to take items from your desk without your permission.
- If you suspect that a child has been abused or neglected, act quickly by sending the student to a counselor.
- Take suicide threats seriously; contact a counselor at once.
- Teach with the door to your classroom closed, to prevent interference from outside.
- Take a stand against drugs and alcohol. Your students need to hear adults speak against underage drinking and drug use.
- Have no tolerance for racial, ethnic, gender, or other prejudices in your classroom.
- If you hold students after school, stay with them until their rides arrive. They need your supervision.
- Never give a student a ride home from school.
- Do not give the keys to your classroom or to your car to a student. If you ask students to retrieve something from your car or your room, accompany them.
- Stand at the door to greet your students as they enter the classroom, and stand at the door as they leave. Use this time to monitor their behavior as well as make a solid connection with each one.
- Whenever you have to reprimand a student, as often as possible, do so in private. Students who are embarrassed in front of their peers may misbehave to save face.
- Make an effort to build student self-esteem whenever you can. Students who feel capable and able to succeed in school tend to focus on positive instead of destructive behaviors.

Create Class Goals

When students work together toward a common goal, something magical happens in a classroom. The synergistic energy generated by the group effort affects students positively. This success, in turn, leads to more success.

There are countless ways to help your students create a class goal. Begin by considering their interests. For example, if your students are interested in recycling, encourage them to act on that interest by undertaking a schoolwide project. Your students may want to participate in an aluminum can drive or create a contest to see which class can read the most books on environmental issues by a certain date. The actual project itself is not as important as the shared goal.

A goal can also be contained within the four walls of your classroom. Choose a problem that you would like to solve, and make it a class goal. For example, if your students have trouble remembering to put their name on their papers, make it a class goal to have names on all papers for a week. To make your class's progress visible, create a large bar graph with five spaces, one for each day of the week. Color in a space for each day that students put their name on all their papers. When you dramatize the goal in this way, your students can see the benefits of working together and have fun at the same time. Here are a few suggestions for worthy goals you can adopt or adapt for your class:

- One hundred percent homework completion for three nights
- No tardies for a week
- No papers without student names for two weeks
- No forgotten textbooks for a week
- No trash left behind after class for five days

Teach and Enforce School Rules

You will prevent many discipline problems and create a positive classroom environment if you take the time to teach and enforce the rules that govern all students in your school. Consistent enforcement is especially important because some of the conflicts you will have with your students will arise from teachers who inconsistently enforce rules. Use the following guidelines to create a positive classroom environment.

- **Know the rules thoroughly.** To teach and enforce school rules successfully, you must be thoroughly familiar with them. Ask colleagues about rules that you are not sure how to enforce.
- **Follow the rules yourself.** Students are quick to point out hypocrisy. For example, a particularly sensitive area for many students is the dress code. You will find it very difficult to enforce the rules for student dress if you violate them yourself.
- **Take the time to teach school rules to your students.** One mistake that many teachers make is assuming that someone else will teach school rules to students. Even

though the administrators at your school may have reviewed the rules with students, you should discuss them again during the first few weeks of school to make sure that everyone knows what to do. You will have to repeat the rules from time to time to make sure that students maintain a clear understanding of them.

- **Connect school rules to real-life rules.** One way to make school rules relevant is to ask students to share some of the rules that adults have to follow at work and the rationale for these rules. When you show how school rules correspond to family or work-related rules, you will make it easier for students to accept school rules.
- **Enforce school rules consistently.** If you have a serious reservation about a particular rule, you should speak with an administrator about it. No matter what you personally think about a school rule, however, you should enforce it. Students are quick to take advantage when teachers are not consistent in enforcement.

Create Classroom Rules

Class rules provide guidelines for acceptable behavior. They will protect your right to teach and your students' right to learn. Rules also send the message that good behavior is important and that you expect students to work productively. Although your students may earnestly try to convince you that rules are not necessary, they really do not want total freedom. Students of all ages benefit from the guidance that classroom rules provide in establishing a tone of mutual respect, trust, and cooperation.

When creating rules for your classroom, you should follow three guidelines to ensure their success. Class rules should be

- ✔ Stated in positive terms
- ✔ General enough to cover a broad range of student activity
- ✔ Easy for students to remember

The rules you create for your classroom should be appropriate to the age of your students. When you create a set of rules, you establish a common language for discussing expectations for good behavior. Here is a step-by-step approach to help you create workable classroom rules:

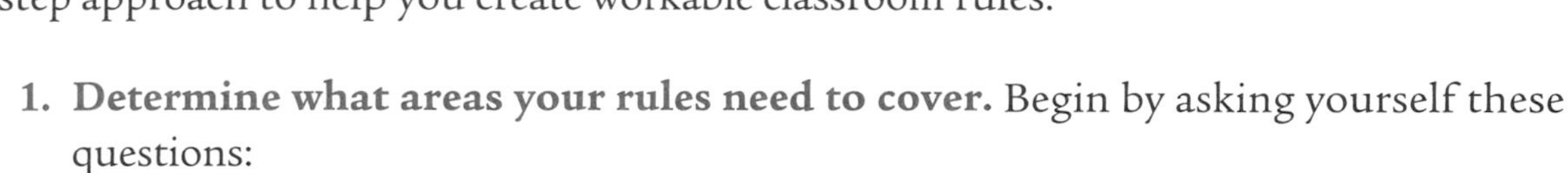

1. **Determine what areas your rules need to cover.** Begin by asking yourself these questions:
   - What are some behaviors that make it possible for students to succeed?
   - What are some behaviors that make it difficult for students to succeed?
   - What limits can I set to guarantee that all students have the right to learn?
2. **Draft a rough set of rules.** After you have determined the areas your rules should cover, write a rough draft. At this point, you may want to show your rules to a colleague to make sure they are in line with school rules and appropriate to the age and ability of your students.

3. **State classroom rules positively.** Take your rough draft and change the wording as needed to state all of your rules in positive terms, conveying a tone of mutual respect and consideration.
4. **State rules so that they are easy to remember.** Can you combine any of your rules to cover a general range of student behavior? For example, you could combine "Bring your textbook every day" and "You will need paper and pens in this class" to read "Bring the materials you will need for class." Your students will also find it easier to recall your class rules if you only have a few. Many experienced teachers recommend having about five rules for middle school and secondary students. Reduce the number of rules for younger students.

If you are not sure whether your classroom rules will work, here are some that experienced teachers have used successfully. Adapt them to meet the needs of your students.

1. Use class time wisely.
2. Do your work well.
3. Treat other people with respect.
4. Follow school rules.
5. Bring your materials to class every day.

If you would like more information about creating class rules that will work well for your students, try visiting Education World (www.educationworld.com). At the home page, use "Classroom Rules" as a keyword to search the dozens of articles and strategies for creating useful class rules for students at all grade levels.

Another resource you should consider exploring if you are interested in allowing your students to participate in the creation of classroom rules is one featuring educator Alfie Kohn's Web site (www.alfiekohn.org). Kohn is author of the landmark book *Beyond Discipline: From Compliance to Community,* published by the Association for Supervision and Curriculum Development in 1996 and 2006.

TEACHING CLASSROOM RULES

In the press of covering the academic material that your students need to learn, it is easy to overlook the importance of actually teaching the classroom rules you have created. A set of well-expressed rules is useless if your students do not know what they are.

You can help your students understand the importance of following rules by spending the time to teach them how to behave correctly. Teaching appropriate behavior is not something you can complete in one class period; rather, it is a process that will last the entire term. It is better to spend a few minutes each day or week with mini-lessons on various aspects of your rules than to spend an hour early in the term and then ignore them afterward.

Students who know how to behave correctly will not lose time in bad behavior. Incorporate the following strategies, and the time you spend teaching the rules will save you precious instructional time later.

- Send a letter about your classroom rules home with your students, thus enlisting the support of parents and guardians.
- Post a copy of your class rules in a prominent spot to serve as a quick reminder for everyone in the class.
- Although teaching classroom rules is a process that will last all term, you should focus on teaching them during the first three weeks of the term in order to let your students know that you are serious about a positive classroom climate. Revisiting the rules periodically will reinforce this early teaching.
- When you are ready to talk about rules with your students, don't try to bluff your way through a brief presentation. Instead, present your rules in a dynamic lesson. Try some of these activities to make the lesson interesting:
  - Have students create a Venn diagram comparing the rules that they have at school with the rules that adults have at work.
  - Place students in groups. Have some groups brainstorm reasons why everyone should follow various rules. Ask other groups to list what could happen if no one followed a rule.
  - Have students write the class rules in their notebook. Ask them to see whether they can improve the wording of a rule or whether they can create examples to explain each one.
  - Have students debate the positive and negative effects on the entire group when students follow or don't follow rules.
  - Ask students to explain the rules to you in their own words.
  - Divide students into groups and assign each group a rule to present in a skit.

Do Your Students Need a Refresher on Class Rules?

To determine whether you should reteach your rules, ask yourself these two questions:

- Do all students understand the rule?
- Do students understand the rationale for this rule as well as its importance?

ENFORCING CLASSROOM RULES

Classroom rules empower teachers who want their students to understand that they are serious about good behavior. By consistently enforcing classroom rules, you can prevent many serious discipline problems. When a student breaks a rule and you care enough to spend the time enforcing that rule, you send a powerful message not just to the rule breaker but also to every student in the class. Thus, by enforcing a classroom rule, you prevent many other infractions.

When a student breaks a class rule, calmly and quietly enforce the rule. Don't threaten, nag, or lose your temper. Instead, try this five-step procedure:

1. Ask, "What rule have you broken?"
2. Help the student understand that the rule applies to this occasion.
3. Ask the student to explain the reasons for the rule.
4. Ask the student to tell you the consequences for breaking the rule.
5. Carry out the consequences you have for students who break that rule.

One fact that you can take comfort in is that frequently students will break a rule not from a desire to misbehave but from a momentary lapse in good judgment. By calmly enforcing your rules, you acknowledge that lapse and remind students not to repeat the offense. Here are a few more tips to help you successfully enforce your class rules:

- The first time that students break a rule, talk privately with them to make sure that they understand the rule and the consequences.
- Before you rush to judgment, determine why your students broke the rule. Do they need more attention from you? Did they run out of meaningful work to do? Do you need to explain the rule again?
- Reward good behavior as often as you can. Rewarding students for behaving well will encourage them to continue.
- Accept that enforcing rules is part of your job as a teacher. Be patient. Your students are going to misbehave from time to time.
- Don't be a pushover. While it may be tempting to make an exception to a rule, think carefully before you do. You should balance the needs of all of your students with the needs of the student who broke the rule.

ENLISTING STUDENT SUPPORT FOR CLASS RULES

Many ways of encouraging students to follow class rules will be more effective than just imposing your teacher power over students. Spending time at the start of a term enlisting your students' support for class rules will result in a more productive classroom environment all year long. Follow these strategies to solicit your students' support:

- Involve students early. The more involved your students are with class rules early in the year, the more likely those rules are to be successful. This success will be generated by the sense of ownership your students will gain through their involvement.
- Have several informal discussions about rule issues; discuss, for example, why rules are useful, how to observe them, or the benefits they bring to every student.
- Have students role-play scenarios illustrating various aspects of the rules.
- Ask students to complete an exit slip (see Section Eleven) describing a positive aspect of a class rule. Share these, if appropriate.
- Occasionally quiz your students orally about the rules in rapid-fire bursts of questions at the start or end of class.

ESTABLISHING CONSEQUENCES FOR BREAKING RULES

When you create your classroom rules, you also need to decide on the consequences that will follow if students break them. You must teach these consequences when you teach the rules so that your students will know what to expect. The consequences you create must meet several important criteria:

- **Consequences should arise logically from the infraction.** For example, if students leave their work area messy, they should have to clean it up.
- **Consequences should fit the infraction.** Asking students to clean their work area after leaving it untidy is a consequence that solves the problem. Asking students to clean their work area because they were late to class does not.
- **Repeated infractions should invoke a hierarchy of consequences so that students know that continued rule breaking will result in consequences that are more serious.** For example, the first time a student forgets a textbook, a reminder or warning is sufficient. If a student habitually forgets his or her textbook, you should consider making a phone call to the student's home or keeping the student after school.
- While consequences will vary depending on the age and ability of your students, when you plan your classroom consequences, consider creating a hierarchy like this:

First offense:	Reminder
Second offense:	Warning
Third offense:	Phone call to student's parent or guardian
Fourth offense:	Fifteen-minute detention

Other consequences that you could employ include the following:

- Loss of small privileges
- Time-out

- Letter to student's parent or guardian
- Parent conference
- Longer detention
- Referral to an administrator

Writing should never be assigned as a consequence of breaking a rule. Having students write sentences such as "I must be respectful" numerous times is not an acceptable consequence because it makes writing an unpleasant task and adversely affects the work of language arts teachers.

The Crucial Step: Monitoring

Almost everyone has had at least one teacher who was able to write notes on the board and tell students in the back of the room to stop making faces at each other at the same time. As a teacher, one of the most important skills for you to develop is monitoring—actively overseeing your students from the moment they enter the room until they leave.

Being acutely aware of what each one of your students is doing at every minute during your class is not relaxing. However, the reward of such vigilance is a peaceful and productive classroom. By paying careful attention to your students, you will help them stay on task and be successful. Furthermore, any problems that might arise will stay small if you are actively working to facilitate instruction through monitoring.

Here are several more benefits that you and your students receive when you know exactly what each one is doing at any given moment. When you successfully monitor your students, you

- Create a positive class atmosphere
- Keep problems small
- Reinforce good behavior
- Keep students on task
- Help students stay focused on learning
- Maintain a strong connection with every student

HOW TO BECOME AN EFFECTIVE MONITOR

Learning to be an effective classroom monitor is not difficult, although it will require effort in order to become a habit. The following suggestions will help you get started.

- **Circulate among your students.** You cannot monitor effectively from your desk. Your students will be far less likely to stray off task if you are moving around the room instead of just sitting at your desk.

- **Place students' desks so that you can easily move around the room.** When you arrange your classroom, make sure to avoid putting desks too close together or against walls so that you can't get around them.
- **Ask students to place book bags and other belongings underneath their desk so that you can move around the room without tripping.** After a day or two of reminders, this should become a habit. (See Section Seventeen for more suggestions on keeping aisles clear.)
- **If students are becoming distracted, stand near them for a minute or two.** Often, a teacher standing near them will be enough to get restless students to settle down and focus on their work. If this does not work, then a quiet word, a glance, or a quick nod will usually suffice.
- **Practice the twenty-second survey.** Before you act, stand in one spot and take about twenty seconds to look over the class to see who is on task and who is not.
- **After your students settle down to work, wait about two minutes before you start walking around to see what they are doing.** Allow time for students to get started on the assignment and for problems to arise.
- **Maintain good eye contact with your students.** Keeping eye contact lets students know that you are aware of them and discourages them from misbehaving.
- **Give all students a share of your attention.** Many teachers tend to focus on only a few students. To determine how evenly you spread your attention, carry a copy of your class roster. When you speak with a student, place a mark next to the student's name. After doing this for a day or two, you will be aware of the unconscious patterns you follow and will be able to adjust your behavior.
- **Don't spend too much time with some students and ignore others.** For example, do not give a student ten minutes of your time while several others are waiting.
- **Try not to allow a large group of students to congregate around you while waiting for help.** Instead, try asking students to put their names on the board so that you can see them in order. Or you could have them take a number from a stack of note cards that you have numbered. You could ask students who have a question that others may also have to write it on the board so that you can address it for everyone.
- **Try creating a checklist for your students to follow as they work.** If they use the checklist, you will be able to check their progress as you come by their desks. You can also ask students to show you each item on their checklist as they work through it.
- **Ask students to write their name on the board when they have finished.** This not only lets you know who is finished but also lets other students know which classmates can help them if you are busy.
- **Be supportive.** Use one of these supportive statements:
  - "At this moment, what are you doing that's right?"
  - "How may I help you?"
  - "When I come by your desk, please show me ________________."

How Students Can Signal for Help

If you arrange signals so that your students can let you know quickly if they need help, you can prevent much of the off-task behavior that can happen when students do not know how to proceed. Try some of the following ideas to allow your students to get help quickly.

- Allow students to ask other students about an assignment before they ask you. This is especially effective if students work in small groups or near study buddies.
- Have students write their questions on the board or on a transparency while waiting for you to answer them.
- Offer students the opportunity to work on alternative assignments while waiting for your help. They can signal you that they need assistance by working on the alternative assignments instead of the class work.
- Tape three note cards together to form a triangle or tent that can stand on a desk. On each side, place a signal that will let you know how a student is doing. A question mark could indicate that the student has a question; a smiling face could mean that the student has no questions; and a frowning face could mean that there is a serious problem.

When You Should Act

Like other teachers, you may sometimes have trouble knowing at just what point you should intervene to stop a problem from becoming serious. When you should act depends on the type of problem. Behavior problems can be divided into two categories: nondisruptive and disruptive.

Nondisruptive behavior problems affect only the student with the problem. Daydreaming, sleeping, and poor work habits are common examples of nondisruptive behavior problems. Try these interventions to end a nondisruptive behavior:

- Move close to the student
- Remind the entire class to stay on task
- Place your hand on the student's desk
- Maintain eye contact
- Praise the work the student has completed
- Offer your help
- Glance at or smile at the student
- Ask if another student could help
- Consider moving the student's seat

Disruptive behaviors involve other students and affect the learning climate. When students become disruptive, your goal must be to minimize the effect on your class. Begin by enforcing your class rules as calmly and quietly as you can. If this does not improve the situation, move the misbehaving student to the hall for a private conversation.

Most of the time, just talking quietly with a student will solve the problem. Listen to what the student has to say, and offer your help. Remind students who misbehave that they do not have the right to interfere with the rights of all students to learn. If you cannot prevent the student from misbehaving again, then you should enforce your class rules, using the necessary consequences. (See Section Fifteen for more information on how to handle disruptions once they begin.)

Catch 'em Being Good!

Take a positive approach to preventing discipline problems in your class. If your students all settle down quickly after lunch, for instance, praise their maturity. When all your students turn in a homework assignment on time, be sure to tell them how much you appreciate their efforts. When you catch them being good, not only will your students understand what you expect of them, but they will also feel encouraged to continue their good behavior. Telling students what they do right is much more effective than nagging them about their mistakes.

One of the easiest ways to increase positive behaviors and decrease negative ones is to chart your students' success. When your students see a chart of their positive behaviors, they will understand that good behavior is recognized and appreciated. Use your computer to make a pie chart, a bar graph, or another type of chart on which to record your class's good behaviors. Display an enlarged printout for your students each day.

You will have hundreds of other opportunities to tell your students when they are successful. Don't hesitate to take advantage of those opportunities; you and your students will benefit from the positive learning environment that will result. Here are some other practical ways to increase positive behaviors:

- Be specific and sincere in your praise so that students know what they did correctly.
- Always point out how the positive behavior will benefit everyone in the class.
- Encourage students to remind each other to behave well for the good of the class.
- Photograph your students when they are working productively or being good, and display these photos as a gentle reminder.
- Periodically ask your students what they did right during class. How did it make them feel? What did they gain from this good behavior?

Harness the Power of Positive Peer Pressure

One of the greatest tools any teacher has is the power inherent in peer pressure. No child, no matter how young or old, wants to look silly in front of classmates. Too often, when students misbehave, they do so because they are not connected to the group; they feel so unattached that they have nothing to lose by failure.

With this in mind, teachers can harness the human desire to perform well in the presence of peers by working to make each child feel that he or she is a valuable, contributing member of the class. To increase the feeling of belonging that you want for your students, try some of these strategies:

- Help students learn about each other. Periodically, use icebreakers and other activities to reveal the strengths, skills, experiences, and talents your students bring to school.
- Make it easy for your students to take risks when they answer questions or try new activities in your class. Promote tolerance and courtesy in order to encourage this spirit.
- Establish study buddies and other peer support opportunities. Teachers who make a consistent effort to include cooperative activities in their lessons find that their students are predisposed to work well together.
- One of the best ways to build positive peer pressure in your class is to have your students work on projects in which they interact with people outside the classroom. An excellent Web site that you can explore to find a shared project for your students is maintained by the Los Angeles County Office of Education at http://teams.lacoe.edu/documentation/projects/projects.html. At this site, you can connect your students to classrooms all over the world in a variety of ways. There are projects for all ages of students and for all types of classes.

Be a Consistent Teacher

As a teacher, you will have to make hundreds of decisions every day. Not only will you have to make many of these decisions quickly, but you will have to make them in front of a crowd of students—all of whom have different needs. You will never have enough time to think through many of the decisions you have to make, so you will have to learn to think fast.

The number of quick decisions you have to make will sometimes make it difficult to be consistent. However, consistency is one of the most important tools you have in preventing problems, because it gives your students a safe framework with well-defined boundaries for their behavior. Consistent classroom management provides a predictable environment with established rules and consequences.

Consistency is crucial to successful management, but it is one of the most difficult skills to develop. You may find it difficult to be consistent if you believe that the consequences for breaking a rule are too harsh, if you believe that overlooking an infraction "just this once" will be acceptable, if the infraction occurs at an inconvenient time or place, or if you have different expectations for students whom you perceive to be less able than others.

You will find it easier to be a consistent teacher if you follow these guidelines:

- Be well prepared and organized so that you will have more energy to make sound decisions under pressure.
- Teach and reteach the rules and procedures you have established for the smooth operation of your class.
- Be careful to enforce the rules for all students every day.
- Do not make idle threats. Mean what you say when you talk with your students about their behavior.

Being fair is most important. If students know that all are on a level playing field, they respect you more.

—Debbie McManaway, 12 years' experience

Talk It Over

How to Manage Your Classroom Through Early Intervention

Use these questions as a springboard for discussions that will help you and your discussion group members grow and develop professionally. Discuss these questions about how you can successfully manage your class through early intervention:

1. Use Self-Assessment 14.1 to help you assess how effective you are at preventing behavior problems. What are your strengths? What are your weaknesses? How can you improve?
2. What anxieties do you feel about how well disciplined your classes are? To whom can you turn for help? What plans can you make to minimize behavior problems in your classes?
3. What classroom rules have you noticed that other teachers in your school use? How can you adapt these for your class?
4. Being a consistent teacher is not always easy. What makes it difficult for you to be consistent? What attitudes can you develop to help you be more consistent? How can your colleagues help you with this?
5. What types of behaviors seem to disrupt your class most often? How can you prevent these disruptive behaviors? Which ones do your colleagues ignore?

6. What effective monitoring techniques have you observed that other teachers use in their classes? Which would work in yours?
7. What difficulties do you have in enforcing school rules? Your class rules? How can you deal with these difficulties? What advice can other teachers in your school give you?
8. How can you tell whether a student is self-disciplined? What can you do to promote this trait in your students?
9. How aware are you of safety issues in your classroom? In your school? When are your students most at risk? What can you do to make sure that every student is safe?
10. What discipline issues have you had to deal with that have surprised you? How did you react? What can you do differently in the future to prevent such problems?

SECTION FIFTEEN

Handle Behavior Problems Effectively

In this section, you will learn

- ✔ How to avoid the most common mistakes when dealing with discipline
- ✔ How to take a problem-solving approach to disciplinary issues
- ✔ How to teach a difficult class and difficult students
- ✔ How to manage behavior contracts, detentions, and referrals
- ✔ How to handle six common school problems

Forgotten pencils, tardiness, defiance, excessive talking—the discipline problems that confront teachers in recent years are more than disheartening. Part of the issue lies in the different types of behavior problems that teachers are supposed to manage successfully. A forgotten pencil can disrupt learning; so can students who openly resist even reasonable requests from their teachers. One of the challenges that all teachers face is knowing the right course of action to take when confronted with this variety of discipline problems.

The behavior issues within your classroom are not the only source of problems. Many factors outside your classroom can have a negative effect on how well you and your students are able to accomplish your goals for each term.

Just a quick glance at cartoons produced for children and teens shows how negative much of what students view can be. Thousands of messages barrage your students, many of which teach them that opposition to authority is admirable and that teachers are nerdy people who exist mainly to interfere in the fun that students could be having.

Another negative influence on the disciplinary climate in your classroom may surprise you as a beginning teacher. You will learn that not every parent supports the orderly environment that you want for your students. When you call a student's home to talk over a problem and find that parents are indifferent or unable to help, you will understand why some of your students find it difficult to behave well in your class.

Your school's climate may also contribute to some of your behavior problems. If students are permitted to misbehave in common areas such as the halls or the cafeteria, it will not be easy for you to impose order in your classroom. Furthermore, in such a chaotic climate, administrators and other teachers may be too overwhelmed to offer the support you need to manage your class effectively.

A final aspect of the disciplinary dilemma that you will have to manage successfully is your inexperience and the ways in which it may contribute to the mix of issues that you have to handle. For instance, one mistake that many new teachers make is being overly lenient at first in order to win their students' trust; they soon find out that such lenience compounds the behavior problems in their classroom. When your own policies are ineffective, you will find it even more difficult to overcome the other negative influences on your students' attitudes toward authority and discipline.

Control Your Anxieties with Proactive Attitudes

Despite your anxiety, you can feel confident that you will soon learn how to manage all of your students' complicated discipline problems. It is understandable that you may feel anxious if you are not able to manage all of them successfully at first. As you gain experience and confidence in your ability to cope with the daily events in your classroom, your anxieties will lessen.

One way to control your anxiety as you learn how to control your class is to adopt proactive attitudes that put you on the right track. These five strategies will keep your confidence level high while your daily experiences help you learn how to handle behavior problems:

1. **Put school rules and classroom rules to work.** If you consistently enforce school and classroom rules, your students will soon stop testing their limits. Because both sets of rules already have consequences attached, you will be able to act quickly, without having to agonize over the right course of action to take.
2. **Motivate and encourage students.** If you are generous with your praise and appreciation, you will establish a strong bond with your students that will help them stay on the right track. When you motivate and encourage students, you improve their self-esteem, which in turn will eliminate many behaviors that arise when students do not feel valued by their teacher or their classmates.
3. **Deliver meaningful, interesting, and well-planned lessons.** Students who are busily engaged in meaningful and interesting work will not have time to misbehave.

When you plan lessons well, students will find it easier to be successful. Success breeds more success, and that will eliminate many problems.

4. **Have confidence in yourself.** You will find it easier to control your emotions as you begin to see that you really can teach and maintain control of a group of students. Do not forget that the most important factor in every successful plan for managing classroom discipline is the teacher. You—and no one else—can control the disciplinary climate for your students.
5. **Take every day as an opportunity to add to your knowledge.** Even your setbacks will teach you something about how to manage your class. As you get to know your colleagues, you will have a large supportive network of people who are willing to help you. And each successful day will make it easier for your students to trust you and for you to learn more about them.

You cannot hold grudges. You need to remember that your students have short memories and trust you to always do the right thing. If there is a problem, settle it, then just continue as if nothing happened.

—Sarah Walski, 25 years' experience

Myths About Discipline

Part of the uncertainty that many new teachers feel is due to prevalent myths about classroom discipline that may seem sound but which are harmful to students in the end. While these myths vary from grade level to grade level and from school to school, some appear to be universal. If a colleague advises you with one of the following ideas, tactfully decline to accept the advice.

- Parents should teach values, not teachers.
- Punishment works.
- Bribing students so that they will behave well works.
- Parents need to do something about their kids' behavior.
- If you have a class participation grade, you can remove points from a student's grade for misbehavior.
- If you are not sure who's guilty, punish the entire class until someone tattles.
- They are old enough to know better.
- A teacher temper tantrum now and then shows that you mean business.
- Assigning punishment work will stop misbehavior.
- Don't smile until Thanksgiving.

Behaviors You Should Not Accept

Almost every teacher has a clear understanding of what the ideal classroom atmosphere should be. Well-disciplined classes share three important characteristics:

1. Students and teacher know and understand the rules and procedures that guide the entire class.
2. The focus is on learning and cooperative behavior.
3. There is a persistent tone of mutual respect and even affection among students and between students and their teacher.

When you and your students are working toward establishing and maintaining a well-disciplined class, you should not have to tolerate behaviors that might destroy the fragile positive atmosphere you have established. Here are ten behaviors that teachers and school districts across the nation have deemed unacceptable in any classroom:

> **Don't sweat the small stuff! Choose your battles! The teacher's reaction to a problem sets the tone.**
>
> —*Patty Muth, 14 years' experience*

1. **Threats and intimidation.** Students are not allowed to threaten or harass each other or you. This prohibition means that no bullying, teasing, sexual harassment, or threats of physical harm can be tolerated.
2. **Substance abuse.** Almost every school now has a zero-tolerance policy in regard to illegal substances at school. All medications should be administered by the school nurse or a designee; even medications such as cough drops are regulated under most zero-tolerance polices. It is against the law for students to have alcohol, tobacco, or illegal drugs on school property.
3. **Interference with others' right to learn.** No student has the right to stop other students from learning. This policy is the rationale behind school dress codes that prohibit students from distracting other students. It also prohibits students from making noises loud enough to interfere with the normal routines of a school day and prohibits many other seriously disruptive actions.
4. **Disrespect for authority.** This behavior includes refusal to comply with a reasonable request from a teacher, administrator, or other staff member. It also includes various forms of defiance, both overt and subtle—for example, talking back, sighing, sneering, and other rude behavior directed at an authority figure.
5. **Failure to complete work.** Teachers should monitor student progress closely enough so that all parents or guardians are aware of the situation if a child refuses to complete work or fails to complete it for some other reason.
6. **Unsafe behavior.** Behaviors considered unsafe range from running with scissors, horseplay, or running in the halls to ignoring safe driving rules in a high school parking lot. Unsafe behavior policies also prohibit students from having matches or other

fire starters at school, leaving school grounds without permission, or using school equipment in an unsafe manner.

7. **Dishonesty.** Students should not forge notes from home, cheat on their work, commit plagiarism, or lie to teachers or other school officials. Teachers are required to report almost all incidents of dishonesty to parents as well as administrators.
8. **Tardiness.** Students are expected to be at school and in class on time. Tardiness to class is not acceptable and is part of the attendance policy in many states.
9. **Truancy.** Almost every state requires local school districts to enforce very strict attendance policies. It is the responsibility of a classroom teacher to maintain accurate attendance records.
10. **Violence.** School districts in all states take violence very seriously. Students are not allowed to fight or to encourage a fight by cheering on the combatants. Regulations against violence include weapons and weapon look-alikes at school.

What Do Your Supervisors Expect from You?

It is not always easy to determine just how permissive or how strict you should be. Many teachers take a long time to figure out what their supervisors expect from them and make many mistakes as they learn to manage their classes. Although expectations for student behavior vary from school to school and from grade level to grade level, there are some common practices that most supervisors are likely to expect you to use in enforcing discipline. As you work to create a safe and productive disciplinary climate, follow these suggestions:

- Prevent as many behavior problems as you can by working to contain or minimize disruptions.
- Establish, teach, and enforce reasonable class rules, including reasonable consequences for breaking them.
- Make student safety a priority; never allow any activity that could endanger your students.
- Help your students stay focused on learning instead of misbehavior.
- Handle most of your own discipline problems, but refer a student to an administrator when your school's guidelines require it.
- Although you are not expected to know every statute of school law, you should know the basic laws pertaining to schools. You should be especially aware of students' rights and your responsibilities.
- Call a student's home early and often when behavior problems arise. Parents and guardians need to be aware of behavior problems before they become serious. Be prepared to show your supervisors documentation that you contacted parents and guardians at appropriate times.
- Maintain accurate documentation of students' behavior. Your supervisors expect you to have an up-to-date file on each of your students.

How to Avoid a Lawsuit: A Teacher's Legal Responsibilities

In the last two decades, the number of lawsuits filed against schools and teachers has increased dramatically. Regrettably, so has the number of teachers who have resigned from a career in education within the first few years. New teachers may feel particularly vulnerable to becoming embroiled in legal problems at school because they are unsure of their responsibilities under the law.

You do not have to become one of those teachers who chooses to opt out of a promising career. In reality, all of the legal policies involving teachers center on one tenet: teachers are obligated to take care of their students—to protect their safety and welfare at school. Because students don't always recognize danger even when warned of hazardous situations, teachers have a duty to anticipate and prevent hazardous situations whenever possible.

What are your responsibilities? Use the guidelines in the following list as a way to make sound decisions for all of your students and for yourself.

- Teachers should learn basic school law. Teachers who understand the laws, policies, and procedures governing their school conduct and duties toward students have a reduced risk of legal problems. A helpful book is *Legal Rights of Teachers and Students,* by Martha M. McCarthy, Nelda H. Cambron-McCabe, and Stephen B. Thomas, which was published in 2003 by Allyn & Bacon.
- Once you have learned the basics of school law, you are obligated to act accordingly. In any case, ignorance of the law is not an excuse for allowing a student under your care to come to harm.
- The rules in your classroom must have a clear educational purpose and must be governed by common sense. The consequences of breaking a rule must be appropriate to the rule. You must publish class rules and the consequences for breaking them for your students and their parents or guardians.
- Teachers are obligated to make their students aware of the risks in activities. Whether the hazard is from running with scissors or operating equipment in a vocational class, students need to be taught how to avoid danger.
- In general, younger students need to be more closely supervised than older students.
- Teachers, parents, students, and school officials must work together to maintain a safe and orderly environment for all students. Sharing responsibility and knowledge is an important way to keep students safe.
- Teachers should never embarrass a student in front of his or her peers. Some of the most violent criminal events at schools in recent years have stemmed, in part, from the isolation experienced by students who were not successful academically or socially.
- One of the best ways to prevent problems is to conduct yourself professionally at all times while you are in school. If your demeanor and dress show that you are serious about your students, your work, and how you manage a class, you will lessen the opportunity for students to act out in anger and disrespect.

- Actively monitor your class. If a student in the front of the classroom is seriously injured while you are in the back of the class checking your e-mail, you could be considered negligent.
- If you have a student who is aggressive or hostile toward others and you ignore the problem, you have neglected to protect the students who may be assaulted. Be aware of potential problems and, if possible, seek administrative assistance before trouble can occur.
- A student's privacy is protected by law. Do not gossip about a student, post grades, or reveal confidential information. Be especially careful about what you transmit electronically or in writing. Keep confidential material in a secure area.
- A student's freedom of speech and expression is protected by law as long as that expression does not disrupt the learning environment. For example, if you do not appreciate a student's fashion sense, you have no legal right to enforce your personal taste.
- Students have a right to due process just as other citizens do. If you are not sure about what course of action to take when a problem arises, use your common sense first. If you are still not sure, call in a school official before you act in violation of a student's right to due process.
- If your students are required to submit a parental permission slip before attending a school activity such as a field trip, that permission slip does not exonerate you from wrongdoing if a student is harmed. A permission slip is not a legal document that will protect you in court.
- You must supervise your students at all times. Special education students, young students, and students whom you know to be behavior risks usually require more intense supervision than others. The types of activities that students are engaging in also determine the level of supervision required. Students playing a rough-and-tumble game at recess require more direct supervision than a group of students reading in a quiet classroom. No matter how mature they are, never leave students unsupervised. *Never.*
- Design activities with safety in mind. Consider the potential for danger to students when you design active classroom games, lab experiments, group activities, or competitive events that could quickly get out of control.
- You must be aware of the requirements and restrictions in a student's Individualized Education Plan or 504 Plan. You are bound by law to follow those requirements.
- Teachers are expected to know about their students' medical needs and behavioral problems as well as any other special factors that could put them in harm's way. Take time to go through students' permanent folders at the start of the term so that you have the knowledge to protect yourself and your students.
- Documentation is necessary to protect yourself and your students. Keep accurate records of parent conferences, interventions, student behaviors, and other pertinent information. It is especially important to document misbehavior. Use Form 15.1 to keep a record that you can refer to if you are asked to give information in court.

FORM 15.1

Behavioral Incident Report

Teacher Name: ______________________________

Student Name: ______________________________

Date and Time of Incident: ______________________________

Place of Incident: ______________________________

Description of Incident:

Actions Taken by Teacher:

Results of Teacher Actions:

Notes:

Parent or Guardian Contact:

Witness(s) Signature: ______________________________

DUE PROCESS

School disciplinary situations can damage the careers of teachers who are not aware of their legal rights and those of their students. One of the most significant rights of students involved in disciplinary actions is the right to due process. Here is a very brief explanation of the process:

1. School and classroom rules must be reasonable.
2. Students must be notified of the rules and policies that govern them.
3. When a student misbehaves, he or she must be made aware of the specific charge.
4. Students have a right to legal counsel.
5. There must be a full investigation.
6. There must be documentation of the incident and the investigation.
7. The disciplinary action must be fair.
8. The student must have an opportunity to file a grievance.
9. The student has a right to a hearing.
10. The student has the right to appeal the disciplinary action.

You May Be the Troublemaker

Your inexperience will cause you to inadvertently make many mistakes. Sometimes the mistakes you make will create discipline problems. The upside is that once you recognize that you have made a mistake, you can take steps to correct it.

Here is a list of common mistakes that many teachers have found to be a source of discipline problems. Along with each mistake, you will find suggestions for effective actions you can take instead.

Mistake 1: The punishment you assign for an offense is inappropriate.
Example: Students receive only a warning for getting into a loud argument in front of the rest of the class.
Suggestion: Because this is a serious offense that could escalate into a more serious altercation, students should be removed from the class and an administrator notified. When you create your class rules, make sure the consequences match the seriousness of the offense.

Mistake 2: You are too permissive, too tentative, too easily sidetracked.
Example: You want your students to have ownership in the class and have allowed them to set the class rules in a democratic fashion. Now your students are not only uncooperative, but they are breaking the rules they established for themselves.
Suggestion: Take the time to think through what you want from your students academically and behaviorally. Act in a decisive manner when you are with your students. You are the

adult in the room. When you allow your students a voice in class decisions, never agree to rules or consequences that make you uncomfortable.

Mistake 3: You are unclear in the limits you set for your students, resulting in constant testing of the boundaries and of your patience.
Example: You have allowed some mild swearing in your class by pretending not to hear it. Now students are not just swearing now and then but using more offensive language.
Suggestion: Be very specific when you set the limits for acceptable and unacceptable behavior for your students. Don't ignore behavior that makes you uncomfortable. Always directly address any student who swears around you. Teach students that swearing is not only inappropriate but disrespectful as well.

Mistake 4: You do not take the time to listen to your students when they are trying to express their feelings about a problem.
Example: Your students are upset over a test question they find unfair. When they try to talk to you, the situation deteriorates until you tell them you do not want to hear more complaints.
Suggestion: Not allowing students to discuss their feelings is a serious mistake that will only worsen a situation as students grow more frustrated. Encourage students to express their concerns in an appropriate manner, and give them chances to do this. When a large group is upset about an issue, you will save time by asking them to write you notes about the problem. You can read the notes later and decide how to respond before you face them again.

Mistake 5: You are inconsistent in enforcing consequences.
Example: You are usually very strict about making students meet their deadlines for projects. However, you decide to let a star athlete have an extra day when his mother writes a note complaining that he didn't have enough time to do the work. Your other students are quick to notice this and complain that it isn't fair. Some of them don't turn in their work on time, either.
Suggestion: Make sure that you are comfortable with administering the consequences for breaking a rule, so that you can be consistent. Make it clear to all students that you intend to be consistent with rules and deadlines.

Mistake 6: You punish one student while overlooking another student's more serious offense.
Example: You reprimand one student for leaving a book bag in the aisle during a test while failing to notice that several other students are cheating on the test.
Suggestion: Take care to assess a situation before you act. Be alert to all of your students' activity, and be consistent in how you handle their misbehavior.

Complete Self-Assessment 15.1 to see how you might improve discipline and create a better learning climate for your students.

SELF-ASSESSMENT 15.1

Classroom Management Techniques to Avoid

Here are some ineffective classroom management practices to avoid. Put a checkmark in the box before any statement that describes how you conducted your class in the past week. Then carefully consider how you can eliminate ineffective management practices from your classroom.

In the last week, I

- ☐ Failed to contact a parent or guardian when I needed to
- ☐ Assigned punishment work
- ☐ Allowed a student to sleep in class
- ☐ Raised my voice
- ☐ Accepted bad behavior from one student and not from another
- ☐ Lost my temper
- ☐ Talked over inappropriate student noise
- ☐ Used negative body language, such as pointing at students
- ☐ Nagged students
- ☐ Allowed a student to ignore me

Until students get to know you, they don't care what you know, they want to know that you care.

—Edward Gardner, 36 years' experience

Think Before You Act

Whenever you have to deal with a discipline problem, take care to understand the reason for the behavior before you act. There are many ways to determine why your students act the way they do. Talk to teachers who have taught your students in the past or to parents or guardians. You can also check permanent records to find out more about your students' past, home situation, and abilities.

To learn about students' behavior, maintain a friendly and supportive relationship with them, listen to what they have to say, and solicit their input when appropriate. When you do, several beneficial things will happen:

- Your students will feel less frustration because you are allowing them to talk about their feelings.
- You will gain an understanding of what caused the problem.
- If there are other causes than what you first noticed, you can act on them.
- You will gain insight into how your students think, feel, and react.
- You and your students will have a common ground for discussing other choices they can make in the future.
- You will probably have prevented this problem from recurring.
- Your bond with your students will be stronger because you have shown them the courtesy of listening and caring about what they had to say.

Figure Out the Reasons for Student Misbehavior

If you make the effort to determine why your students act the way they do, you will benefit by having a clearer understanding of some of the times when your students are going to have trouble staying on task. Here are some common reasons why students misbehave:

- They are excited or upset about an upcoming event or holiday.
- They are having a conflict with a peer.
- They want your attention.
- They want the attention of their peers.
- They finish their work early and want to amuse themselves.
- Their work is too hard or too easy.
- They are distracted by something or someone near them.
- They are upset by something that happened at home.

- They don't know or understand the procedures or rules.
- They are embarrassed.
- They lack the confidence to try for success.
- They don't feel well.
- They are tired of being told what to do.
- They have no realistic goals.
- The work is not relevant to their needs.

Talk to Students

Another approach to handling a behavior problem is to interact directly with the student in private. One way that works well with older students is to have them write out their view of what caused the behavior. When you discuss it with them, you can refer to what they have described to you in writing. Follow these guidelines to make this conversation successful:

- Begin by telling the student that you would like to hear his or her side of the story.
- Listen sincerely, and suspend any judgments.
- Keep probing and talking until the student has shared what he or she needs to say.
- Make sure that you understand what caused the misbehavior.
- Make it clear that you insist on a mutually respectful relationship.
- Do not rush to punish. Instead, tell a student who has misbehaved that you need to think about what you have learned and that you will make a decision overnight.

Take a Problem-Solving Approach

Losing control of your emotions and relying on punishment to effect a change in your students' behavior will not solve discipline problems. What will stop students from misbehaving is a teacher who takes the approach that misbehavior is a problem with a solution.

The first step in adopting a problem-solving approach to misbehavior is to develop a proactive attitude. Refuse to take student misbehavior personally even though you may be hurt, frustrated, and angry. Refusing to give in to your first emotional reaction will de-escalate the situation to a more manageable level.

After you have forced yourself to calm down and control your reactions, you can then complete the rest of the problem-solving process. The following steps will not only help you solve problems but will help you prevent further ones.

Step One: Define the problem.

Step Two: Gather information about the causes from the students who misbehaved.

Step Three: Check to make sure that your students understand the pertinent rules and consequences.

Step Four: Tell your students that you will need to take some time to make a decision.

Step Five: Generate as many solutions as you can.

Step Six: Ask an administrator or a colleague for advice if you are not sure of the right course of action to take.

Step Seven: Decide on the action that will help students not repeat their misbehavior.

Step Eight: Decide how you will implement the solution.

Act Decisively

There are many constructive ways to handle student misbehavior. No matter which approach you choose, you must always act decisively and avoid giving students the impression that you are tenuous about the action you are taking. Here is a list of some of the most common strategies that other teachers have found to be effective in solving discipline problems:

- **Consciously choose to ignore the misbehavior.** Consider the reasons for the behavior so that you can decide whether you can tolerate it. Anticipate the effects of ignoring the behavior before you decide. Use this technique when the misbehavior is fleeting and when no other students are affected—for example, when a student daydreams briefly, gets a slow start on an assignment, or taps a pencil.
- **Delay taking action.** Delay acting when the action you would take could cause further disruption. For example, if a student is taking a quiz in pencil and the correct procedure is to use a pen, you should delay acting if the student's concentration would be disturbed or if the search for a pen would disrupt other students. Talk to the student about the problem after the quiz is over.
- **Use nonverbal actions.** Moving closer to a student and making eye contact are just two of the non-intrusive interventions you can use when the behavior is confined to one or two students only.
- **Give a gentle reprimand.** Often, this will be the only action needed to end trouble. Move close to the student and address him or her in a friendly, firm manner. Word the reprimand in a positive way if possible. Don't allow the student to argue with you or engage your attention further.
- **Confer briefly with a student.** Use a brief conference when you think a short interaction with a student will solve the problem. Use the time to remind a student to stay on task, remind a student of a rule, discuss consequences, and encourage positive actions.
- **Move a student's seat.** If you decide to do this, be as discreet as possible by moving several students at the same time or by advising students at the end of class that they will have new seats when class meets again. Use this technique when students are distracted by their immediate environment or by other students.

- **Arrange for a time-out room.** Arrange this with another teacher in advance so that any time you need to send a student to a time-out, you can do so with minimum disruption. This technique works well for students who are normally well behaved but are upset and need to spend a few minutes out of the classroom to calm themselves. Take care that the students you send to a time-out area have the materials they need to complete their class assignment.
- **Hold a longer conference with a student.** Schedule this type of conference when there are several issues to be resolved or when the misbehavior is serious. The emphasis should be on determining the causes of the misbehavior and finding a solution to the problem.
- **Have students sign a behavior contract.** When you confer with students, you can formalize the solution to a problem with a behavior contract. Use the contract (see Form 15.2 later in this section) to help students acknowledge their behavior and the steps they must take to correct it.
- **Contact a parent or guardian.** If you are having difficulty with helping students control their behavior, ask the other adults in their lives to reinforce your efforts. Too often, teachers hesitate to do this or wait until misbehavior is serious. Early intervention in the form of a request for help is always a good idea.
- **Hold students in detention.** This is a good time to hold longer conferences with students who need to resolve their behavior problems. Use detention time to work together and create a stronger relationship with a student instead of just as punishment.
- **Arrange a conference with parents or guardians.** If a student persists in misbehaving and you have tried several interventions, such as phoning a parent or guardian, with no success, then you should schedule a parent conference.
- **Refer a student to an administrator.** You must make this choice when you have exhausted all other possibilities or when the misbehavior is serious.

Don't Give Up on Your Difficult Students

Of all of the students you will teach, the difficult ones need you most, because too many other people have given up on them. All of your students, even your difficult ones, need to be confident of the following facts:

- You care about them and believe in them.
- It is the misbehavior you don't like, not the student.
- You will never give up on them.

The chief characteristic of children is that they change and grow. Even high school seniors will change dramatically between the first day of school and graduation day. Your chief purpose as an educator is to direct that change and growth so that your students can have productive and peaceful lives.

Be patient. Even though you know they will change and grow over the course of the year, it can sometimes seem almost impossible to maintain your faith in some of your difficult students. When you find your faith beginning to waver, you must resolve to give them every opportunity to overcome their difficulties.

Many experienced teachers can recount stories of unruly, difficult students who are now successful, mature adults who admit to being embarrassed at their poor behavior in school. Before long, you will have similar stories of your own.

Believe in them. I've had many students tell me it was my belief in their abilities that convinced them they could do it. After a while, they aren't just working to please you, but to please themselves. Success breeds success.

—Patty Muth, 14 years' experience

How to Deal with a Difficult Class

Teaching a difficult class can be a debilitating experience. A rude or disrespectful class can turn your enthusiasm into a desire to just make it through one more day. Fortunately, many strategies can be used to turn a classroom full of smart-alecky, unmanageable, or all-around indifferent students into an enjoyable class.

What causes a class to be difficult? The reasons vary.

- Peer conflicts keep students from paying attention to their work.
- Students lack goals.
- An unequal distribution in the ability levels of students is causing frustration.
- A negative label has become a self-fulfilling prophecy.
- There is an unpleasant chemistry between teacher and students.
- There is an unpleasant chemistry among students.
- The classroom is too small to fit all the students.

Perhaps the most serious reason that classes can be difficult lies in the way that students regard themselves and their ability to succeed academically. Students who do not believe they can succeed have no reason to try. Teachers who achieve success with difficult classes turn the negative energy in a class into a positive force by persistently communicating their faith in their students' ability to achieve.

Here are some strategies to help you turn a difficult class into a successful one:

- Smile at your class. If you were videotaped while teaching, would your body language reveal positive or negative feelings about your students?
- Keep the expectations for your class high. Children live up to the expectations of the adults in their lives, so let them know that you expect a lot from them.
- From the first class meeting, establish that you control the class. Demonstrate that you will regulate the behavior in your classroom for the good of all students.
- Call parents or guardians as soon as you can when a problem arises.
- Work on the noise level every day until your students learn to govern themselves. Teach students which volumes are acceptable and which are not. Establish signals to help students learn to control the noise.
- Plan activities to fit your students' short attention span.
- Make sure that activities offer plenty of time for practice and review.
- Never allow students to sit with nothing to do but disturb others. Keep them busy for the entire class period.
- Stay on your feet and monitor. Students who know that you are watching over them will hesitate before misbehaving.
- Tell your students that you expect them to do their work well and that you will help them learn to do it.
- Use nonprint media to catch your students' attention. Art and music are just two media you can use to manage difficult students more easily.
- Make sure that the work you assign is appropriate for your students' ability level.
- Offer incentives other than grades. Students who have never received a good grade may not be motivated by grades. Offer small, frequent rewards instead, such as stickers, computer time, or bookmarks.
- Praise good behavior as often as you can. Difficult students do not always know when they are behaving well. When you praise your class for good behavior, you are encouraging all of your students to repeat the behavior.
- Take time to teach and reteach the rules and procedures that you want your students to follow.
- Be as specific as you can when telling difficult students what you want them to do.
- Give students opportunities to help each other. Students who are sharing their knowledge with a classmate will be so busy being productive that they will not have time to disrupt class.
- Acknowledge the rights of individuals in your class. Showing students that you are fair will ease many sensitive situations.

Hold Successful Student Conferences

Student conferences can be a powerful tool for teachers who want to create a positive disciplinary climate. You can confer with your students for many purposes. You may want to help them work on projects or offer extra assistance after school. You could even offer help when students are working together in a study group.

Student conferences can also be very useful for establishing a positive working environment with a student who has misbehaved. When the two of you sit down together, without the distraction of the rest of the class, and work out a solution to a problem, you both benefit.

Holding a successful conference with a student who has misbehaved is not difficult. Use the following strategies to guarantee success by making it clear that you have given much thought to the student's concerns and to how the two of you can work together to resolve problems.

Before the Conference

- At least twenty-four hours in advance, notify the parents or guardians of any students that you intend to keep after school.
- Make sure that the conference time is workable. Younger students will have to consult their parents for rides home. Be as cooperative about the time as you can.
- Arrange a place to meet that is as free from distractions as possible. Do not confer with students while other students are in the room.

During the Conference

- Be courteous in your greeting. This will set the tone for the rest of the meeting.
- Make the area as comfortable as possible. Offer a pen and paper for taking notes, and sit side by side in student desks or at a table. Do not sit behind your desk.
- To protect yourself from charges of misconduct, when you are meeting one on one with a student, sit near the door to the room, and make sure the door is open. If you believe that a conference will be uncomfortable, arrange for a colleague to be in the same room with you and your student.
- Be very careful not to touch a student for any reason during a conference. Even an innocent pat on the back can be misinterpreted.
- Begin the meeting by stating that the purpose of the conference is to work together to resolve a problem between the two of you. Avoid rehashing unpleasant details, blaming the student, or showing your anger.
- Take the initiative by asking the student to tell you why you are meeting. Make sure that you each have a chance to state the problem as you see it.
- Listen to the student without interrupting. Take notes. Use positive body language to encourage the student to speak.

- When you discuss the student's behavior, focus on the misdeed itself, not on your student's negative personality traits.
- After the student has spoken, restate the problem in your own words. Make sure you understand the problem and express your sincere interest in solving it.
- Be positive but firm in conveying that it is the student's responsibility to change.
- You and your student should brainstorm some solutions. Ask questions about how the student could handle the situation differently.
- Agree on a plan that satisfies both of you. Make sure that you are comfortable with implementing it.
- Calmly explain the negative consequences you will impose if the student fails to carry out his or her part of the plan.
- Once again, state that you are willing to help the student be successful.

At the End of the Conference

- Ask the student if there is anything else that needs to be said. State your willingness to listen again.
- Be very clear that you consider the student's misbehaviors to be in the past and that you will not hold a grudge now that a resolution has been reached.
- Thank your student for taking the time for a conference and for deciding to work with you.

Use Behavior Contracts Effectively

Whether in promoting positive behaviors or eliminating negative ones, behavior contracts are another effective tool. Although you can create other types of contracts for classroom purposes such as daily responsibilities, group projects, or individual assignments, behavior contracts are specifically to help resolve misbehavior.

The behavior problems that can be solved most easily by using a behavior contract are those caused by a student's bad habits: not doing homework, talking back, making rude remarks to peers, not cleaning a work area, among many others. Don't use behavior contracts with students who commit serious misbehaviors or who only misbehave occasionally.

You can also enter into a contract with a parent and a child when the need arises. This is particularly effective in solving homework problems. Everyone wins when a parent is actively involved in finding the solution to a problem and creating the contract.

Behavior contracts are effective because they clarify the problem and its solution for teachers and students, and because they help both teacher and student avoid negative emotions and focus on steps to improve misbehavior. Here's how to use behavior contracts successfully in your class:

- Find a quiet time and place to talk with your student about setting up a behavior contract. An after-school conference is ideal.

- Begin with contracts that have very specific goals that can be achieved in a short length of time. Use small, achievable steps to encourage success.
- Start with tangible rewards rather than intrinsic ones so that the child can see the results of improved behavior immediately.
- Check to be sure that the student has a clear understanding of the problem and the solutions to which you both agree. State this agreement explicitly in the contract.
- Together with the student, fill in a contract form (see Form 15.2). Consider including these items:
  - Name of the student
  - Name of the teacher
  - Beginning and ending dates for the contract
  - A statement of the problem
  - Dates when progress will be checked
  - Specific actions to be performed
  - Rewards
  - Consequences of not meeting the terms of the contract
  - Signatures

Put Detentions to Good Use

If your school district allows you to detain students after school, you can use this time productively if the purpose of a detention is not to punish but to resolve problems. The following suggestions will help you make the process easy to manage.

Before You Issue a Detention Notice

- Take time to learn what your district's policy on student detentions entails.
- Make sure to have plenty of forms on hand so that you will be able to hand out notices as students leave class.
- Before you write out a notice, try to prevent the misbehavior. Privately warn students of the rules they are breaking and of the consequences. No student should be surprised when you issue a detention for misbehavior.
- Decide what you will do if the child refuses to serve a detention. Know your district's policy on this issue before you have to address it.

When You Issue a Detention Notice

- When you must issue a detention notice, do not write the notice while you are upset or in a hurry. If you do, you will appear less than professional.

FORM 15.2

Behavior Contract

Contract between ______________________ and ______________________

Student Teacher

Date: ______________________

Problem to be resolved:

____

____

The student agrees to

____

____

____

The teacher agrees to

____

____

____

Dates for checking progress: ______________________

Reward:

____

____

Consequences of not fulfilling the contract:

____

____

The student's efforts to solve this problem will be considered complete when

____

____

Student's signature: ______________________

Teacher's signature: ______________________

- When you do write the notice, use a dark pen and write neatly. Spell the student's name correctly as well as the names of his or her parents or guardians.
- Be very specific when you write the notice so that the student and his or her parents or guardians know what has happened to cause the notice. If you assign a detention as a result of a third tardy to your class, for example, give the dates of the previous tardies and the consequences that resulted from them.
- Make it very clear to your students that their parents or guardians must sign the notice before you can allow them to serve their detention. You should never cause a parent or guardian worry because their child is late in coming home from school.
- Because students may take detentions lightly and parents or guardians do not, call the student's home to let parents know that you have issued a detention notice to their child.
- Issue the detention notice quietly, matter-of-factly, and at the very end of class to avoid embarrassing students or causing a scene with an angry student.
- When you issue a detention notice, ask the student to sign a brief statement that he or she has received the notice. Be sure to date the statement and keep it in your records.
- If a student crumples or tears the notice, continue to be very calm. If the student does not come back for the notice and to apologize before the end of the school day, contact his or her parents or guardians by phone. You should also lengthen the time of the detention by a few minutes because you will need to discuss this issue with the student.
- Never issue detention notices to a large group of students at the same time; you will appear to have lost control of your class.
- Plan what you want to accomplish with a detained student and how you will reach that goal.

During the Detention

- Be careful to protect yourself from being accused of misconduct by keeping the door open at all times when you are detaining a student. Do not touch the student at all.
- Establish a very businesslike atmosphere. Refuse to tolerate inappropriate behavior.
- If you have more than one student staying for a detention, do not allow them to sit near each other or to be playful.
- Talk with your student about the problem and how it should be resolved. Have the student write out his or her thoughts before trying to talk with you. Such writing is not busywork but a tool to open a helpful dialogue. Try using questions such as the ones on the following list to get your students thinking about the changes they can make to prevent the problem from recurring.
  - What choices can I make other than the ones I made?
  - What are some appropriate behaviors that I have used in this class in the past?

- What are the reasons that I should change my behavior?
- How can I improve my approach to my work, my classmates, and my teacher?
- What are my goals for this class, and how can I achieve them?

After the Detention

- Make notes about what happened during the detention. Keep a record of the conference and a copy of the student's writing.
- Do not give students a ride home. If a parent or guardian has signed the notice, transportation is not your responsibility.
- Do not leave a child alone at an empty school. Wait with the student until his or her ride appears.
- Make it clear to any student you detain that you are optimistic about future behavior improvements and that you will not hold a grudge about past misbehavior.

Manage Referrals to an Administrator with Confidence

In order for the discipline process to be meaningful, teachers who need assistance with students who make learning difficult for others must have some recourse. Usually, this recourse takes the form of an administrative referral.

Referring students to an administrator during your first year as a teacher is, at best, a nerve-racking experience. Consider the answers to the following common questions in order to make the referral process easier for everyone involved.

When should a teacher send a student to an administrator?
There is no question that you should refer a student to an administrator for any of these behaviors:

- Persistent defiance
- Bullying
- Stealing
- Sexual harassment
- Vandalism
- Deliberate profanity
- Bringing weapons to school
- Substance abuse
- Making threats
- Violent behavior

- Truancy
- Cheating
- Persistent disruptions
- Habitual tardiness

How can a teacher maintain credibility with students, parents, and administrators? Referral to the office is a serious step and should not be taken lightly by anyone involved. To safeguard your credibility, you should follow these five guidelines:

1. Don't send students to the office for minor misbehaviors that you are expected to handle successfully, such as
    - Not doing homework
    - Scribbling on desks
    - Rude comments
    - Infrequent tardiness
    - Not working in class
    - Nonviolent peer conflicts
    - Excessive talking
    - Chewing gum
    - Poor work habits
    - Inattention

2. Unless the misbehavior is sudden, such as a fight that requires students to be removed from the room, administrators should not be surprised to receive a referral from you. When you begin to notice a pattern of misbehavior, make an appointment with an administrator to discuss the problem and to ask for help. When you finally refer a student, the administrator will then have a clear understanding of what has happened and what you have done to try to resolve the conflict. By giving administrators this background information, you not only make it easier for them to make the best decisions about how to handle problems but also present yourself as a competent educator who can handle most of your problems.
3. When you write a referral, make sure that the language you use is as professional and objective as possible. Because many different people, including the student and his or her parents, will read the referral, use behavior-oriented, factual language.
4. Call the student's parents or guardians before the end of the day to inform them of the incident and of the referral.
5. Between the time you turn in a referral and the time an administrator acts on it, speak to the administrator in order to discuss the problem and add any details you didn't want to write on the referral form.

How can a teacher avoid making the disruption worse when referring a student?
Following are some suggestions on how to minimize disruption when referring a student:

- Have copies of the referral form on hand so that you will be able to write it quickly and with a minimum of distractions.
- Maintain a student's dignity and privacy in front of classmates. Do not tell the student that you intend to write a referral when you are in the presence of other students. Be discreet. This will also help you avoid an angry outburst that will disturb other students.
- Remain calm, and remind the student of the rules and the consequences for breaking them. Don't threaten or bully a student, even if you are angry.
- Students should not be surprised when they are referred to an administrator for persistent misbehavior. By the time a student needs to be referred to an administrator, you should have intervened several times. If students know the consequences of their actions in advance of taking the actions, they should not be surprised by a referral.

What should a teacher do if he or she disagrees with an action that an administrator has taken?
If you have been working with an administrator to prevent the student's misbehavior and to avoid writing a referral, you should know the action that the administrator intends to take when you refer the student. If the administrator's action turns out to be different from what you had discussed or one that you are not comfortable with, speak with him or her to find out the reason for the decision. Resist the temptation to publicly criticize the decision.

How can a teacher prevent misbehavior from happening again?
Here are some tips on how to keep misbehavior from recurring:

- Learn from your mistakes. Examine the actions that led to the final referral. Determine what other interventions you could have taken early in your relationship with the child to prevent the misbehavior from reaching this point.
- Help students leave the behavior and the referral behind. Make students aware that you view referrals as an end to misbehavior.
- Continue to use a variety of early interventions to prevent misbehaviors from reaching the referral point.

Handling Common School Problems

Although it may sometimes seem as if your school days are beset with tribulations unique to a first-year teacher, experience alone will not allow you to prevent every problem. Some fall into the category of problems that all teachers have to learn to manage. Following are suggestions on how to handle six common problems:

1. Tardiness
2. Absenteeism
3. Overcrowded classes
4. Substance abuse
5. Fighting
6. Harassment

Problem 1: Tardiness

Very few students can attend school for an entire term without being tardy at least once. Students have many reasons to delay their arrival in class, and by the end of the first few weeks of school, you will have heard many creative excuses. Expect your students to suffer from car trouble, traffic, stuck lockers, lost notebooks, arguments with friends, sleepy parents, and mysterious alarm clock failures.

The real reasons for your students' tardiness are not as colorful. Students may be late to class because they do not see an advantage in being on time. Perhaps they are late because you have not communicated the consequences of tardiness to them. Another reason for student tardiness may be that inconsistent enforcement of the consequences has led students to believe that being late to class is not a problem.

Although tardy students are the first to claim that being tardy is not a serious offense and that they are not hurting anyone else, tardy students do disrupt learning. You must raise students' awareness of the negative effects associated with their tardiness:

- Tardy students cause a disruption, no matter how quietly they try to slip into the class. Furthermore, if students see that their classmates can be tardy with no teacher reaction, then they will believe that it is OK for them to be tardy, too. The disruptive effect will multiply if more and more students come tardy to your class.
- Tardy students set a negative tone in a class by tacitly sending a message that the activities you have planned for them are not important enough for them to make the effort to be on time. As a result, the focus in your class may shift from learning to a power struggle between you and the students who are testing the boundaries of your patience.

YOUR RESPONSIBILITIES

- ▶ Make it important for your students to be on time to your class. Begin an interesting and meaningful assignment as soon as the bell rings.
- ▶ You must enforce your policy about tardiness consistently. Be sure that your policy is in line with your school's policies. Chronically tardy students respond particularly well to a policy with escalating consequences because it forces them to take their actions seriously.

- You must involve parents or guardians if students are tardy more than once or twice in a marking period. This is an especially important step if the tardy student is late to school and not just late from another teacher's class.
- Most schools have a policy for handling habitual tardiness. At some point in the process, you will be expected to refer the student to an administrator for action. Be sure to follow your school's procedures in regard to tardiness.
- Model the behavior you expect. Your students will be very quick to point out your hypocrisy if you are tardy and then reprimand them for the same offense.

MISTAKES TO AVOID

- Never embarrass tardy students with sarcastic remarks such as "Glad you decided to join us." Sarcasm will not solve the problem, nor will it earn you respect; instead, it will make tardy students even more reluctant to enter the room.
- Do not delay calling a student's home. The second time a student is tardy, you should contact a parent or guardian to enlist support in handling the problem.
- Do not be a pushover who accepts unreasonable excuses; instead, enforce the consequences for tardiness.
- Never stop what you are doing to interrogate a tardy student in front of the rest of the class; instead, allow the student to slip into class while you continue giving instruction.
- Don't overlook tardiness, or the problem will spread.
- Don't allow students to stand in the doorway before class starts. Students who block the entrance interrupt the smooth start of class because they delay their classmates from getting to their seats on time.

STRATEGIES THAT WORK

- Define tardiness for your students, and be reasonable in your definition. Most teachers will agree that a student who is inside the classroom but not in a seat is not tardy; others are more particular and insist that a student who is not actually sitting down is tardy. Note, however, that the second definition is difficult to justify to your students and their parents.
- Begin class quickly, with assignments that students will find enjoyable. If necessary, grade the work you assign at the start of class so that your students have a reason to be prompt. Make the first few minutes of class as meaningful as the rest.
- The first two weeks of the term are important in establishing your expectation that students will arrive promptly. If you make tardiness control a priority as the term begins, you will avoid many problems later.
- Speak with a tardy student privately to determine why he or she was late to class.

- Your attendance records must be accurate. It is sometimes confusing to stop class and change an absence mark to a tardy mark, but you must do so in order to ensure that your records remain accurate. When you refer a student to an administrator or when you talk to parents, you will need to be able to give the dates.
- Move a chronically tardy student to a seat near the door in order to minimize disruptions. When you pass out materials and the student is not present, place materials on the desktop to prevent disruption if he or she is late.
- Find out about the background of tardy students. Often, their tardiness is the result of a disorganized family life in which children have not been taught to be punctual.
- Be consistent in enforcing your procedures in regard to tardiness. If students see that you are not comfortable enforcing your policies, they will not strive to be punctual.
- Whenever you talk with your students about their tardiness, put the responsibility for their behavior where it belongs—on them. Ask tardy students what steps they plan to take to eliminate the problem. Offer support, but remain firm in your expectations.

Problem 2: Absenteeism

In the last few decades, a profound social shift has resulted in an increased demand for educated workers in the United States. As the contrast between the abundance of high-paying jobs for educated workers and the lack of jobs for uneducated workers becomes more stark, it is becoming more and more evident that students need to stay in school.

Many factors may contribute to a child's poor attendance. A consistent pattern of poor attendance usually develops from their earliest days onward. For instance, when a family is in turmoil, children find it difficult to attend school. Frequent illnesses may also be a factor, especially with the rise in respiratory illness among young students.

Another factor that causes some students to miss school is that their family does not value education and does not encourage regular attendance. Students who are parents themselves find it almost impossible to overcome the difficulties associated with having a child and attending school. Sometimes older children have to stay home to take care of younger siblings or other family members for various reasons.

Take an active role in encouraging students to attend school regardless of the reason for their absenteeism. Encouraging your students to attend school on a regular basis is one of the most important and most difficult tasks you will face in your career.

YOUR RESPONSIBILITIES

- Be aware of the attendance patterns of your students. Find out the reasons for a student's absenteeism so that you can offer assistance.
- When you realize that a student has an attendance problem, do not ignore it. It is up to you to help that student in the most appropriate way.

- Students who feel connected to their school, their classmates, and their teachers rarely miss school without good reason. Encourage regular attendance by building a strong relationship with each of your students. Children should feel that they are missed when they are absent.
- Your classroom should be a place where students feel challenged and capable at the same time. If classes are too difficult or are not challenging, a student may feel that there is little reason to attend.
- Students should know that you disapprove of absence without good reason. Contact the parents or guardians of absent students so that everyone involved knows that you believe it is important for every student to attend school.
- Maintain accurate attendance records. It is not always easy to keep up with attendance records, but students and administrators need to have an accurate accounting of attendance throughout the term.

MISTAKES TO AVOID

- Don't assume that absent students want to miss school.
- Don't allow a student to be absent without determining the reason.
- Ignoring attendance problems will only encourage students to miss more school.
- Don't make it too difficult for students to make up missing work. Arrange times that are convenient for both of you to meet, if necessary. Give the child the assignments that were missed and a reasonable length of time in which to complete them.

STRATEGIES THAT WORK

- Follow your school district's procedures for reporting and handling attendance, especially if you want to seek assistance for truant students.
- Consider sending a letter home with any student who misses a third day of your class. Keep a copy of the letter as documentation that you have contacted the student's parents or guardians.
- Contact the parents or guardians of students who have excessive absences to ask them to work with you on the problem. Some parents may request that you contact them whenever their child is absent. Try to honor this request whenever you can.
- Encourage students and their parents to record the days that children miss school on a calendar. Some parents do not realize just how often their child is out without a reminder such as this.
- Ask a counselor to speak to students who are having trouble with their attendance so that the students will have a clear picture of their options. Many believe that they can drop out and then pick up a GED certificate later, not realizing how difficult the test for this certificate can be.

- Some parents or guardians do not value school and do not encourage regular attendance. Help parents of students who have excessive absences understand the importance of regular attendance and the long-term consequences for students who do not attend school.
- Talk to students about their absences. If your students are having family problems or social problems, seek help for them. Have them talk to a guidance counselor in order to enlist further support for maintaining regular attendance.
- Make your students aware that their attendance is important to you and to their classmates. Always greet them pleasantly when they arrive in your class, to show your concern.

Problem 3: Overcrowded Classes

Overcrowded classes are common in many school districts due to a population boom and tight school budgets. Rows of mobile classroom units surround many schools, while other schools have many teachers who must "float" from classroom to classroom because there isn't space for them to have their own classroom. Still other schools have many classrooms in which there are just too many students for anyone to be comfortable.

Although overcrowded classrooms may be inescapable, the problems associated with them are not. Your attitude is the most important factor in coping with the demands of a large class. Careful planning, strong connections with students, and interesting lessons—not the number of students you are required to teach—are the determining factors in the success of your classroom.

YOUR RESPONSIBILITIES

- You are expected to provide the same quality of instruction for a large class as you would for a small one.
- Student safety is even more of a concern when classes are crowded. You should be aware of activities with the potential to be unsafe and determine how you will successfully manage them.
- You still need to create strong bonds with your students, to keep them from being lost in the crowd.

MISTAKES TO AVOID

- Don't miss the opportunity to enlist your students' help in managing the situation. If you create a team spirit, you will find it easier to manage the challenge of a crowded classroom.
- Don't delay in returning papers. Although keeping up with paperwork is more challenging with a large class, the size of the class makes it even more important to do

so. Falling behind will not only cause you more stress but also deprive students of attention and feedback that is already spread too thin.

- Don't neglect class routines. Routines are especially important for creating an orderly environment in a large class.
- Don't overlook the essential task of getting to know your students as individuals. Make sure that your students know that you are aware of them as people, not as just faces in the crowd.
- Don't allow small problems to grow into large ones. Monitor, contact parents, teach courtesy, and use other strategies to prevent problems from becoming serious.
- Don't let noise get out of control. Deal proactively with the noise levels that can accompany a large class.

STRATEGIES THAT WORK

- Monitoring is even more important in large classes; it is crucial to maintain an orderly environment. Stay on your feet, and remain alert.
- Room arrangements are very important in overcrowded classes. Pay attention to traffic patterns, and arrange the furniture in your class to accommodate your students. Have enough desks so that every student has a place to sit. Reduce clutter by storing equipment that you are not using.
- Be very organized. You will need to have enough materials, books, and handouts for every student. Create a seating chart, and insist that students adhere to it. Keep your own desk area organized and tidy.
- Create and enforce routines for class activities. Teach your routines early in the term, and reinforce them as necessary. Students should be able to predict what they are supposed to do.
- Keep student movement to a minimum by encouraging students to dispose of trash at the end of class and to sharpen pencils at the start.
- Be alert to the opportunities for cheating that can arise in an overcrowded classroom. Monitor vigilantly during tests and quizzes.
- Speak with every student every day. Greet students at the door to let everyone know that you are not only aware of them as people but concerned about them, too.
- Create small groups within the larger group to increase students' sense of belonging. When students have partners to support them, they will feel like part of the group instead of just one of many.
- A large courteous class is much easier to handle than a small rude one. Insist that all students treat you and each other with courtesy.

Problem 4: Substance Abuse

Students are barraged with mixed messages about cigarettes, alcohol, and drugs. On television, they see public service announcements warning them that all three substances can be deadly, yet in the same hour, they may watch programs in which substance abuse is taken lightly or, even worse, treated as a cool choice made by grown-ups. It's not surprising that so many confused students appear to be biding their time until they are old enough to experiment with illegal substances.

Many teachers do not have a clear idea about how they can help students resist the lure of drugs and alcohol. They are not sure what to do when students brag about a weekend party or reek of cigarette smoke. Many teachers want to believe that educating students about substance abuse is someone else's job. The problem with this assumption is that many families either are unable to cope with the problem or are themselves the root of the problem.

YOUR RESPONSIBILITIES

- You are expected to know and follow your district's guidelines on substance abuse by students.
- You are expected to involve other adults to help a student as soon as you determine that a problem exists.
- You are expected to be a role model and to discourage students from experimenting with illegal substances.
- You are expected to be a supportive and caring adult who will help students with substance abuse problems.

MISTAKES TO AVOID

- Don't ignore substance abuse problems among your students; this problem does not go away by itself.
- Don't overreact. For example, if a student makes a passing mention of a weekend party, don't lecture or notify a counselor. Instead, speak privately with the student about making sound decisions.
- Don't ignore your school's policies on students with substance abuse problems.
- You should not attempt to handle a serious substance abuse problem without involving other adults. If you have a student with a substance abuse problem, keep in mind the serious nature of the problem and recognize that it needs to be handled with support from all of the adults in a student's life.
- Do not forget that you are a role model. Teachers who talk about the fun they had at college parties do not help students to make wise choices for themselves.
- Do not lose sight of the fact that students are under the legal age for smoking, drinking, and taking drugs, no matter how old they may seem.

STRATEGIES THAT WORK

Prevention of Substance Abuse

- You do not have to spend hours of instructional time teaching students about illegal substances. Instead, when the subject arises, be clear about your position on the issue.
- Give your students the facts about substance abuse, thus enabling them to make wiser choices based on real information rather than the opinions of their friends, who may be just as confused as they are.
- Many students, especially younger ones, are simply not aware of the health risks and the social consequences of substance abuse. Make sure that students are aware of these risks as well as the legal penalties for substance abuse.
- Your school district may have programs to help students who are struggling with substance abuse. In addition, the guidance counselors at your school are good sources of information about community resources.
- Make sure that your students understand school policies concerning student use of tobacco, alcohol, and drugs, including the consequences for violating those policies.

How to Intervene If You Notice Substance Abuse

If you notice that a student has violated your school's policies on substance abuse, you should intervene. Follow these steps:

1. Remove the student from class and quietly question him or her to determine whether there is a problem.
2. Don't overlook the problem. Immediately and calmly put your school's policies into effect.
3. Contact the person at your school who is designated to handle substance abuse problems, and explain the problem as you see it. That person will conduct a search, if necessary, and will involve the child's parents and other appropriate personnel.
4. Help the student see you as a supportive and caring person. Students with substance abuse problems need support and assistance, not blame.

Problem 5: Fighting

Any teacher dreads the signs that a fight is imminent. The potential for serious injury is very real when students set out to hurt each other. And because other students often gather around to encourage the participants, they are also at risk.

After a fight is over, the effects can disrupt classes for the rest of the day. Students do not want to settle down, preferring instead to discuss the fight blow by blow. Even worse, a fight often triggers a series of other conflicts as anger and adrenaline run high throughout the school.

In the last few years, there has been a dramatic increase in the number of fights at school as students bring conflicts from their neighborhoods to school. In recent years, conflicts have been more likely to involve the use of weapons. As an educator, you can do a great deal to reduce violence by taking a proactive stance.

YOUR RESPONSIBILITIES

- You are expected to follow your school district's procedures for handling student fights.
- Your school district will expect you to act quickly to prevent fights by reporting student rumors.
- You should stop students from harassing each other in your presence. Encourage them to report incidents of bullying to administrators.
- You are expected to keep all of your students as safe as you can when a fight erupts.
- You are expected to take reasonable measures to stop fights without putting yourself or others in danger.
- You may be expected to provide an accurate witness report and appear in court.

MISTAKES TO AVOID

- Do not try to restrain violent students without help from other adults. Teachers who inadvertently hurt students while stopping them from fighting have been sued successfully. Other teachers have been injured themselves.
- Don't leave the fight area. Send students for help instead.
- Don't allow a fight to hinder the rest of the day's instruction. Settle students down quickly. A written assignment usually will focus their attention on their work.
- If you are assigned to hall duty, cafeteria duty, or any other duty, don't miss it. Be on time and be alert. A strong adult presence deters many fights.

STRATEGIES THAT WORK

Preventing Fights

- Familiarize your students with your school's policy concerning students who fight at school. Remind them of the severe penalties that they will have to pay for fighting.
- Teach students how to mediate peer conflicts. If your school has a conflict resolution program, refer students who are at risk for violent behavior.
- Make sure that your students are aware of their options in a peer conflict situation. They should not have to fight as a way of resolving problems.

- Be alert to the signs that a fight is building: rumors, a high level of excitement, remarks about what will happen later.
- If you see that two students are beginning to square off, remind them of the serious penalties for students who fight. Often students will take this as an opportunity to back down without losing face because they can claim that they do not want to be expelled.
- Immediately contact an administrator about a possible fight. Also, contact the parents or guardians of the students who are threatening to fight.
- Make sure that all of your students are aware of the school policy on weapons and how to report weapons to an adult.
- Teach your students about bullying and sexual harassment. Make sure that they understand the limits they should observe when relating to one another and what they should do if they are bullied or harassed.
- Encourage good behavior by refusing to allow students to insult each other, even in jest. Good-natured insults can quickly generate anger and violence.
- Teach your students that they can be punished for inciting others to fight and for blocking the area so that adults cannot get through to stop a fight.

During a Fight

- Immediately get help from other adults by sending students to fetch them. Do not try to restrain or step between students without another adult present.
- The safety of all students at the scene is your first concern.
- Be very clear with students who are watching the fight that you want them to leave the area or, if the fight is in your classroom, to sit down.
- Be very careful about how you approach violent students so that no one, including yourself, is injured.

Fights with Weapons

- If you hear a rumor that there is a weapon in the building, contact an administrator at once. You should not attempt to handle this situation by yourself.
- When a weapon is used during a fight, do not allow other students to take it. The weapon may be used as evidence. If you can, confiscate it and turn it over to an administrator.

Fights That Result in Injuries

- Send a student for the school nurse. Deal first with any injured students and then with the other students at the scene. Do not leave the area.

- Assist the more seriously wounded students first. Be careful that the aid you offer does not injure students further.
- Protect yourself and others from contact with blood or other body fluids.
- If you are even slightly injured, seek medical attention promptly.

After a Fight

- As soon as you can, jot down the details of what happened. As a witness to the fight, you may be called on to remember these details in court, sometimes months after the incident, so be as specific as you can when you write your notes.
- If a fight took place while students were under your supervision, contact their parents or guardians so that you can work together to prevent a recurrence.
- Model the calm response you want from your students. Resume teaching immediately, without rehashing the fight or allowing students to do so.

I had five sixth-grade students who were known for frequent misbehavior. I made a promise to each of their parents that I would call each evening. I kept my promise for the entire school year. Those students had the best year because they knew they had to behave. Their behavior improved, and life at home improved.

—Yann Pirrone, 15 years' experience

Problem 6: Harassment

Schools are not always safe places for teachers. Each year, thousands of teachers report that they have been insulted and threatened by their students. School can be an even tougher place for students. Every month, thousands of students report that a classmate has physically attacked them. Others report that they have been too afraid to attend school on at least one occasion. These statistics reveal only what is reported to authorities; far more harassment occurs than is ever reported.

The worst aspect of the problem of harassment is that teachers have been slow to react to complaints from victims in the past. Some teachers seem to feel that victims of harassment bring it on themselves or are overreacting. Many teachers, despite recent incidents of school violence, are still inclined to overlook harassment. The situation is exacerbated by the fact that many teachers are not sure about when they should intervene.

The first step you can take to stop this serious threat is to understand exactly what harassment is. It can take two forms: physical abuse and verbal abuse. When students are abused physically, teachers are usually quick to respond. Furthermore, because of highly publicized court cases involving sexual harassment (both verbal and physical) teachers also tend to take threats and taunts of a sexual nature very seriously, acting quickly to deal with them. However, verbal abuse in the form of rumors, racial slurs, name calling, and teasing is the most widespread form of harassment, and unfortunately, it is far more likely to be tolerated by teachers.

YOUR RESPONSIBILITIES

- You are expected to take necessary steps to prevent harassment by teaching your students about it and by supervising them adequately.
- Be alert to signs that a student is being harassed by others. Act promptly.
- You must know your school's policy about harassment and your responsibilities.
- Because harassment is such a serious offense, you must involve administrators, parents or guardians, and other support personnel according to the guidelines specified by your district if one of your students is involved in harassment.

MISTAKES TO AVOID

- Never ignore the situation. If you observe an incident, no matter how mild it may appear to you, take action.
- Don't make things worse for the victim by causing him or her unnecessary public humiliation. Be sensitive to the embarrassment such students feel at being a target and having to ask for help.
- Don't ever assume that victims bring it on themselves.
- Don't neglect to teach your students about harassment, the forms it can take, the consequences of perpetrating it, how to report it, and why they must report incidents to adults.

STRATEGIES THAT WORK

Before an Incident Occurs

- Make teaching social skills part of your classroom procedures, no matter how old your students are. Some of your students simply do not know which behaviors are appropriate and which are not.
- Strive to build a sense of teamwork among your students so that they learn to value everyone's contributions to the class.
- Promote acceptance by praising students when they are helpful to each other. It is particularly effective when you can label an entire class as helpful, initiating a positive self-fulfilling prophecy.

- Boost the self-esteem of all students, particularly those who may be tempted to harass others because of a poor sense of self-worth and those who may be a target of harassment.
- Make sure that students have the basic skills they need to deal with peer conflicts.
- Be aware of how students treat each other. Listen carefully to what they have to say to and about each other.
- When you notice several signs of trouble—students have targeted someone for disrespect or a student is having trouble adjusting to school—document them and report your findings to an administrator.

After an Incident Occurs

- Put the school's procedures into action by speaking with an administrator. It is important to prevent more abuse by acting quickly.
- Meet with the student whom you suspect of harassment and ask him or her to tell you about the incident. Then ask for the details in writing. It is important that you not speak with the victim first so that there will be few reprisals for tattling.
- Meet with the victim to discuss the incident. Have this student write a report of the incident, too.
- Support the victim. Often, just talking with an adult will help relieve some of the anxiety that the child is feeling.
- Talk with the parents or guardians of both students to let them know what has been reported. They should understand not only what happened but that there is a school policy about harassment and that the incident has been reported to an administrator. Elicit their support in working with you to prevent further abuse.
- Work with both students together to solve their differences. The abuser should apologize to the victim. At the end of their conference, both students should have a better understanding of their behavior.

Twenty-Five Discipline Don'ts

1. Don't waste time trying to prove that you are right and your students are wrong. Instead, work together with your students to solve problems.
2. Don't let a situation strip you of your objectivity or cause you to lose your temper.
3. Don't be inconsistent.
4. Don't take student misbehavior personally. Distance yourself emotionally from student misdeeds and remain objective.
5. Don't create problems by tempting your students. Don't leave valuables lying around; don't leave your room unsupervised; and don't allow opportunities for misbehavior because you are not monitoring.

6. Don't confront a student in front of the class. Not only will this create a disruption that will upset everyone who watches, but the misbehaving student may act even worse in reaction to the embarrassment. Talk to misbehaving students privately whenever you can.
7. Don't force a student to apologize. This will only humiliate the student and is not likely to result in a sincere apology. Instead, you should work with both students, helping them to resolve their differences so that an apology can be sincere.
8. Don't subtract points from a student's grade because of misbehavior. A grade reflects a student's academic progress, not his or her behavior.
9. Don't touch an angry student. Your innocent touch could be misconstrued.
10. Don't neglect to intervene when a problem is small enough to be handled simply.
11. Don't label students in a negative way. Their behavior may be bad, but they are not bad people.
12. Don't be too quick to send a student to an administrator. Handle your own problems as often as you can.
13. Don't move straight to a referral for a pattern of small offenses. Establish a management plan in which consequences build in severity as misbehavior continues.
14. Don't assign double negative consequences. Not allowing a student to join classmates at recess and assigning a detention is an example of a double negative consequence. To be effective and fair, an offense should have a single appropriate negative consequence, not multiple ones.
15. Don't remain angry with students who have misbehaved. Knowing that you are still angry will not encourage students to behave better after they have made a mistake.
16. Don't ignore improper behavior. Allowing students to make fun of each other or just rolling your eyes as they do are two ways of ignoring improper behavior.
17. Don't attempt to threaten or bully your students into behaving well. It won't work.
18. Don't just tell students to stop; tell them what they must do to be successful.
19. Don't hide a serious problem such as cheating in an attempt to help a student. Involve other concerned adults, and follow your school's policy.
20. Don't punish students in anger. Calm down and think before you act.
21. Don't assign academic work as punishment. The consequence should be appropriate to the misbehavior.
22. Don't punish an entire group of students for the behavior of only a few of its members.
23. Don't be confrontational. Take a problem-solving approach instead.
24. Don't order an angry student to comply with your demands.
25. Don't bargain with your students in order to coax them into behaving better. Enforce your rules instead.

Talk It Over

How to Handle Behavior Problems Effectively

Use these questions as a springboard for discussions that will help you and your discussion group members grow and develop professionally. Discuss these questions about how to handle behavior problems effectively:

1. What are your skills in handling students who have misbehaved? What can you improve about how you deal with misbehaving students? How can you capitalize on your strengths? How can you improve a weakness in handling misbehavior?
2. Why do students misbehave in your class? Can you notice a pattern or a time when misbehavior is most likely to occur? What can you do to prevent problems from happening? What can your colleagues suggest to help you prevent discipline problems?
3. What plans do you have in place for handling serious student misbehavior such as fighting? What is your school's policy about teacher intervention in a student fight? What can you do to keep your students and yourself safe when serious misbehavior erupts?
4. What do you do that causes your students to misbehave? What can you do to solve this problem?
5. In this section you will find a list of twenty-five discipline don'ts. Which ones will be easiest for you to remember? Which ones will be difficult? Can you add to this list? Where can you go to for help with discipline issues at your school?
6. Share ideas about what you have done to work with a difficult class. What strategies work well? What have you observed other teachers doing that you could adapt for your class?
7. Which students cause you the most trouble? What can you do to help solve their problems? Who in your school can give you advice?
8. Discuss what your supervisors expect from you in terms of discipline. How strict do they expect you to be? How can you find out what is expected of you? How will you know if you are too strict or too permissive?
9. What attitudes can you adopt to increase your confidence in your ability to cope with discipline issues? How can you improve your ability to manage the discipline concerns in your classroom?
10. With your colleagues, brainstorm about the characteristics of a well-behaved class. How can you eliminate unproductive behaviors and promote positive ones? How will you know when you have succeeded?

SECTION SIXTEEN

Manage Diversity in Your Classroom

In this section, you will learn

- ✔ How to work successfully with gifted students
- ✔ How to work well with special needs students
- ✔ How to help students who are capable but who are underachieving
- ✔ How to work with at-risk students and students living in poverty
- ✔ How to celebrate the cultural differences in your classroom

When you decided to become a teacher, you may have made your decision based on your love of a particular discipline or you may have chosen education because of an inspiring role model in your past. Although many teachers give these as reasons why they were first attracted to a career in education, most teachers remain in the profession because they enjoy being with their students.

You can expect your class to include an intricate mixture of students with different ability levels, ethnic backgrounds, family situations, maturity levels, and school experiences. You can also expect that while these differences can create a rich experience for all of your students, they can also present many challenges throughout the year.

Although teachers may often wish for a class of motivated youngsters who are capable of behaving well all the time, experienced teachers know that the challenging students are most fascinating to teach because their successes are the most satisfying.

> **We *all* have a gift! Let those gifts shine. Everyone can do something in a special way.**
>
> —*Sandra Council, 23 years' experience*

When you look at your class roster, remind yourself that every one of your students deserves the best instruction you can deliver every day. When you take this attitude, you will be the kind of teacher that your students need you to be.

In this section, you will explore several types of students that you may be fortunate enough to have in your class. Use the suggestions and strategies for each type to help students reach their full potential while under your tutelage.

Gifted Students

Gifted students are usually fun as well as difficult to teach. When a lesson interests a gifted child, he or she will take the lesson far beyond the boundaries of the material. Gifted students are also a challenge to teach. They are impatient with topics they don't perceive as interesting, and they can be especially impatient with teachers and peers whom they perceive to be less than capable. To learn more about teaching gifted students, consult some of the many books and Web sites that other teachers have found valuable:

- **Carol Ann Tomlinson (www.caroltomlinson.com).** A noted authority in the field of gifted education, Tomlinson has written several practical and helpful books for teachers. In particular, her book *The Differentiated Classroom: Responding to the Needs of All Learners,* published by the Association for Supervision and Curriculum Development in 1999, contains useful information for all teachers of gifted students.
- **National Association for Gifted Children (http://www.nagc.org).** At this site, you will find excellent resources for educators: links to Web sites with advice for those who teach students with high potential, research articles, and helpful information about teaching gifted children.
- **TeachersFirst (www.teachersfirst.com/gifted/spot.html).** This site offers reading lists, strategies for teachers, links to other Web sites, book lists for students, and information on how to modify instruction to appeal to multiple intelligences.

When you have gifted students in your class, you will need to modify the content of the material or modify the learning process to meet their needs. Use or adapt the following guidelines for modifying the content and process of your instruction to accommodate the needs of your gifted students.

MODIFYING LEARNING PROCESSES FOR GIFTED STUDENTS

- ▶ Many gifted students do well with project-based instruction. When you assign a project to gifted students, give a reasonably loose structure and then allow them to take the project as far as they need to. (See Section Eleven for more information on helping students with projects.)

- Gifted students are self-directed learners. Take this characteristic into consideration when you modify the process of learning, allowing students to have a strong voice in how they will accomplish their goals.
- Set a rapid pace for instruction. Gifted students quickly grow bored with the slower pace of undifferentiated instruction.
- Focus on higher-level thinking skills throughout a unit of study; gifted students quickly master the recall and comprehension levels.
- Be as flexible as you can in the nature of the work you assign gifted students.
- Use technology as often as you can. Your gifted students are likely to become proficient at accessing resources on the Internet with just a bit of guidance from you.
- Allow gifted students to work together. They benefit from being able to bounce ideas off each other.

Modifying Lesson Content to Challenge Gifted Students

- Focus on the broad concepts in a unit of study. Gifted students will quickly grasp the details of an assignment.
- Provide content that will not only challenge gifted students to learn but appeal to their particular interests. For example, if one of your students is interested in a sport, capitalize on this in teaching mathematics, physics, history, or other lessons.
- When you work with gifted students, use information from a variety of sources and ask students to synthesize the information. For a gifted child, a textbook is only a jumping-off point from which to begin exploring a topic.
- Encourage student input in the selection of material. You may have a general unit of study, but allow students to study the details that most interest them. For example, you may teach a general unit on space first and then have each student work on a particular aspect of space, such as planets, asteroids, or comets.
- Don't ask gifted students to just solve problems; have them use real-life situations to formulate their own problems. For example, you could ask students to anticipate and solve the problems that they would experience if they were to create a new city or to solve a current problem in their own neighborhood.
- Focus on depth of content rather than more content. For example, reading three excellent books on a topic of study is better than asking students to read five books of lesser quality.
- Plan to move instruction out of the classroom whenever possible in order to study material firsthand. Enrich lessons with trips to museums and other appropriate points of interest.

TEACHING GIFTED STUDENTS IN A GROUP OF STUDENTS WITH MIXED ABILITIES

- Although allowing gifted students to serve as peer tutors is acceptable, be careful not to overuse this technique. It reinforces what they already know, but it doesn't provide enrichment of their own skills in the subject they are tutoring.
- When working in groups, place gifted students with other high-achieving students as well as with less able students.
- Provide a modified assignment as often as you can.
- Work closely with the parents of gifted students so that you can fulfill each child's needs and reduce their frustrations when lessons don't appeal to their abilities or learning styles. Parents or guardians often are excellent and knowledgeable advocates for their gifted children.

> The teacher may provide more scaffolding or prompts for special needs students: a specific list of resources or Web sites, a visual (for example, a teacher-made story board), or examples of past student projects that could be used as a template or guide. For gifted students, you may let them use their talents to do the assigned task through any method they feel would meet the objective.
>
> *—Stephanie Mahoney, 29 years' experience*

Special Needs Students

Special needs is a very broad term that encompasses a wide range of disabilities or conditions. Special needs students will be the treasures of your first year as a teacher when you learn to work with them successfully.

In years past, most teachers did not see students with special needs in their classes. Special needs students were segregated in special classrooms or centers, where they had little contact with the general school population. This practice ended with the passage of Public Law 94-142, which mandated that children be educated in the "least restrictive environment"—that is, that children with special needs be mainstreamed to the greatest possible extent. Because of this law, students who have special needs are now frequently part of ordinary school life.

The Internet provides a great deal of information about students with special needs. To learn more about this topic, try these Web sites:

- **LD OnLine (www.ldonline.org).** This site advertises itself as the world's largest Web site for students with learning disabilities and attention disorders. It offers advice on motivation, an excellent glossary of educational terms, many practical strategies, information about social skills for students with learning disabilities, and an online forum.

- **Council for Exceptional Children (www.cec.sped.org).** This site is the "voice and vision of special education." It offers current information on trends, online courses, information about national and local policies, guidelines for various types of exceptionalities, and an excellent overview of the field.
- **Learning Disabilities Association of America (LDA) (www.ldaamerica.org).** In existence since 1963, LDA offers current strategies for handling practical concerns such as homework policies and test accommodations. Their site is supportive as well as informative for teachers who have students with specific learning disabilities.

You can expect to have many types of special needs students in your class, from students who need only a slight accommodation to help them learn to students with severe disabilities. How successfully you handle this challenge will depend on your attitude. Along with having a positive attitude, the following general strategies can guide you as you teach your students with special needs:

- **Accept your students' limitations and help them overcome them.** Although some teachers think students with disabilities that are not as obvious as others just need to try harder, trying very hard is not enough to create success for many of these students. Students who do not understand the work or who need extra help will not be successful, no matter how much effort they put forth.
- **Be proactive in dealing with special needs students.** Make sure you understand their specific disabilities and the required accommodations.
- **Give your best when teaching special needs students.** They deserve your best effort. When you take this view, you will be in a good position to help them. Expect to work closely with the special education teachers assigned to help you modify your instruction to meet the needs of every learner in your class.
- **Accept responsibility for your students' success.** Don't anticipate extensive additional training on how to help your students with special needs. Continue to educate yourself about how to work well with your special needs students by reading professional literature, researching relevant Web sites, attending workshops, and observing special education teachers as they teach.
- **Be sensitive to the needs of each student, and anticipate them whenever you can.** For example, be sure to seat students with special needs where they can see and hear you without distractions.

> **Teaching special needs students is so rewarding and worthwhile. I feel so needed and important to my students. It's a wonderful feeling.**
>
> *—Paige Adcock, 10 years' experience*

- **Use the resources available to you.** Study students' permanent records in order to understand the instructional strategies that have worked well in past school years. As soon as possible, contact the special education teacher who is working with the students in your class so that you can learn the specific strategies that will help them learn successfully. Some of the other adults who can help you learn about your students are parents, the school nurse, counselors, and previous teachers.
- **Talk with each special needs student about his or her concerns.** Make it easy for your special needs students to communicate with you. Even young children can tell you when they learn best and what activities help them master the material.

INSTRUCTIONAL STRATEGIES FOR SPECIAL NEEDS STUDENTS

Following are some helpful ideas for teaching special needs students. Because students' needs vary, not all of the ideas will be appropriate for every one of your special needs students.

- Limit the materials you ask special needs students to manage at any given time. They should only have the materials necessary for the successful completion of a lesson on their desk.
- Limit the number of practice items. For example, instead of fifteen drill sentences, ask special needs students to complete ten.
- Consider each special needs student's preferred learning style when you create assignments. When you can, modify the assignment to better fit their needs. If you can provide alternative materials, do so.
- Be sure to provide prompt feedback when a special needs student completes an assignment.
- Limit the amount of written work that you assign to special needs students.
- Offer a variety of activities. Change the pace several times in each class so that students will find it easy to stay on task.
- Structure your classroom routines so that students can predict what they are expected to do. Go over the daily objectives at the start of the class, and offer students a checklist to keep them on task all day.
- Be generous with your praise when your special needs students do something well.
- Give very clear directions. Ask special needs students to restate what you want them to do. On written work, use bold type or other eye-catching design elements to distinguish the directions from the rest of the text.
- Offer collaborative learning opportunities whenever you can. Working with other students reinforces learning, gives special needs students an opportunity to interact in a positive way with classmates, and often builds their confidence as learners.
- Help your students with special needs understand their progress. Set small achievable goals, and celebrate together when students reach them.

COLLABORATING WITH SPECIAL EDUCATION TEACHERS

When special needs students began to be included in all classrooms, special education teachers and general education teachers formed teams to help students who required special accommodations. The unique features of this type of collaboration are that, frequently, both teachers are present in the classroom at the same time and they take joint responsibility for the education of all students in their class.

These collaborative teams of teachers face an important challenge: how to share the duties of the class so that they have common goals for delivering instruction, assessing progress, and managing behavior. Successful collaboration is likely if team teachers see themselves as equal partners who are actively engaged in all parts of the teaching process.

The general education teacher's responsibilities usually include the following:

- Creating activities to teach the content
- Finding and adapting resource material for all students
- Delivering effective instruction
- Meeting the curriculum requirements of all students

The special education teacher's responsibilities usually include these:

- Adapting material to meet the needs of special needs students
- Adapting activities to match the learning styles of special needs students
- Modifying assessments
- Meeting the curriculum requirements of special needs students

What makes it possible for two teachers with different educational backgrounds to work together in a successful collaboration? The primary requirement for a positive working relationship is a commitment on the part of both teachers to work together for the common good of their students. Both teachers should also agree to

- Plan lessons together
- Follow the same classroom management procedures
- Discuss controversial class events in civil tones and in privacy
- Assume equal responsibility for what happens in class
- Present a united front to students
- Share resource materials
- Schedule time to work together on a regular basis

WORKING SUCCESSFULLY WITH PARA-EDUCATORS

Para-educators are professionals who assist special education teachers and general education teachers by working directly with students. Para-educators are often the people with whom special needs students have the closest contact.

Para-educators can assume a variety of tasks in the classroom, depending on the needs of their students. As part of an inclusion team or as teaching assistants in your classroom, the para-educators you work with will be able to help you and your students.

To learn more about how to work well with a para-educator, search the Web site of the National Resource Center for Paraprofessionals (www.nrcpara.org). Here you will find materials, information about the roles and responsibilities of paraprofessionals, and paraprofessional discussion boards.

Tips for Teaming with Para-Educators

The following tips will help you work effectively with para-educators.

- Include para-educators in meetings with parents and administrators about students. Para-educators can often offer valuable insights about the students they work with.
- Once you determine the strengths and special skills of the para-educators you work with, tap into those skills to help your students. For example, if you have a para-educator who reads aloud in an engaging way, encourage him or her to read to students.
- You and the para-educator should decide together what the para-educator's role should be in various aspects of class. Plan specifically what duties and responsibilities you are both comfortable with, and remain flexible as the term progresses.
- Anticipate and clarify issues that might cause problems. For example, what kinds of interventions should the para-educator undertake if students are misbehaving?
- Unless a para-educator is also a certified teacher, do not leave him or her in charge of your class while you are absent from the room. The law requires that a certified person supervise students.
- Maintain open lines of communication by scheduling a regular time to discuss any problems or concerns that may arise.

Students with Attention Disorders

Students with attention deficit disorder (ADD) or attention deficit/hyperactivity disorder (AD/HD) usually require intervention from supportive adults in order to be academically successful.

If you are not a special education teacher, a special education teacher will probably talk to you at the beginning of the term about your students with attention disorders. That teacher will suggest appropriate accommodations and will review the student's Individualized Education Plan or Section 504 form with you.

To learn more about how you can help students with attention disorders, search the Internet, beginning with the Web site of the Attention Deficit Disorder Association (www.add.org). This site offers many practical tips, links to other sites, articles on a variety of issues pertaining to attention disorders, and information on legal issues of concern to students with attention deficit disorders.

Here are some general guidelines to assist you in teaching students with ADD or AD/HD:

- Enlist support from other professionals and from the parents and guardians of ADD and AD/HD students. These people will be an excellent source of support and advice as you work together to assist students.
- ADD and AD/HD students do not always have effective school-related skills such as note taking or following directions. Take time to show them how to accomplish some of the tasks that other students find easy to do.
- Clearly define classroom procedures for ADD and AD/HD students, to help them stay on task. They will benefit from seeing as well as hearing directions and other information.
- Monitor unobtrusively by placing students with attention disorders near you. You should also seat them with their backs to other students so that they will be less easily distracted. Other distractions to consider are doors, windows, computer screens, pencil sharpeners, and high-traffic areas.
- Provide ADD and AD/HD students with extra assistance during transition times; it is not always easy for them to adjust to a change.
- When you give directions, be sure to give them one step at a time. Because ADD and AD/HD students tend to be easily overwhelmed by large tasks and need guidance in planning how to accomplish their work, you should help students understand that each task is a sequence of smaller steps.
- Photocopy parts of a text that students may find particularly difficult, then highlight key parts. Using this example, show your ADD and AD/HD students how they can do the same thing themselves to help them focus on important information in the text.
- ADD and AD/HD students usually do well when they can listen to an audiotape of a text as they read the selection; the soundtrack helps keep them focused on the text. Contact the publisher of your textbook, a special education teacher in your building, or your state's textbook adoption committee for copies of tapes.
- ADD and AD/HD students often benefit from using a computer; it enables them to work quickly and competently and removes much of the tedium they associate with written work, making it easier for them to stay on task.

- Peer tutoring is often very helpful for ADD and AD/HD students, allowing them to reinforce skills and to share advice about study skills.
- Review frequently so that students with attention disorders have the basic skills and facts mastered before you move on to the next topic.

In the 1960s, a student was placed in my general mechanics class because he could not read. I asked him what he liked to do. He said he liked to mess with motors. He had taken his diesel tractor motor out and put it in an old pickup truck. This is what he drove to school. In the spring, the motor went back in the tractor for spring plowing. Other teachers had told me this boy was dumb.

—Edward Gardner, 36 years' experience

Students with 504 Plans

A 504 plan is a legally binding document that protects students who have a documented physical or mental disability that limits their ability to learn. Students with 504 Plans are students whose disabilities do not need to be addressed by a teacher specifically trained to teach special education students. Instead, 504 Plan students have needs that can be addressed with modifications by a general education teacher.

Disabilities that a 504 Plan student might have include ADD or AD/HD, chronic illness, anger management problems, impaired vision or hearing, obesity, or being confined to a wheelchair. While these students do not qualify for special education programs, their 504 Plans spell out special accommodations they must receive. The accommodations in a 504 Plan may include extra time on assignments, a special set of textbooks, services such as special transportation, or classrooms that are wheelchair accessible. The most frequent 504 Plan accommodations are those that modify regular education instruction to meet the needs of the protected student.

To find out more about how you can help students with 504 Plans, begin your Internet search with the Web site of the U.S. Department of Education (www.ed.gov). At the home page of this site, use "504" as a keyword to search for more information. At the time of publication, many articles about 504 Plans were available.

When the school term begins, you will receive copies of the 504 Plans for your students. You will also meet with the 504 Plan administrator for your school to discuss each plan and what your specific responsibilities are.

Although each 504 Plan is unique because it is tailored to the needs of the child it protects, typical accommodations that you might see include these:

- Preferential seating
- Extended time on assignments
- Extra books or materials
- Reduced amount of practice
- Frequent parental contacts
- Early parental notification when problems arise
- Written copies of notes that you present orally
- Assistance with organizational skills

You must follow the 504 Plan exactly. 504 Plans are different from other school documents in that if you fail to follow them, the parents or guardians of the child have the right to sue not just the school district but the classroom teacher as well. Even if you are personally uncomfortable with an accommodation, you must make that accommodation.

I really believe that kids want to do well in school. No one spends seven hours a day motivated for failure. Teachers have to meet kids where they are educationally. Just because a student is in ninth grade doesn't mean he or she is ready for high school challenges and curriculum. Curriculum can be taught and mastered without having to water it down. Give the students a chance to succeed, and keep raising the bar.

—Charlene Herrala, 24 years' experience

Students Who Are Underachievers

Few students have gone through all of their school years without having moments when they could have done better. Occasional underachievement is to be expected, but this behavior becomes problematic when it is the overriding pattern in a student's school life.

Chronic underachievement is a problem for students of many ages and capabilities. Their parents are often quick to tell you that their child is either lazy or just doesn't try hard enough. The students often label themselves in these negative ways, too.

As you begin to work with underachieving students, you may find yourself calling their parents or guardians often and you will find yourself frustrated when no punishment you can devise solves the problem. In fact, many underachievers accept punishment as their due.

Chronic underachievement is not just a bad habit. It is often an elaborate defense mechanism that students adopt to protect themselves from their anxiety about failing. Often, underachieving students have successful, highly goal-oriented parents who are very involved in their life. Parents of underachievers usually spend lots of energy trying to understand and help their children.

The problem compounds itself when underachievers are gifted students. These students often must live up to their parents' high expectations and their own exacting standards. They opt for certain failure instead of trying and possibly failing. The contrast between their potential and what they achieve is frustrating for everyone who works with them.

Working with underachieving students can be made less frustrating with a combination of these strategies:

- Accept that underachievers' shortcomings are not the result of laziness, even though they may see themselves as lazy and worthless. Their anxiety levels often paralyze them.
- Work with parents and guidance counselors to help underachievers, but be aware that overinvolvement can sometimes increase a student's anxiety.
- Underachievers need extra motivation. They seldom find the work intrinsically interesting. Successful teachers strive to make assignments so appealing that all students will want to do their work. 
- Don't expect your underachieving students to be more than briefly motivated by their own success. Too often, after a successful school experience, underachievers will stop putting forth any effort—a situation that frustrates their family and their teacher.
- Often, underachievers do not turn in work even when they have completed it. Work out a plan with the student and his or her parents to guarantee that work will be turned in to you on time.
- Underachievers need assistance in establishing their priorities so that they can work with a purpose. Use a checklist to show students how to accomplish their assignments.
- Have extra supplies on hand for the times when an underachiever will forget to bring them to class.
- Teach study skills, time management, and organization strategies so that the work will not be burdensome for an underachieving student who is easily overwhelmed by school tasks.
- Be matter-of-fact about assignments. Expect students to do them, and offer extra help and encouragement. If you allow your anger to show or if you reprimand underachieving students harshly for not completing the work, they will have difficulty completing it.
- One of the most effective strategies is to bolster self-esteem in your underachievers. Be positive and supportive as you encourage effort and the attempts to work.
- Offer help soon after you make an assignment in class. For many underachievers, the hardest part of an assignment is getting started. Often, they will make several beginnings before giving up.

- ▶ Be aware that underachievers seldom ask for help. Be proactive in offering assistance.
- ▶ Underachievers have a perfectionist approach to their studies that results in incomplete work—the opposite of what they wanted to accomplish. Offer frequent and unobtrusive encouragement to combat this.
- ▶ Most underachievers passively accept criticism from the disappointed adults in their lives. They tend to use the negative labels to excuse themselves from not working. Don't allow students to give you excuses such as "I am just lazy" or "I never do well in math."
- ▶ Form a close connection with underachieving students whenever you can. If they feel that you are counting on them, they have more incentive to work than if you indicate that you do not care whether or not they do their work.
- ▶ Boost students' self-esteem by encouraging them to tutor less able students. Often, underachievers will do for other students what they will not do for themselves.

At-Risk Students

At-risk students are those who are very likely to drop out instead of graduate. Like most students, their future success depends on their getting as much education as they can. While there are many promising programs and a great deal of support available for students who are at risk in this way, too many students still drop out of school.

Students can be at risk for dropping out for many reasons. Here are just a few of the possible contributing factors:

- Family problems
- Poor academic skills
- Substance abuse
- Pregnancy
- Emotional problems
- Chronic peer conflicts
- Repeated failure in school
- Inadequate parental supervision
- Undiagnosed learning problems
- Chronic illness

At-risk students depend on their teachers to help them stay in school. While the strategies listed will benefit all your students, it is especially important for you to reach out to those who are at risk. Adapt the following ideas to meet the needs of your at-risk students.

- ▶ Be persistent in your efforts to motivate at-risk students. Do not hesitate to let them know you plan to keep them in school as long as you can.

- Spend time helping your students establish life goals so that they can see a larger purpose for staying in school. Without a purpose for learning, school may seem like an exercise in futility and dropping out may be seen as an easy choice.
- Set small goals that will help students reach a larger one. If you can get them in the habit of achieving at least one small goal each day, they can build on this pattern of success.
- Involve students in cooperative learning activities. Feeling connected to their classmates empowers and supports students who may be considering quitting school.
- Invite guest speakers or older students to talk with younger ones about the importance of staying in school.
- Offer open-ended questions so that at-risk students can attempt answers without fear of failure.
- Be generous with praise and attention. Your kind words may often be the only ones your at-risk students will hear all day.
- Assign work that is relevant and meaningful. If students see a purpose for their work, they may decide to stay in school.
- Seek assistance from support personnel and family members. It takes many determined adults to change a student's mind once he or she has decided to drop out.
- Check on students when they are absent. Call their home. Show your concern.
- Create situations in which at-risk students can be successful. Perhaps they can tutor younger students, mediate peer conflict, or help you with classroom chores. Focus on their strengths.
- Offer extra help and assistance to all of your students, but particularly to those at risk of dropping out.
- Tailor activities to students' preferred learning styles. When the work seems too difficult, at-risk students can often be successful if their teacher uses another modality to teach the material they need to know.
- Connect to at-risk students in a positive way. Make sure that they understand that they are important to you.

Love children, or stay out of the classroom.

—*Carolyn Marks Bickham,*
16 years' experience

To learn more about at-risk students, begin with the Teachnology Web site (http://www.teach-nology.com). You can access a wealth of information on how to help your students at risk of dropping out of school by using "at risk" as a keyword to search the site. You will find links to other sites, articles, motivational tools, and strategies for teachers.

Students Living in Poverty

Millions of school-age students in America live in poverty. You don't have to teach in a blighted urban area or a depressed rural region to teach students who are from a poor family.

The lives of poor students are often very different from those of their more affluent peers. They cannot look forward to an abundance of presents at Christmas or on their birthday. Back-to-school shopping is not an exciting time of new clothes and school supplies. Even small outlays of money are significant to students living in poverty; a locker fee, a soft drink for a class party, or a fee for a field trip may be out of their reach. In addition, because they do not wear the same fashionable clothes as their peers, poor students are often the targets of ridicule.

Economically disadvantaged students have a very difficult time with succeeding in school. One of the most unfortunate results of their economic struggles is that students who live in poverty often drop out of school, choosing a low-paying job to pay for the luxuries they have been denied instead of an education.

Ways to Help Disadvantaged Students

Despite the bleak outlook for economically disadvantaged students, you can do a great deal to make school a meaningful haven for them. You can help your students who live in poverty by implementing some of these suggestions:

- When you suspect that their peers are taunting disadvantaged students, act quickly to stop the harassment.
- Students who live in poverty have not been exposed to broadening experiences such as family vacations, trips to museums, or even eating in restaurants. Spend time adding to their worldly experience if you want poor students to connect their book learning with real-life situations.
- Listen to your disadvantaged students. They need a strong relationship with a trustworthy adult in order to succeed.
- Work to boost the self-esteem of students who live in poverty by praising their school success instead of what they own.
- Provide access to computers, magazines, newspapers, and books so low-income students can see and work with printed materials. School may be the only place where they are exposed to print media.
- Keep your expectations for poor students high. Poverty does not mean ignorance.
- Don't make comments about your students' clothes or belongings unless they are in violation of the dress code.
- Students who live in poverty may not always know the correct behaviors for school situations. At home, they may function under a different set of social rules. Take time to explain the rationale for rules and procedures in your classroom.
- Be careful about the school supplies you expect students to purchase. Keep your requirements as simple as you can for all students.
- Arrange a bank of shared supplies for your students to borrow from when they are temporarily out of materials for class.

- Do not require costly activities. For example, if you require students to pay for a field trip, some of them will not be able to go.
- If you notice that a student does not have lunch money, check to make sure that a free lunch is an option for that child.
- Be very sensitive to the potential for embarrassment in even small requests for or comments about money that you make. For example, if you jokingly remark, "There's no such thing as a free lunch," you could embarrass one of your low-income students.
- Make it clear that you value all of your students for their character and not for their possessions.
- For more information on how to help your economically disadvantaged students, visit aha!Process (www.ahaprocess.com). aha!Process is an organization that was founded by Ruby Payne, a leading expert on the effects of generational poverty on students. Her book *A Framework for Understanding Poverty,* published in 1996 by aha!Process, is significant because it explains how the silent culture clash between students and teachers in classrooms has a harmful effect on students.

Students Who Are Not Native Speakers of English

In recent years, the number of non-English-speaking students has greatly increased in many U.S. schools. The cultural diversity of these students enriches our classrooms even as it presents a perplexing problem for teachers who do not speak their students' native language.

With sensitivity, courtesy, and insight, you can help your minority-language students. Here are some strategies that should make this process easier for you and your students who speak little English:

- Keep in mind that not only do students who speak little English have to learn the content that your other students must learn, but they have to learn it in a foreign language.
- Make a point of learning to pronounce the names of your non-native students correctly. Insist that your other students do so, too.
- Be aware of cultural differences and sensitive issues. For example, in many cultures, it is rude to maintain eye contact.
- Make a point of giving as many directions as you can in writing as well as orally.
- Label items in your classroom to help students learn simple words.
- Keep resources on your students' home countries on hand for other students to read. Library books and Internet sites are good sources of such material.
- Arrange for your students to interact. Students who can communicate with each other about their work tend to do better. It is also easier for students to learn English if other students engage them in conversation as much as possible.

- Use a variety of learning styles to help your students master content as well as a new language. Graphic organizers and other useful study devices will help students who are learning English as well as your other students.
- Encourage students to read aloud to you whenever it is appropriate. Be careful that your corrections of English learners are helpful and not overwhelming.
- Set realistic expectations for your students who speak little English. They are not going to be able to do as much work as your other students if the work involves intensive interaction with a text because it will take them longer just to figure out the language.
- Don't rush to answer questions or fill in words when students are struggling to think through their responses. You must be patient and supportive if you want your students to learn successfully.
- Find bilingual dictionaries in the languages that your students speak. Encourage them to use the relevant bilingual dictionary frequently. Model its use yourself.
- Use audiotapes and other technology appropriate to the age and ability levels of your students. Students benefit from both seeing and hearing the language.
- Keep your language simple. If at all possible, use words that students will be likely to know.
- Many useful Web sites are available to help teachers of non-native students. Search some of the following for good ideas about how to help your students.
    - **Tower of English (http://towerofenglish.com).** Here you will find links to hundreds of other useful resources to help you teach your non-native students.
    - **Dave's ESL Café (http://www.eslcafe.com).** This excellent site offers a wealth of useful information, resources, links, and insights into teaching students who are not proficient in English.

Celebrate the Cultures in Your Class

Although teaching students from many cultures can be challenging, one of the most enduring successes of the public school system in America is the variety of cultures that meet peacefully in thousands of classrooms each day. In classroom after classroom, students of all different races and cultural backgrounds study together. At a time when school systems are scrutinized and criticized from many sides, classroom diversity is one of our nation's greatest assets.

Although some people try to define culture in ethnic or racial terms, a broader definition is more accurate. Every person belongs to a variety of cultural groups delineated by such features as geography, age, economics, gender, religion, interests, or education levels. If you ignore the cultural differences among your students, you will create strife and tension. Conversely, if you choose to accept and celebrate those differences, you will find those differences to be a rich resource for your class.

By teaching your students to value their differences, you are creating a truly global classroom. And by expanding students' appreciation of each other, you are showing them how to appreciate the rest of the world.

Here are some general guidelines you can use to incorporate the many cultures in your classroom into a successful unified group:

- Expose your students to a wide variety of cultures throughout the term. This exposure will enable them to be more tolerant of each other's differences.
- Make discussing the differences in cultures in your class an important part of what you and your students do together. You can manage a few minutes every now and then for an informal discussion without losing valuable instructional time.
- Accept that the concerns of a parent or guardian who is not part of your culture may be different from the concerns that you have. If you are sensitive to the potential difference when you speak with parents, you will find yourself asking questions that will help you determine what their goals for their children are before you attempt to impose your own beliefs.
- Stress the importance of an open-minded attitude about people whose beliefs or lifestyles are different from those of your students. Make sure you model that acceptance yourself.
- Promote activities that will increase your students' self-esteem. Students who are self-confident are not as likely to taunt others in order to feel good about themselves.
- Even if you have lived in your community all of your life, take time to learn about its various cultural groups. Understanding how these groups are represented in the school system will help you understand your students better.
- If students learn racism or intolerance at home, you will have a very difficult time stopping it in class. Your first step in combating intolerant attitudes should be to make your position of tolerance very clear to your students through what you say and what you do.

To learn more about how to incorporate a multicultural approach in educating your students, explore these Web sites:

- **New Horizons for Learning (www.newhorizons.org).** When you click on the "Teaching and Learning" tab, you will find information about topics such as emotional intelligence, cultural bias, diversity at school, and multicultural education. You can also explore many other resources and topics at this excellent site.
- **Southern Poverty Law Center (www.tolerance.org).** This Web site offers a wealth of different resources to help teachers promote tolerance and "dismantle bigotry." It has many classroom activities for students of all ages. One of the most interesting links allows site visitors to test their hidden biases.

Avoid Gender Bias in Your Classroom

Gender bias is one of society's most insidious unconscious attitudes. The problem with gender bias lies in the damage it can cause. For example, many girls do not think they can excel at mathematics because they see it as a subject suitable for boys. Another example of the effects of gender bias is that boys who are loud and rude often receive far less substantial punishment than girls who are loud and rude because their teachers adopt a "boys will be boys" attitude.

You can help yourself and your students understand and mitigate gender bias in your classroom by raising your awareness and by being proactive. Here are some strategies that can help:

- Make sure that you communicate the same expectations for academic achievement to both genders. Males and females can be equally capable students in any subject.
- Balance the genders that you use in examples and problems.
- Use language that includes both genders. For example, replace *mailman* with *mail carrier* and *chairman* with *chairperson.*
- Pay attention to how you give attention. Do you focus more on the males in your class than you do on the females?
- Do not allow students to group themselves according to gender. Make sure that you balance genders when you create groups in your class.
- When your students have classroom duties, do not assign them along gender lines. Girls can carry things and boys can tidy up a mess.
- To learn more about gender bias in our classrooms, visit David Sadker's Web site (www.american.edu.sadker), where you will find useful information, advice, insights, and an overview of the issue of gender bias.

Talk It Over

How to Manage a Diverse Classroom

Use these questions as a springboard for discussions that will help you and your discussion group members grow and develop professionally. Discuss these questions about how to manage the diversity in your school:

1. What do you anticipate as your biggest challenge in dealing with the differences among your students? What can you do to meet this challenge? Where can you find assistance with this problem?
2. Who is at risk of failure in your class? What should your attitude toward these students be? What schoolwide programs can help the at-risk students in your class? What can you do to help them stay in school and be successful?
3. What are some of the different cultures in your class? How do they reflect your community? How can you promote awareness and appreciation of these cultures?
4. What do you already know about your students with special needs? How do your supervisors expect you to help these students? How do the students themselves expect you to help them? Who at your school can help you learn the best ways to help your students with special needs?
5. Which of your students have attention disorders? What behaviors clue you in to their problems with attention? What can you do to make sure that you help these students achieve academic success? Where can you find out more about this topic?
6. What strengths do you have that will help you meet the diverse needs of your students? How can you use your strengths to help all the students in your class reach their full potential?
7. What can you do to ensure that you work effectively with the special education professionals at your school?
8. What are your biases in regard to gender? What can you do to make sure that you treat male and female students fairly?
9. What do you do in your class to be sensitive to the needs of your students who live in poverty? What experiences can you draw on to help you be more sensitive? Where can you learn more?
10. How can you help the students in your classroom transcend their differences? Which of the strategies in this section will help you? How can you create a positive classroom culture in which all students are valued?

SECTION SEVENTEEN

Troubleshoot Twenty Common Problems

In this section, you will learn

- ✔ How to use troubleshooting principles
- ✔ How to cope with school situations such as assemblies and video viewing
- ✔ How to minimize disruption from problems such as theft, passing notes, and eating in class
- ✔ How to cope with problems arising from new technology, such as inappropriate use of cell phones and cheating by copying from online sources
- ✔ How to deal with individual misbehavior such as defiance and talking back

Because you have hundreds of decisions to make at school each day, it is impossible to choose the best one in every situation. And because you work with unpredictable fellow humans under complex circumstances, there will not always be an absolute best choice for many of the perplexing problems you will face. There are, however, some basic principles that can guide your thinking when you want to successfully manage a school situation. When you begin planning solutions to school problems, let the following principles guide your actions.

- Solve the problem instead of punishing the child.
- Follow school rules and policies.

- Make sure that the punishment fits the crime.
- Maintain a positive relationship with each student.
- If your first attempt is not successful, try another one. Then another one . . . as many as it takes.
- Ignore as much as you can.
- Begin with small interventions. Save the office referrals for serious problems.
- Minimize disruptions by maximizing students' time on task.
- When things are not going well, try to see the problem through your students' eyes.
- Think before you act.
- If you are not sure what to do, talk to your colleagues, your mentor, and the administrators at your school.
- Involve parents or guardians while the problem is still small.
- Preserve your students' dignity and you'll preserve your own.

In this section, you will find suggestions on how to handle some of the problems you may experience during your first year as a teacher. Because these problems are ubiquitous, there are many suggestions on how to deal with each one. Only you can judge which ones will work best for your students.

Problem 1: Heavy Backpacks Blocking the Aisles

Your school does not have a policy concerning student backpacks. Your students carry around all of their school belongings in backpacks that sometimes seem to weigh more than they do, and their backpacks block the aisles in your class.

SUGGESTIONS

This is a problem with two parts that you must handle separately. First, deal with the weight of the backpacks. Then, tackle the issue of the obstructions and disruptions in your class.

Backpack Weight

- This situation certainly requires collaboration with other teachers. When you speak with colleagues, suggest that you stagger homework deadlines so that students can leave some of their belongings in their locker, in the classroom, or at home.
- Talk to your students to let them know how concerned you are about their health and their stress level. Ask for their suggestions on how to solve the problem.
- Consider involving parents in finding solutions.
- Find out why students feel the need to carry so much. Do they need more time to go to their locker? Do they need advice on how to manage their materials?

Obstructions and Disruptions in Your Class

- When students have backpacks in class, expect them to place their backpack under their desk or as close to them as possible in order to leave a safe aisle.
- Take a team approach to keeping backpacks stowed safely. If they are involved in creating the solution, students will be able to police themselves and each other. Working together on the problem will increase the chances of successful resolution.
- See if you can provide a safe place for students to keep their backpacks other than near their desks.
- Teach students that it is disruptive to constantly search for materials in their backpack during class. Encourage them to keep their belongings as organized as possible in order to reduce search time.

Problem 2: Disruptive Cell Phones

Because cell phones are a recent development in school life, school officials are still trying to formulate a workable policy. Cell phones are becoming more and more of a nuisance in class. They ring during tests, and your students send each other text messages instead of working.

SUGGESTIONS

- Although school administrators everywhere may still be trying to formulate a workable cell phone policy, your school district probably has one in place. Enforce it.
- If your school district's policy is unclear, consider these suggestions for elements of a workable policy in your classroom:
    - All cell phones should be turned off while students are in your class.
    - All cell phones should be completely out of sight.
    - If a phone rings during class, the child's parents or guardians will be contacted.
    - If a student is caught sending a text message during class, the child's parents or guardians will be contacted.
    - Don't confiscate a cell phone unless you absolutely have to. Make sure you have a safe place to store it, where there is no chance of it being stolen. If you have to take a student's phone, turn it over to an administrator as soon as possible.
    - When you send home an introductory letter to parents and guardians at the start of the term, notify them of your policy on cell phones.
    - Be alert to the ways that students can use their phones to cheat in class. Monitor carefully.
    - At the start of tests and quizzes, be careful to warn students to turn off their phones. Post reminders, and encourage students to help each other remember the policy.

- Do not use your own phone in front of your students when you should be teaching.
- If cell phones continue to be a problem, ask your colleagues for suggestions on how to solve it.

Problem 3: Fire Drills

You have just handed out quiz papers to your students when the bell signaling a fire drill rings.

SUGGESTIONS

- ▶ You should expect a fire drill at least once a week during the first month of school. Before the first fire drill, you should teach your students the procedures you want them to follow.
- ▶ Make sure you have the evacuation route posted during the first week of school. Go over it with your students as soon as you can.
- ▶ Select a responsible student to lead the others to a designated spot where you can meet with them and check to make sure that everyone is safe. Make sure that your students know to stay in this spot until you give them permission to leave.
- ▶ Take your class roster outside with you so that you can call roll.
- ▶ If your students are taking a test or a quiz during an evacuation, expect that the integrity of the test or quiz has been compromised. Either disregard the objective portions or allow students to use the assessment as a study guide for a retest the next day.

Problem 4: Drumming on Desks

Students drum on their desks with a pencil or pen, not staying on task and distracting other students.

SUGGESTIONS

- ▶ Pay attention to the times when the drumming happens and who it disturbs. Is there a pattern? Is anyone being disturbed?
- ▶ Consider the reasons for the behavior. Is it a bad habit, a means of stress relief, or a way to attract attention? Is there some other cause?
- ▶ If you overreact, other students may begin drumming to annoy you.
- ▶ Consider establishing a signal with the student, who may not be aware when he or she is drumming.
- ▶ Give the student a pad to drum on. This will lessen the noise and reduce the distraction.

- Suggest that the student soften the noise by adding an eraser to the end of the pencil or pen.
- Move the student to a place in the room where the drumming will not disturb others.
- Sometimes playing soft classical music will mask the sound of the drumming or distract the student from drumming entirely.

In answer to the question "What skills should all teachers have?":

Patience
Knowledge of the subject
Patience
Kindness
A love of young people
Patience
Flexibility
Patience

—*Luann Scott, 31 years' experience*

Problem 5: Eating in Class

One of your students sneaks food and drinks into your classroom as often as possible. A school rule states that students are not to have food or drinks in class, but other teachers allow it.

SUGGESTIONS

- You have little choice but to enforce the school rule when the situation first occurs. At the start of the term when you discuss the rules of your class, be sure to tell students that you intend to honor the rule in your classroom.
- If you are uncomfortable with the rule, talk to your mentor or an administrator about how strict you should be about enforcing it. If you are the only teacher in your school who refuses to allow students to have water in class, for example, you will not be perceived as fair.
- There are many reasons for rules about food in class. Before you decide to allow it, consider the maturity of your students. Will it be a distraction? Will it cause a mess? Will students abuse the privilege? If students have food in class, are you promoting the healthy lifestyle you want for them?
- Don't eat in front of your students if they are not allowed to eat in class. It is rude, and you will be perceived as a hypocrite.

Problem 6: Note Passing

Your students persist in passing notes to each other when they should be working on school assignments.

SUGGESTIONS

- Keep this problem in perspective. It is not necessarily a negative thing for students to want to write notes to each other.

> **All teachers should have patience and understanding and should know that tomorrow is another day.**
>
> *—Julie Savoy, 3 years' experience*

- Don't take a note from a student; it was not written for you to read.
- Don't read the note. Don't display the note. Your students will resent it if you overreact in this way. In addition, think about what you would do with any knowledge you learn from the note. Are you prepared to deal with the intimate details of your students' personal lives?
- You can turn an incident of note passing into an advantage by taking a creative approach. Capitalize on students' interest by providing opportunities for them to write to each other. Have a silent class day when everyone must communicate only in writing. Or allow students to write to each other at the start or end of class.
- When you see a student writing a note in class, you do not have to overreact. Just ask the student to put the note away. Move close to the student to make sure the note has been put away. Teacher proximity is usually the best deterrent for a student who wants the contents of a note to remain private.
- If a student refuses to put the note away, the problem is not with the note, but with the child's defiance. See "Problem 18: Defiance" later in this section and Section Fifteen for help in handling difficult students.
- Keep your students so busy that they do not have time to pass notes in class.

Problem 7: Public Displays of Affection

As you greet students at the start of class, two students block the hallway with their fond farewells.

SUGGESTIONS

- Resist the urge to lecture these students about how embarrassing their behavior seems. Instead, convey your understanding and concern.
- Don't make the situation more troublesome by calling attention to them or mentioning it in front of other students.
- Discuss the situation with the two students:
  - Your school probably has a policy on public displays of affection. Discuss it with them so that they will understand that you have not singled them out.
  - Sometimes students are just not sure how to express their affection. Be careful to explain which hallway behaviors are acceptable and which ones are not. Be very specific.
- If a conference with the two students does not change their behavior, contact their parents or guardians.

Problem 8: Dress Code Violations

While you are monitoring homework at the start of class, you notice that one of your students is wearing a T-shirt with a message that promotes alcohol. This is a violation of the dress code.

SUGGESTIONS

- Make sure that you are familiar with the dress code rules before you try to explain them to your students.
- Be careful not to violate the dress code yourself. It will be impossible for you to enforce it if you are also in violation.
- Make sure that your students understand the rules. If violations seem to be a problem with your students, post the dress code so that they can check it for themselves.
- Always handle dress code issues privately. If a child refuses to comply with your requests, enforce your school's policy or send the student to the administrator in charge of dress code issues.
- Be alert to gang activity expressed through student clothing. Speak with other staff members to learn about specific gang colors and types of clothing in your area.
- Be careful to preserve the child's dignity when enforcing the dress code. Sometimes a student does not have anything else clean to wear. And if a student is wearing inappropriate clothes in order to be defiant, you certainly do not want to give the student an audience by attempting to discuss the issue where others can overhear.

Problem 9: Excessive Noise

Your class is too loud! You sometimes have to shout to be heard. When your students work productively in groups, you don't mind the noise as much as when your students are engaged in personal conversations and off-task activities.

SUGGESTIONS

- Never talk over noise or shout to be heard in your classroom.
- Don't allow noise to get out of control. Once students are very loud, you will have to take extreme measures to get them to stop being noisy. You'll find it easier if you begin to control noise levels as soon as class begins.
- You should not try to assume control of a noisy class without enlisting the cooperation of your students. Ask for suggestions from your students about how to manage noise.
- Some noisy activities are just not acceptable. Teach your students that it is never acceptable to talk during a movie, talk when you are giving instructions or lecturing,

shout at any time, talk during a test or other quiet activity, or talk across the room to classmates.

- When you plan activities that have the potential to be noisy, consider moving to a part of the building where you can't disturb other classes.
- Don't plan group activities without teaching students how to control the noise level of their groups. One way to do this is by using distances as noise measurements. For example, students should find a one-foot voice useful for working in pairs and a three-foot voice useful for working in groups. When you give directions for an assignment, tell students the acceptable noise level for the activity.
- Model the noise level that you want from your students. If you speak softly, your students will follow your lead. If you shout, you will dramatically increase the noise level in your class because students will see this as permission for them to shout, too.
- Be consistent in enforcing the noise levels that you expect from your students. Set reasonable limits and stick to them so that students will learn to manage their own noise.

Problem 10: Inappropriate Behavior at Assemblies

Your students have been excited all week about an eagerly awaited assembly; however, during the assembly, they are rude, talking nonstop throughout the performance.

SUGGESTIONS

- In advance of the next assembly, teach your students the behaviors that you will expect to see from them. Make sure that this lesson includes the consequences for good and bad behavior.
- When you teach students the good behavior you expect from them, focus on the reasons for it; for example, everyone has the right to enjoy the performance without distractions and those performing deserve the respect of their audience.
- Many students are used to loud interactions at concerts and movies. Discuss the difference between behaviors that are appropriate for those events and behaviors that are appropriate for a school assembly.
- Reduce distractions by encouraging students to leave their personal belongings—such as combs, makeup, and book bags—in the classroom.
- If you are going to sit with your students during the assembly, make sure that you create a seating chart for them. If possible, have them sit in a block where you can easily speak to each student rather than in a long row. Having assigned seats will send the message that you expect good behavior during the assembly.
- Model the good behavior that you expect from students. Don't take papers to grade. Instead, sit with your students and be attentive.

Problem 11: Restless Students During a Video Viewing

You show a video that other teachers have recommended, but only a few of your students watch. Most are bored and restless.

SUGGESTIONS

- Always preview a video that you are going to show to make sure it fits the needs of your students. While you are watching, create a worksheet for students to complete as they watch. You can also plan the points where you will stop the video for discussion.
- Talk to your students in advance about the courteous and attentive behaviors you will expect from them while they watch the video.
- Make sure that every student can see. Allow time for students to move their chairs if they need to.
- Don't make the room too dark. You should avoid glare, but total darkness will make it impossible for your students to do their assignment.
- Plan a closing activity for your students in which you hold them accountable for what they should have learned during the video and during any discussions.

Problem 12: Lost Papers

You hand back a set of homework papers and notice that some of your students do not have their papers. You tell them that you never received their work. They, in turn, assure you that they did the work, turned it in on time, and you must have lost it.

SUGGESTIONS

- Be very organized about how you manage student papers. By appearing very organized, you will prevent many false accusations because students will not think that they can take advantage of your disorganization.
- Grade papers and hand them back as quickly as you can. The longer you delay in returning papers, the harder it will be to keep track of them.
- If you use an in-basket to collect work from students as they finish it, be sure to move their papers to a labeled folder before the next class can add theirs to the stack.
- If you are unable to check a set of papers within a day or two, at least check to make sure that all students have turned in work. This will preclude any surprises for students who are expecting to receive graded papers.
- Do not be absolute in denying your guilt. Instead, try to solve the problem by first asking students whose papers are missing to check their own notebook or locker to

see whether they could have taken the papers from the room accidentally. If the papers do not turn up, offer the students time to redo the work and turn it in.

Problem 13: Sleeping in Class

Day after day, some of your students have trouble staying awake in class. Other students notice the sleepers and expect you to react.

SUGGESTIONS

- Because sleeping students are not involved in class, they can't learn. For this reason, you must not overlook this passive misbehavior. Don't let your students miss valuable instructional time.
- Before you act, you need to know the cause. Speak to sleepy students in private to find out why they want to sleep. Do they stay up too late at home? Is there a medical problem? Do they have after-school jobs that require long hours? Are they bored with school?
- When you speak with a student about sleeping in class, don't be unpleasant. Instead, decide how to work with the student on the problem.
- If talking to a student does not solve the problem, call his or her parents or guardians to elicit their support.
- Try not to disrupt the entire class by calling too much public attention to a sleeper.
- Never ask other students to wake up a sleeping classmate. Not only does this interrupt their work, but it puts them in an awkward position.
- When you see that a student is becoming sleepy, allow that child to stand up, move around, or perhaps go to the water fountain.
- When students decide that they cannot succeed in a class, they sometimes choose to sleep rather than be frustrated. Involve such students in activities that they can be successful in and that they will enjoy more than napping through class. Give them a reason to stay awake.
- Few students can sleep through a lively, active class. If you notice that several of your students are tempted to sleep, reconsider the way you are presenting information.

Problem 14: Crying

Although you are not aware of a cause, one of your students is visibly upset and crying.

SUGGESTIONS

- Spare the child's already tender feelings by showing your understanding and sympathy instead of becoming impatient.

- Allow the student to leave the room, accompanied by another student if necessary, to regain composure. This will also minimize the potential for additional class disruption.
- Talk to the student in order to determine the cause. Offer assistance, if appropriate.
- Be careful to work with the student even if the cause is not one you find worthwhile. Being uncaring will not end the tears.
- Contact a parent or guardian about the situation, regardless of the age of the student. There may be more to the matter than you realize.
- If the tears seem to be chronic or if the student is immature, seek advice and insight from the child's previous teachers or the school nurse in addition to parents or guardians.
- Show your concern for a student who was upset enough to cry at school by quietly checking with him or her about the incident the next day.

Problem 15: Feigned Illness

One of your students begins complaining that she doesn't feel well, even though you just observed her laughing and chatting with her friends moments earlier.

SUGGESTIONS

- Keep in mind that students feign illness for many reasons: to gain sympathy; to get attention; to escape from work; to escape from the consequences of not completing homework; boredom; or problems at home.
- If this behavior is repeated, it can become a serious problem. For this reason, you should involve the child's parents or guardians and the school nurse as soon as possible after the first instance.
- You must act as if the child is ill. Your role is not to determine whether the child is really ailing. Imagine the consequences if you were to ignore a serious medical issue because you assumed that the student was pretending. Send the child to the clinic.
- Do not excuse the child totally from missed assignments; accept them late or schedule a make-up date if necessary.
- As soon as you can, contact the student's parents or guardians to check on the child's well-being. If the child is really ill, you can work with the parents or guardians to manage missing work. If the child is feigning illness, the child's parents or guardians can work with you.
- Take the time to determine what is causing the child's stress. What can you do to help with the causes of this behavior?

Problem 16: Inappropriate Comments

One of your students is in the habit of blurting out irrelevant comments whenever you present material, give oral directions, or just speak to the class. While these comments are not defiant, they are unsuitable and unappreciated.

SUGGESTIONS

- Be careful to think before you react; then, be careful to react in a professional manner. Never allow yourself to respond with a cutting remark in front of a student's classmates. You may make the behavior worse if you take a confrontational approach.
- Students often make comments in a bid for attention. If the comments are not disruptive or defiant, you may be able to stop this behavior by ignoring it as much as you can.
- Talk to the student privately. Be sure to guide the conversation by
  - Adopting the attitude that this is a problem for the two of you to solve
  - Planning what you want to say before you meet with the student
  - Explaining why the comments are inappropriate
  - Using "I" messages and working with the child to solve the problem
  - Suggesting a better way for the student to communicate with you
  - Praising as much of the student's positive behavior as you can
- If the problem persists, contact the student's parents or guardians to enlist their support.

Problem 17: Talking Back

You tell a student who has not yet turned in a test paper that the time for the test is over and that you must have all papers. The student becomes belligerent and loudly tells the class that you don't know anything about teaching.

SUGGESTIONS

- Although it is natural that you would have something to say in your own defense, resist the temptation to argue or reprimand the child in front of the class.
- Ask the student to step into the hall for a private conference when you are calm enough to manage the situation well. Talk with the student about the effects of disrespect on you and on the rest of the class. Take a problem-solving approach to the situation instead of escalating the confrontation and ill will.

- Make an agreement with students who feel the need to talk back; tell them that you want to hear what they have to say and are willing to listen but that they need to speak to you privately and respectfully. When you take this friendly attitude, you offer students a chance to approach you in a positive manner, a way to deal with frustrations, and an opportunity to learn how to resolve conflicts in a respectful manner.

When working with students who are performing below grade level, meet kids where they are educationally. Many times, students will mask their poor performance with poor behavior to save face. Students prefer misbehavior over lack of ability as a reason for failure. Give the students work they can do.

—Charlene Herrala, 24 years' experience

Problem 18: Defiance

One of your students has made a mess while working on a project in class. When you ask that the mess be cleaned up, your student refuses, saying, "Why should I?"

SUGGESTIONS

- Absolutely refuse to reply to a defiant student in a rude way. Silence is better than a sarcastic retort or insisting on compliance. Do not argue or raise your voice.
- A first approach to try is looking surprised and saying that you thought you heard wrong. This gives the student a chance to back down. If this happens, just carry on with class. Later, meet quietly with the student and discuss the situation calmly.
- Another approach many teachers have found effective is talking quietly and privately with the student. Begin by asking the student to tell you what is wrong and offering your help. A confrontation will only make things worse.
- If the situation persists, you must involve the student's parents or guardians and an administrator. Meet with them and the student to work out a plan to solve the problem.

Problem 19: Theft

You leave the money you collected for a class trip on your desk for just a few moments while you help a student in the front of the room. When you return to your desk, you realize that the money has been stolen.

SUGGESTIONS

Preventing Theft

- Be aggressive in preventing theft. Don't leave your personal belongings in the open or on your desk. Many teachers do not carry very much cash at school and leave their credit cards at home.
- Be very careful about how you handle money you collect from your students. To avoid problems, deposit it as quickly as you can.
- Remind your students that they can prevent theft by taking good care of items that are attractive to thieves: calculators, headphones, pens, money, jewelry, electronic devices, cell phones, hats, CDs, books, notes, and yearbooks.
- Always lock your classroom on leaving, and never give your keys to students. Discourage students from taking items from your personal space at school.

Dealing with a Theft

- If the stolen item belongs to you, don't threaten your students. Instead, offer a small reward for its safe return. Promise to ask no questions, and honor that promise.
- If the stolen item belongs to a student, remain calm and follow these steps:
  1. Don't use the words *steal* or *theft.*
  2. In a matter-of-fact manner, ask that anyone who may have picked up the item by mistake return it. Don't expect students to tell on each other, and don't expect a student to confess in front of the class.
  3. If no one returns the item, notify an administrator. An administrator's help will be necessary if your students need to be detained.
  4. Don't accuse students or continue to talk about the situation unless an administrator is involved. Try to maintain as normal a class atmosphere as you can, to minimize the disruption.
  5. When you catch a student stealing, keep that information as private as possible. You will have to involve an administrator and the student's parents or guardians, but try to preserve the student's dignity.
  6. Work with the student to help him or her learn from the mistake and move forward. Make sure to maintain a strong relationship with students who make

mistakes so that you can help them improve their self-esteem enough to resist the temptation in the future.

Problem 20: Cheating by Copying from an Online Source

As you grade a student's research project, you notice that the language is very different from the student's usual work. You suspect that the student has cheated by lifting material from an online source.

SUGGESTIONS

- Before you confront the student, check the Internet to determine whether your suspicions are correct.
- If you find that the student has cheated, be sure to print the proof.
- Speak with the student in private; discuss your suspicion and the evidence from the Internet.
- Be careful to maintain a problem-solving approach with the student. Becoming angry or confrontational will not help the student.
- Follow your school's policy on cheating. This will probably involve informing an administrator, contacting the child's parents, and a loss of points for the assignment.
- Be sure that you teach your students how to do research and the other skills they will need to complete their assignment. If you discuss online cheating with them at the start of an assignment, students are less likely to be dishonest.
- Reduce the opportunities for students to cheat by designing assignments that are not conducive to online cheating.

Talk It Over

How to Troubleshoot Problems

Use these questions as a springboard for discussions that will help you and your discussion group members grow and develop professionally. Discuss these questions about how to troubleshoot problems at your school:

1. With your colleagues, brainstorm a list of problems that come up each day. Which ones affect the entire school and which ones are specific to individual classrooms?
2. Use your brainstormed list to select one or two problems. Generate a plan to solve each one. How will you know when you have succeeded?
3. How well do your students handle disruptions to the entire class, such as assemblies and fire drills? How can you manage these better?
4. When do your students tend to be defiant? How can you prevent this? What suggestions do your colleagues have about how to deal with this problem?
5. What are some mistakes about discipline that you are determined to avoid? How can you make sure that you will be able to avoid them?
6. What is the best way to handle problems with dishonesty in your classroom? What do your students tend to be dishonest about?
7. Which school rules would you like to modify? Why? Who would benefit? Who can you speak to about the issues you have?
8. When are your students most likely to be off task? How can you help them stay focused on their work?
9. What attitudes can teachers develop that will make managing problems a challenging opportunity for growth instead of a hassle?
10. What have you learned about how to be a self-directed teacher?

Index

A

B

C

D

E

F

Q

R

Also by Julia G. Thompson

Discipline Survival Kit for the Secondary Teacher

Paper ISBN: 978-0-87628-434-6
www.josseybass.com

This unique, hands-on resource is packed with tested ideas and strategies to help you create a classroom environment where good conduct and high achievement are the norm, where students become self-motivated and take responsibility for their actions, and where you experience the satisfaction that only a career in education can bring!

For easy use, the *Discipline Survival Kit* is organized into nine key areas of classroom management and printed in a big 8 by 11-inch format for photocopying the scores of full-page forms, checklists, and other ready-to-use tools. You'll find practical advice in each of the following sections:

The Discipline Dilemma: Crowd Control or Self-Discipline explores your role as a classroom leader and how you can become a proactive teacher

Getting Ready to Make a Good Impression gives you the organizational skills necessary to establish a positive learning environment from the first day forward

Door to Door: Using Class Time Wisely shows you how to maximize class time and how to minimize disruptions

A Partnership Approach to Discipline contains ways to promote positive discipline practices by teaching your students how to relate better to you, to other adults, and to each other

Preventing Discipline Problems gives you the methods you need to prevent discipline problems

Dealing with Problems Once They Occur helps you know what to do once misbehavior has occurred in your classroom

Strategies for Solving Specific Problems provides practical solutions to a broad range of specific problems that many secondary teachers encounter

Moving Beyond Crowd Control to Promote Self-Discipline shows how to begin the process of moving your students toward becoming self-disciplined learners, and

The Most Important Factor in Discipline: The Teacher focuses on the teacher's important role in the discipline process and how to reach your full potential as a classroom leader.

In the author's words, "Without a mannerly classroom environment, no lesson, no matter how creative, how beautifully planned, or how artfully delivered, can be successful. There are many ways to help students learn to be successful while managing their own actions." You'll find hundreds of them in this resource.

Other Books of Interest

Teaching with Fire: Poetry That Sustains the Courage to Teach

Sam M. Inrator and Megan Scribner

Cloth ISBN: 978-0-7879-6970-7
www.josseybass.com

"*Teaching with Fire* is a glorious collection of the poetry that has restored the faith of teachers in the highest, most transcendent values of their work with children . . . Those who want us to believe that teaching is a technocratic and robotic skill devoid of art or joy or beauty need to read this powerful collection. So, for that matter, do we all."

—**Jonathan Kozol, author of** ***Amazing Grace and Savage Inequalities***

Those of us who care about the young and their education must find ways to remember what teaching and learning are really about. We must find ways to keep our hearts alive as we serve our students. Poetry has the power to keep us vital and focused on what really matters in life and in schooling.

Teaching with Fire is a wonderful collection of eighty-eight poems from well-loved poets such as Walt Whitman, Langston Hughes, Billy Collins, Emily Dickinson, and Pablo Neruda. Each of these evocative poems is accompanied by a brief story from a teacher explaining the significance of the poem in his or her life's work. This beautiful book also includes an essay that describes how poetry can be used to grow both personally and professionally.

Teaching with Fire was written in partnership with the Center for Teacher Formation and the Bill & Melinda Gates Foundation. Royalties will be used to fund scholarship opportunities for teachers to grow and learn.

Sam M. Intrator (Northampton, MA) is professor of education and child study at Smith College. A former high school teacher, administrator, and son of two public school teachers, he is the editor of *Stories of the Courage to Teach* and *Living the Questions*.

Megan Scribner (Takoma Park, MD) is a freelance writer and editor who has worked with numerous foundations and educational organizations.

Other Books of Interest

The Reading Teacher's Book of Lists, 5th Edition

Edward B. Fry and Jacqueline E. Kress

Paper ISBN: 978-0-7879-8257-7
www.josseybass.com

"*The Reading Teacher's Book of Lists* should be on the bookshelf of every reading teacher in the English-speaking world! It is a tremendous resource that I have used over and over again throughout my career. The fifth edition is the best yet! It has more useful information than any of the previous editions. You can be assured that I will make good use of Dr. Fry and Dr. Kress's classic book."

—Timothy Rasinski, professor of education, Kent State University

Written for anyone who teaches reading, *The Reading Teacher's Book of Lists* is the thoroughly revised edition of the best-selling foundational reading reference book. This classic resource is filled with 218 up-to-date lists that teachers can use to develop instructional materials and plan lessons that might otherwise take years and much effort to acquire. The book is organized into eighteen sections that are brimming with practical examples, key words, teaching ideas, and activities that can be used as-is or adapted to meet the students' needs. It covers everything from Greek and Latin roots to teacher's correction marks, word plays, prefixes, oxymorons, vocabulary, and more.

This revised fifth edition contains a complete overhaul of teaching methods sections and includes new sections on electronic resources, new literacies, building fluency, and reading in content areas. It is an essential resource with endless uses.

Edward B. Fry (Laguna Beach, CA), is a professor emeritus of education at Rutgers University (New Brunswick, NJ). At Rutgers, Dr. Fry was the director of the Reading Center and taught graduate and undergraduate courses in reading, curriculum, and other educational subjects. A respected author and speaker, he has also written *The Vocabulary Teacher's Book of Lists* for Jossey-Bass (ISBN 0-7879-7101-4). Dr. Fry is internationally renowned for his Readability Graph, which is used by teachers, publishers, and others to judge the reading difficulty of books and other materials.

Jacqueline E. Kress (Elizabeth, NJ) is dean of education at New York Institute of Technology. She has designed numerous educational programs, including programs for at-risk students, students with special needs, and standards-based K–12 and college-level curricula. Dr. Kress is also the author of *The ESL Teacher's Book of Lists* for Jossey-Bass.

Other Books of Interest

Enriching the Brain: How to Maximize Every Learner's Potential

Eric Jensen

Cloth ISBN: 978-0-7879-7547-0
www.josseybass.com

"Eric Jensen's *Enriching the Brain* is an outstanding, reader-friendly resource filled with the best information available on how to teach and bring out the best in every child. This is a must-read for every educator, parent, or anyone who works with children."
—Jonathan Erwin, educational consultant and author, ***The Classroom of Choice***

"Many young people with gifts and talents underachieve. This book gives quality information about the scientific-based practices needed to turn around all learners, including the low performers and the gifted. It's all about the power to change."
—Joseph S. Renzulli, director, The National Research Center on the Gifted and Talented, University of Connecticut

Debunking the belief that the brain has a fixed capacity, this provocative book explains why students deserve better, and how the way we teach, parent, and run our schools can dramatically change (and enrich) the brain of every single learner, not just the gifted.

Eric Jensen argues that educators greatly underestimate students' learning potential—even suggesting that today's test-driven schooling practices may be shortchanging young brains. Pointing to IQ studies as well as neuroscience research, he explains why the idea of the "fixed brain" is a myth and how certain types of learning conditions can actually "enrich" the brain. Novelty and challenge are crucial for enrichment as are stimulating learning environments, physical exercise, and solid nutrition. Attention to the preschool years is essential.

Jensen explores the unique brains of special needs and gifted children, and how poverty and even television can place young brains at risk. Urging educators to move beyond no-frills approaches to schooling, he calls for an enrichment-based educational framework that would customize schooling for every learner, and he also includes strategies that parents and educators can take to enrich learning in the home, the school, and the classroom.

Eric Jensen is an internationally recognized educator known for his translation of neuroscience into practical classroom applications. A former teacher, he is the author of over twenty books, including the widely acclaimed *Teaching with the Brain in Mind*. He is a long-time member of the Society for Neuroscience and the New York Academy of Sciences. Jensen is currently a trainer, consultant, and cofounder of Jensen Learning Corporations.